Reports of the Research Committee
of the
Society of Antiquaries of London
No. XXXV

The Glass Beads of the Prehistoric and Roman Periods in Britain and Ireland

By

MARGARET GUIDO, F.S.A.

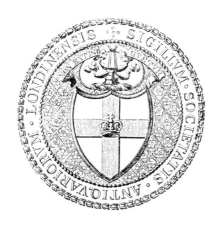

Published by
The Society of Antiquaries of London
Distributed by
Thames and Hudson Ltd.
1978

ISBN 0 500 99026 3

PRINTED IN GREAT BRITAIN BY
THE EASTERN PRESS LIMITED
OF LONDON AND READING

In grateful memory of
Tessa Verney Wheeler, F.S.A.

PREFACE

IT is a strange fact that no serious study of ancient European glass beads has as yet been attempted: the reason probably lies in the very daunting size of the subject, the enormous variety of material to be studied and our almost total ignorance about the location of local glass bead factories. Nevertheless a beginning was certainly made in 1960 when Dr. Thea Elisabeth Haevernick published her classic study of glass armlets and some varieties of Celtic beads.[1] This largely Central European study paved the way for what all countries, by subdividing types of beads into meaningful classes, now need to do much more fully, so that a true overall picture can be obtained. At present, owing to the area chosen for her study, the distribution maps published by Dr. Haevernick inevitably show a concentration around the Upper Rhine, Switzerland, Czechoslovakia, and Austria which repeats itself for each class of armlet or bead under discussion, but now, particularly as we know that beads and armlets were produced in workshops both large and small all over Europe, the study needs to be extended both in depth and extent; Britain and Ireland, so conveniently two islands without artificial frontiers, readily present themselves for the first intensive study.

Armlets in the British Isles have already been the subject of some research,[2] and an interesting outcome of the study was that many were regarded as of native British manufacture. If this was so for armlets, how true might it be for beads? A result of the present study is to draw attention to several areas of Britain in which beads were almost certainly manufactured and certainly distributed.

We need to make a country-by-country analysis, starting with Bronze Age glass beads, on which some notes are published below. So far we only know that during the last millennium B.C., apart from the big production centres in the Near East, Egypt, and the Eastern Mediterranean, large-scale bead production took place also in Northern Italy,[3] and in Carniola where thousands of beads have been reported from graves at Magdalenska, Gora, Vinica, St. Veit and other sites and subsequently dispersed.[4] Central Europe, too, particularly perhaps Bohemia, had centres of production and we now know that there were many smaller centres all over the Celtic world (see pp. 29–37), including Britain.

---

[1] Haevernick, T. E. (1960). This has recently been supplemented for Czechoslovakia, by Venclová, N. (1971). The latter publication is especially useful for its illustrations, and there is a short résumé in English.

[2] Kilbride-Jones, H. E. (1938), followed by Stevenson, R. B. K. (1954-6). One of these armlet classes, made apparently in Britain and thought to have been post-Agricolan in date, is now known to have been earlier. See Harden, D. B. and Price, J., in Cunliffe, B. (1971 b) and p. 78, n. 1, below. See also Stevenson, R. B. K., in Rivet, A. L. F. (ed.) (1966), fig. 3, p. 27, and forthcoming in *GAJ* iv (1976).

[3] Red and blue glass for bead-making in the early first millennium B.C. has been reported from Frattesine in Northern Italy not far from the mouth of the river Po. Barfield, L. (1971), 100.

[4] Mahr, A. (ed.) (1934). Over 2,000 beads were discovered in one of the necklaces from St. Veit, and it was written, 'it is really surprising to watch the never-ending variety of beads offered by practically each individual grave'. Most of the beads from the Mecklenburg Collection are either at Harvard or in the Ashmolean Museum at Oxford.

Some of the La Tène Celtic beads, both on the Continent and in Britain, are of such exquisite craftsmanship that it is surprising to find hardly any reference to them in works concerning Celtic art. For instance, in a recent exhibition of 'Early Celtic Art'[5] drawn from many parts of Europe, not a single example of this craft was displayed: only one exhibit, and that atypical, showed a group of marble, shale, and amber beads. Again, in discussing Iron Age crafts, Cunliffe (1975) makes no mention of glass. It is time that La Tène glass beads were recognized not only for their artistic qualities but for their chronological and cultural significance as well.

I am grateful to Dr. D. B. Harden not only for first suggesting my undertaking this study, but also for so generously working to improve the text in innumerable details, and to the very many museum curators and private individuals who have co-operated with me by allowing me access to their collections. The resulting Schedules printed at the end of this book (mostly under the old county system) must be incomplete in certain respects, even if every attempt has been made to find all available material, and over 150 museums have been visited. But very many beads have been noted only from excavation reports, and it is for this reason that it has been impossible in the majority of cases to be certain of the method by which a bead was made (see pp. 7–8). Where possible, each bead has been drawn and coloured on a card which has been filed in its Group or Class as defined in this study; the resulting corpus will be deposited in the care of the Society of Antiquaries, Burlington House.

The work has been helped by the generous provision of grants from the Central Research Funds of London University and from the Leverhulme Trust, to both of which foundations I am grateful. I am indebted to Mr. George Boon for many stimulating discussions and to Dr. R. G. Newton for having kindly checked through that part of this study concerned with chemical components in glass and for making alterations and improvements to it; to Dr. Michael Avery for discussing his suggested dating of Meare in Somerset in advance of his publication and to very many curators and excavators who have shown me recently discovered and sometimes stratified beads. Lastly I want to thank Mr. Nick Griffiths for his beautiful coloured drawings, reproduced here as pls. I and II, and for his other drawings.

It is necessary to stress that the conclusions reached in the discussion are often relevant only to the British Isles, and should not be applied without due caution to other areas of Europe. It is equally important for the reader to understand my usage of the words *Classes* and *Groups*.

I have used the word *Class* for beads which show identical or similar forms and decoration —or in certain Scottish Classes (see Classes 13 and 14) a divergence of decoration despite which there is no doubt that they really belong to the same Class. These can all be studied for what they can reveal to us both of their cultural and chronological settings, and of the movements of peoples or trade contacts which lay behind their distribution patterns. They are coherent and significant, and are as valid as 'type fossils' as are many bronzes and other small classifiable objects.

In the *Groups*, on the other hand, I include miscellaneous beads which appear similar only because they have no very notable characteristics; they are therefore not so useful to us as

---

[5] See the Catalogue of that title published by the Edinburgh University Press in 1970 for the Arts Council of Great Britain.

coherent Classes can be, and it is also certain that the schedules of Groups often include beads of widely different dates and cultural backgrounds—even post-Roman ones. It would therefore be quite meaningless to study them for what could be gleaned about their archaeological cultures from their distribution. They simply represent a corpus which by more advanced glass analysis (chemical, spectrographic, microprobe tests, ratio of lead isotopes or whatever the method may be) can ultimately be broken down into significant Classes.

CONTENTS

PART IV. IRON AGE BEADS OF BRITISH DESIGN AND ORIGIN

PART V. ROMAN PERIOD BEADS

THE SCHEDULES

INDEX

LIST OF PLATES

(between pages 102 and 103)

LIST OF FIGURES

ABBREVIATIONS AND BIBLIOGRAPHY

The abbreviations are mainly of journals cited in both the Bibliography and the Schedules. However, certain monographs (e.g., Wheeler, *Maiden Castle*) are given in an abbreviated form (*MC*) applicable to the Schedules only; when cited in the text, they appear in a slightly different form (Wheeler, R. E. M. (1943)) for which reference should be made to the Bibliography.

ABBREVIATIONS

A   *Archaeologia.*

AA   *Archaeologia Aeliana.*

AANHSC   *Ayrshire Archaeological and Natural History Society Collections.*

AB   *Archaeologia Belgica.*

AC   *Archaeologia Cambrensis.*

ACt   *Archaeologia Cantiana.*

AGC   *Ayr and Galloway Collections.*

AH   *Archaeologia Hungarica.*

A.M.   Ashmolean Museum.

An   *Antiquity.*

AnJ   *Antiquaries Journal.*

ANL   *Archaeological News Letter.*

Ar   *Archaeometry.*

ArJ   *Archaeological Journal.*

AR   *Archaeological Review.* (C.B.A.)

BAJ   *Bedfordshire Archaeological Journal.*

BBCS   *Bulletin of the Board of Celtic Studies.*

BIAL   *Bulletin of the Institute of Archaeology in London.*

B.M.   British Museum.

BPI   *Bullettino di Paletnologia italiana.*

BRGK   *Berichte der Römisch-Germanischen Kommission.*

Brit   *Britannia.*

BSAC   *Bulletin de la Société Archéologique Champenoise.*

BSPF   *Bulletin de la Société Préhistorique Française.*

CA   *Current Archaeology.*

Cam   Hawkes, C. F. C., and Hull, M. R., *Camulodunum: First Report on the Excavations at Colchester 1930–1939.* (Reports of the Research Committee of the Society of Antiquaries of London, xiv, 1947.)

C.B.A.   Council for British Archaeology.

CLAJ   *County Louth Archaeological Journal.*

C.M.   Cambridge Museum of Archaeology and Ethnology.

EAH   *Essex Archaeology and History.*

FF   *Forschungen und Fortschritte* (Korrespondenzblatt (Nachrichtenblatt) der deutschen Wissenschaft und Technik.)

Ga   *Gallia.*

GAJ   *Glasgow Archaeological Journal.*

GDV   *Germanische Denkmäler der Völkerwanderungszeit.*

Ge   *Germania.*

GECJ   *General Electric Company Journal.*

Gl   Bulleid, A., and Gray, H. St. George, *The Glastonbury Lake Village*, i (1911), ii (1917).

HA   *Helvetia Archaeologica.*

HH   Bushe-Fox, J. P., *Excavations at Hengistbury Head, Hampshire, 1911–12.* (Reports of the Research Committee of the Society of Antiquaries of London, iii, 1915.)

JBAA   *Journal of the British Archaeological Association.*

JCNWAAHS   *Journal of the Chester and North Wales Architectural, Archaeological and Historical Society.*

JDANHS   *Journal of the Derbyshire Archaeological and Natural History Society.*

JGAHS   *Journal Galway Archaeological and Historical Society.*

JGS   *Journal of Glass Studies.*

JMM   *Journal of the Manx Museum.*

JNNHSFC   *Journal of the Northamptonshire Natural History Society Field Club.*

JPEK   *Jahrbuch für prähistorische und ethnographische Kunst* (Berlin).

JRAI   *Journal of the Royal Anthropological Institute.*

JRGZM   *Jahrbuch des Römisch-Germanischen Zentralmuseums, Mainz.*

JRIC   *Journal of the Royal Institution of Cornwall.*

JRS   *Journal of Roman Studies.*

JRSAI   *Journal of the Royal Society of Antiquaries of Ireland.*

MA   *Monumenti Antichi* (Accademia dei Lincei, Rome).

MAGW   *Mittheilungen der Anthropologischen Gesellschaft in Wien.*

MAn   *Monmouthshire Antiquary.*

MAr   *Medieval Archaeology.*

MC   Wheeler, R. E. M. (1943), *Maiden Castle, Dorset* (Reports of the Research Committee of the Society of Antiquaries of London, xii, 1943).

Me i   Bulleid, A., and Gray, H. St. George, *The Meare Lake Village,* i (1948).

Me ii   Bulleid, A., and Gray, H. St. George, *The Meare Lake Village,* ii (1953).

Me iii   Cotton, M. A. (ed.), *The Meare Lake Village,* iii (1967).

Ne   Curle, J., *Newstead: A Roman Frontier Post and Its People. The Fort of Newstead in the Parish of Melrose* (1911).

N.M.A.   National Museum of Antiquities, Edinburgh.

N.M.W.   National Museum of Wales, Cardiff.

NS   *Notizie degli Scavi.*

NSJFS   *North Staffordshire Journal of Field Studies.*

O   *Oxoniensia.*

Of   *Offa.*

Os   Whiting, W., etc. (1931), *Report on the Excavation of the Roman Cemetery at Ospringe, Kent.* (Reports of the Research Committee of the Society of Antiquaries of London, viii, 1931.)

P   *Préhistoire.*

PAI   *Proceedings of the Archaeological Institute* (later *Archaeological Journal*).

PCAS   *Proceedings of the Cambridge Antiquarian Society.*

PCNHSS   *Proceeding of the Coventry Natural History and Scientific Society.*

PDAS   *Proceedings of the Devon Archaeological Society.*

PDNHAS   *Proceedings of the Dorset Natural History and Archaeological Society.*

PHFCAS   *Proceedings of the Hampshire Field Club and Archaeological Society.*

PNNAS   *Papers of the Norfolk and Norwich Archaeological Society.*

PPS   *Proceedings of the Prehistoric Society.*

PRIA   *Proceedings of the Royal Irish Academy.*

PSANHS   *Proceedings of the Somerset Archaeological and Natural History Society.*

PSAL   *Proceedings of the Society of Antiquaries of London.*

PSAS   *Proceedings of the Society of Antiquaries of Scotland.*

PSIA   *Proceedings of the Suffolk Institute of Archaeology.*

PZ   *Praehistorische Zeitschrift.*

RA   Revue archéologique.

RAECE   Revue archéologique de l'Est et du Centre-Est.

R.C.H.M.   Royal Commission on Ancient and Historical Monuments (England).

R.G.K.   Römisch-Germanische Kommission.

R.G.Z.M.   Römisch-Germanisches Zentralmuseum, Mainz.

Rich i–v   Bushe-Fox, J. P., *Reports on the Excavations of the Roman Fort at Richborough, Kent.* (Reports of the Research Committee of the Society of Antiquaries of London vi, 1926, vii, 1928, x, 1932, xvi, 1949 and xxiii, 1968.)

SAC   Sussex Archaeological Collections.

S.A.L.   Society of Antiquaries of London.

SDNQ   Somerset and Dorset Notes and Queries.

SJ   Société Jersiaise.

SNQ   Sussex Notes and Queries.

TBGAS   Transactions of the Bristol and Gloucestershire Archaeological Society.

TBNHS   Transactions of the Buteshire Natural History Society.

TCW   Transactions of the Cumberland and Westmoreland Antiquarian and Archaeological Society.

TDA   Transactions of the Devonshire Association.

TDGNHAS   Transactions of the Dumfries and Galloway Natural History and Antiquarian Society.

TLAHS   Transactions of the Leicestershire Archaeological and Historical Society.

TLSSAHS   Transactions of the Lichfield and South Staffordshire Archaeological and Historical Society.

TNDFC   Transactions of the Newbury and District Field Club.

TPBAS   Transactions and Proceedings of the Birmingham Archaeological Society.

TRIA   Transactions of the Royal Irish Academy.

TSAS   Transactions of the Shropshire Archaeological Society.

TWNFC   Transactions of the Woolhope Naturalists' Field Club.

TZ   Trierer Zeitschrift.

UJA   Ulster Journal of Archaeology.

Ver   Wheeler, R. E. M. and T. V., *Verulamium, a Belgic and Two Roman Cities.* (Reports of the Research Committee of the Society of Antiquaries of London, xi, 1936.)

VCH   Victoria County History.

WAM   Wiltshire Archaeological and Natural History Magazine.

WCFC   West Cornwall Field Club.

YAJ   Yorkshire Archaeological Journal.

BIBLIOGRAPHY

Abercromby, J. (1912). *Bronze Age Pottery of Great Britain and Ireland*.

Alcock, L. (1964). *Dinas Powys*.

—— (1973). *Arthur's Britain*.

Allen, D. F. (1944). 'The Belgic dynasties of Britain and their coins', *A* xc, 1–46.

—— (1961). 'The origins of coinage in Britain: a re-appraisal', in Frere, S. (ed.) (1961), 97–308.

Ammianus Marcellinus. *Incerti Auctoris: Epitome de Caesaribus*, xli.

ApSimon, A. M. and Greenfield, E. (1972). 'The excavations of Bronze Age and Iron Age settlements at Trevisker, St. Eval, Cornwall', *PPS* xxxviii, 302–81.

Arbman, H. (1940). *Birka I*.

—— (1940–43). *Birka I: Die Gräber*.

Atkinson, D. (1930). 'Caistor excavations', *PNNAS* xxiv, 93 ff.

Avery, M. (1968). 'Excavations at Meare East, 1966', *PSANHS* cxii, 21–39.

Avery, M., Sutton, J. E. G. and Banks, J. W. (1967). 'Rainsborough, Northants., England: Excavations, 1961–5', *PPS* xxxiii, 207–306.

Baillie-Reynolds, P. K. (1938). Collected reports of *Excavations on the Site of the Roman Fort of Kanovium*.

Barfield, L. (1971). *Northern Italy*.

Bateson, J. D. and Hedges, R. E. M., (1975), 'The scientific analysis of a group of Roman-age enamelled brooches', *Ar* xvii, pt. 2, particularly p. 182.

Baur, P. V. C. (1938), *see* Kraeling, C. H. (1938).

Beck, H. C. (1928). 'Classification and nomenclature of beads and pendants', *A* lxxvii, 1–76.

—— (1934). 'Glass before 1500 B.C.', *Ancient Egypt and the East* (June), 7–21.

—— (1936). *Beads and Magic*.

Beck, H. C. and Stone, J. F. S. (1935). 'Faience beads of the British Bronze Age', *A* lxxxv, 203–52.

Benadik, B. (1959). 'sklo v ts keltskom hrobovom inventâri na Slovensku' (Glas im keltischen Grabinventar in der Slowakei) in *Acta Universitatis Carolinae, Philosophica et Historica*, iii (Prague), 27–224.

—— (1962). 'Chronologické vztahy keltskych pohrebisk na Slovensku', in *Slovenská archeológia*, x–2, 371–5.

Biddle, M. (1970) in *CA* xx, 245–6.

—— (1972). 'Excavations at Winchester, 1970: Ninth interim report', *AnJ* lii, 93–131.

—— (forthcoming), *Winchester Studies*, iii, parts I and II.

Birley, E. B. (1953). *Roman Britain and the Roman Army*.

Boisserain, U. P. (ed.) (1955). *Historia Romana*.

Boon, G. C. (1945). 'The Roman site at Seamills, 1945–46', *TBGAS* lxvi, 258–95.

—— (1950). 'The Roman villa in Kingsweston Park. . . .', *TBGAS* lxviii, 5–58.

—— (1957). *Roman Silchester* (extensively revised 1974).

—— (1966). 'Gilt glass beads from Caerleon and elsewhere' in *BBCS* xxii, pt. I, 104–9.

—— (1972). *Isca*. N.M.W.

—— (1977), 'Gold-in-Glass beads from the ancient world', *Brit* viii, 193–207. .

Borlase, W. C. (1872). *Naenia Cornubiae*.

Borlase, W. C. (1879). 'Archaeological discoveries in the parishes of St. Just-in-Penwith and Sennen', *JRIC* xxi, 190–212.

Boulanger, Cl. (1902–5). *Le Mobilier Funéraire (Gallo-Romain et Franc) en Picardie et en Artois.*

Bowen, E. G. (1954). *The Settlements of the Celtic Saints in Wales.*

—— (1972). *Britain and the Western Seaways.*

Branigan, K. (1971). 'Wessex and Mycenae: some evidence reviewed', *WAM* lxv, 89–107.

—— (1972). 'The Surbo bronzes—some observations', *PPS* xxxviii, 276–85.

—— (1973). 'Gauls in Gloucestershire', *TBGAS* xcii, 82–95.

Břeň, Jiři (1966). *Třisov: A Celtic Oppidum in South Bohemia.*

—— (1972). 'The present state of research into the problems of Celtic oppida in Central Europe', *BIAL* x, 13–22.

Bretz-Mahler, Denise (1971). 'La civilisation de La Tène I en Champagne: le facies marnien', *Ga* supplément xxiii.

Brewster, T. C. M. (1971). 'The Garton Slack chariot-burial in East Yorkshire', *An* xlv, 289–92.

Brill, R. H. and Wampler, J. M. (1965), see Young, W. J. (1965) (ed.).

Brizio, E. (1899). 'Il sepolcreto gallico di Montefortino presso Arcevia', *MA* ix, 617–808.

Brunton, G. (1930). *Qau and Badari III.*

—— (1937). *Mostagedda.*

Budge, E. Wallis (1907). *Account of the Roman Antiquities Preserved at Chesters.*

Bulleid, A. (1924). *The Lake Villages of Somerset.*

Bulleid, A. and Gray, H. St. G. (1911). *The Glastonbury Lake Village*, 2 vols.

—— (1948). *The Meare Lake Village*, i.

—— (1956). *The Meare Lake Village*, ii.

—— (1967). *The Meare Lake Village*, iii (ed. Cotton, M. A.).

Burley, E. (1955–6). 'A catalogue and survey of the metal-work from Traprain Law', *PSAS* lxxxix, 118 ff.

Bushe-Fox, J. P. (1915). *Hengistbury Head, Hampshire.* (S.A.L. Research Report, iii.)

—— (1949). *Excavations at the Roman Fort at Richborough, Kent*, iv. (S.A.L. Research Report, xvi.)

Caley, E. R. (1962). *Analysis of Ancient Glasses.* (Corning Museum of Glass Monographs, i.)

Callander, G. (1911). 'Notice of the discovery of two vessels of clay on the Culbin Sands, . . . with a comparison of the Culbin Sands and the Glenluce Sands and of the relics found on them', *PSAS* xlv, 158–81.

Charleston, R. J. (1963). 'Glass "cakes" as raw material and articles of commerce', *JGS* v, 54–67.

Cheesman, G. L. (1914). *The Auxilia of the Roman Imperial Army.*

Childe, V. G. (1929). *The Danube in Prehistory.*

Christlein, R. (1966). *Das Alamannische Reihengräberfeld von Marktoberdorf in Algäu.*

Clarke, G. (1972), in Biddle, M. (1972), 94–8 and forthcoming in *Winchester Studies*, iii, part II.

Clayton, J. (1880). 'Description of Roman remains discovered near to Procolitia, a station on the Wall of Hadrian', *AA* viii, 1–39.

Clifford, E. M. (1961). *Bagendon: A Belgic Oppidum.*

Cole, H. (1966), in *JGS* viii, 46–7.

Coles, J. M. (1959–60). 'Scottish Late Bronze Age metalwork: typology, distributions and chronology', *PSAS* xciii, 16–134.

Coles, J. M. and Simpson, D. D. A. (eds.) (1962). *Studies in Ancient Europe.*

Collis, J. R. (1971). 'Markets and money', in Jesson, M. and Hill, D. (eds.).

Collis, J. R. (1974). *Oppida: the Beginnings of Urbanisation in Temperate Europe* (unpublished Cambridge Ph.D. thesis).

Collingwood, R. G. and Wright, R. P. (1965). *The Roman Inscriptions of Britain*, i.

Corder, P. (1955). 'The re-organisation of the defences of Romano-British towns in the fourth century', *ArJ* cxii, 20–42.

Cotton, M. A. (1967), see under Bulleid, A. and Gray, H. St. G. (1967).

Cunliffe, B. (1968) (ed.). *Excavations at Richborough, Kent*, v. (S.A.L. Research Report, xxiii.)

—— (1971 a). 'Some aspects of hill-forts and their cultural environment', in Jesson, M. and Hill, D. (eds.) (1971).

—— (1971 b). *Excavations at Fishbourne 1961–9*, i and ii. (S.A.L. Research Reports, xxvi–xxvii.)

—— (1972). 'The Late Iron Age metalwork from Bulbury, Dorset', *AnJ* lii, 293–308.

—— (1974). *Iron Age Communities in Britain*.

—— (1976). *Iron Age Sites in Central Southern England*. (C.B.A. Research Report, 16).

Cunnington, M. E. (1923). *The Early Iron Age Site at All Cannings Cross Farm, Wiltshire*.

Curle, A. and Cree, J. (1915–24). Reports on Traprain Law in *PSAS* xlix–lviii.

Curle, J. (1911). *Newstead: A Roman Frontier Post and its People*.

—— (1931–2). 'An inventory of objects of Roman and provincial origin found on sites in Scotland not definitely associated with Roman constructions', *PSAS* lxvi, 277–397.

Daniel, Glyn (1958). 'The chronology of the French collective tombs', *PPS* xxiv, 1–23.

Davis, J. B. and Thurnam, J. (1865). *Crania Britannica*.

Déchelette, J. (1904). *Les Fouilles du Mont Beuvray de 1897–90*.

—— (1914). *Manuel d'archéologie préhistorique, celtique et Gallo-Romaine*, ii, 3me partie. *Second âge du fer ou époque de la Tène*, 1314–27.

De Paor, M. and L. (1961). *Early Christian Ireland*. (3rd ed.)

Dewar, H. S. L. and Godwin, H. (1963). 'Archaeological discoveries in the raised bogs of the Somerset levels', *PPS* xxix, especially pp. 39–40.

Diaconu, G. (1965). *Tirgşor*.

Dudley, D. (1968). 'Excavations on Nor'nour in the Isles of Scilly, 1962–66', *ArJ* cxxiv, 1–64.

Duncan, G. S. (1960). *Bibliography of Glass*. (Society of Glass Technology, Sheffield.)

Ebert, M. (ed.) (1924–9). *Reallexikon der Vorgeschichte*.

Eck, T. (1891). *Les Deux Cimetières Gallo-Romains de Vermand et de Saint-Quentin*.

Eogan, G. (1964). 'The Later Bronze Age in Ireland in the light of recent research', *PPS* xxx, 268–351.

Favret, P.-M. (1927). 'La nécropole Hallstattienne des Jogasses', *RA* xxvi, 80–146.

—— (1936). 'Les nécropoles des Jogasses à Chouilly (Marne)', *P* v, 24–119.

Feachem, R. W. (1966). 'The hill-forts of Northern Britain', in Rivet, A. L. F. (ed.) (1966), 59–88.

Fell, C. (1936). 'The Hunsbury hill-fort, Northants.', *ArJ* xciii, 57–100.

Foster, I. Ll. and Alcock, L. (ed.) (1968). *Culture and Environment*.

Fowler, E. (1964). 'Celtic metalwork of the fifth and sixth centuries, A.D.', *ArJ* cxx, 98–160.

Fowler, P. J. *et al.* (1970). *Cadbury Congresbury, Somerset*. (Dept. Extra-Mural Studies, Bristol University.) See also *CA* xxiii (November).

Fox, A. (1961). 'South-western hill-forts', in Frere, S. (ed.) (1961), 35–60.

Fox, C. (1923). *The Archaeology of the Cambridge Region*.

—— (1943). *The Personality of Britain*. (4th ed.)

—— (1958). *Pattern and Purpose*.

Frere, S. S. (1961) (ed.). *The Problems of the Iron Age in Southern Britain.*
—— (1967). *Britannia. A History of Roman Britain.*
—— (1972). *Verulamium Excavations,* i. (**S.A.L.** Research Report, xxvii.)

Gillam, J. P. (1958). 'Roman and native A.D. 122–197', in Richmond, I. A. (ed.) (1958), 60–90.
Goodchild, R. G. (1947). 'The Farley Heath sceptre', *AnJ* xxvii, 83–5 and refs.
Goodchild, R. G. and Kirk, J. R. (1954). 'The Romano-Celtic temple at Woodeaton', *O* xix, 15–37.
Gozzadini, G. (1870). *L'Antico Necropole a Marzabotto nel Bolognese.*
Gray, H. St. G. (1942). 'Glass beads found in a cist burial at Clevedon', *PSNAHS* lxxxviii, 73–6.
Greenwell, W. (1877). *British Barrows.*
—— (1890). 'Recent researches in barrows in Yorkshire, Wiltshire, Berkshire, etc.', *A* lii, 1–72.
—— (1906). 'Early Iron Age burials in Yorkshire', *A* lx, 251–312.
Griffith, F. Ll. (1902–7). *El Amarna.* (Archaeological Survey of Egypt, vols. xiii–xvii.)
Grimes, W. F. (1939–45). *Excavations on Defence Sites 1939–45.*
—— (ed.) (1951). *Aspects of Archaeology in Britain and Beyond.*
Grinsell, L. V. (1971). 'Somerset barrows (part ii)', *PSANHS* cxv, 43–137.
Guido, M. (forthcoming). 'The glass beads from Lankhills, Winchester', in Biddle, M. (forthcoming).

Hachmann, R. (1976). 'The problem of the Belgae as seen from the Continent', *BIAL* xiii, 117–37.
Haevernick, T. E. (1960). *Die Glasarmringe und Ringperlen der Mittel- und Spätlatènezeit auf dem Europäischen Festland.* (R.G.K.)
—— (1972). 'Perlen mit zusammengesetzten Augen', *PZ* xlvii, Heft I, 78 ff.
Haffner, A. (1971). *Das keltisch-römische Gräberfeld von Wederath-Belginum.*
Harbison, P. (1970). *Guide to the National Monuments of Ireland.*
—— (1971). 'The Old Irish chariot', *An* xlv, 171–7.
Harden, D. B. (1947), see Hawkes, C. F. C. and Hull, M. R. (1947), esp. pp. 306–7.
—— (1967), in Stead, I. M. (1967), 14–16.
—— (1968). 'Ancient glass I: pre-Roman', *ArJ* cxxv, 46–72.
—— (1969). 'Ancient glass II: Roman', *ArJ* cxxvi, 44–77.
Harden, D. B. and Price, J. (1971), in Cunliffe, B. (1971 b), 317–68, especially 366–7.
Harding, A. and Warren, S. E. (1973). 'Early Bronze Age faience beads from Central Europe', *An* xlvii, 64–6.
Harding, D. W. (1970). 'The "New" Iron Age', *CA* xx (May), 235–40.
—— (1972). *The Iron Age in the Upper Thames Basin.*
—— (1974). *The Iron Age in Lowland Britain.*
Hawkes, C. F. C. (1959). 'The ABC of the British Iron Age', *An* xxxiii, 170–82.
—— (1961). 'Gold ear-rings of the Bronze Age, East and West', *Folklore*, lxxii, 438–74.
—— (1968). 'New thoughts on the Belgae', *An* xlii, 6–16.
Hawkes, C. F. C. and Hull, M. R. (1947). *Camulodunum.* (S.A.L. Research Report, xiv.)
Hawkes, S. C. (1975). Note in *ArJ* cxxxii.
Hawkes, S. C. and Dunning, G. C. (1961). 'Soldiers and settlers in Britain, fourth to fifth century', *MAr* v, 1–70.
Héléna, P. (1937). *Les Origines de Narbonne.*
Hencken, H. O'N. (1950). 'Lagore Crannog: An Irish royal residence of the 7th–10th centuries A.D.', *PRIA* liii, 1–247.
Henry, F. (1965) (revised ed.). *Irish Art in the Early Christian Period to A.D. 800.*
Hoare, R. Colt (1812). *Ancient Wiltshire.*

Hodson, F. R. (1962). 'Some pottery from Eastbourne, the 'Marnians' and the pre-Roman Iron Age in Southern Britain', *PPS* xxviii, 140–55.

—— (1964). 'Cultural grouping within the British pre-Roman Iron Age', *PPS* xxx, 99–110.

Hogg, A. H. A. (1951). 'The Votadini', in Grimes, W. F. (ed.) (1951), 200–20.

—— (1957). 'Four Spanish hill-forts', *An* xxxi, 25–32.

Hughes, M. J. (1972). 'A technical study of opaque red glass of the Iron Age in Britain', *PPS* xxxviii, 98–107.

Hull, M. R. (1958). *Roman Colchester.* (S.A.L. Research Report, xx.)

Jacobsthal, P. (1944). *Early Celtic Art.*

Jesson, M. and Hill, D. (eds.) (1971). *The Iron Age and its Hill Forts*

Jope, E. M. (1957). 'A burial group of the first century A.D. near Donaghadee, Co. Down', *UJA* xx, 73–95.

—— (1960). Note in *UJA* xxiii, 40.

—— (1962). Reported in *An* xxxvi, 30.

Keller, E. (1971). *Die spätrömischen Grabfunde in Südbayern.* (Münchner Beiträge zur Vor- und Frühgeschichte, 14.)

Keller, J. (1965). *Das keltische Fürstengrab von Reinheim.* (R.G.Z.M.)

Kenney, J. F. (1929). *Sources for the Early History of Ireland,* i.

Kenyon, K. M. (1948). *The Jewry Wall Site, Leicester.* (S.A.L. Research Report, xv.)

Kilbride-Jones, H. E. (1938). 'Glass armlets in Britain', *PSAS* lxxii, 366–95.

Knowles, W. J. (1879). 'Ancient Irish beads and amulets', *JRSAI* xv, 523 ff.

Koehl, W. Z. (1882). *Neue prähistorische Funde aus Worms und Umgebung,* i. (Behrens Germ. Denkmäler, i.)

Kraeling, C. H. (ed.) (1938). *Gerasa, City of the Decapolis.*

Krämer, W. (1958). 'Manching. Ein Vindelikisches Oppidum an der Donau', in *Neue Ausgrabungen in Deutschland.*

—— (1961 *et seq.*). Various reports in *Ge* xl *et seq.*

—— (1964). *Das keltische Gräberfeld von Nebringen (Kreis Böblingen).*

Krämer, W. and Schubert, F. (1970). *Die Ausgrabungen in Manching.*

Kunkel, O. (1961). 'Zur Frage keltischer Glasindustrie. Nach einer Manchinger Fundgruppe', *Ge* xxxix, 322.

La Baume, P. (1967). *Das fränkische Gräberfeld von Junkersdorf bei Köln.*

Laing, Ll. (1975). *The Archaeology of Late Celtic Britain and Ireland, c. 400–1200 A.D.*

Leeds, E. T. (1926). 'Excavations at Chun Castle in Penwith, Cornwall', *A* lxxvi, 205–40.

Lethbridge, T. C. (1931). 'Recent excavations in Anglo-Saxon cemeteries in Cambridge and Suffolk', *PCAS* n.s. iii.

Lucas, A. (1959 ed.). *Ancient Egyptian Materials and Industries.*

McKerrell, H. (1972). 'On the origin of British faience beads, and some aspects of Wessex-Mycenae relationship', *PPS* xxxviii, 286–301.

MacKie, E. W. (1965 a). 'The origin and development of the broch and wheelhouse building cultures of the Scottish Iron Age', *PPS* xxxi, 93–146.

—— (1965 b). 'Brochs and the Hebridean Iron Age', *An* xxxix, 266–78.

MacKie, E. W. (1969). 'Radio-carbon dates and the Scottish Iron Age', *An* xliii, 15–26.

Mahr, A. (ed.) (1934). *Prehistoric Grave Material from Carniola*. (Catalogue of the Mecklenburg Collection.)

Mallowan, M. E. L. (1966). *Nimrud and its Remains*, ii. (Appendix III by Axel von Saldern, 623 ff.)

Mann, L. McL. (1905–6). 'Prehistoric beads of coarse vitreous paste', *PSAS* xl, 396–402.

May, T. (1904). *Warrington's Roman Remains*.

—— (1922). *The Roman Forts of Templebrough, near Rotherham*.

—— (1930). *Catalogue of the Roman Pottery in the Colchester and Essex Museum*.

Megaw, J. V. S. (1970). *Art of the European Iron Age*.

Milne, J. G. (1948). *Finds of Greek Coins in the British Isles*. (Ashmolean Museum, Oxford.)

Moreau, F. (1892). *Album Caranda*.

Morel, L. (1898). *La Champagne souterraine; matériaux et documents. Ou résultats de trente-cinq années de fouilles archéologiques dans la Marne*.

Müller Beck, H. and Ettlinger, E. (1962–63). 'Die Besiedlung der Engehalbinsel in Bern', *BRGK* xliii–xliv, 107–53.

Müller-Karpe, H. (1959). *Beiträge zur Chronologie der Urnenfelderzeit nördlich und südlich der Alpen*.

Myres, J. N. L. (1969). *Anglo-Saxon Pottery and the Settlements of England*.

—— (1973). *The Anglo-Saxon Cemeteries of Caistor-by-Norwich and Markshall, Norfolk*. (S.A.L. Research Report, xxx.)

Neuburg, F. (1949). *Glass in Antiquity*.

Newton, R. G. (1971 a). 'A preliminary examination of a suggestion that pieces of strongly coloured glass were articles of trade in the Iron Age in Britain', *Ar* xiii, 11–16.

—— (1971 b). 'Glass trade routes in the Iron Age', in *XXth Congress on Glass Studies* (Versailles). (British Glass Industry Research Association, Sheffield.)

Newton, R. G. and Renfrew, C. (1970). 'British faience beads reconsidered', *An* xliv, 199–206.

Nolte, B. (1968). *Die Glasgefässe im Alten Ägypten*.

O'Kelly, M. J. (1962–4). 'Two ring-forts at Garryduff, Co. Cork', *PRIA* lxiii, 17–125.

Oppenheimer, A. L., Barag, D., Von Saldern, A. and Brill, R. (1970). *Glass and Glass-Making in Ancient Mesopotamia*.

Ordnance Survey (1956). *Map of Roman Britain*.

—— (1962). *Map of South Britain in the Iron Age*.

ÓRíordáin, S. P. (1942). 'A large earthen ring-fort at Garranes, Co. Cork', *PRIA* xlvii, C., 77–150.

—— (1954). 'Lough Gur excavations', *PRIA* lvi, C., 297–459.

—— (1964). *Tara: The Monuments on the Hill*. (2nd ed.)

Párduez, M., in *AH* xxv and xxx.

Peacock, D. P. S. (1971). 'Roman amphorae in pre-Roman Britain', in Jesson, M. and Hill, D. (eds.) (1971).

Petrie, W. M. F. (1888). *Tanis*. (Egypt Exploration Fund.)

—— (1902–1907). *Archaeological Survey of Egypt*, xiii–xvii.

Pič, J. L. (1906). *Le Hradischt de Stradonitz en Bohême*.

Piggott, S. (1952–3). 'Three metal-work hoards of the Roman period', *PSAS* lxxxvii, 1–50.

—— (1953). 'Bronze double-axes in the British Isles', *PPS* xix, 224–6.

—— (1957–8). 'Excavations at Braidwood Fort, Midlothian, and Craig's Quarry, Dirleton, East Lothian', *PSAS* xci, 61–77.

Piggott, S. (1959). 'The carnyx in Early Iron Age Britain', *AnJ* xxxix, 19–32.

—— (1970). *Early Celtic Art*. (Arts Council Exhibition Catalogue.)

Pirling, R. (1966). *Das römische-fränkische Gräberfeld von Krefeld-Gellep.*

Pitt-Rivers, A. H. L. F. (1887). *Excavations in Cranborne Chase,* i.

—— (1888). *Excavations in Cranborne Chase,* ii.

—— (1892). *Excavations in Cranborne Chase,* iii.

—— (1898). *Excavations in Cranborne Chase,* iv.

Powell, T. G. E. (1958). *The Celts.*

Quiggin, A. H. (1949). *A Survey of Primitive Money.*

Raddatz, K. (1957). 'Zu den magischen Schwertanhängern des Thorsberger Moorfunders', *Of* xvi, 81–4.

Radford, C. A. R. (1951). 'Report on the excavations at Castle Dore', *JRIC* n.s. i A (Appendix Volume).

Raftery, B. (1969). 'Freestone Hill, Co. Kilkenny: an Iron Age hill-fort and Bronze Age cairn', *PRIA* lxviii C., 1–108.

—— (1972 a). 'Irish hill-forts', in Thomas, C. (ed.) (1972), 37–58.

—— (1972 b). 'Some late La Tène glass beads', *JRSAI* lii, Part 1, 14–18.

Ralston, I. and Büchsenschütz, O. (1975). 'Late pre-Roman Iron Age forts in Berry', *An* xlix, 8–18.

Reinecke, S. (1911). *Altertümer unserer heidnischen Vorzeit,* v.

Renfrew, C. (ed.) (1974). *British Prehistory: a new outline.*

Richmond, I. A. (1954). *The Roman Fort at South Shields: A Guide.*

—— (1956). 'Roman Britain in 1955', *JRS* xlvi.

—— (ed.) (1958). *Roman and Native in North Britain.*

Richmond, I. A. and Thompson, E. A. (1944). 'Roman Britain in 1943', *JRS* xxxiv.

Riefstahl, E. (1968). *Ancient Egyptian Glass and Glazes in the Brooklyn Museum.* (Brooklyn Museum, New York.)

Rivet, A. L. F. (ed.) (1966). *The Iron Age in Northern Britain.*

Rooksby, H. P. (1962), in *GECJ* xix, No. 1, 20–6.

—— (1964). *Physics and Chemistry of Glasses,* i.

Rooksby, H. P. and Turner, W. E. S. (1959 and 1961), see under Turner.

Ross, A. (1967). *Pagan Celtic Britain.*

Rynne, E. (1961). 'The introduction of La Tène into Ireland', in *Bericht über den V internationalen Kongress für Vor- und Frühgeschichte.* (Hamburg, 1958.)

Sandars, N. K. (1957). *Bronze Age Cultures in France.*

—— (1968). *Prehistoric Art in Europe.*

Sayre, E. V. (1963), 'The intentional use of antimony and manganese in ancient glasses', in *Advances in Glass Technology.* Part 2, ed. Matson, F. R. and Rindone, G. E., pp. 263–82. (Additional Papers from the VIth International Congress on Glass, Washington, D.C., 1962.)

Schaeffer, F. A. (1926). *Les Tertres funéraires préhistoriques dans la Forêt de Haguenau.* (i. Les Tumulus de l'Âge du Bronze.)

Schmidt, E. (1924). 'Le cimetière gaulois du Mont de Vraux à la limite des territoires de Juvigny et de Vraux', *BSAC* (1924), 15–20.

Seligman, C. G. and Beck, H. C. (1938). 'Far Eastern Glass: some Western origins', in *Bull. Museum of Far Eastern Antiquities,* x.

Simpson, G. (1964). *Britons and the Roman Army, A Study of Wales and the Southern Pennines in the First to Third Centuries.*

Simpson, M. (1968). 'Massive armlets in the North British Iron Age', in Coles, J. M. and Simpson, D. D. A. (eds.), 233–54.

Slade, F. (1871). *Catalogue of the Collection of Glass formed by Felix Slade*, with an introduction by A. Nesbitt.

Smith, A. C. (1884). *British and Roman Antiquities of North Wiltshire*.

Smith, C. Roach (1852). *Collectanea Antiqua*, ii and iii.

Stanford, S. C. (1972). 'Welsh Border hill-forts', in Thomas, C. (ed.) (1972), 25–36.

—— (1974). *Croft Ambrey*.

Stead, I. M. (1965). *The La Tène Cultures of Eastern Yorkshire*. (Yorks. Philosophical Society.)

—— (1967). 'A La Tène III Burial at Welwyn Garden City', *A* ci, 1–62.

—— (1971), in Butler, R. M. (ed.), *Soldier and Civilian in Roman Yorkshire*.

Steer, K. A. (1958). 'Roman and native in North Britain: the Severan re-organisation', in Richmond, I. A. (ed.), 91–111.

Stevens, C. E. (1966). 'The social and economic aspects of rural settlement', in Thomas, C. (ed.) (1966).

Stevenson, R. B. K. (1954–5). 'Native bangles and Roman glass', *PSAS* lxxxviii, 208–21.

Stone, J. F. S. (1940). 'A Round Barrow on Stockbridge Down, Hampshire', *AnJ* xx, 39–51.

—— (1952). 'Report on beads from Knackyboy Cairn, St. Martins, Isles of Scilly', *AnJ* xxxii, 30–4.

Stone, J. F. S. and Thomas, L. C. (1956). 'The use and distribution of faience in the Ancient East and prehistoric Europe', *PPS* xxii, 37–84.

Sulimirski, T. (1970). *The Sarmatians*.

Thomas, C. (1966). 'The character and origins of Roman Dumnonia', in Thomas, C. (ed.) (1966), 77 ff.

—— (ed.) (1966). *Rural Settlement in Roman Britain*. (C.B.A. Research Report.)

—— (1971). *Britain and Ireland in Early Christian Times, A.D. 400–800*.

—— (ed.) (1972). *The Iron Age in the Irish Sea Provinces*. (C.B.A. Research Report.)

Thompson, F. H. (1965). *Roman Cheshire*.

Todd, M. (1973). *The Coritani*.

—— (1975). *The Northern Barbarians* 100 B.C.–A.D. 300.

Tress, H. J. (1962). *Glass Technology*, iii, 95–106.

Turner, W. E. S. and Rooksby, H. P. (1959). *Glastechnische Berichte, Sonderband* v. (Intern. Glaskongress 32K, Heft VIII, 17–28.)

—— (1961). 'Further historical studies based on x-ray diffraction methods of the reagents employed in making opal and opaque glass', *JRGZM* viii.

Van der Sleen, W. G. N. (1967). *A Handbook on Beads*. (Journées internationales du Verre, Musée du Verre, Liège.)

Venclová, N. (1971). 'Pravěké Sklo v Čestoslovensku', in *Zpravy*, xiii. (Annonces de la Société Tchécoslovaque d'Archéologie.)

Viollier, D. (1916). *Les sepultures du second âge du fer sur le plateau suisse*.

Von Sacken, E. F. (1868). *Das Gräbfeld von Hallstatt in Oberösterreich*.

Wacher, J. (1974). *The Towns of Roman Britain*.

Wainwright, G. J. (1967). *Coygan Camp*.

Warne, C. (1866). *The Celtic Tumuli of Dorset*.

Webster, G. (1969). *The Imperial Roman Army of the First and Second Ceeturies A.D.*

Weinberg, G. Davidson (1969). 'Glass manufacture in Hellenistic Rhodes', in *Archaiologikon Deltion*, xxiv, 143–51.

Wedlake, W. J. (1958). *Camerton*. (Camerton Excavation Club.)

Wenham, L. P. (1968). *The Romano-British Cemetery at Trentholme Drive, York.*

Werner, J. (1956). *Beiträge zur Archäologie des Attilla-Reiches.* (Bayerische Akademie der Wissenschaften, xxxviii.)

Weyl, W. A. (1951). *Coloured Glasses.* (Monograph of the Society of Glass Technology.)

Wheeler, R. E. M. (1941). 'Hill-forts of Northern France . . .', *AnJ* xxi, 265–70.

—— (1943). *Maiden Castle, Dorset.* (S.A.L. Research Report, xii.)

Wheeler, R. E. M. and Wheeler, T. V. (1936). *Verulamium, a Belgic and Two Roman Cities.* (S.A.L. Research Report, xi.)

Wilde, W. R. (1861). *Catalogue of the Antiquities in the Museum of the Royal Irish Academy.*

Willvonseder, K. (1937). 'Die ältesten Glasfunde aus Österreich', in *FF* xiii, 3 ff.

Young, W. J. (ed.) (1965). *Application of Science in the Examination of Works of Art.*

TECHNICAL AND ARCHAEOLOGICAL CONSIDERATIONS

PART I

TECHNICAL CONSIDERATIONS

THE CHRONOLOGICAL LIMITS OF THE STUDY

THE date covered by this study cannot be exactly defined. The beginning of the term 'Iron Age' in this context must signify the earliest post-Bronze Age beads imported into these islands, but as our archaeological knowledge of the first millennium B.C. deepens it is becoming increasingly clear that, whereas one part of Britain may have been in a retarded and persisting Bronze Age culture, other parts were already in regular contact with the European Hallstatt and La Tène Continental mainland; we must therefore remain open minded as to whether there was ever an interval between what are listed on p. 20–22 as 'Bronze Age' imports and those discussed in this study, though such an interval now seems less probable. We need more close dates and these are now beginning to be provided by radiocarbon analysis and other modern techniques. It is clear that the last five centuries B.C. witnessed an increase of Celtic bead production to a culmination in the first century A.D. when the Roman Conquest temporarily brought it to an end and beads of Roman types came to the fore instead, until they in turn were supplanted by Teutonic types after the Roman evacuation of Britain.

Apart from a brief discussion of Bronze Age beads the dates for this study are therefore very approximately *c*. 700 B.C.–A.D. 410. This period embraces the earliest Iron Age imports from the Continent, and the beads of the pre-Roman and Roman Iron Age (or Romano-British period in those parts of Britain occupied by the Romans) and ends with the arrival of numbers of Germanic settlers. The Iron Age cultural divisions 'A', 'B', and 'C' are hardly used as our knowledge is still too imprecise for this not to be misleading to foreigners. For the same reason I have only hinted at regional cultural sub-divisions. Approximate dating by centuries has seemed less confusing. To keep the dating terminology simple I have used the term Roman Iron Age for parts of Wales and Scotland not occupied by the Romans, and the word Roman is used as distinct from Romano-British only when there is reason to believe that the site in question was preponderantly more Roman than native in culture. Through lack of knowledge, however, there is inevitably a considerable degree of elasticity. This study has been made when excavations have recently shown that our whole concept of the Iron Age needs revision. As D. W. Harding has stressed 'sites which formerly were seen as single-period settlements may now be viewed as the product of prolonged or successive occupations, and groups of sites which might hitherto have been assigned to a single historical context may now be regarded as cumulative over a longer period of time'.[1]

With regard to the terminal date—the end of the Roman period—this too, though more

[1] Harding, D. W. (1970). Among recent accounts of the British Iron Age see, *inter alios*, Harding, D. W. (1974); Hawkes, C. F. C. (1959) and (1968); Rivet, A. L. F. (ed.) (1962); Hodson, F. R. (1962); Cunliffe, B. (1974); Frere, S. (ed.) (1961); Thomas, C. (1966); Todd, M. (1975); and Renfrew, C. (ed.) (1974). See also Ordnance Survey Maps, *Southern Britain in the Iron Age* and *Roman Britain*.

precise, must remain hazy within a few decades. We know that non-Roman peoples were already entering Britain before the end of the occupation, and yet that the Roman way of life, and therefore the objects they used, persisted in large areas of Britain after the formal abandonment by Rome in A.D. 410 or more significantly perhaps about A.D. 442 when the *foederati* revolted and brought an end to the Roman way of life. After that date the barbarian incursions began on a large scale and broke up the central imperial power, but it must be borne in mind that for at least half a century before and after that final date, the picture varies from place to place within Britain, some much affected by the new modes, some remote and lingering in an ever more threatened Roman tradition, and some which had never been more than lightly brushed by Roman culture but which were at the same time halted in a state of non-development of their native heritage based on those lingering Bronze Age or Celtic traditions in which they had been isolated by the Roman occupation. Each area must be studied for its *local* history, and Ireland in particular can be seen to have followed its own insular history (discussed on pp. 39–42). Only time and further study will elucidate these problems. The cultural complexity of the British Isles is clear to all who work here, but must be stressed again for foreign scholars. I must also emphasize that many of the beads here listed in '*Groups*' as apart from those in '*Classes*' (see p. vi) may prove in time to fall outside the limits of this research.

Yet another difficulty which at present impedes research is the relative lack of adequate description and illustration of Gaulish, Gallo-Roman, Frankish, and other Continental Iron Age beads, and of Roman and non-Roman beads from beyond the frontiers of the Roman Empire, not to mention early Germanic beads, Celtic beads in Italy and Spain, etc. No doubt, therefore, in the course of time not only will some of the beads listed in the present Schedules turn out to have had a Continental origin, but for the same reason many of the beads at present regarded as 'probably Germanic' (or more properly 'non-Continental-Roman') and therefore excluded from this study should, had they been recognized, have been included within the chronological limits selected for this study.[1] The very foundations, both archaeological and historical, are not as yet ready for a more definitive study. For this reason, and because relatively few glass beads come from well-dated contexts, and the great majority are from unscientific early excavations, the classification here adopted cannot lay claim to finality.

THE FORMS AND USES OF BEADS AND THEIR DECORATION

Here (and it must be emphasized that the following remarks apply only to the British Isles) the nomenclature follows what appears to be a logical system. The suggested classification put forward for a world basis in Canada has not been used,[2] because with a highly complex system of classification, a badly made bead can very easily be removed from the Class or

---

[1] There are a number of reports on these beads, well illustrated in colour, e.g., Moreau, F. (1892); Boulanger, C. (1902–5); Pirling, R. (1966). For Frankish beads see, *inter alios*, La Baume, P., *Das Frankische Gräberfeld von Junkersdorf bei Köln*, and the forthcoming and very important publica-tion of Schretzheim, near Dillingen, on the Danube, by Koch, U., in *GDV*, forthcoming.

[2] Occasional Papers in Archaeology and History, No. 1, *Canadian Historic Sites* (Queens' Printer for Canada, Ottawa, 1970–1).

type to which reason and experience tell us it more properly belongs. The essential requirements will vary from country to country, or more properly from one cultural or geographical area to another, and as long as students of beads clearly define the nomenclature they have adopted, it will one day be possible for beads from much wider areas to be correlated and classified. For the same reason the classifications proposed by H. C. Beck[1] and W. G. N. Van der Sleen[2] have not been followed.

The forms used in the present study are explained in the text when they relate to undecorated beads. In the Classes, but not the Groups, the characteristics of form, colour, translucency or opacity, and other details are defined, and many Classes are called after a characteristic site where they have been found. This will help to obviate confusion between two apparently comparable but really unrelated Classes. Beck suggested in 1928 that 'to describe a bead fully it is necessary to state its form, perforation, colour, material, and decoration'; by today's standards this is quite inadequate. To these requirements should be added: dimensions, translucency or opacity, method of manufacture (wound, drawn, blown, hand-moulded, etc.), and, where relevant or possible, some kind of analysis. The approximate or exact date of archaeological context in which it was found is equally essential, and its position in relation to a burial may provide a clue as to how it had been used—for not all were on necklaces. Some were arranged in a panel on a child's breast in a grave at the Forum in Rome,[3] others were used as decorations on ear-rings,[4] as brooch-runners,[5] or as hair ornaments.[6] In some examples, particularly of Class 6, the beads were used as talismans attached sometimes to the sword hilt.[7] Others may have been used as finger-rings for the dead: the German Totenringe.[8] Sometimes, too, metal pins may be decorated with glass beads.[9] It must not be assumed that the presence of beads necessarily denotes a female burial, for writing in the Catalogue of the Mecklenburg Collection,[10] Dr. F. de Tompa points out, 'It goes without saying that horse-trappings . . . denote men's graves, and in the latter case this is corroborated by the fact that the tomb also contained ten arrowheads. . . . This grave, moreover, was very rich in glass beads, and it would therefore be rash to assume that the discovery of many beads in a grave denotes it as a female.' In some modern primitive societies the men wear more beads than the women.

[1] Beck, H. C. (1928), 1–75.

[2] Van der Sleen, W. G. N. (1967). This is particularly important for its section on Dutch sixteenth- and seventeenth-century trade beads, sometimes used as currency by explorers like Sir Samuel Baker, and sometimes in exchange for other commodities among backward communities. See also Quiggin, A. H. (1949).

[3] NS (1902), 96–111 and (1903), 123–70.

[4] See, e.g., Mahr, A. (ed.) (1934). Grave 56 from Vinica, of mid-La Tène date, produced a pendant in the form of a little human mask with a small blue glass ear-ring. During Roman times this was not a common usage in Britain, but became more so in post-Roman times.

[5] Very common on the Continent, but not so in Britain.

[6] Mentioned in the Ulster Cycle and probably reflecting late Iron Age and Roman Iron Age fashions. See the Annals of Ulster, ed. and trans. in 4 vols. by Hennessy, W. M. (Dublin, 1887–1901), and K. H. Jackson, The Oldest Irish

Tradition: A Window on the Iron Age (1964).

[7] It is interesting to note in this connection that Pliny (NHist xxix, 52–4) refers to a Gaulish leader having been put to death by order of Claudius for wearing an amulet. Such talismans may have commonly been worn round the neck. A few years ago I was myself offered a bead amulet against the evil eye by a young fisherman in the Aeolian Islands off Sicily. I had been photographing his boat.

[8] Petrikovits, H. von, Novaesium (Führer d. Rheinisches Landesmuseum in Bonn, 1957), 42, 111.

[9] PPS xxx (1964), 159 ff. Many Roman references might also be given.

[10] Mahr, A. (ed.) (1934), 60, concerning a burial at St. Veit near Sittich, Carniola, of the last few centuries B.C. One might also mention a Gaulish tomb at Introbio (Valsassina), in Italy, containing a La Tène II iron sword, etc., and four large beads; NS (1918), 91.

Necklaces are of course particularly valuable for showing at least a partial cultural and chronological overlap for certain bead types; all the more deplorable for the student has been the habit of dealers and even some museum curators who have strung together for convenience beads from more than one site or from different contexts on a long-occupied site, giving a false impression that they are all of one date. It must be remembered, that there are genuine instances of early beads being found and reused on necklaces of later dates.

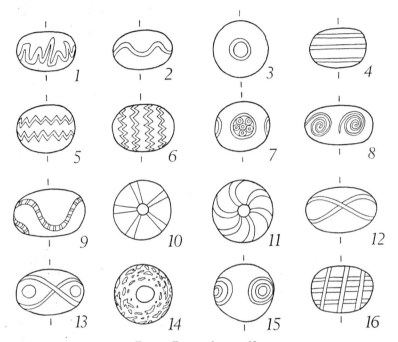

FIG. 1: Decorative motifs.

Decoration (see fig. 1)

The principal methods of decoration for beads were as follows, but there are, of course, a great many varieties on this theme. The decoration was usually applied and then 'marvered' (rubbed smooth on marble) into the surface while the glass was still warm.

(1) *Scrabble*: Less well made than the wave bands (2). The applied trail has often snapped and been restarted so that overlapping is found, and in addition the design is more pinched and angular, and the trail of varying thickness. The scrabble is often unmarvered in late or post-Roman examples.

(2) *Wave*: Generally simply a wavy band of a different colour applied to the circumference of the bead.

(3) *'Eyes'*: Generally surrounded by a ring or rings different in colour from the body colour of the bead.

(4) *Bands*: Straight trails applied around the circumference.

(5) *Chevrons* in contrasting colour. Note that on the earlier beads this design normally runs at right angles to the perforation. In Irish and post-Roman beads it is parallel to the perforation and is called:

(6) *Zig-zag:* Vertical chevrons.

(7) *Compound eyes*: Many small eyes contained in a larger eye.

(8) *Spirals*: Most commonly white or yellow on a dark ground, or yellow on a colourless ground.

(9) *Cables* of two twists marvered on a different coloured ground.

(10) *Spoke-like rays* in contrasting colour radiating from the perforation.

(11) *Whirls* in contrasting colour radiating from the perforation.

(12) *Double swag*: Figure-of-eight bands crossing on the circumference of the bead.

(13) *Double swag with eyes*: As (12) but with spots or eyes in the spaces enclosed by the swags.

(14) *Mottled.*

(15) *Concentric rings.*

(16) *Criss-cross or network.*

Note that the decoration may not have been well marvered or not marvered at all. In such cases the applied trails stand out and are not flush with the bead surface.

METHODS OF MANUFACTURE

The simplest description of bead-making is given by Van der Sleen[1] from whose work these short notes are taken.[2]

Glass is made in thick earthenware crucible containers from 2 to 200 lb. of mixed pulverized quartz or sand quartz with some lime and soda, potash or nitre, sometimes lead. Generally before heating, iron or copper, manganese or cobalt colouring is added. The ingredients are then thoroughly mixed and heated in one or more firings to a red-hot, viscous state. A 'gathering' of the glass is then drawn out to make a shiny glass rod which quickly solidifies. These rods or canes are then cut down to useful lengths for making the oldest and simplest kind of beads—wound beads.

Wound beads

The glass cane is melted at one end and folded round a wire. The rest of the rod is cut off and the wire with the glass ring turned and heated till the ring is rounded. In cooling the metal contracts more than the glass and the beads can be pulled off. A tapered bead results from a gradually thinning thread of glass being wound round a wire. If larger beads are needed the cane is wound several times round the metal wire or other core. These resulting beads are then called multiple wound beads.

---

[1] Van der Sleen, W. G. N. (1967). See also *JRAI* lxxxviii, 203 ff. and Neuburg, F. (1949).

[2] See also Riefstahl, E. (1968). This includes a history of glass-making in Egypt up to the early Roman period.

Drawn beads

The melted 'gathering' of glass is in this case worked into a gob of funnel shape enclosing a large air-bubble in the glass. This gob (hollow and therefore not a 'cane') is then elongated by drawing. Cut into lengths these rough 'beads' must then have their corners polished off. When still hot, drawn beads can be made into other shapes by pressing them or using small moulds. They can also be bi-coloured—say red with a white core. The first stage is made by pulling out a tube of white glass and then it is 'marvered' or rubbed smooth on marble. This is then rolled over half-molten red glass which adheres to it. Alternatively the white 'bead' can be dipped into a crucible containing molten glass. A drawn tube can also be pinched at regular intervals to be broken off into segments of the required length.

Folded beads

These are flattened glass canes folded round a wire. The line where the melted ends joined is often visible.[1]

Pressed beads

While still half molten the incipient bead is pressed into hexagonal or square or biconical shapes.

Spiral beads

The half-molten canes are wound spirally round a wire which, if tapered, would produce tapered segmented beads of the type common on Roman sites.

Blown beads

Used exceptionally for hollow beads (blown glass was not invented until the first century B.C.). Some large beads were apparently made by blowing them like a vessel, but these are very rare in Britain. The invention made glass-ware much cheaper to produce.

Hand-perforated beads

Drops of molten glass are perforated with a tool while still hot. This is a very simple form of bead-making and may well have been used by unpractised natives making their own beads in native villages and hill-forts. The perforation is sometimes enlarged by filing, and striations can be seen.

Dr. Haevernick [2] reproduces a vivid picture of Africans spinning molten glass on two sticks until they are cool and well rounded as annular or ring beads. A characteristic of this type is that the inner circumference of the bead (or armlet) is smooth and tapered.

COLOURS AND OPACIFIERS USED FOR GLASS BEADS

A variety of colours were popular in pre-Roman and Roman times in Britain; the commonest ones in use during the Iron Age were translucent or seemingly opaque blue (a variety of shades but mostly 'cobalt'), opaque yellow, and opaque white (which was reserved for decoration of applied waves, spirals, eyes, and so on). Terracotta red (Pliny's *haematinum*) and occasionally, but rarely, glass which appears black may also have been in use before

[1] Knowles, W. J. (1897), 523 ff.
[2] Haevernick, T. E. (1960), Textafel A, taken from Fro-benius, *Und Afrika Sprach*, Band 2 (1912). Her work includes full references to bead-manufacturing techniques.

the Roman conquest. Translucent greenish-blue glass was introduced before the Romans and is discussed below, as is also colourless translucent glass. After the conquest opaque emerald green became increasingly popular for cylinder and polygonal beads (see pp. 95–8).

Glass can be regarded as being composed of a mixture of oxides, the main ones being silica (SiO_2), rarely less than 60 per cent, lime (CaO), soda (Na_2O) and potash (K_2O). Alumina (Al_2O_3) is usually present, derived from clays in the sand. Magnesia (MgO) and iron oxide (Fe_2O_3) are rarely if ever absent, and traces may be present of the oxides of lead, antimony, barium, etc. The presence of Al_2O_3 and Fe_2O_3 may well have resulted from the clay crucibles used.[1]

Purple may be obtained by adding manganese; deep blues are generally held to result from cobalt, but this is not invariably the case, and copper without cobalt may give a blue colour, which depends on the composition of the glass itself. 'Probably the colouring power of cobalt minerals was not fully understood in the west in the Iron Age.'[2]

Pale blue-green is produced by copper or by iron in the reduced state but not cobalt; reddish amber colour and some browns are probably due to sulphur and/or a carbon compound in combination with iron, but not leaving any trace in spectrographic tests (horse manure has also been known to have been added to produce this colour). White was used almost exclusively for decoration, and yellow was produced by adding lead oxide to produce colorants such as lead antimonate.[3] Deep greens, browns, and ruby red can be obtained by the addition of copper, and dark bottle-green glass, which does not seem to appear in these islands much before the first century A.D. and which was never commonly used for beads, can be obtained by substituting certain igneous rocks in place of sand.

From earliest glass-making times opacity was achieved through the inclusion of calcium, lead,[4] or some other antimonate, by adding phosphates or fluorides or by the presence of undissolved silicates. With the discovery of the technique of glass-blowing, now known to have been in the first century B.C., tin oxide, or copper and tin oxides began to replace the earlier opacifying agents.[5]

As Earle R. Caley has pointed out in reference to Roman glass, opacity may be caused by various factors: the presence of stannic oxide or dispersed cuprous oxide, or intense colourization caused by the presence of a high proportion of iron.[6] It can also be caused simply by insufficient heating to disperse bubbles. (Glass, faience, frit, paste, and other terms are best defined in *MAr* xv, 50, n. 32.)

A. *TRANSLUCENT GLASS*

COLOURLESS GLASS

Colourless glass is known to be deliberately obtained by the addition of either manganese or antimony to the natural greenish-coloured glass, which takes its colour from the iron

[1] Weyl, W. A. (1951). Also Tress, H. J. (1962) for ruby glass. There is a valuable discussion in *A History of Glass-making* by R. W. Douglas and S. Frank (Foulis and Co., 1970). See also Saleh, S. A., George, A. W. and Helmi, F. M. in *Studies in Conservation*, xvii (1972), 143–72.

[2] Jope, E. M. (1957). This contains useful information about glass colouring.

[3] Newton, R. G. (1971 a).

[4] Large folded sheets of lead were found in the Hellenistic glass factory in Rhodes.

[5] For discussion of lead tin oxide opacifier see Rooksby, H. P. (1962), 20–6, and (1964). See also Turner, W. E. S. and Rooksby, H. P. (1959) and (1961).

[6] Caley, E. R. (1962).

contained in the sand, or any other form of silica which must be its main ingredient. Manganese and antimony can be used either together or separately, and while antimony was utilized at least as far back as the seventh century B.C., manganese was perhaps not used until the first century A.D. and was in constant use after the sixth to fifth century A.D.[1] Where the colourless glass was produced is not yet clear. Certainly on the Continent it was used by at least the fifth century B.C. or earlier; there are big annular beads and armlets sometimes found in association with La Tène I bronze torcs from which they may have hung[2] and in the fourth century B.C. the Gauls were using colourless glass,[3] but this may have reached them as lumps of glass from an area as yet unidentified, but possibly South Russia or in the Eastern Mediterranean. D. B. Harden has pointed out[4] that both Greece and Etruria were on the route to Gaul, and we know that this glass was in use in mainland Greece from the fifth century B.C., and spherical (or 'globular') beads have often been found in Greek grave groups as well as in Etruria and elsewhere.

By La Tène II and possibly before that, both beads and armlets of clear glass were being produced in Central Europe, and their distribution can be studied from the maps prepared by Dr. T. E. Haevernick.[5] As has already been mentioned, however, areas of France and Spain and the whole of the British Isles play a very marginal part in her study, and this lack, as far as Britain is concerned, can be overcome by looking at the distribution of Classes 5, 10, and 11, all of which date from at least one or two centuries and maybe more before the Roman conquest.

In Britain the use of colourless glass was to a large extent discontinued during the Roman period for beads, but on the Continent it was probably imported into the west from Egypt and possibly Northern Italy: we do not yet know. Pliny mentions that the first stage of glass was subsequently re-fused in a separate furnace and the product was colourless glass called *vitrum purum*. This was regarded as the best. In a third fusion the various colorants were added.[6] In Britain the colours may often have been arrived at accidentally by the impurities or trace elements in the raw material. There are kaolin-bearing whitish sands (which would produce almost colourless glass) in Devon and Cornwall, as well as in Derbyshire and Staffordshire, but there is so far no evidence for their exploitation in prehistoric times.

That Meare in Somerset[7] may have been a distribution centre during the last three or so centuries B.C. for small opaque yellow annular beads (Class 8) and for colourless glass beads often decorated with opaque yellow spirals and other designs (Classes 10 and 11) is more than probable, for large quantities of these beads were discovered there, and as yet there do not seem to be any known parallels for them on the Continent (see pp. 32–3). If colourless glass beads of the prehistoric or Roman periods are plotted on a distribution map, it is shown that nearly all the find-spots lie in the western part of Britain, with evidence for movement up

[1] Cole, H. (1966), 46–7; Sayre, E. V. (1963). Note that Bontemps (*Chemical News*, 16 Aug. 1862) proved that manganese was used for window glass at Pompeii to counteract impurities. See also *A* xlvi (1880), 65–163.
[2] Déchelette, J. (1924).
[3] e.g., examples in the museums at Épernay, Châlons-sur-Marne, Rheims, Soissons, etc.
[4] Harden, D. B. (1969).
[5] Haevernick, T. E. (1960). Some of these are so small

that they appear to resemble ring-beads somewhat comparable to our Hanging Langford Class (see pp. 51–3) and some were evidently links in chains, or hung from women's torcs as in pre-Roman Gaul.
[6] Caley, E. R. (1962).
[7] Bulleid, A. and Gray, H. St. George (1948 and 1956), followed by Cotton, M. A. (ed.) (1966). See also Avery, M. (1968), 21–39.

the Bristol Channel and up the Irish Sea to Northern Ireland and to Wigtownshire and the Scottish Isles in the last two or three centuries B.C. During the earlier Roman period some colourless segmented beads in which gold or metal foil was encased between layers of clear glass[1] were imported from the Near East—probably indirectly—and became more common in the third and fourth centuries. This method was commonly used on the Continent in the Celtic Iron Age. See Haevernick's Group 20, but pre-Roman beads with metal foil do not appear to have reached these islands.

One or two miscellaneous finds of Meare spiral beads (Class 10), which cannot be dated, come from Ireland, but there is a possibility that Ireland (which through nearly all its history went its own individual way) may have seen a renaissance of colourless glass in the fifth century and later, when large quantities of beads were manufactured there, particularly in Antrim where suitable sands are present, specially at Muckish Mount in Donegal.[2]

TRANSLUCENT NATURAL GLASS (German, *naturfarbenes*)

This glass takes its slightly greenish colour from the iron contained in the sand. It does not seem to have been popular in Britain much before the Roman period, but immediately before and after the conquest, and probably acquired from Gaul, this glass was widely used by the natives, not only for armlets of Types I, II, and III,[3] some of which were perhaps distributed from Traprain Law (East Lothian) (see pp. 35–6), but also for cable beads (Class 9) whose distribution suggests a certain concentration around the lower Severn and movement up the Irish Sea, and is complementary rather than similar to that of the Type I armlets. Both the beads and the armlets are so far regarded as native British products which were manufactured at some as yet unidentifiable place or places around the first half of the first century A.D. or shortly before. Before that this glass was rare in Britain though plain annular beads of this glass seem more concentrated around Cornwall and the Bristol Channel area than elsewhere. Their place of origin is as yet unknown. This was the type of glass which was more readily available to the native people once the Romans had established military or civil bases from which broken glass bottles and other waste could be pillaged or bartered,[4] and it is consequently only to be expected that it was used mostly for simply made annular beads throughout Roman times and on into the Saxon period; the peak period of its use seems to have been during the first to early third centuries.[5] It does not seem to have reached to any noticeable extent beyond the Forth-Clyde area, though a few examples come from the Culbin Sands, nor does it appear in Ireland with one or two rare exceptions in associations which can be proved to be earlier than the renaissance in glass-working after the fifth century.

It is strange that the various types of armlet do not appear to have been common in the Culbin area, especially as at the time of their popularity glass bead-making had become a large industry there (see Classes 13 and 14), although as mentioned above, a bronze snake

---

[1] See pp. 93–4.

[2] For the problems concerning Ireland, see pp. 39–42, below.

[3] See Preface, footnote 2.

[4] Note, too, the presence of a glass rod 5.5 cm. long from a second- to third-century site at Whitchurch in Somerset;

ArJ cxxii (1965), 25.

[5] Harden, writing on the Colchester glass vessels, mentions that very little glass seems to have entered Colchester in pre-Conquest times. It is much commoner in earlier Claudian levels, and increases considerably in the Neronian period. See Hawkes, C. F. C. and Hull, M. R. (1947).

armlet with inset blue glass came from the Culbin Sands. May this apparent lack of production of armlets there have been partly due to the natives' difficulty in getting hold of bottle-glass waste from Roman sites? It has been shown in a number of examples that analyses of the armlet glass and bottle-glass reflect similar composition,[1] and show the same trace elements. Nevertheless it would be carrying the conclusions unwisely far to claim that such was always the case: it remains unproven. Certainly both in some beads and armlets the core was made of the natural green glass and then covered with rarer cobalt or other coloured glass. It is interesting to note that when mechanically aerated this glass becomes milky white in colour, but this variety is extremely rare in British pre-Saxon beads. It may also be noted that among the imported glass gaming-pieces from a Belgic burial at Welwyn Garden City (late first century B.C.) some were of opaque white.[2]

TRANSLUCENT YELLOW, AND LIGHT GREEN, AMBER-COLOURED (REDDISH), AND GREENISH-GOLD GLASS

Pale yellow and light green glass (stronger in colour than the 'natural' glass) was preponderantly used for annular beads, and while a number of these have come from Roman towns such as Silchester (Hants) which had a long period of occupation, there are reasons for regarding these beads as being popular among the native Britons rather than the Romans, and a native element is apparent from many of the sites of their discovery. None is so far known to have come from very early Iron Age sites, but some may prove to have been as early as the third to second century B.C.[3] and to have continued into at least the second century A.D.; in the fourth century, at least at Lankhills cemetery, Winchester, little biconical beads of this yellow glass were present and may have been imported from the Rhineland. (See below, pp. 97–8.)

The difficulty we meet here is that only by testing the glass in some way will it be possible to reduce the various green and yellow beads into more precise Classes. At the moment they represent Groups only.[4]

Two colours can be studied a little more closely: amber-coloured (reddish) and greenish-gold.

Translucent amber-coloured glass (reddish) seems to have been unknown in Britain before the first century B.C., and even then was never very popular, although a few small annular beads, almost the only form used for beads in this glass, except for rare cable beads,[5] linger into the Roman period. In several cases it was used as inlay in native type armlets.[6] The beads with their fairly concentrated southern distribution—Weston-under-Penyard; Kenchester; Whitcombe, Dorchester; High Rocks, Tunbridge Wells (probably just pre-Roman); Verulamium; Hamworthy; Hunsbury, Northants. (pre-Roman); Bredon, Worcs.; Bath; The Verne, Portland;[7] and no doubt a few others—may either have been imported from

[1] Stevenson, R. B. K. (1954–5), especially 216–21.

[2] Stead, I. M. (1967).

[3] It is to be expected that some green beads may have reached Britain in the last centuries B.C., being already known on the Continent where they were widespread, e.g., light green annular beads from the early Hunsrück-Eifel Culture (about 600–400 B.C.) in Neuwied Museum. Translucent yellow glass seems to have been almost equally early.

Both may be 'natural' glass.

[4] See definition on pp. vi–vii.

[5] See below, pp. 77–9.

[6] Kilbride-Jones, H. E. (1938), and see cable beads (Class 9), pp. 77–9.

[7] For all these see the Schedules of annular beads, pp. 139–64.

the Continent or made up from lumps of imported glass. Only analysis may one day tell us. It is interesting to find that there are large numbers of amber-coloured beads, both annular and globular, from Irish collections: there are about a hundred examples from the Bell and Grainger collections in Belfast alone. Though their date is unknown, it is quite probable that they are later than the fifth century when glass-working began to be practised on a large scale in Ireland.

Translucent greenish-gold glass. Beads (here called 'Bulbury glass' after a site in Dorset near Poole Harbour (see p. 30) have such an individual and strong colour, as well as a predominantly southern distribution at about the period (? second century B.C. to second century A.D.) that it is worth regarding them as possible imports. Where they came from we do not yet know (but at least in one case the site where these beads were found produced a Roman or Venetic type of anchor,[1] and Amorica may have been the source). The sites yielding Bulbury glass[2] are Silchester, Hants (a Roman town); Verulamium, St. Albans, Herts. (dated 10 B.C. to A.D. 40); Portland, Dorset (first century A.D.); Kingscote, Glos. (?first century A.D.); Irchester, Northants. (Iron Age 'B' or early Belgic); Porthmeor, Cornwall (early Roman probably); Bulbury, Dorset (eight examples with mirror, etc., of first century A.D.); St. Mawgan-in-Pyder, Cornwall (? first century B.C. or A.D.); Worthy Down, Hants (? second to first century B.C.); and Whitton Roman villa, Glamorgan (probably first century B.C. or A.D.). Very similar glass comes from Usk, Monmouthshire (dated A.D. 55–60); Prestatyn, Flint (almost certainly Roman period); and Meare, Somerset (probably second to first century B.C.),[3] as well as from ' Rochester and Alnham,' Northumberland; and Carrawburgh (a bead with a yellow wave decoration from a settlement dating from approximately A.D. 122–383). A large cable bead (Class 9) in this glass came from St. Giles' Hill, Winchester, apparently reused in a later context, and should belong between the first century B.C. to second century A.D. A recent example not yet published comes from Hengistbury Head, Dorset, associated apparently with Dressel IA amphorae of the second to mid-first century B.C. Maybe this glass was distributed from here.

This small group is worthy of being tested to see whether analytically any of these beads are of identical glass, and the non-destructive techniques which have recently become available may well answer a number of such questions.

TRANSLUCENT BLUE GLASS

Among the earliest imported glass beads in Britain were the small annular beads of cobalt or prussian blue glass (Group 6) beginning around the mid-first millennium B.C. (see fig. 22). Others are of blue, almost translucent cobalt-coloured, glass decorated with blue and white eyes (the type known from the Marnian graves at Arras in Yorkshire, Class 1) and from Swallowcliffe and other sites in the south, at present thought to date from about the fifth to fourth century B.C. This cobalt blue (sometimes loosely used here to describe the colour and not necessarily implying the use of cobalt rather than copper) as well as lighter translucent blue continued to be favoured among imported and British Celtic beads (see Classes 1, 3, and

[1] Cunliffe, B. (1972), 293–308.
[2] All in the annular bead Schedules except for one from
Carrawburgh which has a wave decoration.
[3] Nos. G6. EV and G9.

6) up to the time of the Roman conquest. Then, apart from annular beads with white, or less commonly, yellow waves (Group 5 (A)) which continued right through Roman and Saxon times, they became less used except for simple annular beads and for the small biconical ones (pp. 97–8) and other small beads of non-Celtic origin in the later Roman period. The reason for this is probably twofold: imported beads were probably not any longer being traded to Britain, nor was the glass pot-metal which may have been available in pre-Roman times for manufacture in this country (though its scarcity at Meare is difficult to explain). During the Roman period, as Stevenson has suggested, the common ribbed blue glass melon beads (nearly as common at the mainly second-century Newstead [1] as the faience ones) may have provided a source for blue beads or armlets made by native craftsmen. For a discussion of glass melon beads see below, p. 100.

Many of the small annular blue beads which continue right through the Iron Age and probably through the Roman period as well as the Saxon and Viking periods have no special characteristics, and many of those not found in datable associations, but listed in the Schedules (pp. 155–62), may well be post-Roman.

As far as the armlets of Scottish northern type are concerned it has already been mentioned that Stevenson[2] noted that in some instances the cobalt glass had been used extremely sparingly over the ordinary translucent blue-green core—supporting the suggestion made above that cobalt blue glass became increasingly rare after the late first and early second century A.D.

Translucent bright sky-blue glass was much used in the early Roman period.

PURPLE TRANSLUCENT GLASS

This colour was never very commonly used in Britain. Some very thick annular beads of Class 7 appear to be black unless held to a strong light. In its raw state this coloured glass was found at Hengistbury Head near Christchurch, Dorset,[3] evidently ready for distribution and reuse in the second or first century B.C. Similar glass seems to belong to the first century A.D. or late B.C. at Loughey, Donaghadee in Ireland,[4] and was used sometimes for large Celtic ray and whirl beads on the Continent.[5] Its use died out after the beginning of the Roman period in this country.

TRANSLUCENT RED AND CRIMSON GLASS

This was never common in Britain, and the rare examples were Continental imports, perhaps sometimes reused to decorate native glass armlets.[6] Opaque red glass, particularly terracotta-coloured, was slightly more common, and it is often hard to be sure if the glass was translucent or opaque.

A burial at Clevedon, Somerset (see Group 8), was found with some barrel-shaped and

---

[1] Curle, J. (1911).
[2] Stevenson, R. B. K. (1954–5).
[3] *HH*. Purple glass also came from a primary context from a broch in Tiree. See MacKie, E. W. (1965 b), 270.
[4] Jope, E. M. (1957), 82–4 and (1960), 40.
[5] Haevernick, T. E. (1960), and one example from Glastonbury. (See Class 7.)

[6] See pp. 35–6. Used either as oblique bands or spots, e.g., Braidwood Fort, Midlothian (*PSAS* lxxxiii (1948–9), 10); Dod Law, near Wooler, Northumberland (*ibid.* lxxxvii (1952–3), 202); Dunagoil Fort, Bute (*TBNHS* lix (1925)). It is also known from Continental armlets of La Tène III. See Haevernick, T. E. (1960) and, e.g., Krämer, W. (1958), Taf. 1, etc.

apparently hand-moulded colourless glass beads covered with a fine film of crimson translucent glass,[1] accompanied by beads of yellow opaque glass (Class 8) and one of Class 11. This burial should probably be attributed to the second or first century B.C. The extreme delicacy of this thin glass makes its survival difficult, but it is worth noticing in this context that Warne, excavating in the last century in Dorset at Shapwick,[2] found what was described as a 'ruby coloured barrel-shaped bead which had evidently undergone the action of fire' in a barrow with a cremation. Three stratified pieces of red glass dated to phase 2 (now thought to belong to the third to second centuries B.C.) came from refuse tips at Meare in Somerset which may have been the glass factory which produced the Clevedon beads.

On the Continent, too, pre-Roman red or crimson glass is uncommon and it may be true to a certain extent as J. L. Pič suggested[3] that red amber (and one might suggest coral) was preferred by the Celtic peoples. But unrefined carmine-coloured glass was found at Manching which may have been a glass-producing centre.[4] O. Kunkel also noted semi-finished products there.[5] This glass was represented both in bracelets and beads at Třisov.[6]

Opaque red glass was mostly used in Britain for decoration on Celtic bronze-work such as the Battersea and Witham shields, the brooch from Datchet, and other pieces—sometimes used in a *cloisonné* technique [7]—but it never reached popularity for beads either during the Iron Age or subsequently.

BEADS WHICH APPEAR TO BE BLACK

Beads which appear to be black were never common in Britain before the beginning of the fifth century: they were then imported from Germanic sources and also appear, from their numbers there, to have been manufactured in Ireland as well. In Britain some beads and armlets appear to be black until held to the light when they are shown to be very dark green, brown or purple. In fact with very dark beads it is sometimes impossible to be sure either whether the glass was opaque or translucent, or what was its colour.

A small annular 'black' bead came from the Iron Age village at Meare in Somerset (Taunton Museum, no. G49. EV),[8] and others from Roman sites such as South Shields, Weston-under-Penyard, and Corbridge. Globular beads of 'black' glass are equally rare; one came from Hunsbury fort (Northants.), perhaps second or first century B.C., and a few came from Roman towns, though during the Roman period jet from Whitby or occasionally shale may have been preferred. The real popularity of 'black' glass, as mentioned above, came at the very end of Roman times, introduced by Germanic peoples, whose beads were frequently decorated in opaque red, yellow or blue (see pl. II, no. 4).

---

[1] Gray, H. St. George (1942), 73–6. (See Group 8, p. 71.)
[2] Warne, C. (1866), 39–40.
[3] Pič, J. L. (1906).
[4] Krämer, W. (1961).
[5] Kunkel, O. (1961), 322.
[6] Břeň, J. (1966), 136–7.

[7] Fox, C. (1958). What appears to be a red glass stud or half a bead has recently been found at Burton Fleming in an Iron Age cemetery in Yorkshire. (Information from T. C. M. Brewster.)
[8] They are known, though rarely, in the Continental Iron Age. See Krämer, W. (1964).

B. *OPAQUE GLASS*

YELLOW OPAQUE GLASS

Yellow opaque glass is obtained by the admixture of lead and also antimony and tin. As a ground colour this was extremely popular in Britain for some centuries from about the third century B.C. or earlier, and on the Continent it was frequently used for single or double-tier beads with blue and white eyes (Class 4).[1] These beads (perhaps Phoenician or Carthaginian) possibly originated somewhere in the Mediterranean area and remained popular for some centuries. They were among the varieties still being produced in the late third to early second century B.C. factory at Rhodes.[2]

In Britain one of the earliest beads made of opaque yellow glass came from All Cannings Cross in Wiltshire,[3] belonging perhaps to the fifth or fourth century B.C. It has a brown wave around it somewhat like an example from Les Jogasses in France,[4] probably nearly contemporary. A somewhat similar bead has recently been found at Beckford, Worcestershire with stamped wares (unpublished) and a little later perhaps are some beads from the Queen's Barrow at Arras in Yorkshire, where opaque yellow glass has been used for the wave decoration.[5] Apparently dating from about the third to second century B.C., though lingering on into the first century A.D., are the small annular beads (Class 8) which appear to have been manufactured, perhaps from imported glass, at Meare in Somerset[6] and in the Culbin Sands area of Moray (see pp. 34–5). At about the same time the so-called Meare spiral beads (Class 10) and the possibly contemporary or slightly later variants (Class 11) were being made at Meare and apparently imitated by the turn of B.C. to A.D. at Culbin (Class 13) where decorated annular beads (Class 14) were also being made. Approximately at the same time some beads of well-known Celtic Continental type decorated with opaque yellow design (Classes 5, 6, and 7) were being imported, some into the main area of Belgic settlement in the south-east, and some further to the west. This glass was also popular for the native armlets now thought to have been made in the first century B.C. to first century A.D.[7] After the conquest, however, a sharp decline is detected, and it may have been that the native Britons had been cut off from their main source of supply of this variety of glass, whose origin may lie somewhere in Central Europe. Throughout the Roman period this glass seems to have been rare, but was again, of course, very popular in the Migration period.[8]

An attempt has recently been made by Dr. R. G. Newton[9] to discuss whether opaque yellow glass from several different beads and armlets in the pre-Roman or early Roman Iron Age, if examined by milliprobe X-ray fluorescent spectrometer and neutron activation analysis, could be found to have been made of glass metal from the same source. The results suggested that two of the armlets tested showed that the glass from which they were made

---

[1] e.g., from Santa Lucia di Tolmino (about 450–300 B.C.) in Italy (*NS* (1930), 426), and from Vraux, Marne, in France, probably fifth century B.C. (in the museum at Châlons-sur-Marne). There are others in St. Germain and in many Continental collections.

[2] Weinberg, Gl. Davidson (1969).

[3] Cunnington, M. E. (1923).

[4] Favret, P.-M. (1936), 24–119.

[5] Stead, I. M. (1965).

[6] Bulleid, A. and Gray, H. St. George (1948 and 1956)

and especially Cotton, M. A. (ed.) (1967).

[7] See p. 58.

[8] I have examined a number of Frankish beads which might, at first sight, be confused with the Iron Age ones (Class 8), but they are generally less regular, and the tone of yellow more lemon-coloured; they also tend to be more globular in shape. See, for example, Christlein, R. (1966).

[9] Newton, R. G. (1971), and also *Ar* xv (1973), 53–7 and 74–6.

could have had the same origin, but that a bead of earlier date from Overton in Wiltshire (Class 11) had a noticeably lower manganese content and could not have been derived from the same 'stock'. This result was only to be expected. It is hoped that further, and much more extensive, work on these lines will produce more positive results.

OPAQUE RED AND TERRACOTTA-COLOURED GLASS

This, though not uncommon amongst Gaulish beads and again extremely popular in Frankish and Germanic beads, was never, until the post-Roman period, very much favoured in Britain. Perhaps it may have been technically difficult to make.[1] One of the pre-Roman annular beads from Meare was a yellow one which had been coated with terracotta-coloured glass paste, suggesting that the latter was rare. As already mentioned in the discussion of translucent red glass, it is not always possible to be quite certain at first glance if some glass was translucent or opaque; if thin enough, however, it can be seen to be translucent. It was in any case never commonly used for beads in Iron Age or Roman times in Britain. It appears in a few exotic Roman beads, perhaps imported from far away parts of the Empire, and it is also found as eyes in beads of Class 3 and as bands or chevrons in the early Germanic beads from the fourth century A.D. and later, when glass paste was more commonly used.

Lead was used as a pigment or as an agent in making red glass but it is not known quite when it was first used. At Tara in Ireland a lump of red 'opaque' glass was discovered in a context thought to date between the first to third century A.D., but so far lead sulphide ore has not been recognized from Ireland and its provenance is therefore unknown.[2] Since yellow and red may be obtained from the same lead, perhaps some red annular beads (which apart from colour are identical with the Class 8 yellow beads) from Airrieoland Crannog, Ayrshire, may in fact have been intended to be yellow but owing to firing or some accidental or intentional change had become red. Another samian-coloured red drawn bead came from Milking Gap, Northumberland.

Bright sealing-wax-coloured red beads have recently been found in a probably first-century A.D. context at Kingscote, Glos. This colour is discussed in Bateson and Hedges (1975).

OPAQUE BLUE GLASS

(a) *Cobalt blue.* In its opaque form this glass is very rare until the Roman period and particularly the later part of it when many beads were imported from other parts of the Empire. It was widely used for small segmented beads and long biconical beads, both plain or decorated with red or white bands or chevrons as well as for other smaller forms of Roman beads and polygonal beads. It is also worth noting that the decorated annular beads made in Scotland (Class 14) often employ opaque blue, but whether this was deliberate or accidental

[1] A recent study of Iron Age opaque red glass has been made, and is valuable for technological data and references. Hughes, M. J. (1972).

[2] For Tara, see *TRIA* xxx (1892–6), 277–93. Dr. Robert Brill is continuing his researches into lead sulphide ores which occur in many deposits in the ancient world. These different deposits in say Spain, Greece, England, etc., produce differing amounts of lead isotopes in galena ores, so that although their exact provenance cannot as yet be identified, at least a geological similarity can be claimed. For example a chip of lead from a first century Roman vase from Caerleon matched the locally mined lead very closely.

is unknown. In all probability, chance impurities may have given rise to many colours, unsuspected even by the beadmakers themselves, for it is improbable that the craftsmen were so sophisticated that they knew the exact proportions of trace elements required to give the colours they selected.

(b) *Sky blue*. Most of the beads made of sky blue glass are smallish annular, globular, or occasionally rather larger oblong beads. A rare example from Water Tower Street, Chester, was associated with a coin of Vespasian: it is small and barrel-shaped with a white wave and painted gold band round one end and is almost surely an import. One of the earliest pre-Roman examples of this glass came from Castle Dore in Cornwall [1] where the first occupation mainly belonged to the second century B.C., but on the whole the maximum popularity for this colour was reached in the first two or three centuries A.D., and this tallies with the Roman Continental sites as well. This glass was sometimes used in England and abroad for small oblong square-sectioned beads, sometimes threaded on a wire.[2] Surface finds in a shiny condition should be regarded with suspicion in this country where there was a widespread revival of this glass colour in Victorian and later times, both for bobbin weights for lace-making and for children's games.

'BLACK' OPAQUE GLASS

As has been mentioned above, p. 15, it is often difficult to be sure with weathered or thick 'black' glass whether it is really opaque or very thick translucent. The remarks made there may be taken as relevant for opaque glass as well.

OPAQUE DARK BROWNS, PURPLES AND GREENS

Opaque dark browns, purples and greens were particularly common in the Culbin Sands glass used for Classes 13 and 14 and in all probability were accidentally coloured by impurities. Only opaque green was popular in Britain after the Roman conquest, and particularly in the third to fifth century this glass was commonly used for many polygonal beads, small segmented beads, cylinder and cut cylinder beads, and others; originally these may have been poorer imitations of emeralds. Many other opaque colours reappear in quantity with the intrusive beads which began to filter into this country early in Roman times, but especially after the third century when barbarian inroads are attested, and then reached their crescendo during the next centuries.[3] By the fifth century the Kentish and Thames cemeteries reflect a mixed population of Britons, *foederati*, and Saxons.

[1] Radford, C. A. R. (1951).
[2] As for instance from Croft Ambry, Herefordshire. Stanford, S. C. (1974).
[3] See *ArJ* cxx (1963), 134. At Lankhills Cemetery at Winchester, graves with burials containing South German beads and other objects of the fourth century were recently discovered, and the full report by the Winchester Research Unit is forthcoming.

We also know that defences against Saxon raiders were hurriedly adapted at Richborough, Kent, and other sites in the last quarter of the third century when the 'Saxon shore forts' were begun by Carausius and Allectus, so some Saxon beads may have come into Britain earlier than we at present suspect.

PART II

ARCHAEOLOGICAL CONSIDERATIONS

THE EARLIEST GLASS BEADS IN BRITAIN

IT is now clear that there were sporadic examples of glass beads reaching Britain by the second millennium B.C. and these, if they came by the western sea routes and not direct from the Continent, must take their place alongside, though not perhaps altogether contemporary with, the various other imports from the Eastern Mediterranean characterizing the Wessex Culture in the south (see below). As, however, that culture is still under discussion, with some favouring for it a long and others a short duration, it follows that the dating of some of our glass beads must await the verdict. Beads may be prior to it, some others

● *Second and Early First Millennium Glass Beads*   ○ *Early Date uncertain*

FIG. 2: Distribution of second- and early first-millennium B.C. glass beads.

19

may post-date it, and link, without any identifiable gap, with the earliest Iron Age beads imported by about the sixth century B.C. from the northern Continent.

Not all early beads may have been brought in by trade. The accidental discovery of glass in different places can easily have come about, as pointed out by Renfrew, when sea-weed was used as fuel for smelting copper.

Unfortunately most British examples come from badly documented excavations; no attempt was made in early publications to illustrate beads, and details of many of them and of their associated objects are now lost. Others may exist, but without any known provenance. To make matters even more difficult, many early excavators failed to distinguish between primary and secondary burials. All the same, and despite the occasional confusion between glassy faience and true glass, there are examples which clearly indicate a second-millennium B.C. date, and these fall comfortably into place beside many Continental glass beads, some of which are discussed below.

The glass beads of early date from Britain are as follows:

England

Boscregan, St. Just-in-Penwith, Carn Creis (Cornwall). An oblong bead with bands wound around it, once filled with colour now missing. Found with cremations, faience, and shale beads, and a V-bored button under a barrow. Presumably Wessex Culture. (Borlase, W. C. (1879), pl. 16, no. 3.) This sounds like a banded bead of Mediterranean type.

Rillaton, Linkinhorne (Cornwall). 'A few glass beads with a Wessex culture ogival dagger and gold cup.' Possibly faience. Now lost. At least the gold cup, dagger, and beads were apparently secondary in an earlier cairn. (Borlase, W. C. (1872) and *ArJ* xxiv (1867), 189.)

Thirkel-low, Frith, nr. Buxton (Derbyshire). Again possibly faience. *PSAL* xv (1893–5), 425.

Moretonhampstead, Moor Barton Farm (Devon). 'A glass bead, and with it a spearhead [i.e. dagger] of copper and a small amulet of soft stone', the latter perhaps a whetstone. Again possibly Wessex Culture. (*Devonshire Barrows* (Devon Association Reports, xxi, 31).) According to R. P. Carrington's notebook in the Devon Record Office at Exeter the beads were 'blue and white'. All the finds were in a stone cist.

St. Alban's Head, Portland (Dorset). Green glass bead 'in form merely a drop of glass pierced through', with a pot which might be Bronze Age. (*ArJ* vii (1850), 385).

Winterborne St. Martin (Dorset). Bronze Age urn with glass and faience beads. (ApSimon, A. M. and Greenfield, E. (1972), 357).

Stockbridge (Hants). 'A small transparent glass bead of pale bluish colour . . . crudely and badly made, having lost its shape whilst being fired.' Originally regarded as intrusive, this bead is probably contemporary with the Middle Bronze Age burial. (*PPS* iv (1938), 251 and B.M. Registration No. 1939 5–6, 20. See also Stone, J. F. S. (1940).)

Carnforth at Yealand (Lancs.). Found in 1778 in a barrow containing urns with cremated bones. Large blue glass bead 2·5 cm. in diameter. (Baines, E., *History of Lancashire*, iv (1836), 581, and *A* vii (1785), 414.)

Knackyboy Cairn, St. Martin's (Scilly Isles) with a faience star bead. Also found were an irregular greenish-blue, semi-translucent bead, and a large globular blue glass bead. These were with a cremation burial with urns, etc., and were thought to belong to the late second millennium B.C. (Stone, J. F. S. (1952).)

Chewton Mendip (Somerset). 'Small opaque blue glass bead, perforated' from cist in cairn with grape cup, amber beads, bronze knife dagger, etc. (Grinsell, L. V. (1971), 99.)

Marksbury (Somerset). Barrow destroyed in about 1827. A skeleton was found and 'near its neck a glass bead larger than a walnut'. (Possibly a secondary burial?) (*PSAHNS* cxv (1971), 108.)

South Chard, Tatworth (Somerset). Bright greenish-blue globular bead, 11 mm. in diameter, with a Middle or Late Bronze Age pot, awl, thirty amber beads, etc. Taunton Museum. Thought by Gray to date from the early first millennium B.C. (*PSAHNS* xcvii (1952), 184–5. See also *AnJ* xviii (1938), and Abercromby, J. (1912), ii, pl. xc 1, fig. 433 and pl. cviii, figs. O14 and P.43.)

Wookey Hole, Cheddar (Somerset). One small opaque blue bead from a Bronze Age barrow. (Balch, H., *Wookey Hole* (1914), 150.)

Kingston Deverill (Wiltshire). Objects (lost) included bone tweezers, glass, amber, and jet beads, with cremations in a bowl barrow. (Hoare, R. Colt (1812), i, 75, pl. ix.)

It should be noted that so-called 'yellow glass' beads from Pensthorpe, Norfolk (*ArJ* vi (1849), 409) and from Barrow Amesbury G44 (in both cases associated with segmented faience beads) are now known to have been calcite. See Stone, J. F. S. (1940), 43–4.

Ireland

Although in some periods of her prehistory Ireland suffered a certain time-lag in comparison with other more advanced parts of the British Isles, during the Early and Middle Bronze Age her richness in gold kept her in communication with Europe via the western sea routes. There is reason to suppose that at least some of the glass beads from Irish contexts go back into the second millennium B.C. Nor should it be forgotten that the Massiliote Periplus quoted by Avienus refers to trade between Ireland and possibly Brittany.

Carnduff (Co. Antrim). Blue bead from a megalith which produced Neolithic ware. (Wood-Martin, W. G., *Pagan Ireland* (1886), 299.)

Gortnacargy, nr. Bawnboy (Co. Cavan). Small blue glass bead with Irish Late Bronze Age character urn. Possibly first millennium B.C. (*PPS* xxiv (1958), 212.)

Mullaghmore (Co. Down). From a ritual site with pottery of apparently Bronze Age date. (ÓRiordáin, S. P. (1954), 357.)

Pollacorragune (Co. Galway). In a cist in the top of a tumulus containing a Class I razor. (*JGAHS* xvii, 48.)

Lough Gur (Co. Limerick), Site C. Small greenish-blue wire-wound bead, apparently from a local Bronze Age context. Technically this bead resembles those from the XVIIIth Dynasty in Egypt, and also some from Southern France. (ÓRiordáin, S. P. (1954), 354–8.)

Aghnaskeagh (Co. Louth). Blue glass bead from Bronze Age cairn, with cremations and a pot, apparently primary. (*CLAJ* viii (1935), fig. 4, facing p. 245.)

Lough Crew (Co. Meath). One bead of translucent greenish glass. (*PSAS* xxx (1895–6, 342.)

Two blue glass beads on an amber necklace came from Antrim and are in the Beck Collection, and a similar necklace is in the Murray Collection; both in Cambridge Museum of Archaeology and Ethnology. (See Beck, H. C. (1936), 14, pl. III, and *A* lxxxv (1936), 212.) Date uncertain.

For the later Irish Bronze Age, see Eogan, G. (1964).

Scotland

Gilchorn, Arbroath (Forfar). Small irregular, drop-shaped whitish glass bead, partially opalescent, and with signs of a spiral band at one end. (N.M.A., Edinburgh.) Found with a cinerary urn, etc. This bead was compared by Dr. D. B. Harden with XVIIIth Dynasty beads, now in the Ashmolean Museum in Oxford. (*PSAS* xxv (1890–1), 447–56.)

Glentrool (Kirkcudbrightshire). With a Middle or Late Bronze Age hoard perhaps dating from about the twelfth century B.C. (see discussion below). (*PSAS* lv (1921), 32–3.)

Adabrock (Isle of Lewis). Blue bead about 12 mm. in diameter, now weathered with small greenish spots. With a hoard containing Class II razors. Perhaps about eighth century B.C. (see below). (*PSAS* xlv (1910–11) and lvii (1922–3), 33.)

Eddertoun (Ross-shire). Streaked glass bead found in a cairn with what sounds like a cordoned urn, cremation, and a small bronze point. (*PSAS* v (1862–4), 311–15.)

Wales

Llanbabo (Anglesey). This bead might have been faience. From a cairn. (*PSAL* xix (1902), 50.)

The problems concerning early glass-making and the trade of beads across Europe from factories in the Near East and elsewhere would present a valuable subject for research. At first the products from these early factories may have been bartered or exchanged for Baltic amber, which many scholars now think travelled across the Continent via the eastern end of the Alps to reach the head of the Adriatic somewhere near Aquileia at least by the late third or early second millennium B.C. Research concerned with the earliest glass (as distinct from faience or frit) beads to have found their way across Europe, even to Britain, by this date, is confined to regional, or at best national, lists, but no attempt has as yet been made to draw the information together to obtain an approximate chronological sequence. Nor do we know when glass beads were first made in European factories. Like amber, with its magnetic power, glass beads, particularly when decorated with an eye or spiral, have always been regarded as having magical qualities, and were therefore greatly in demand, and though the earliest beads must have been undecorated, they were presumably prized because of the newly discovered material of which they were made—glass. Subsequently the addition of decoration prompted their supposed efficacy against the 'evil eye' and as such talismans they have been valued right through history from Pliny's description of 'serpent's eggs' among the ancient Gauls, and the 'Druid's eggs' or 'adder's eggs' reported by the seventeeth-century historians of Britain to the amulets superstitiously dangled by car drivers in the Middle East today.

It is not the place here to enter into a detailed discussion of the date of the earliest glass factories in the Near East, but information of basic importance is given in Harden, D. B. (1968), both in the text and footnotes. It is sufficient here to mention that glass had already been discovered by the third millennium B.C., for a fragmentary glass rod in the Berlin Antiquarium bears the insignia of Amenemat III (XIIth Dynasty, 2050–2000 B.C.) and Harden cites a lump of dark blue glass, for resmelting, from Abu Shahrain (Eridu) in Mesopotamia, of at least as early a date. Other important sources include Petrie, W. Flinders (1888); Griffith, F. Ll. (1902–7); Axel von Saldern in Mallowan, M. E. L. (1966); Oppenheim, A. L. *et al.* (1970); Brunton, G. (1930) and (1937); Beck, H. C. (1934); many articles in *Iraq*, particularly vol. xvi, part 1 (1954), 83; Reports of the Oxford Excavations at Faras (Nubia) in *Liverpool Annals*, viii–x; and Nolte, B. (1968). Oppenheim, A. L., in *J. Amer. Orient. Soc.*, xciii (1973), 259–66, cites linguistic evidence in cuneiform texts, saying that Egyptian glass-workers were using imported glass cakes from Syria.

An article on the spread of gold jewellery across Europe (Hawkes, C. F. C. (1961)) is also relevant to some of the trade routes followed in the case of glass products, and is valuable for drawing attention to gold penannular ear-rings and hair-rings which reached Bronze Age Ireland from the Eastern Mediterranean.

It is possible that glass beads were being made in European secondary factories by the later second millennium B.C. or at least the early first, and were at first, no doubt, imitations of the imported ones from the Near East.[1] Dates in the second millennium for Northern European glass beads would once have been considered very early, and, in fact, talking of the finds from a Breton dagger grave (contemporary with the Wessex Culture) at Landivisian (Finistère) in 1934, Professor Piggott regarded a glass bead as 'an unexpected and puzzling feature'.[2]

Although some of the British examples, with a notable concentration in south-west England (fig. 2), cannot be closely dated, the evidence of funerary associations suggests that at least the Boscregan (St. Just-in-Penwith), Chewton Mendip, Stockbridge and Kingston Deverill burials belong to some phase of the Wessex Culture of the second millennium, a culture whose duration, as mentioned above, has not yet been determined,[3] but which drew imports (or models to copy) from both the Eastern Mediterranean and Central Europe. Not far removed in date would be the beads from Gilchorn, Arbroath, in Scotland and Lough Gur in Ireland, both of which are paralleled from XVIIIth Dynasty Egypt (sixteenth to fourteenth century B.C.).

About sixty or more glass beads have come from French megalithic tombs. Daniel, G. (1958) lists examples from the Dolmen de Pilandes-Costes (or Truan) (Aveyron); Fournes II gallery grave (Aveyron) with fragments of metal and a V-bored button; Grotte de St. Jean d'Alcas (St. Jean de Paul) (Aveyron); Grotte Monier (Var); Grotte de Bringaret (Aude) and the possibly Hallstatt date Romanin ossuary near St. Rémy (Bouches-du-Rhône). Other French examples come from Treille, Mailhac (Aude) where eight small blue glass beads were found with a faience mace-head and degenerate Beaker fragments[4]; while those from the Dolmen à Grailhe (Gard)[5] were dated by Beck to 2000–1500 B.C. Others are reported by Arnal from Grotte Landric, St. Baulize, and other dolmens in Aveyron, and others include the above-mentioned dagger grave at Landivisian (Finistère), Le Comb Bernard, Magny-Lambert (Côte-d'Or); Vinets, Ramperup (Aude), etc., referred to by Sandars, N. K.

---

[1] For possible local imitation of faience beads, see p. 34.

[2] Piggott, S., in *PPS* v (1934), 193.

[3] For the latest discussion of this, see *VCH Wiltshire* I (ii), 352–7 (1973), Branigan, K. (1970), and Burgess, C. in

Renfrew, C. (ed.) (1974).

[4] *Ampurias* xi (1949), 25.

[5] Beck, H. C. (1934), 7.

(1957) and Schaeffer, F. A. (1926). The majority seem to have been distributed from the Mediterranean coast.

In support of a second millennium date for some glass beads are some barrel-shaped ones, some of glass and some of faience, associated with Mycenaean sherds of L.H. IIIA from La Portella, Salina, in the Lipari Islands.[1] This date would be slightly earlier than some East Mediterranean imports into Britain, such as the Pelynt sword fragment from Cornwall, thought by Branigan to belong to L.H. IIIB.[2] but possibly contemporary with the bronze double axes.[3]

As far as the rest of the European mainland is concerned, only a few references can here be suggested, but the time is fast approaching when a coherent study might profitably be made. For Central Europe see Childe, V. G. (1929), Dehn in *Germania* xxix (1951); Harding, A. (1971), 'The Earliest Glass in Europe'; *Archeol. Rozhledy* xxiii. 2; Godmer Gessner, V., 'Vom Problem der Spätbronzezeitlichen Glasperlen' in *Festschrift Reinhold Bosch*, 80–98 (Aarau; also Kuhn in *JPEK* (1935), 130, for Egyptian beads in Central Europe). For Germany see Reinecke, S. (1911). For Holland see *Analecta Praehistorica Leidensia*, viii (1975), 97 and note references in Butler, J. J. (1969), *Nederland in der Bronstijd* (Bussum). For Austria see Willvonseder, K. (1937) who gives valuable glass references among many referring to faience. For Czechoslovakia see Venclová, N. (1971) who lists about ten examples from Bohemia but emphasizes the rarity of Middle Bronze Age glass beads in comparison with those of the Late Bronze and Hallstatt periods, Leheckova, E. (1972), *Vorgeschichtliche Glasperlen aus Böhmen und Mähren* (Annales du 5me Congrès de l'Association Internationale pour l'Histoire du Verre, Prague, 6–11 juillet, 1970, S. 31–40, Liège) and Moucha, V. (1958), 'Faience and glassy faience beads in the Unétice Culture in Bohemia, *Epitymbion Roman Haken* (Prague). For Denmark see Brønsted, J., *Danmarks Oldtid II* (1939), 118.

A well-documented glass bead from Glentrool in Kirkcudbrightshire may be some centuries later than the earliest glass beads to reach Britain, and may belong to the twelfth to eleventh centuries B.C., approximately contemporary with the Knackyboy beads from the Isles of Scilly. Coles has written: 'The Glentrool hoard [bronzes] has analogous material in Ireland and in Somerset, and is the northern representative of the Ornament horizon in South England, dated mainly by its contacts with Period III in Northern Europe.'[4]

Not long after this may be the beads mentioned by Brønsted from Humlum (district of Ringkøbing) in Denmark found with a gold wire arm-ring of about 1000–800 B.C. but by this time glass-works were probably already producing glass in a number of European countries, first perhaps at the head of the Adriatic, and then in Central Europe. A few centuries later, the end of the earlier series in Britain may be marked by the bead from a group at Adabrock in the Isle of Lewis, again discussed by Coles. This group included what appears to have been part of a cross-handle-holder bowl of von Merhart's Class B2b, and other finds which date it approximately to the seventh to sixth centuries B.C., to a period, that is, when north-eastern Scotland, between Moray and Tay, was in direct contact with the north-western German plain (Cole's Adabrock and Tarves phases), and when the Celtic

---

[1] *BPI* lxv (1956), 61. See also Karo, G., 'Schatz von Tiryns' in *Athenische Mitteilungen*, lv (1930), 119–40, especially 125 and 129 ff., fig. 2, pl. iv.

[2] Branigan, K. (1970) and (1972), especially 282–3.
[3] Piggott, S. (1953).
[4] Coles, J. M. (1959–60).

world had been opened up to increased Mediterranean trading after the founding of Massilia around 600 B.C.

Enough information, therefore, emerges to permit us to recognize that in Britain no real hiatus intervened to separate the early beads from the later ones discussed in the present study. There was simply and understandably an increasing intensification in their production and trade during the last five centuries B.C.

IRON AGE AND ROMAN BEADS OF CONTINENTAL ORIGIN OR INSPIRATION IN BRITAIN

THEIR CULTURAL AND CHRONOLOGICAL VALUES, AND THEIR MANUFACTURE AND DISTRIBUTION

During the last five or so centuries which constitute the middle and late Iron Age in Britain, some of the following Classes and Groups of beads were almost certainly imported into England. These will be described in the order here indicated, and will be found on pages 45–71.

(i) DECORATED CLASSES OF THE IRON AGE

Class 1. Small dark blue beads with blue and white eyes ('Arras' type) (pp. 45–8).

Class 2. Large globular beads with white concentric rings ('Welwyn Garden City' type) (pp. 48–9).

Class 3. Large annular beads with three coloured eyes set in white ('South Harting' type) (? imported or British made) (pp. 49–50). Almost certainly copied in Britain.

Class 4. Opaque yellow beads with two registers of blue and white eyes ('Findon' type) (pp. 50).

Class 5. Clear colourless annular beads with opaque yellow lining to perforation ('Hanging Langford' type) (pp. 51–3). Possibly copied in Britain.

Class 6. Large dark blue annular beads with bosses inlaid with white or yellow spirals ('Oldbury' type) (pp. 53–7).

Class 7. Celtic whirl and ray beads (pp. 57–9). Probably copied in Britain.

Following these Classes will be the Groups. The reader should be reminded of the division of beads into Classes and Groups stated in the Preface to this study. The Groups below serve here only as a useful corpus which it is hoped will one day be analytically classified.

(ii) DECORATED OR UNDECORATED GROUPS (both Iron Age and Roman in date)

Group 1. Large or medium annular with streaky or mottled design (pp. 59–60).

Group 2. Miscellaneous spiral decorated beads (p. 60).

Group 3. Miscellaneous horned beads, some with eyes or spirals (pp. 60–1).

Group 4. Compound-eyed beads with small eyes set in roundels ('Garrow Tor' type) (pp. 61–2).

Group 5. Miscellaneous wave-decorated beads (pp. 62–5).

Groups 6 and 7. Undecorated annular and globular beads (pp. 65–71).

Group 8. Exotic beads of Iron Age date (p. 71).

The cultural and chronological values of beads vary from one to another. Sometimes a given Class may last for several hundred years; at other times one may have been produced and have died out within a span of two or three generations. But beads, being small and attractive, may often have been regarded as precious and curious things which might be handed down as heirlooms or rediscovered many generations after their manufacture and loss, and reused on much later necklaces. It should, in time, be possible to use them, just as one uses metal brooches, etc., to indicate tribal concentrations, folk movements, and commercial contacts, both within Britain itself and in the wider context of Europe.

Among the earliest recognizable imported beads in these islands, apart from some miscellaneous Bronze Age examples (a short list of which is given on pp. 20–2), are perhaps the Arras beads of our Class 1, p. 45–8. These, though widespread in the sixth century B.C. and perhaps before in the Mediterranean lands and in Southern Europe, probably reached Britain from the Marne area around the fifth or fourth century B.C. and are found from Wessex to the graves of the Parisi in Yorkshire. Some other Classes not yet closely datable but possibly including the earliest blue beads with white waves (Group 5 (A)) and the opaque yellow beads with two rows of blue and white eyes (Class 4) may also have come in around this time, but only further examples from well-dated contexts will prove the validity of this supposition. We are handicapped, as a glance at any of the Schedules will indicate, by the comparatively few beads from well-dated archaeological deposits: the great mass come from old excavations or chance finds. It is only to be expected that a great many beads came across to England during the last few centuries B.C. but some of the trade may have been from Britain to the Continent once the bead factories had begun production in Britain.

During La Tène II and III there was a partial and slow cultural infiltration from Belgium and elsewhere, though perhaps it was not until the second century B.C. that large numbers of people crossed the channel as invaders, settlers, traders or refugees. The distribution of certain classes of beads may one day be found to tally with that of other finds such as the various coin types studied by D. F. Allen.[1]

A great difficulty in Britain lies in the fact that only relatively few Iron Age beads have been found in associated groups, and Professor Piggott's words should be borne in mind: 'Since Iron Age society was socially stratified, distribution maps of domestic things, e.g., pottery, did not necessarily correspond with those of fine metal work, or coins [or perhaps glass beads]. Only in cemeteries would the three come together, and these are still undiscovered.'[2] As mentioned above, when closer dating is available, it may be possible in conjunction with other finds, such as coins, to connect certain beads with known tribal areas.

Those not familiar with the topography or the local archaeological problems in Britain may be puzzled to see from the maps here published that certain regions never seem to have received beads as trade objects. It is impossible here to attempt more than a very superficial explanation of this phenomenon, but certain facts are worth mentioning. A study still of basic importance is Fox, C. (1943).

In the Iron Age it may reasonably be expected that the areas of Britain most likely to be

[1] Allen, D. F. (1961), following (1944). For the districts of Belgic Gaul occupied by the various tribes see Hawkes, C. F. C. (1968), De Laet, S. J., in *Helinium*, i (1961) and Hachmann, R. (1976).

[2] Reported in *An* xxxiii (1959), 187.

THE IRON AGE TRIBES OF BRITAIN: Approximate territories

FIG. 3: The Iron Age tribes of Britain.

actively trading with or to be settled by small groups of Continental peoples were along the south and south-east seaboards in areas most accessible from the opposite shores. This is clearly demonstrated from the distribution patterns of beads of the third to first centuries B.C., when trade activities were at their height and when, especially after the disturbances of the Cimbri and Teutones around 100 B.C. and then at the time of Caesar's conquest of Gaul, settlers were presumably crossing the Channel and working their way inland or even sometimes coming up the Bristol Channel. That some of the British natives wished to acquire even greater numbers of beads than reached them from the Continent is shown by the presumed bead factory at Meare in Somerset which from about the third to the first century B.C. exported up the Bristol Channel and the Welsh marches as well as up the western sea-ways, and also by the pre-Agricolan North Scottish and Votadinian bead factories in the Culbin Sands, and perhaps at Traprain Law in East Lothian. (For a description of the local factories, see below, pp. 32–7.) All the same certain blank areas on the maps need to be explained, and the explanation seems to be at least partly an economic one; beads were luxuries which could be bought only when the essential needs had first been satisfied. The inhabitants of areas such as Devon and Cornwall (the Roman *Dumnonia* [1]), trading tin and other commodities especially to the Breton Veneti, had barren uplands to farm and only a rela-tively narrow coastal fringe: they could not have been rich in certain basic requirements, and the acquisition of these would have had to take priority over luxuries. Even after the Romanization of much of the rest of Britain, *Dumnonia* remained to a considerable degree unaffected by Roman influences. Much the same would have applied to most of Wales and mid- and northern Scotland, and also, perhaps again for economic reasons, to certain tribal areas such as Brigantia—again poor mountainous land. The territory of the Iceni in Norfolk and Suffolk, much of the centre of which was heavy clay land and perhaps not intensely occupied, lay outside the vigorous trading areas occupied by the Belgae and was moreover suppressed and impoverished by the Romans after the uprising under Boudicca. There are, then, social, economic, and political reasons for the lack of luxuries, and it must be remembered that some of these backward areas may have had nothing to offer in exchange. It must not be forgotten either that certain tribal areas in Britain (e.g., the Coritanian territory around Lincoln and Leicester) remain relatively unexplored archaeologically (see, however, Todd, M. (1973) and (1975)).

Continental politics must also have affected cross-channel trade to southern Britain, and such an explanation has been suggested by Barry Cunliffe to account for the distribution of certain hill-forts in south Britain.[2] It is noticeable that the earlier beads reaching Britain arrived along the south and western coasts and in the Bristol Channel area, but after the pacification of Gaul in the mid-first century B.C. the trade contacts appear to have shifted eastwards to Kent, Surrey, and Sussex. This was the rich Belgic territory which could afford to import luxuries. It has been suggested that some parts of the south of Britain may have been regarded at this time as hostile territory.[3]

Professor J. Břeň has recently published some notes on Celtic *oppida* on the Continent.[4] He regards these as distribution centres for specialized products such as glass, iron, coins, etc. For instance amber imported from the Baltic was perhaps distributed from Staré Hradisko in Moravia, iron objects and unfinished stone sculpture from Havranok, and glass beads, armlets, and other artifacts, from Stradonitz. He makes a plea for the word *oppidum* to apply only to a fortified Celtic settlement of the first century B.C. concentrating on the manufacture or distribution of some particular commodity: 'the decisive criterion and yardstick is the importance of the *oppidum* as a manufacturing and industrial centre as seen against the background of the extensive agricultural hinterland.'

---

[1] Thomas, C. (1966). Finds of actual Roman glass, pottery and metalwork are (outside Exeter) startlingly few and far between.

[2] Cunliffe, B., in Jesson, M. and Hill, D. (eds.) (1971).

[3] Peacock, D. P. S., in Jesson, M. and Hill, D. (eds.) (1971).

[4] Břeň, J. (1972) with footnotes to recent publications of Central European *oppida*.

These conclusions have already received support from J. Collis.[1] He sees Hengistbury Head in Dorset as a distribution centre for Roman amphorae and late La Tène bronzes, in direct contact with Central France, and this evidence is supported by the foreign coins reaching the same centre.[2] Collis writes: 'In the first century B.C. there was a sudden rise of major marketing centres, each with a network of satellite sites or sub-centres, and a peripheral zone from which it draws its supplies. There is extensive "international" trade between these individual centres, and perhaps foreign traders resident controlling the trade.' It is interesting to note (see p. 30) that Hengistbury may also have been distributing raw glass (see also remarks on pp. 32–3 below concerning Meare in Somerset).

Most of the imported beads which are more fully discussed in Part III below are well known from Continental sources, mostly in La Tène II and III, but their immediate point of departure for Britain cannot be ascertained until extensive work has been done in both excavation and collation, particularly in France. The ultimate source for many of the La Tène III Celtic beads, at least, lies in Central Europe, particularly in Switzerland, along the lower course of the river Main, the middle Rhine, and Czechoslovakia. They have above all been found in Celtic *oppida* such as Manching, Třisov, Stradonitz (in huge quantities, suggesting they were manufactured there), Hockstetter, the Dürrnberg, close to the Hallein salt-mines near Salzburg, Staré Hradisko (an amber-distributing centre), and many other sites.[3]

The closest dating for these *oppida* seems to come from Třisov (though not all need be strictly contemporary). At Třisov[4] the beginning of the settlement, dated by Nauheim type brooches should, Břeň wrote, 'not be earlier than the sixties of the first century B.C.', or very little later, and its end is dated from spoon-shaped and Stradonitz brooches (the latter probably ending with the appearance of the so-called 'tongs-shaped' brooches at the close of the first century B.C. or first few years A.D.). At Stradonitz, he points to the sudden end of the *oppidum* and associates it with the coming of the Marcomanni into Bohemia in the year 9 B.C. or when the Romans occupied the Bavarian Alps. At all events the first century B.C. seems to have been the main period of active life in these *oppida*, and it follows that many of our imported beads will fit within or at least overlap that chronological horizon. At the same time the disturbed conditions in Gaul would have led to many people crossing to Britain and Ireland. Certainly there was a noticeable intensification in cross-channel contacts during that time. The Roman occupation of Britain immediately after A.D. 43 may have lessened the import or production of native beads, and the few discovered in slightly later contexts must be survivals from pre-Roman days. Thereafter with few exceptions (see pp. 37–9) the imported beads were standard Roman types, and large gaily decorated beads were destined not to reappear until the post-Roman migration period; then Britain received both the Teutonic beads from north-eastern Europe and some Irish beads from the very prolific centres in that country.

No factory has so far been definitely identified in these islands, and the few known glass

[1] Collis, J. R., in Jesson, M. and Hill, D. (eds.) (1971), and (1974).

[2] Milne, J. G. (1948).

[3] See above, p. 28. A recent and important paper concerning beads from Czechoslovakia is cited on p, 24.

For additions to Haevernick, T. E. (1960) see also Benadik, B. (1959) and (1962). For Manching, see Krämer, W. (1958) and Kunkel, O. (1961), p. 322.

[4] Břeň, J. (1966).

furnaces of Roman date probably produced glass vessels and perhaps window glass rather than beads, like their Continental counterparts at Cologne, and in Normandy during the second century. These British furnaces were at Mancetter (Warwickshire),[1] Wilderspool Lancs.),[2] and Caistor-by-Norwich.[3] Wasters from glass-making in the late second to early third century A.D. have also been found at Colchester, Wroxeter,[4] and Leicester.[5] Recently blue glass waste and lumps of raw glass have been found at Castleford, Yorks.

On the European mainland bead factories have not yet been identified, though beads of La Tène date and earlier are so common in Central Europe, around the Upper Rhine in particular, as well as in north Italy and the north of Yugoslavaia (Carniola), that factories will no doubt one day be discovered there. Northern Italy certainly received a new impetus from the eastern Mediterranean (the home of glass-making in Europe) just before and during the Etruscan period. Recently an important late third- to early second-century B.C. bead factory has been identified in Hellenistic Rhodes.[6]

As far as the Iron Age peoples of Britain are concerned, they no doubt at first used imported beads received by various routes, mainly from Europe, brought in by trade or settlers; the origins of many of these beads are fairly accurately known. But there is certainly reason to believe that by La Tène II at least, and during the last three centuries B.C., glass beads were being manufactured here in Britain too—not simply faithful copies of Continental beads, but highly individual both in form and decoration.

Some years ago R. J. Charleston suggested that lumps of glass-metal were probably imported and made up in this country,[7] and his theory that such a trade was carried on has been supported by the finding of two purple glass armlets and lumps of purple glass in the crude state at Hengistbury Head, near Christchurch, Dorset.[8] Sir A. Church to whom these were submitted wrote, 'the rough pieces of purple glass shown to me appear to be the so-called "pot-metal" from which, by refusion, etc., various objects may afterwards be fashioned'. Whence this pot-metal was imported, we do not yet know. Charleston's hypothesis is again borne out by the distribution of a particular yellowish-green glass of a very distinctive colour centred round South Dorset and Hampshire, and here called 'Bulbury' type glass from a hill-fort in which beads made of it [9] were found. Another important article on the subject has been published by R. G. Newton.[10] The reuse of bits of glass armlets as pendants has also been suggested,[11] as well as the reuse of Roman pillar-moulded glass.[12] For the reuse of bottle glass and other broken Roman glass, see above (p. 11). It is also interesting to note that a block of red glass found at Tara in Ireland was submitted for tests and the lead in it was said to have had an Italian origin.[13]

[1] A recent discovery mentioned by Frere, S. (1967), 290.

[2] Thompson, F. H. (1965).

[3] Atkinson, D. (1930), 93 ff.

[4] At Wroxeter early Flavian to Antonine glass slag fragments of imported glass for reuse, blobs of melted glass, and open furnaces were all recently discovered. See *Brit* iv (1973), 287.

[5] Wacher, J. (1974), 353.

[6] Weinberg, G. Davidson (1969). See also G. von Merhart in *Bonner Jahrbuch* (1942), 147.

[7] Charleston, R. J. (1963). While mainly concerned with the post-medieval period, this paper refers to earlier glass on pp. 58–9.

[8] Mentioned above, p. 14. *HH*, 63.

[9] See p. 13, above.

[10] Newton, R. G. (1971).

[11] *PSAS* lxv (1931), 201. It must be remembered that technologically it is easier to mould glass or turn it into vitreous paste than it would be to make glass from its mineral components.

[12] Stevenson, R. B. K. (1954–5), 216.

[13] Young, W. J. (ed.) (1965) and Charleston, R. J. (1963), note 29 on p. 159.

In the publication of the post-Roman site of Dinas Powys in Wales some of the broken glass of Teutonic origin was thought to have been brought to the site for reuse. Fused glass was found there and it was pointed out that 'it is very much easier to reheat existing blocks of glass to make beads, etc., than to manufacture glass from the constituent minerals. It seems clear that the former process was within the technological competence of craftsmen . . . whereas the latter was not. This, of course, would explain the fragments of Teutonic or even Oriental glass which have been found on many western sites of this date.'[1] It might also explain the cargoes of waste glass in classical period wrecks in the Mediterranean.

On the Continent instances of the reuse of glass are not infrequent, and it is now thought that some of the great *oppida* mentioned above for their dating may have been used as distribution centres of glass products and metalwork.

As early as the first part of the first millennium B.C. lumps of blue and red glass appear to have been used at Frattesine in north Italy [2]—the earliest yet recognized on the European mainland. In the Viking site of Birka[3] in Scandinavia large quantities of broken glass led to the same conclusion about the reuse of glass waste. There seems then no reason to doubt the existence of this practice.

IRON AGE BEADS OF BRITISH ORIGIN OR DESIGN

That glass beads were actually made in Britain, even if actual glass-works themselves still elude us, has only become apparent as a result of the present study, when the writer plotted the distribution of Class 13 beads following a hint made by Graham Callander in 1911 when he wrote [4] : 'I believe that time will show that these beads are more numerous in the north-east than in the South of Scotland.' He was right (see fig. 34), and other evidence points to their manufacture at several other sites.

So far, as mentioned above, only a few presumptive bead factories of Iron Age or early Roman date can be identified in Britain; presumptive in the sense that although no actual glass-working refuse has yet been recognized on any large scale, the distribution of certain bead types is so concentrated in those localities that the evidence points to their having been bead-producing centres. This hypothesis is strengthened by the fact that the beads from these sites are of distinctly individual design, and contrast with those from distribution centres marketing Continental imports.

The British-made beads are as follows:

Class 8. Small opaque yellow annular beads with flattened surfaces (pp. 73–6) perhaps made both at Meare and in the Culbin Sands.

Class 9. Cable beads. Large annular beads decorated with a two-colour twist or cable (pp. 76–9). Probably made, like the comparable armlets, both in England and South Scotland.

Class 10. Meare spiral beads: rather globular colourless translucent beads with fine yellow spirals covering the surface (pp. 79–81). Made at or near Meare.

[1] Alcock, L. (1964).   [3] Arbman, H. (1940–3) i.
[2] Barfield, L. (1971).   [4] Callander, G. (1911), 178.

Class 11.   Meare variants: related to above group but bearing yellow chevrons, waves, criss-cross, etc. (pp. 81–4). Also made at or near Meare.

Class 12.   Stud beads (p. 84).

Class 13.   North Scottish spiral-decorated beads: various colours with yellow spirals (pp. 85–7).

Class 14.   North Scottish decorated annular beads: varied colours. Designs often based on rays combined with ladder patterns (pp. 87–9). Both these last Classes were probably made in the Culbin Sands area.

Some of the beads at present relegated to Groups in this study may also have been made in Britain.

■ Glass Bead Factories   ▼ Other Sites of Importance

Fig. 4: Suggested glass bead factories and other sites of importance.

The possible factories will now be briefly described:

Meare

Meare, like nearby Glastonbury, lies on low-lying raised bog-peat in western Somerset, in an area which has experienced variations in its coast-line and height above sea-level, and which is known to have become increasingly water-logged to a maximum degree shortly before the Roman conquest.[1] The western part of the site was excavated over a number of years by Bulleid and Gray[2] and the three volumes of their report show that the site was particularly rich in finds. Some of the mounds of the eastern group, only a few of which were examined by Bulleid and Gray, have been partly excavated and reinterpreted by Avery.[3] (All finds from this site, now in the Taunton Museum, are prefixed by the letters EV.)

Briefly Avery's results, kindly given to me before his full publication, reinterpret the character of the stratified deposits in the mounds, and permit a sub-division of phases as follows: the significant ones are Phase 2 (thought to belong to the third century B.C., perhaps even earlier) and Phases 3 and 4, of the later first century B.C. and the early first century A.D. During some part of the second century B.C., the areas so far excavated were temporarily abandoned, in favour, probably, of other nearby land as yet unidentified.

Phase 2 antedates the decorated ware and La Tène III brooches, and may be contemporary with the La Tène I or II brooches from the site. During this period Meare spiral-decorated beads of Class 10 and most of the variants of Class 11 were being made, as well as some of the small annular beads of Groups 6 and 8. During Phases 3 and 4 small beads, as well as large clear annular beads with yellow waves (Class 11 (g)), appear to have been made. The numerous other beads cannot yet be assigned to their phases.

The enormous number of beads from Meare can only be explained in one of two ways: either, being not far from the coast, the village could have acted as an emporium or distribution centre for foreign goods, as has been suggested for certain types of *oppida*, or the beads were actually manufactured in the locality. Whilst there were almost surely some instances of copying Continental beads, the vast majority of them seem to be of purely British design, and their local origin must be regarded as highly probable. One speciality of the factory was the production of translucent colourless glass, often decorated with opaque yellow motifs.

Glastonbury

This site lies close to Meare and may also have produced beads. Parts of it were excavated by Bulleid and Gray[4] and, as a result of the new work at Meare, it seems that its earliest phase post-dated Meare Phase 2 and coincided with Phases 3 and 4, and that it was abandoned in the early first century A.D. There are fewer beads from this site, and possibly they were obtained from the nearby Meare factory, but the difference in their character is fairly marked, and local production is very likely.

It is difficult to say what tribal group was occupying the area including Meare and Glastonbury in the last centuries B.C. Perhaps the Durotriges, centred on Wessex, extended into this district, for this is suggested by the distribution of their coins which do, albeit rarely, reach Somerset.[5] On the other hand it is possible that the Dobunnic territory may have stretched down this far along the south border of the Bristol Channel: their trade relations were noticeably close (see map, fig. 3). The Dumnonii certainly did not reach this part of Somerset, and the extent of Belgic influence is not yet clear. On the whole it seems

[1] Dewar, H. S. L. and Godwin, H. (1963), and for discussion of flooding, see Williams, M., *The Draining of the Somerset Levels* (1970).

[2] Bulleid, A. and Gray, H. St. George (1948), and Cotton, M. A. (1967).

[3] Avery, M. (1968). A fuller report is expected.

[4] Bulleid, A. and Gray, H. St. George (1911).

[5] Allen, D. F. (1961), Map VII. Map reproduced in Cunliffe, B. (1974), p. 97.

most likely that the Durotriges, receiving raw glass from Hengistbury Head (which also may have been a factory), and possibly from unidentified harbours on the Somerset coast, had their main factories at these two sites.

Culbin Sands, Moray

These sand dunes run for miles near the mouth of the Findhorn river in Scotland, and are subject to constant changes in form as the result of strong winds and tides. They cover a land surface occupied in prehistoric and Roman times.

The first suggestion that glass was manufactured in this area was made as long ago as 1871, and among the autograph letters in the Library of the Society of Antiquaries of Scotland in Edinburgh is one from C. Innes to Major Chadwick referring to a bead necklace 'of glass or vitreous paste coloured with oxide of iron', and mentioning 'some curious information from Dr. Gordon of Birnie of the remains of kilns near Elgin where such glass ornaments were manufactured'. Lumps of fused glass of various colours are in the N.M.A. (Nos. BIB 63 and BIB 69).

Perhaps these sandhills may have had a long history for glass- or faience-making. Faience beads of star, quoit or segmented shapes which have a notably Scottish distribution may have been made locally in Scotland, as first suggested by Mann,[1] as at least fifteen of these came from Culbin where analogous slag is said to have been found. These beads are thought to belong to the mid-second millennium B.C.[2] But the question of their origin remains uncertain, for a more recent study denies that they were made in Scotland[3] and repeats the long-held view that they were made in the Near East.

At all events there is no evidence for glass-making in Culbin between this period and about the second or first century B.C. and the first century A.D. At this time the territory of Buchan, Moray and Mar seems to have been inhabited by the Vacomagi and their more easterly neighbours, the Taexali,[4] both of which tribes may have been merged in a wider Caledonian confederacy by the end of the second century and have been ancestors of the later Picts. It is interesting to note here that the area is characterized by a distinctive, though as yet undated local type of hill-fort,[5] often unfinished, and possibly hastily constructed at the time of the Agricolan invasion, or at the time of Severus. Were these, perhaps, the same tribesmen as those responsible for the bronze snake-armlet inlaid with blue glass (now in the N.M.A.), and also for the more massive Castle Newe type armlets, the Deskford carnyx-bell,[6] etc.?

Although no glass factory has as yet been identified, the maps make it clear that one must have been producing beads and probably armlets for a hundred years or so, perhaps more, before the Agricolan conquest, when marketing outlets or the possibility of acquiring glass

---

[1] *PSAS* xl (1905–6), 496–502. See *ibid.* iv (1860–2), 55, and for possible glass-making crucibles from the sands, *ibid.* xlv (1910–11), 158–81. Half-finished beads are recorded in *PSAS* xxv (1890–1), 508–10.

[2] Beck, H. C. and Stone, J. F. S. (1928); Stone, J. F. S. and Thomas, L. C. (1956) and Newton, R. G. and Renfrew, C. (1970).

[3] McKerrell, H. (1972). Note that other faience beads

came from Stevenston and Glenluce Sands in Ayrshire and Wigtownshire respectively. See, however, Harding, A. and Warren, S. E. (1973), 64–6.

[4] Richmond, I. A. (1958) and Steer, K. A. (1958).

[5] Rivet, A. L. F. (ed.) (1966).

[6] See Simpson, M., in *Studies in Ancient Europe* (Leicester, 1968) and Piggott, S. (1959).

waste were stopped after the Roman victory at *Mons Graupius* in A.D. 85. Moreover a number of half-finished beads and glass slag have been discovered there. A Roman glass bottle from Brackenbraes, Turriff, reflects some intercourse between the Taexali and the Romans.

Who these people were and where they had come from is quite obscure. The beads they made were gay, colourful, and highly individual, and their limited distribution (see maps, figs. 34 and 36) suggests little outside trade and perhaps only a short period of manufacture. One can, however, detect that these not very competent glass-workers had seen three or four types of bead which they were inspired to copy in their own idiom. They must have seen some Meare spiral beads of Class 10 which might have reached them from the west via the Great Glen: these they imitated without being able, or perhaps wanting, to obtain the same translucent, colourless ground. Their own productions, perhaps full of local and fortuitous impurities, were mostly 'black', green, brown or blue, all fairly dark, sometimes opaque, but all with yellow spirals (Class 13).[1]

Another of their designs (Class 14), no two of which are identical, shows a combination of the whirl and ray patterns of some Celtic beads (Class 7), albeit in a hardly recognizable form owing to their inferior technique, and the twisted cables (now reduced to a sort of ladder pattern) of Class 9. A certain quantity of small yellow annular beads similar to Class 8 made first at Meare in Phase 2 of the site, but enjoying a long popularity, may also have been produced at Culbin.

Beads from this factory are probably survivals if they post-date the late first century A.D.

Glenluce Sands, Wigtownshire

Numbers of beads have also come from these sands. For a discussion of them, see Callander, G. (1911).

Traprain Law and Newstead

The evidence for bead-making at these sites is very tentative. Traprain Law [2] stands on a high rocky outcrop dominating parts of East Lothian, to the north of the Lammermuirs. It was first inhabited long before the Iron Age, but reoccupied from at least Flavian times as the capital of the Votadini, a tribe whose territory extended down the coastal area between the Tyne and the Forth. It is possibly to be equated with the *Curia* mentioned by Ptolemy.[3]

This many times fortified settlement was allowed to remain in being throughout the Roman occupation, a fact which argues for some collaboration, and a great number of Roman as well as native objects were found during many seasons of excavations, unfortunately undertaken before scientific methods were adopted.

Local industries thrived at Traprain, and some of the metalwork (e.g., dress-fasteners of certain types) [4] stems from south-west English cultural traditions. Since, therefore, there were trade contacts between Southern Scotland and the Somerset region it is not surprising to find that the idea of making beads was also adopted in the north, and in fact the actual migration of craftsmen from Meare and Glastonbury cannot be discounted. In a paper

[1] A 'Pictish' (*c.* ninth-century) date for these has been recently claimed in *PSAS* cv (1972–4), 197–8, but the Croy, Inverness-shire bead is in fact more probably a survival. See also Laing, Ll. (1975), 336.

[2] Curle, A. O. and Cree, J. (1915–24). For more recent reassessments see Hogg, A. H. A., in Grimes, W. F. (ed.) (1951), 200–20, and *PSAS* lxxxix (1955–6), 284.

[3] Richmond, I. A., in Richmond, I. A. (ed.) (1958).

[4] Gillam, J. P., in Richmond, I. A. (ed.) (1958).

published in 1938 Kilbride-Jones suggested that several types of glass armlets, sometimes decorated with a cable of two-colour twists, seem to have centred on, and perhaps been made at, Traprain Law notably in the first and second centuries A.D.[1] Fused lumps of coloured glass have indeed been found there, and a number of crucibles containing coloured glass slag. Although exactly similar in technique, so far only one cable bead (Class 9) comes from the large numbers of varied examples from the site and in fact these beads show a notably more southern distribution. Newstead (at the time thought to have been an administrative centre frequented by many natives and one of the frontier posts where traders may have had to present themselves) has produced glass armlets and cable beads, as well as glass melon beads, all of which might have reached there from Traprain, only about forty miles away. But so far the melon beads are rare at Traprain. At least sixty beads have been recovered from Newstead, where the occupation was not a long one. Possibly it had a glass factory, and in Flavian times olive-green glass was not uncommon there.

The idea of the cable motif may have originated at either Glastonbury or Meare, from whose sphere of influence several early and tentative attempts to obtain a twist effect have been found.[2] A more successful result could have been achieved at Traprain where a busy industrial centre may be envisaged; its cable-decorated products (if indeed they were made there and this is still only surmised) reached up to Moray to inspire the Taexali and Vacomagi to imitate them, even if in a crude way, at their Culbin Sands factory.

Wilderspool (Lancs.)

This site in the territory of the Cornovii,[3] stood beside the Mersey on the outskirts of Warrington, between Chester and Manchester, and seems to have grown up around a ford across the river, as it stands on a deposit of glacial sand among otherwise swampy land; it therefore controlled an important point in the communication system. It was excavated many years ago but unfortunately its true character was not established. Possibly the earliest occupation at Wilderspool was a military one associated perhaps with Agricola's campaigns in the late first century A.D.[4] but the presence of native beads of both cable (Class 9) and Oldbury types (Class 6) hints at an earlier date in that century or even before. By the end of the first century some industries had been begun there, including potteries and, perhaps, a glass bead factory, for the site has produced not only a large number of beads but also lumps of glass slag and a small crucible containing 'black' glass paste. What appears to be an unfinished bead of opaque white glass with red and blue patches was also found. The evidence is presumptive rather than conclusive.

Other sites

Particularly after the Claudian invasion, glass waste or imported metal was made up at innumerable sites.[5] The natives in the hill-forts in Wales, Scotland, and elsewhere must

[1] Kilbride-Jones, H. E. (1938) followed by Stevenson, R. B. K. (1954–5), and in Rivet, A. L. F. (1966). For crucibles with plain glass outside and red, yellow, and possibly blue glass inside, see *PSAS* lvii (1923), 206. A glass rod for bead-making is mentioned in *ibid.* l (1915–16); it was thought to be first- to second-century in date.

[2] See pp. 77–8, below.

[3] See Richmond, I. A. and Foster, I. Ll., in Alcock, L. (ed.) (1968) and Webster, G. (1975).

[4] Thompson, F. H. (1965).

[5] Note that Strabo (iv.6.3.) wrote that the pre-Roman Britons imported glass utensils, but did not explicitly mention beads.

frequently have obtained bits of Roman glass, and as already mentioned Stevenson suggested in 1954 [1] that a purple and white marbled British type armlet from the hill-fort of Traprain Law, East Lothian,[2] might have been made from a reworked Roman pillar-moulded bowl from a different level on the same site.

Glass canes for bead-making have been identified from a number of places and may represent the first stage of bead manufacture from reused glass. For some of these sites see Castlehill Fort, Dalry, Ayrshire,[3] Caerhun, the Roman fort of *Kanovium*,[4] the Romano-British settlement at Woodyates,[5] Covesea Cave (Moray),[6] the native hill-fort of the Votadini at Traprain Law (East Lothian),[7] and the Romano-British temple at Lamyatt Beacon, Somerset (publication forthcoming), and from Caerwent in Monmouthshire.[8] What appears to be red vitreous slag came from Airreoland Crannog [9] in Ayrshire. Large blue melon beads may have been reused by native peoples. A number of these as well as blue glass slag came recently from Castleford, Yorks. (so far unpublished).

ROMAN BEADS
(see also pp. 91–102)

With the Roman occupation, particularly after the mid-second century A.D., the picture alters. The native beads die out and the Romans in Britain never appear to have been much interested in jewellery not made with precious or semi-precious stones: the rest of their repertoire was very limited. It is surprising perhaps to find that the native British taste for variety in form and colour died out at so early a date. But this observation, albeit in another context, had already been made by E. T. Leeds in 1933. He wrote: 'It is an incontestable fact . . . that from about 250 to the end of the Roman period, objects other than pottery which exhibit in any degree the influence of Celtic art in their decoration are distinguished by nothing so much as their scarcity.' His words are certainly applicable to beads.

The Roman villas, nearly all of which for climatic or economic reasons lie to the south of a line between the Tees near Middlesbrough and the Dee at Chester,[10] rarely produce beads other than the small standardized types common to the northern Roman Empire: the finds are nearly all from towns (supply centres, one imagines), such as Cirencester, etc., from Roman military sites, particularly along the Roman Wall, to which they were presumably brought by camp-followers, or from sites such as Cold Kitchen Hill, Wiltshire,[11] which was in all probability a sacred precinct where offerings might be expected. Recently large numbers of late Roman burials have been discovered at Cirencester (Gloucestershire), and Poundbury, near Dorchester, Dorset, as well as at Lankhills near Winchester, and at least in this last cemetery bracelets and other offerings were sometimes deposited in the graves. There is some evidence to suggest that offerings were not commonly placed with burials

[1] Stevenson, R. B. K. (1954), 216, followed by Newton, R. G. (1971). The latter paper gives some results of microprobe analyses.

[2] Curle, A. O. and Cree, J. (1920–1), 153–206.

[3] *PSAS* liii (1918–19), 123 ff.

[4] Baillie-Reynolds, P. K. (1938).

[5] Pitt-Rivers, A. H. L. F. (1887), pl. xliv, 23 and 24.

[6] In the N.M.A., Edinburgh, no. H.M. 212.

[7] *PSAS* l (1915), fig. 26, no. 1.

[8] Forthcoming in *MA* 1974 or 1975.

[9] *PSAS* xxiii (1889), 148, and *AGC* vii (1894), 34.

[10] Stevens, C. E. (1966), 126–7.

[11] *WAM* xliii (1925–7), 180–91, and 327–32.

for some decades from about A.D. 320–30, and this may explain the rarity of early fourth century necklaces.[1] By the latter part of the fourth century, however, at Lankhills[2] and Cirencester, for instance, the practice of making offerings to the dead was reintroduced— perhaps under the influence of incoming central European *foederati* and craftsmen, who, outside the Roman Empire, had never lost their love of bead necklaces. For more information about non-Roman elements in Roman Britain, see pp. 101–2.

During the Roman period, and apart from their ornamental use, beads also appear to have been made specifically for use as votive offerings at sacred shrines, wells, and temples. There are, in fact, several such sites some of which have yielded numbers of beads, both of Roman and immediately pre-Roman Celtic types, notably Coventina's Well at Carrawburgh, Northumberland (*Procolitia*),[3] Farley Heath[4] (temple) in Surrey (where the spread of Iron Age coins may have begun in the first century A.D.), Cold Kitchen Hill, Wiltshire (presumed sacred site),[5] and Lamyatt Beacon (temple) near Bruton in Somerset,[6] to mention a few of the better known instances.

Coventina's Well contained offerings of many varieties, including over 14,000 coins, pins, glass, potsherds, etc. The pre-Roman and Romano-British temple at Woodeaton (Oxford),[7] also produced large numbers of coins, etc., and these facts prompted Anne Ross to write, 'it would seem that a workshop existed on the site, which manufactured articles for dedication in the shrine or shrines'. She adds, what is certainly apposite for the numbers of badly made segmented beads (see below pp. 91–3) from both Lamyatt Beacon and Cold Kitchen Hill, 'the rather shoddy nature of many rings, bracelets and pins suggests that they were manufactured, not for hard wear but for immediate dedication'. In fact, as the same writer points out, 'markets were an integral part of Celtic religious festivals'.[8]

Only presumptive factories for the production of Roman beads have as yet been discovered either in Britain or on the Continent, but the general uniformity of the design of beads leads one to imagine that the demand for them was not extensive and may have been covered by relatively few factories. The richer Roman citizens in the towns on the Continent and certainly in Britain showed little interest in decorated beads, perhaps considered barbarous, and preferred semi-precious stones, and at least by the third and fourth centuries very small glass beads, sometimes threaded on wire as bracelets or necklaces; the poorer people showed even more conservative and humdrum taste. In the early Roman period a few bright and large beads of Celtic type still survived, but by the third century they had almost all disappeared from circulation, and large gaily coloured beads were only reintroduced after the Roman Empire had fallen. Late Roman beads are very small and very common. It is interesting to find the fourth-century historian Trebellius Polio referring to the fashions among late Roman women of wearing numbers of beads (*De Gallieno . . .*).

A few definitely Roman types (or types of the Roman period current in the Empire) can be recognized, manufactured both inside and outside the confines of Roman territory and

---

[1] Hull, M. R. (1958), 250–9, and Wenham, L. P. (1968), 46–7.

[2] See Clarke, G., in Biddle, M., *Winchester Studies* (forthcoming).

[3] Clayton, J. (1880).

[4] Goodchild, R. (1947).

[5] *WAM* xliii (1925–6) 180–91 and 327–32, and *ibid.* xliv (1928), 138–42.

[6] Information before publication from Mrs. Crystal Bennett and Mr. Roger Leech.

[7] Goodchild, R. and Kirk, J. (1954).

[8] Ross, Anne (1967), especially 46–8.

large numbers in Egypt, Nubia, etc. (see refs. on p. 102). Sarmatian and other exotic beads can be found in Britain, and the recently discovered fourth- to fifth-century cemetery at Lankhills near Winchester has necklaces which can be paralleled in the Danubian area. Yet others, notably the colourless or 'amber'-coloured reddish glass beads enclosing sheet gold or other metal (see p. 93) came at least originally from more sophisticated glass factories in Egypt or perhaps Syria. It is only to be expected that Roman auxiliaries and their camp-followers brought in beads from the lands of their origin, and that Britons serving overseas in the Roman army would bring back souvenirs from the countries to which they had been posted.[1] Branigan (1973) has made a strong case for the presence of Gaulish and Germanic people moving across to Britain, particularly to the Gloucestershire–Somerset area, at times of disturbance near the frontier on the Continent between about A.D. 270–300. They were settlers, and must have left traces of their material equipment as well as their native types of villas, mosaics, etc.

By the third and fourth centuries, as mentioned above, Germanic peoples were coming to England,[2] but their beads cannot be allocated to their proper origin until we know far more in detail of the Gallo-Roman and non-Roman areas from which beads were obtained. At the moment all that we can do is to try to recognize them as non-Roman. Their *floruit* in Britain at all events mainly falls outside the limits of the present enquiry, and calls for a separate study. Discussing the Anglo-Saxon cemetery at Caistor-by-Norwich in 1973, J. N. L. Myres writes that the 'culture so closely mirrors that of fourth century Schleswig and Fünen as to imply a fairly direct transference in considerable numbers from Continental Anglia. And certainly from the end of the fourth century, perhaps earlier, there was a considerable body whose direct antecedents were among the less coherent Saxon peoples of the lower Elbe valley and the vast lands extending to the Weser and Ems'. It should be noted, however, that others, e.g. Hawkes, S. C. (1975), adopt a more cautious view.

IRISH BEADS

We do not know when beads began to be manufactured in Ireland: but there are several indications to suggest that the period of their real popularity was not earlier than the fifth or sixth century and so falls outside the scope of this book.

Yet there is growing evidence that Continental and British made Iron Age beads reached Ireland before the Roman period began in the rest of the British Isles. The part played by the so-called Irish Sea province has recently been discussed by a number of scholars[3] and it has been shown by several that the Irish Sea acted as a barrier rather than a bridge between the rest of Britain and Ireland during the Iron Age and Roman periods—even if

[1] For some notes on the military movements in the Roman period see p. 102. In Eastern Britain there were many Nordic inhabitants for a century before the *Adventus Saxonum* of A.D. 443–5. See *JBAA* (1972).

[2] 'By the fourth century even inland towns like Winchester were being provided with garrisons of Germanic mercenaries, for the Roman army could no longer protect them.' Biddle, M., in *CA* xx (May 1970), 246. Among the many important works concerned with this period see Alcock, L. (1973); Hawkes, S. C. and Dunning, G. C. (1961); Corder, P. (1955); Myres, J. N. L., 1969) and John Morris, *The Age of Arthur: A History of the British Isles from 350–650* (1973).

[3] Thomas, C. (ed.) (1972).

trade or sporadic settlers brought both Iron Age and Roman objects into Ireland. That this sea bore much traffic can be shown by several pieces of evidence, and these are supported by the distribution of some of the beads discussed in this study. A. H. A. Hogg [1] has drawn attention to the great diversity in the hill-forts along the west coast of Wales; there is also a connexion between some second- century B.C. to first-century A.D. south-western wide-spaced multivallate hill-forts in Wales and in Devon and Cornwall with undated ones in Iberia,[2] and such a connexion is emphasized by the 'duck-stamped' pottery and La Tène I fibulae of Iberian type from Cornwall.[3] Hogg has also noted that 'chevaux-de-frise' defences were common in Iberia, Wales, Scotland, and Ireland.[4] Barry Raftery [5] has made an important contribution to Irish studies in isolating two main classes of Irish hill-forts; the wide-spaced multivallate ones (only in certain respects comparable with those described by Aileen Fox, referred to above) which have a notably south and west distribution, and the other classes bordering and inland from the Irish Sea: these have not yet been dated. The distribution of the two classes is almost mutually exclusive. It is possible, therefore, that more Iberian influences may have come into Ireland and also south-west England than are at present recognized, though the vague similarities are far too tenuous to support a serious thesis.[6] To make matters more difficult there is a serious dearth of dating evidence.

The evidence for La Tène Celts in Ireland is still very meagre,[7] but it is apparent that, during the few centuries before and after Christ, imported beads occasionally reached Ireland, either directly from the Continent, or indirectly as a result of movements up and down the Irish Sea and from the rest of Britain. Some of the foreign metal objects may reflect immigration movements into Ireland, others may have been copies, made locally, of a few acquired examples. It has been suggested that small groups arriving from overseas could have caused considerable social upheaval,[8] but on the whole the continuity from the late Bronze Age to the Early Christian period seems to have been largely unbroken. Jope, however,[9] has pointed out that connexions between British and Irish metal workshops began in the first century A.D. which ultimately produced a continuum in metalwork in the British Isles, and from then onwards Roman provincial styles and techniques pervade much of the Irish work.

Thus present evidence suggests that Ireland may not have had much interest in glass during the Roman occupation of Britain. Perhaps it was the difficulty in obtaining raw glass, combined with the lack of glass technicians, that explains why a site of such regal importance as Tara yielded such small and miserable specimens of beads, acquired in all probability from some area (Wales perhaps) under Roman influence.[10] By the first century B.C. at least some Gaulish settlers may have established themselves in Ireland and their beads should be searched for.[11]

[1] In Thomas, C. (ed.) (1972).
[2] Fox, A. (1961).
[3] Leeds, E. T. (1926–7), 227–38.
[4] Hogg, A. H. A. (1957).
[5] Thomas, C. (ed.) (1972).
[6] Kenney, J. F. (1929), *passim*.
[7] Rynne, E. (1961).
[8] Harbison, P. (1971), 174–6 and (1970).
[9] Jope, E. M. (1972), 30.
[10] ÓRíordáin, S. P. (1954). Other Roman material might have reached Freestone Hill, Co. Kilkenny. See Raftery, B. (1969), 1–108, especially p. 96. The small annular beads of blue and other colours (not examined by me) suggest a Roman date and Romano-British origin, although one decorated bead appears to have come from another, not identified, context. As Alcock writes, curragh-loads of raiding Irish gathered treasures from the richer areas of Western Britain. Later, even the young Patrick was kidnapped by them.
[11] Powell, T. G. E. (1958), 120.

In the rest of the British Isles there was a Celtic political resurgence in the fourth to fifth centuries A.D. after 'the shift of power from Roman to native barbarian authorities',[1] but when this renaissance did begin (and it probably started after St. Patrick's mission in the fifth century), the decorative motifs which emerged were not identical with those of earlier times. As Elizabeth Fowler stresses in another context, we are not dealing with either a survival or a revival so much as a reinterpretation, and this observation seems to be applicable to Ireland. Here a stagnant civilization was increasingly fired by the early Church to produce beautiful things. In her important study, *Irish Art in the Early Christian Period to A.D. 800*,[2] Françoise Henry writes: 'The Christian art which will develop in the framework of the complex and changing circumstances just outlined passes first through a Phase of formation corresponding more or less with the time when Ireland was almost completely isolated from the Continent by pagan England, and so approximately covers the end of the fifth, the sixth and part of the seventh centuries.' Only after this formative period did the real *floruit* of true Christian art reach its height between 650–800, and I think that the main output of Irish glass beads may have corresponded with this latter period, even if it began in a more tentative way somewhat earlier. The monasteries grew in size and wealth in the later seventh century and inspired an outburst of craftsmanship.[3]

It is probable therefore that this Irish glass-making renaissance took place at too late a date to be included in the terms of reference of this study. It is possible that the people responsible for the introduction of 'Late Roman B and C Wares' from North Africa, Egypt, the Levant, etc., may have brought with them glass-wares to be imitated, or even skilled Mediterranean glass-workers between about A.D. 500 and 700. Combed and ribbed amphorae came in from the Aegean and Asia Minor a little later; and it is interesting to find that these all seem to have arrived—perhaps together with monastic ideas—direct from the East Mediterranean.

In North Wales (raided by Scotti from Northern Ireland in the late third and fourth centuries), there are no recognizably Irish beads, and this is also so in south-west Wales when the Irish founded Dyfed in about the late fourth century A.D. and in Argyllshire where the Dalriadic Kingdom was founded in the fifth century. We must remember that there was, during Françoise Henry's phase of formation, considerable activity along the western sea routes which alone in the fifth to sixth centuries were able to maintain contact with what remained of Roman civilization in Gaul and the Western Mediterranean,[4] and Bowen also points out that 'there is archaeological evidence to show that following the withdrawal of Roman control from Britain many Irish immigrants crossed the Irish Sea'. Their influence is particularly well-marked in south-west Wales. The evidence is negative it must be admitted, but if Irish glass-working was thriving in the fourth to fifth centuries it might be reasonable to expect their products to be found in the lands to which they emigrated, particularly in Dyfed in Wales and Dalriada in Scotland. Future evidence may provide an explanation, but at present it is difficult to infer that Irish bead production was significantly

[1] Fowler, E. (1964), 134.

[2] London, Methuen. Revised edition, 1965.

[3] De Paor, M. and L. (1961) (3rd ed.), 110 ff. It must be remembered that the seaways from the Coptic East to Ireland had remained open without serious interference. See also Thomas, C. (1971), and a valuable discussion of beads in Hencken, H. O'N. (1942).

[4] Bowen, E. G. (1954).

active before about the sixth century;[1] but we sadly lack dated examples. Jewellery, church plate, and the great illuminated manuscripts belong chiefly to the artistic achievements of the seventh to ninth centuries; glass-work may have reached the peak of its technological and artistic ingenuity in Ireland at the same date.

[1] Although originally imported from Egypt in Roman times, millefiori glass seems to have been made in Ireland, and possibly Wales as well, during these centuries. For instance the industrial waste at Garranes (fifth-sixth centuries) described by ÓRíordáin, S. P. (1942), and at Lagore (later) included crucibles and composite glass rods. See Hencken, H. O'N. (1951).

For Wales see Alcock, L. (1963), 10–12. There is one piece from Scotland, perhaps of Irish origin, from Luce Bay, Wigtownshire. (*AnJ* 1 (1970), 332–3).

It is interesting to note that some of the beads from the Dalriadic stronghold of Dunadd in Argyllshire were imported Gallo-Roman beads, not, as might have been expected, Irish, unless they were Irish copies.

DESCRIPTION OF BEAD CLASSES
AND GROUPS

PART III

BEADS OF CONTINENTAL ORIGIN OR INSPIRATION

(i) Decorated Classes (Iron Age) (pp. 45–59)
(ii) Decorated or undecorated Groups (Iron Age or Roman dates) (pp. 59–71)

(i) DECORATED CLASSES OF THE IRON AGE

CLASS I

Arras Types I and II (Schedules, pp. 105–7) (pl. I, no. 1 and figs. 5 and 6)

FIG. 5: Arras type beads of Class I:
left, Type I; *right*, Type II. Scale 1/1.

The characteristics of these two types are that they are both normally about 12 mm. in diameter and 10 mm. in height. They are invariably dark blue, decorated with white rings round blue eyes. In *Type I* the fewer and larger eyes are defined by white rings marvered into the ground colour of the bead, and these white rings have often fallen out and leave only the circular groove around the eye which is part of the ground of the bead; *Type II* has many more eyes and they are what have been called 'stratified', i.e., they are made by filling a saucer-like depression first with opaque white and then adding a central blue blob which, overlying the white, appears to be brighter and more translucent than the ground colour.

These are possibly among the earliest Iron Age beads to have found their way to this country, and though their precise dating is still elusive they can be dated approximately to certain Iron Age contexts which will themselves, within a short time, through the use of radio-carbon and other newer dating methods, be much more precisely understood.

Type I is much the less common of the two varieties, and is only present in Britain at Cowlam Barrow L and Arras (Queen's Barrow, Market Weighton, in Yorkshire) and from a site (Lake, or Winterbourne Stoke in Wiltshire), whose dating will be discussed below.

Type II is more widespread and shows a distribution (see fig. 6) which extends from the Bristol Channel and Wessex area via the Jurassic Way into Yorkshire.

The 'Arras' culture (the earliest phase of which is known as the Cowlam phase or Phase I) has produced various finds including both Type I and Type II beads and has received considerable attention in recent years.[1] The graves both at Arras itself and at Cowlam and elsewhere in East Yorkshire were excavated in the last century.[2]

The two graves which most concern us here are Grave L at Cowlam and the so-called Queen's Barrow at Arras, characteristic respectively of Phase I and Phase II of the culture.

Grave L at Cowlam produced one Type I bead and some blue beads with white waves, and also two important bronze objects, a brooch paralleled from a Münsingen Ia context in Switzerland, and a bracelet which also has a late Hallstatt or early La Tène analogy from the Continent. A comparable bracelet and brooch were found together in a grave at Yvonand (Switzerland) and are cited by Stead. Switzerland has, it should be noted, also produced Type I beads.[3]

It is not clear yet whether these Cowlam graves and the subsequent ones from Phase II of the Arras culture reflect a direct intrusion from the Marne district of Northern Champagne (for cart or chariot

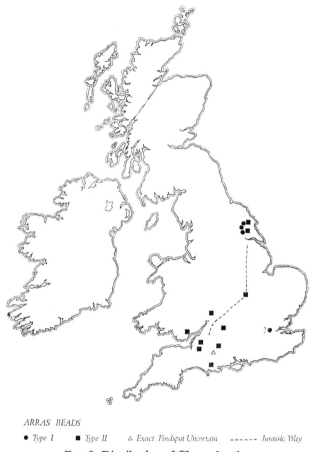

ARRAS BEADS

● *Type I*   ■ *Type II*   △ *Exact Findspot Uncertain*   ------ *Jurassic Way*

FIG. 6: Distribution of Class 1 beads.

[1] Vital to the discussion is Stead, I. M. (1965) and (1971). Note also Harding, D. W. (1974), 173–6, and Bretz-Mahler, D. (1971). The French Marnian sites still await detailed and full discussion in the light of modern excavations.

[2] Many barrows at Arras were excavated as early as 1816 by the Rev. Mr. Stillingfleet; the finds are in the Dept. of Prehistoric and Romano-British Antiquities in the B.M. One was examined by Greenwell and published in Greenwell, W. (1877), 208–9 and in (1890) and (1906). See also *ArJ* xxii (1865), 97–117 and 241–64.

[3] Viollier, D. (1916), pl. 22, no. 122.

burials are also characteristic of both the French and English sites). It has been written, 'while certain resemblance to Champagne is present there are equally clear affiliations with the more southerly La Tène complexes in Burgundy and even Switzerland'.[1]

The second phase of the Arras culture is best represented by the Queen's Barrow, Arras. Here 28 beads of the Cowlam (Type I) variety and 18 of Type II were found, together with 'natural' greenish glass beads with yellow waves and blue beads with white waves. Also present were other finds particularly bronze bracelets of a knobbed type, one of which was also found in one of the Cowlam graves (Barrow LI).

There was therefore an overlap between the Cowlam phase and the rather later Arras or second phase. Chronologically neither is very clearly assignable, but since a number of Type II beads have been found from approximately datable contexts in Britain (see below), the Cowlam phase may have begun around the fifth century or so, and Harding may be right in regarding the Arras culture as part of a Marnian contact which mainly affected southern Britain and which he also tentatively identifies with certain pottery forms.[2]

At least the Type II, and probably the Type I beads as well, originated apparently in the eighth or seventh century in Phoenician lands (there are a number for instance from Bet Shean which were found with a late seventh-century glass amphoriskos, in the museum at Jerusalem). Thence they spread to Corsica, Minorca, Italy,[3] Yugoslavia,[4] Czechoslovakia,[5] and Austria (Hallstatt).[6] Almost surely they were copied in Central Europe as they occur in the Vosges, Aisne (the Caranda cemetery whose beads are in the museum at Rennes), and others come from a Somme chariot burial (Beck Collection). In Châlons-sur-Marne Museum there are beads of this type in the Bérard Collection; they are also recorded from Marson, Marne (in the British Museum), and from the Mont-de-Vraux cart or chariot burials[7] as well as from Bergères-les-Vertus and Bussy-le-Château (both Marne).[8]

The Type II beads from Britain include examples from Meare, Somerset(? third to first century B.C.); Swallowcliffe, Wilts. (? fifth to fourth century B.C.); Arras (Queen's Barrow, which also produced the Type I beads referred to above)[9] (?third century B.C.); Conderton Camp, Bredon, Worcs. (from a late phase of the second main period not yet published but almost certainly third or second century B.C.); Whitton near Barry, Glamorgan (perhaps first century B.C.); Hunsbury, Northants. (? third to first century B.C. hill-fort, strongly influenced by the Yorkshire Iron Age,[10] and also receiving lead from the south-west); Maiden Castle, Dorset[11] (an earlier stray found in a deposit of the late second to early first century B.C.). Recently some more beads of this type were discovered at Garton Slack near Driffield, Yorks., with an inhumation burial (perhaps of the third century B.C.) near but not associated with a rich cart burial.[12]

[1] An xl (1966), 234.

[2] Harding, D. W. (1974), particularly his Chapter 10, pp. 157 ff.

[3] Gozzadini, G. (1870), pl. xv, fig. 13; others, from Palestrina, dated fourth to second century B.C. are in the Villa Giulia, Rome, and others come from many sites in Etruria as well as from Cumae, etc.

[4] Wissenschaftliche Mitteilungen des Bosnisch-Herzogowinischen Landesmuseums, Band I, Heft A (Sarajevo, 1971). Arras Type II beads dated from associations to c. 250–110 B.C.

[5] Venclová, N. (1971), fig. iii, 1.

[6] Von Sacken, E. F. (1868), pl. xvii, figs. 32, 37.

[7] Schmidt, E. (1924), 15–20.

[8] In the museum at St. Germain-en-Laye. Others may be cited from fifth-century graves at Villeneuve-Renneville and Gaurgancon, and from late fifth- to early fourth-century graves at Pierre-Morains, 'Les Champs Écus' (all in the museum at Épernay).

[9] Davis, J. B. and Thurnam, J. (1865). See also the Proceedings of the York meeting of the Archaeological Institute (1892).

[10] ArJ xciii (1936). In this connexion it is necessary to remember that Hunsbury, lying on the Jurassic Way, also yielded an Arras cart-burial type bridle-bit and two-linked snaffle-bit of Polden Hill type, reflecting southern British and Yorkshire influences passing up and down the route. See ArJ cx (1953), 212–13.

[11] Mistakenly compared with a bead of later type from Newstead, Roxburghshire.

[12] Note in An xlv (1971), 289. Report forthcoming.

The dating, being somewhat vague, leaves us in doubt whether the beads of Type II at least (and possibly Type I) were first introduced into Yorkshire from the Continent and so through the course of trade found their way down the forest-free Jurassic belt[1] to Wessex and the Bristol Channel area or whether they first entered the south coast ports and spread northwards.

(A word of warning should be given. A similar but larger bead with Type II affinities was discovered in a Viking grave at Ballinaby, Islay, in the Hebrides[2]: this is probably a later version of an early design after a long interval, and unlikely to have been a reused early bead.)

CLASS 2

Welwyn Garden City type beads (Schedules, p. 107) (pl. I, no. 2 and fig. 7)

Perhaps it seems somewhat arbitrary to claim that only two beads can be called a Class, but nevertheless it is worth drawing attention to them as other comparable beads may turn up in the future.

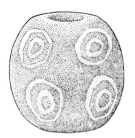

FIG. 7: Class 2: Welwyn Garden City type. Scale 1/1.

These beads, from Hertfordshire and Sussex, respectively, are rather big, globular beads[3] made of dark blue glass into which two registers of eyes enclosed by two irregular white circles have been marvered. These 'eyes' are both very much larger and more irregular than those on the Arras Type beads just discussed (pp. 45–8). A small fragment of such a bead might readily be confused with one of the Oldbury type (Class 6, pp. 53–7, below) if the full development of the globular form and the white rings were incomplete.

Both these beads are relatively closely datable. The Wiggonholt (Pulborough) one, found in a large pit full of Romano-British pottery of the first to second century A.D. and a coin of Vespasian, was only a fragment and almost certainly came from some earlier occupation material. The Welwyn Garden City one, of which less than half the bead was included with the burial, is more satisfactorily dated, as it came from a rich late La Tène III grave, one of a group of comparable burials in south-east England, in this instance with grave goods including some Italian imports which place its date within the last quarter of the first century B.C.;[4] both of these beads of course might have been old and prized when buried.

Where these beads were made is not yet clear, but they belong to a tradition which one would expect to find in northern Italy, where there are a number of large globular beads as distinct from the more numerous annular beads in Central Europe. It is believed that glass bead factories were operating in

[1] See Grimes, W. F. in Grimes, W. F. (ed.) (1951), 144–71.
[2] *PSAS* xiv (1879–80), 51 ff.
[3] In my opinion the Welwyn Garden City bead was incorrectly restored in the published drawing. It appears to be globular rather than annular, and to have a rather narrow perforation.
[4] Stead, I. M. (1967), fig. 10c.

northern Italy and at the head of the Adriatic,[1] and Beck illustrates a somewhat comparable though earlier small bead from Italy.[2] It may be significant to note that the Welwyn Garden City bead, buried perhaps as a prized fragment or as a die for a game, came from a cremation in a large rectangular grave without any mound, in which not only the tomb type itself, but also the coloured glass gaming pieces found in it, find their nearest parallels from Montefortino in the Marche, belonging to the Gaulish tribe known as the Senones: these graves were, however, three centuries earlier than the Welwyn Garden City burial. The latter, which is one of a group of eight of the same type, all confined to the southeast of Britain, contained a silver cup and amphorae of Dressel Type I [3] of Italian origin. Four other comparable graves are recorded from the Continent and cited by Stead: two from Arras in the Marne and two from Presles-et-Bores (Aisne) but other comparable beads are not yet known to me.

The Welwyn Garden City burial also produced a fragment of a brownish glass armlet with an opaque yellow scrawl around its circumference, and a brown and yellow bead: both are types similar to late Celtic ones from the Continent.

The pottery is characteristic late La Tène III Aylesford–Swarling ware, with some Continental imports.

To sum up: the beads belong to the latter part of the first century B.C., and lingered, at least as survivals, until the Roman conquest. Their possible origin is in Italy or the head of the Adriatic, but this cannot be affirmed with any certainty so far as our present knowledge allows.

CLASS 3

Large annular beads with eyes of blue or other colours ringed with white (South Harting type) (Schedules, pp. 107–10) (pl. I, no. 3 and II top left, and figs. 8 and 9).

FIG. 8: Class 3: South
Harting type. Scale 1/1.

These are fairly large annular beads with a diameter of approximately 20–30 mm. and a height of about 15–20 mm. Almost invariably they are made of dark blue glass, and they generally have three equidistant eyes, marvered flush with the surface of the bead. These eyes are often of different coloured glass but are always surrounded with an opaque white ring. Occasionally there are only two eyes, and related specimens may have two or more registers of eyes.

These are not Roman beads and certain British examples belong to about the first century B.C. (e.g., Wookey Hole, Somerset), but the majority seem to fall within the early Romano-British period, and it is improbable that many survived into the third century. They are present in England, Wales, and Scotland but not in Ireland.

Continental beads of somewhat similar type are known from the Marne district and elsewhere—e.g., from Recy Voie Chantereine with yellow rings round the eyes found with ring beads whose affinities lie with our Hanging Langford beads (see pp. 51–3). Some smaller examples are also recorded from Gaulish graves but exact parallels are not readily found.

---

[1] See Harden, D. B. (1967).
[2] Beck, H. C. (1928), 43, no. A.7.b.
[3] For a discussion of these amphorae and their major concentration in Wessex, and more especially in Trino-vantian territory to the north of the lower Thames around Colchester and Welwyn see Peacock, D. P. S. (1971), 161–79.

SOUTH HARTING BEADS

● *South Harting Type Bead*   □ *Type Uncertain*

FIG. 9: Distribution of Class 3 beads.

A glance at the distribution map shows that the type is widespread and was carried northwards to early Roman sites in Scotland. It is possible that, as they seem to be commoner in Britain than in France or other parts of the Continent, they were manufactured in this country—but this apparent absence of exact parallels from across the Channel may only reflect our lack of knowledge, particularly of Gaul in the first century B.C.

CLASS 4

Opaque yellow beads with two superimposed rows of blue and white eyes (Findon type) (Schedules, p. 110) (pl. I, no. 4, and fig. 10).

Although a well-defined class on the Continent, only a few of these beads seem to have reached the British Isles, though in various sizes they are very common over the Mediterranean area and parts of Central Europe, as are their blue-green counterparts, not recorded from Britain.

In England, unfortunately, both the Woodeaton example and the one without provenance from the Nightingale Collection were found without associations.

The Findon one, from a ritual site with pottery of Park Brow affinities, is in our present state of

FIG. 10: Class 4: Findon type. Scale 1/1.

knowledge rather vaguely dated to probably the fourth or third century B.C., and the long period during which these beads were popular on the Continent makes it impossible to be more precise.

In Italy they are common, and are found for instance at Palestrina[1] in the fourth to second century B.C. (in the Villa Giulia Museum in Rome) and many other sites, including earlier Etruscan tombs.[2] Nearer to Britain they are known from France with Arras type beads at Vraux[3] and other Marnian cemeteries, e.g., five or six examples from St. Étienne-au-Temple, and ten from Bergères-les-Vertus.[4] Others came from Villeneuve Renneville near Épernay (fifth century B.C.) (this was of the almost equally common double variety in which one bead is made with another similar element above it), and from the Nécropole de Pernants (with La Tène I chariot burials, etc.). The latter was found close to, and perhaps originally hung from, a torc on the left shoulder. They are also found at similar dates on Punic sites in the Mediterranean world.

In Bohemia they may have continued in fashion into the second to first century B.C. at Stradonitz.[5] Others can be quoted from Mladší Doba Zelezná; Tumulus XIII, Grab 36 at Šmarje (Sankt Marein); Magdalenska Gora (Slovenia); and from the salt mine site at Hallein (in the Keltenmuseum, Hallein in Austria). In Holland the type is represented in the fourth to third centuries B.C. (in Leiden Museum).

It is impossible at present to try to locate their cultural and chronological range on the Continent, but one thing is fairly certain: their absence in the vast majority of late pre-Roman sites indicates that they were only surviving as rare heirlooms as late as the first century B.C. which may be the date of the one from Stradonitz. Their initial production in the Mediterranean area may go back to the sixth century or even before.

CLASS 5

Clear colourless annular beads with opaque yellow round the inside of perforation (Hanging Langford type) (Schedules, pp. 111–12) (pl. I, no. 5, and figs. 11 and 12).

These annular beads are generally about 20 mm. in diameter and about 6 mm. in height; the straight perforation measures about 10 mm. across. Around the perforation on the inner side of the bead, an irregular and discontinuous band of opaque yellow glass has been applied in such a way that it glows through the clear colourless glass like its prototypes which may have had gold foil enclosed to give the same though more brilliant effect.[6] It is possible that the smaller 'armlets' (sometimes under 50 mm. in diameter) and the beads were hung from torcs.

Exactly how the opaque yellow was applied is not known, but Déchelette when describing Continental La Tène II armlets decorated in the same technique, says: 'Mon. Viollier estime plutôt que la pâte jaune a été étendue au pinceau une fois le bracelet froid.' An alternative suggestion is that the

---

[1] *NS* (1907), 144.

[2] Examples of the sixth to fifth centuries B.C. are in the Ashmolean Museum at Oxford, and others come from Staré Vačc in Yugoslavia.

[3] Châlons-sur-Marne Museum. See also Bretz-Mahler, D. (1971).

[4] St. Germain-en-Laye.

[5] Pič, J. L. (1906). For other Czech ones see Venclová, N. (1971), fig. ii.

[6] These are noted by Haevernick, T. E. (1960): Groups 1 (armlets decorated with enclosed gold foil) and 20 (beads of the same type, which she notes are often found on the Continent in a melted state in cremation graves).

FIG. 11: Class 5: Hanging
Langford type. Scale 1/1.

yellow was applied to the mould itself and then fired to the bead when the molten glass was poured in.[1] The techniques of lining clear glass with opaque yellow first perhaps began to be used for glass vessels and armlets rather than for beads on the Continent, and some early ones, perhaps fourth to third century B.C., have been noted from Montefortino in Italy,[2] and others are quoted from Monte Rolo San Vito, and from Corroy in the Marne.[3] In the museum at Mainz there is one from the Rhein-hessen, and there are second- to first-century B.C. examples from the Dürrnberg, Hallein, in Austria.[4]

The earliest of the British examples may be around the second century B.C. An armlet of this type comes from Castle Dore in Cornwall,[5] a site whose first occupation is unlikely to have been much after about 100 B.C. Another, perhaps of the first century B.C. or early first century A.D., was found at Ballacagen, Isle of Man.[6] This had a comparable yellow coating inside but also had moulded cable patterns which may mean that it was a local British production (see Class 9 beads). This finds a partial analogy in a badly made armlet from Kintore, Aberdeenshire.[7] A bead from the hill-fort of Hunsbury, Northamptonshire, also probably belongs to the second to first century B.C.

The two Meare examples may belong, not to the earliest phases of the site, but more probably to the second to first century B.C. (see above, pp. 32–3.)

The hill-fort of Hanging Langford in Wiltshire has not yet been dated, but the finds, while including a La Tène I type fibula, are predominantly Belgic and approximately dated first century B.C. to first century A.D.

Both at Maumbury Rings, Dorchester, Dorset,[8] and Nor'nour in Scilly the beads come from what may be early Romano-British contexts. The Irish bead could have been traded up the western sea-ways, and the Faversham, Kent, bead was evidently a reused earlier one found in a Saxon context. There are other instances of such reuse. In the British Museum a bead of this Class has been reused in a Frankish necklace from the Rhineland, and in the Ashmolean Museum in Oxford a bead of Oldbury type (Class 6) has been found in a Saxon grave at Ducklington.

The distribution pattern (fig. 12) is unlike that of the other colourless beads with opaque yellow designs which may have been manufactured at or at least distributed from Meare in Somerset, and which do not seem to have Continental analogies. The hypothesis must therefore be that the Hanging Langford Class beads came as imports into the south-west of England, perhaps from northern France or Brittany. They may of course have subsequently been copied in Britain, probably, if anywhere, at Meare.

Continental beads comparable to the British ones are not uncommon. To mention only a few, examples come from Recy Voie Chantereine in the Marne,[9] found with beads of *oppida* types such as were found at Stradonitz (second to first century B.C.) and from Manching, of the same date.[10]

[1] Viollier, D. (1916).

[2] Brizio, E. (1899).

[3] Morel, L. (1898), pl.

[4] *MAGW* (1926), 324–6 and Abb. 2.

[5] Radford, C. A. R. (1951), App. 68–9.

[6] *JMM* v, no. 72.

[7] Kilbride-Jones, H. M. (1938), 305.

[8] Recently incorrectly compared to a Bulbury-type bead in *A* cv (1974–5), 197–8. Incorrectly drawn in fig. 20, no. 10.

[9] Châlons-sur-Marne Museum.

[10] Krämer, W. and Schubert, F. (1970).

HANGING LANGFORD BEADS

● *Hanging Langford Type Bead* ▲ *Related Armlet*

FIG. 12: Distribution of Class 5 beads.

Others come from the Worms district [1] and from Corseul, Côtes-du-Nord.[2] Their departure point from the Continent cannot yet be indicated.

It seems convincing that the period of their *floruit* in Britain lasted from the second century B.C. to the first century A.D., dying out after the Roman conquest.

CLASS 6

Large blue annular beads with marvered white or yellow spirals (Oldbury type) sometimes with swags between the spirals (Colchester type) (Schedules, pp. 112–17) (pl. I, no. 6a and b and II, top left and figs.13 and 14).

Beads which have been called the 'Oldbury' type from the site in Kent where such a bead was discovered and well illustrated, have the following characteristics: they are roughly 25–30 mm. in diameter and rather more annular than globular, about 15–20 mm. in height. The perforation, almost invariably cylindrical, is approximately 10 mm. wide. The glass (with the few exceptions mentioned below which may not belong to the same period) is dark, almost opaque, blue, appearing to be nearly black sometimes unless held to the light. The ornament generally consists of three, more rarely two,

[1] Worms Museum.　　　　　　　　　　[2] B.M. Dept. of Prehistoric and Romano-British Antiquities.

registers of trailed and marvered spirals, carefully made in opaque white, or less commonly yellow glass, round the circumference of the bead often on small bosses (perhaps vestigial 'horns').

A variant of the Oldbury Class is here called the Colchester Class (B). It is distinguished by having opaque yellow glass double swags running between the spirals.

Both these Classes belong to a well-known Continental Celtic type which can be ascribed to the last 150 years or so B.C., and they are particularly common during the later first century B.C. This date perfectly well accords with the evidence from the British Isles where quite a number come from datable

Fig. 13: Class 6: *left*, Oldbury type
(A); *right*, Colchester type (B). Scale 1/1.

contexts. The beads from the Iron Age site of Oldbury itself unfortunately came from a fox's earth from a twice-occupied fort which, though originally thought to be later, has been reconsidered.[1] It is now thought to belong to the early first century B.C. in its initial phase and to have been refortified about a century later 'by people whose pottery was largely if not predominantly Belgic in character'. The defences of the refortification had an unusual flat-bottomed ditch of a kind well represented in the Seine-Inférieure.[2] Of about the same date was the Maiden Castle (Dorset) bead, stratified in a deposit of the early first century B.C., and both the Meare and Glastonbury (Somerset) beads should belong to the early first century or so, as the Meare one does not apparently belong to the first phase of that settlement in the third century.

The Breiddin in Montgomeryshire produced a bead which 'could have been associated with a timber-built round-house assigned to the first century B.C. to first century A.D.', and another came from the Iron Age fort of South Cadbury in Somerset. Yet another has recently come from Beckford near Tewkesbury, and another from Danebury, Hants, thought to belong to the early first century B.C.

These beads survived into the early Roman period, and on one or two occasions were rediscovered and reused in Saxon times [3] but they were only survivals by Roman times as their importation was presumably brought to an end with the conquest. However, some dated examples are known. The Colchester bead was possibly pre-conquest in date, belonging, according to Harden, D. B. (1947), to Period III (dating from A.D. 43–8) or IV (from A.D. 48–65). Roman period examples of Oldbury type include the following: Dorchester (Dorset) [4]; Burnt Fen (Cambridge); Yewden (Bucks.); Old Winteringham (Lincs.), probably Claudian; Chichester (Sussex), with objects of late Antonine date.

The Irish examples are unfortunately almost all without provenance except for one from Dun-na-mara (Co. Tyrone). These beads may have reached the east coast of Ireland through trade, or have been carried by refugees moving northwards (see below). It is, however, possible that such beads may have been imitated in Ireland once the local glass-workers really developed their skills in a period which appears to fall well outside the scope of this study (see pp. 39–42).

The pattern of distribution (shown in fig. 14) points to a main area of import centred along the south

[1] In view of new evidence from Rainsborough Camp, Northants. See *PPS* xxxiii (1967), 207 ff.
[2] *AnJ* xxi (1941), 265–70.
[3] E.g., from a Saxon grave at Ducklington (Ashmolean Museum).
[4] From the Colliton Park villa. See R.C.H.M. *Dorset*, vol. ii (South-East), pt. 3.

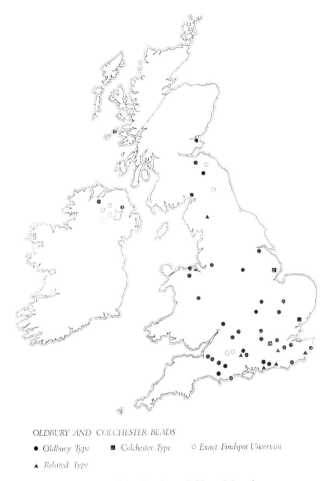

OLDBURY AND COLCHESTER BEADS

● *Oldbury Type*   ■ *Colchester Type*   ○ *Exact Findspot Uncertain*

▲ *Related Type*

FIG. 14: Distribution of Class 6 beads.

coast, particularly around Kent, Essex, and the Thames estuary, and in Dorset. Some may have come up the Bristol Channel or perhaps reached Somerset and Gloucestershire from the southern counties. From these areas they also spread northwards by both west and east sea routes to reach Northern Ireland and south and west Scotland—perhaps between A.D. 43 and 71 if not before. Their greatest density is shown to be the area of Belgic settlement or influence in south-east England, and these beads may possibly find a place among the many objects of so-called 'Belgic' type which reached the south of Scotland: cauldrons and cauldron-chains,[1] certain types of brooches and polychrome enamelling,[2] a bronze brooch of Type Bii from Craig's Quarry, Dirleton,[3] loop or ring-ended torcs such as those from Snettisham (Norfolk) and Cairnmuir (Peebles), and the related Castle Newe torcs which are apparently skeuomorphs of the loop-ended variety.[4]

In Ireland, it is hard to explain all the examples as coming from ports of call up the western seaways, for as Jope has shown,[5] a number of other south-east English objects of early first-century A.D. date

[1] *PSAS* lxxxvii (1952-3), 17-19, with map.
[2] From Traprain Law, East Lothian; *PSAS* lxxxix (1955-6), 135.
[3] *PSAS* xci (1957–8) 72–4.
[4] *AnJ* xxxix (1959), 31.
[5] *UJA* xx (1957), 85 8.

found their way to Ireland, and their distribution suggests that they were brought by individuals rather than by groups of intending settlers. Alternatively they might have reached Northern Ireland from Scotland, for at that time the two areas shared a common school of metalworking.

Continental analogies for these beads are not difficult to find, and they belong to the last two centuries B.C. and the first few decades of the first century A.D. It is possible that the Oldbury beads resulted from a blending of two earlier bead types, both known in Switzerland and Central Europe in La Tène II. One is an annular blue bead with a single row of white or yellow spirals (see pl. I, no. 6c) and the other a heavy cylindrical blue glass bead with projecting horns surrounded by white rings (see fig. 19, no. 2). Both of these types occur in England but are rare. (See Schedules, pp. 122–4, for the first type.)[1] The second class is represented so far only from one site in Britain, at Cooling in Kent (see fig. 19) but on the Continent they are noted by *inter alios* Viollier [2] from Zollikofen and Berne. The resultant Oldbury type combines the spirals with the horn element which dwindles into bosses or may be entirely flattened.

Whether or not such an ancestry is acceptable, beads of Oldbury or Colchester types are known from Celles-les-Condé (Aisne) found with mostly La Tène II objects,[3] and others from Loisy-sur-Marne and La Vigne aux Morts (both Marne) are in the museum at Châlons-sur-Marne. Another with yellow spirals came from an inhumation grave a little to the north-west of the *oppidum* (? of the Vindelici tribe) of Manching in Upper Bavaria.[4] There is only one fragment which appears to belong to this type from the *oppidum* of Manching [5] occupied from the early second century until the later first century B.C. One of Colchester type came from Heppenheim, Rheinhessen,[6] from a grave (457) with a warrior's iron sword, etc. The importance of this lies in its being, like that from near Manching, a male grave, and there seems little doubt from the position of the finds that the bead was attached to the sword as a talisman (see below). Another Colchester Class bead is in the Speyer Museum, and is very much burnt; apparently both the swags and spirals were yellow. A related bead came from a hillfort at Waldfischbach near Birmisens, South Palatine.[7]

The evidence is therefore consistent in pointing to a date for these beads on the Continent in the last two centuries B.C. and they no doubt lingered in use a little later than the end of the first century B.C. when so many of the *oppida* were sacked. It is possible that sometimes such beads may have served as a loop for a strap to draw the sword firmly to the scabbard. The use of attaching a bead to the sword is not without precedent, and Joachim Werner showed [8] that the custom went back to the Sarmatians in the first century B.C. and that during the empire of the Huns it spread to other peoples. He suggested that it reached the British Isles in about A.D. 500, perhaps introduced by Franks. The glass rings were replaced by metal ones after the seventh century A.D. In the light of the evidence from Heppenheim (if the bead was a sword-ring rather than a talisman) the introduction into Northern Europe may have been earlier than the first century B.C. and need not have been of Sarmatian origin. On the whole I find it more convincing to explain the Heppenheim bead as a talisman.

Most of the related spiral beads from Britain can also be matched from Continental sites, but I have not been able to find any analogy for the two colourless examples with yellow spirals, both of which come from collections. It is possible that they are later Irish copies of Oldbury beads, or that, like the

---

[1] e.g., Worthing, which had a second-century B.C. parallel from Ludwigshafen, and others from Worms, Manching, etc.

[2] Viollier, D. (1916), pl. 32, nos. 11 and 12.

[3] *BSPF* lv, fasc. 10 (1958), 671. Note that from this site came a 'creuset pour perles en bronze', showing that at least some kinds of beads were being made there.

[4] Reinecke, S. (1911), pl. xiv, no. 230a. One from Grave

III (Weber, 1903) was accompanied by a pot, iron sword, spearhead, bronze spiral arm-ring, etc. See also Jacobsthal, P. (1944), pl. 248d and Pič, J. L. (1906), pls. 6, 7 and 8.

[5] Krämer, W. (1958).

[6] Koehl, W. Z. (1882), I S. 16, Abb. 20.

[7] Kindly shown to me in 1965 in advance of publication.

[8] *Beiträge zur Archäologie des Attila-Reiches* (1956), 26–37. See also *A* ci (1967) and Raddatz, K. (1957), 81–4.

many other variants of colourless glass decorated with opaque yellow designs, they were perhaps made at Meare in Somerset. (See Class 11.) It is interesting to note that Ireland also produced the only two colourless examples of Class 7 known from the British Isles (see below).

CLASS 7

Large annular beads with whirl or ray design in contrasting colours (Celtic whirl and ray types) (Schedules, pp. 117–20) (pl. 1, no. 7 and II, top right, and figs. 15 and 16).

These two varieties of decoration are generally applied to large annular beads on a blue or purple, brown, or light yellow ground and they may have a straight or rounded hour-glass perforation. The whirls or rays emerge from the perforation (see fig. 15). In addition some of the beads have circumferential bands of a contrasting colour, usually underlying the whirls. For facility of study these beads of Class 7 have been sub-divided into *Type (a)*, blue or purple ground; *Type (b)*, brown or yellowish-brown ground; and *Type (c)* various other colours. Of the three types Type (a) is the commonest.

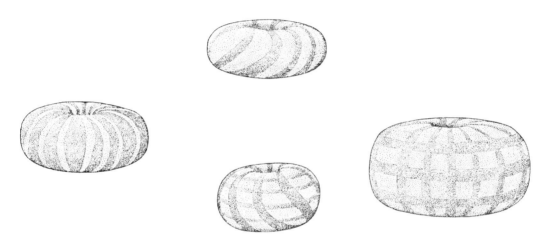

FIG. 15: Class 7: *upper*, Billericay, Essex—blue and yellow whirls; *left*, Salisbury Plain, Wilts.—'black' with yellow rays; *right*, Kirkmaiden, Wigtownshire—dark cobalt blue and yellow criss-cross; *lower*, Colchester, Essex—opaque whitish with purple whirls and light blue bands. Scale 1/1.

TYPE (a)

Several of these have been found in relatively well-dated associations and they can also be paralleled from many Continental Celtic sites. The earliest so far dated British example came from a 'rath' at Walesland in Pembrokeshire, and a radio-carbon date of 210–90 B.C. was obtained from its associations; another (? late second century B.C.) has been found at Danebury, Hants; others come from the villages of Meare and Glastonbury in Somerset (one only from each, and both probably late second to first century B.C.). There is little likelihood that these beads were among those manufactured or distributed from Meare. Their importance probably ceased with the Roman occupation of southern Britain. One came from an early Romano-British rubbish pit at Kelvedon in Essex, one from Norsey Wood Camp with Belgic and pre-Belgic pottery and another from first- to early second-century A.D. fort defences at Wick Wood in Wiltshire. Another fragmentary one was stratified A.D. 130–230 at Caerleon, Monmouthshire: these are survivals, and any examples later than the Claudian conquest can be regarded as such.

The date of these beads falls within the approximate period 150 B.C. to A.D. 50. Their distribution pattern (see fig. 16) reveals the familiar port of entry up the Bristol Channel, with a scatter up the Irish sea coasts and round the Thames estuary. The Irish evidence is tantalizingly inadequate. At Edenderry (Co. Offaly) the association of one of these beads with some bronze implements must either imply that the bead was accidentally associated with earlier implements, or, less improbably, that the bronzes were types which survived in use into the second to first century B.C. The remaining Irish examples came from collections and are therefore worthless. (Others not included in the Schedules were once in the Pitt-Rivers Museum at Farnham, Dorset (now closed down) marked 'Ireland'.)

TYPE (b)

The three dated examples of this type all support a date in the first century B.C. They come from Hengistbury Head in Dorset, Welwyn Garden City with a Belgic burial (probably last quarter of the first century B.C.), and from Glastonbury Lake Village whose occupation ended not long after this time.

TYPE (c)

Includes beads with green, white or colourless glass. The green and colourless glass examples come from Ireland and are not closely datable; the Colchester bead, with an opaque white ground, pale blue

WHIRL AND RAY BEADS

● *Type a*   ■ *Type b*   ▲ *Type c*   ○□△ *Exact Findspot Uncertain*

FIG. 16: Distribution of Class 7 beads.

circumferential bands and purple whirls is said to have come from a burial of the mid-first century A.D. and the Seamills one from a Flavian context. The two Irish beads with yellow whirls on colourless glass might have been made at Meare where such a combination of colours was a speciality. But note that two colourless examples of Class 6 also came from Ireland.

Continental parallels for this class are easily found from a wide variety of Celtic *oppida* in Central Europe, especially from Stradonitz where they may have been made, for over 100 examples were found there (see p. 29), as well as from Italy, the south and north-west of France, Hungary, Roumania, Poland, Jersey, and elsewhere.[1] The size is nearly always large and the colours vary considerably, making use of blue, grey, brown, indigo, black, crimson, etc., glass. (Note that somewhat comparable beads also occur in Alamannic sites and care needs to be taken about dating unassociated beads.[2])

The British distribution adds to that already plotted by Dr. Haevernick for central Europe and north Italy, and merely emphasizes what we already know, that, either through trade or movements of peoples, these beads arrived on the southern coasts of England in numbers which show a sharp increase during the last century or so B.C. and the early first century A.D. A date around the second to first century B.C. would seem to fit many of the Continental ones, for some of the *oppida* are thought to have ended their life in the last twenty years of the first century, or a little earlier. The overall picture seems, therefore, to be perfectly consistent. What is not clear, however, is how many of the British ones were copies of Continental prototypes. Their occurrence at the very productive glass-working centres at Glastonbury and Meare, and the fact that the clear glass ones with opaque yellow whirls from Ireland do not seem to have Continental parallels, leaves this question an open one.

(ii) DECORATED OR UNDECORATED GROUPS (BOTH IRON AGE AND ROMAN IN DATE)

GROUP 1

Large or medium annular beads with streaky or mottled design (Schedules, pp. 121–2 fig. 17)

These beads are common on the Continent and have been catalogued by Dr. Haevernick (1960) as Group 24 of her study (*Ringperlen mit hellgesprenkelter Oberfläche*). She emphasizes that the ground colour is usually blue which is spattered with white or yellow dots of varying sizes, and their distribution is not very widespread. She describes them as varying from 22 to 45 mm. in diameter and 9 to 19 mm. in height,

FIG. 17: Group 1: annular
mottled beads. Scale 1/1.

[1] Haevernick, T. E. (1960), *passim*, and references up to 1959. Also Déchelette, J. (1904), and others from Corrent, etc. Hélèna, P. (1937) for the *oppidum* of Montlaurès near Narbonne. For Jersey see *SJ* xiii (1932). For Trísov (South Bohemia) see Břeň, J. (1966). For Stradonitz see Pič, J. L. (1906), pl. vi; Manching, see Krämer, W. (1958), Haffner,

A. (1971), Farbtaf. B., etc.

[2] The large criss-cross decorated bead from Kirkmaiden in Wigtownshire can also be closely paralleled from Central Europe. See Pič, J. L. (1906), Tab. VI (for Alamannic beads somewhat resembling Celtic ones, see Garscha, F., *Die Alamannen in Südbaden* (R. G. K. Berlin, 1970)).

and she lists 14 examples from Germany, 7 from France, 2 from Switzerland, 2 from Italy, 5 from Austria, and 1 from Hungary; a much larger number come from Czechoslovakia where they may have been made, for no fewer than twenty-four examples came from the Stradonitz *oppidum*, previously cited, which is now regarded as the most prolific Central European glass centre of the first century B.C. Probably it was from here that the few true examples of this type reached the British Isles, and their probable date, when ascertainable, e.g., Hamworthy (Dorset), Colchester (Essex), Hengistbury Head (Dorset), all probably dating from about 50 B.C. to A.D. 50, shows that they began to be imported very sporadically soon after their manufacture. There are some other examples from Britain which may or may not belong to this group, and some may be local imitations, or survivals into a Roman context. Others may even have an Irish origin, possibly as late as the sixth to ninth century A.D. or so.

All that one can safely say is that some of these beads were imports from the Celtic Continent around 50 B.C.–A.D. 50, but this date should be considered with caution.

GROUP 2

Miscellaneous spiral-decorated beads (see also Classes 6, 10, and 13) (Schedules, pp. 122–4) (pl. I, no. 8 illustrates two examples) (fig. 18)

There is nothing to add here to the information given in the Schedules. Among the beads mentioned there must undoubtedly be some of post-Roman date. They differ widely and seldom have exact

FIG. 18: Group 2—miscellaneous spiral decorated beads (see also Classes 6, 9 (fig. 26, no. 5), 10 and 13, and Groups 3 and 8): *left*, Meare, Somerset; *centre*, Traprain Law, E. Lothian; *right*, Worthing, Sussex. Scale 1/1.

counterparts, or at least they are not recognized. For the time being each newly discovered bead must be dated from its associations and, if exactly similar, from dated beads in these lists. It appears, however, that annular beads, often opaque, and with a spiral around the whole bead's upper and lower surfaces in pale blue or another colour, are of Saxon date; they are, therefore, excluded from these Schedules.

GROUP 3

Miscellaneous horned beads, some with eyes or spirals (Schedules, pp. 125–6) (fig. 19)

It is clear that these beads do not in any way form a Class: they must have reached Britain in rare instances from as yet unidentified Continental workshops. It is impossible with our limited knowledge of the Continental beads to find exact analogies, and indeed one is tempted to suggest that the natural greenish glass examples must be regarded as datable within the same approximate brackets as have been proposed for the undecorated annular beads of the same glass (second to first century B.C. and throughout the Roman period) and to regard the horns or spirals as a *jeu d'esprit* on the part of the maker who was availing himself of two well known features: the protruding horn, and the decorative spiral. Thus I should be inclined to date both the Newstead (Roxburghs.) and the Tarporley (Cheshire) beads which are identical—made of natural glass with horns decorated with blue on white spirals—within the early Roman period of the occupation of Newstead which ran from approximately A.D. 80 to 120.

FIG. 19: Group 3—horned beads, some with eyes or spirals (see also Group 8, no. 2 in fig. 23): *left*, Tarporley, Cheshire; *right*, Cooling, Kent. Scale 1/1.

The curious bead from Skeffington (Leics.) may also belong to this context. The same date or slightly later might be proposed for the two beads on a blue ground with yellow eyes on horns from Silchester (Hants) and one from Chesters Fort (Northumberland) occupied from about A.D. 122 to 383. The rest may belong to this roughly defined period with the exception of Lagore and other Irish beads. At Lagore there was almost certainly material derived from earlier occupation close by, for there are other early beads (Meare Class 10, pp. 79–81). The Hunsbury, Cooling and Donaghadee examples may all be pre-Conquest and horned beads are not uncommon in Continental Celtic beads of La Tène II and III.[1]

The 'black' bead with greenish-yellow horns from Icklingham, like the majority of such dark beads, is likely to belong to the beginning of the Teutonic period.

From the Continent it is not at all rare to find horned beads.[2] They have always been widely used both in time and space, but are rare in Britain. They certainly continue into the Frankish period.[3]

GROUP 4

Compound eyed beads with small eyes set in roundels ('Garrow Tor' type) (Schedules, p. 127) (pl. I, no. 9, and fig. 20)

These beads, which, in the British Isles at least, are not common, are generally slightly more annular than globular and about 15 mm. in diameter.[4] The classic ground colour is turquoise, but more rarely

FIG. 20: Group 4—Garrow Tor type. Scale 1/1.

dark blue and into this ground three fairly large mustard-coloured roundels are inset, surrounded by white rings, and with, inside, like eggs in a nest, regularly arranged blue eyes ringed with white. These eyes are stratified as in Arras Type II beads (see p. 45).

---

[1] See Schedules, p. 178. For Donaghadee, see fig. 23, no. 2.

[2] See, for instance, Reinecke, S. (1911) v, 236 and 237, and Taf. 14. Many of much earlier date come from the Eastern Mediterranean.

[3] Examples in the museum at St. Germain (possibly reused beads of Roman date). See also *GDV* xiii, forthcoming, with very valuable coloured plates of beads of sixth- to seventh-century date from Schretzheim on the Danube. Information, in advance of publication, from Dr. Ursula Koch.

[4] On the Continent, on the other hand, they have a tendency to be more globular.

Three not closely dated English examples come from Cirencester [1] (unstratified), from Silchester (unstratified) [2] and from an Iron Age hut in the Garrow Tor settlement,[3] Bodmin Moor, Cornwall. The occupation at Silchester began well before the Roman conquest (there was a La Tène I brooch from the site) and the Garrow Tor huts may go back to the fourth or third century B.C.[4] In addition to the English beads there are four examples from Ireland which, for reasons of colour or shape, while being closely similar to the English beads, are sufficiently distinct to warn us against a contemporary date. One cannot help feeling that here, as in some other types of bead, the decoration attracted much later Irish glass-workers to copy the pre-Roman Continental and English ones, or at least to use them for free versions of their own invention.

We are now left with the necessity of finding an origin for the English beads, particularly for the earlier one from Garrow Tor.

The well-known and richly accompanied princess's burial from Reinheim (Kr. St. Ingbert) near Saarbrücken [5] has been attributed to the fourth century B.C., and while the otherwise precisely similar beads from that grave are somewhat larger than their English counterparts, they must undoubtedly have been ancestral to them and perhaps even produced in the same workshop. Similar or related beads also come from the Marne [6] area and from elsewhere on the Continent, and even from the Near East.[7]

Introduced then into Britain around the fourth to third century B.C., these beads may either have continued to be imported from the Continent until the first century B.C. or thereabouts or, in rare cases, have survived into Roman times, and it seems likely that then, after an interval of some centuries, they were reinterpreted in their own idiom by Irish glass-workers sometime after the fifth century A.D.

GROUP 5

Miscellaneous wave decorated beads (Schedules, pp 128–39) (pls. I and II, no. 10 a–h, and fig. 21)

For convenience of study these are sub-divided as follows:

(A) Translucent blue annular or globular beads with opaque white or yellow wave.

(B) Opaque blue annular or globular beads with blue or purple wave.

(C) Green or natural greenish translucent glass annular beads with white, yellow or blue wave.

(D) 'Black' (dark green or other very dark colours, appearing black).
    (i) Annular with white wave.
    (ii) Annular with irregular yellow scrawl.
    (iii) Annular with various coloured waves.
    (iv) Globular with yellow wave.

[1] In the Corinium Museum, Cirencester.

[2] *A* cii (1959), 53, fig. 8.

[3] Regarded as one of the earlier Iron Age sites in Cornwall. See Thomas, C. (1966), 75.

[4] Others, of unknown provenance, are in the B.M. (one in the Slade Collection). See Nesbitt (1871), 10, fig. 18.

[5] Now in the Saarbrücken Museum. See Keller, J. (1955), 13–44, and Megaw, J. V. S. (1970), 76.

[6] Bergères-les-Vertus, Crons (St. Germain Museum, no. 12.012). See Keller, J. (1955 b) 209; Bussy-le-Château (St. Germain, no. 15195); St. Remy sur Bussy, Grave 5 (St. Germain, no. 67839).

[7] These were discussed by Seligman, C. G. and Beck, H. C. (1938), 1–64. Haevernick, T. E. (1960) extended her study of these beads (1972) and divided them on a worldwide basis into Classes *A* (genuine and characteristic beads of the class), *B* (Italic types with yellow knobs)—the use of knobs (little horns) was common in Italy where the Punic face-bead design may have broken down into a meaningless but still recognizable series of knobs under Celtic influence—*C* (millefiori beads), and *D* (beads made from vase glass). Together they cover a very long period of time.

Note also that in a tomb at Aléria in Corsica (Tomb 87) compound beads were dated by a red-figure lekythos to *c*. 400–375 B.C. (Jehasse, J. and L., *La Nécropole préromaine d'Aléria*, xxx supplément to *Gallia* (1973), pl. 162).

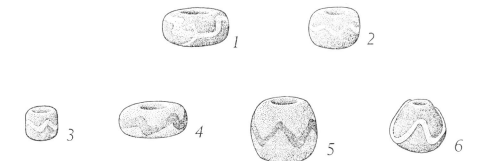

FIG. 21: Group 5—miscellaneous wave-decorated beads: 1. Caerleon, Mon.—blue with white waves; 2. Almondbury, Yorks.—dark greenish-blue with yellow wave; 3. Meare (East Village), Somerset—translucent green with yellow wave; 4. Glastonbury, Somerset—slaty blue with blue-black wave; 5. Hamworthy, Dorset—opaque blue with purplish wave; 6. Mildenhall, Wilts.—shiny black with unmarvered yellow wave. Scale 1/1.

(E) Opaque yellow annular beads with coloured wave.

(F) Opaque annular beads with yellow wave.

(G) Translucent 'amber' (reddish-brown) beads with yellow wave.

(H) Translucent colourless beads with yellow wave. (See Class 11, pp. 81–4.)

(I) Translucent greenish gold with yellow wave.

(A) TRANSLUCENT BLUE ANNULAR OR GLOBULAR BEADS WITH OPAQUE WHITE OR YELLOW WAVE (fig. 21, no. 1)

These beads, almost invariably annular in form, represent such a long-lived type that a distribution map would be meaningless except to emphasize their apparent absence in Ireland and their extreme rarity outside the Roman occupied lowlands of Scotland and Wales. The earliest known from England are those from the Arras (Yorkshire) graves, perhaps attributable to the fourth and third centuries B.C., from the Cowlam Barrow L with Arras Type I bead and from the Queen's Barrow, Arras, with Type II (see pp. 45–8). Not much later we have some examples from Meare in Somerset (about third to first century B.C.) and Longbridge Deverill, Wilts., perhaps third century B.C. Another (c. 100 B.C.) has recently been found at Danebury Camp, Hants. None of these early beads is very strongly coloured in comparison with the rich cobalt blues of the Roman period, but as the same light blues reappear in post-Roman examples, this can hardly be regarded as significant. The 'waves' on these earlier beads are fairly evenly and carefully applied, while during the Roman and post-Roman periods the size of the bead may be larger (16 mm. or so in diameter), the colour is stronger, and the occasionally yellow but usually white thread has often been so thinly drawn out during its application that it may have broken more than once and the marvering is less careful. The waves are haphazard and sometimes make bows or knots. This, however, can only be regarded as a reflection of greater or less skill in craftsmanship.

These beads are not common on the Continent, though how widespread they were is not yet known. They occur, for instance, in some graves of the Hunsrück-Eifel I period (c. 650–500 B.C.) [1] and in the early sixth century B.C. from Fendringen, Switzerland, [2] and further south and east they may be yet

[1] *TZ* xvi–xvii (1941–2), 210, fig. 10.　　　　[2] *HA* v (1971), 2–6.

earlier. It is, however, quite impossible to date one of these beads visually, for they continued to be used (sometimes as reused Romano-British beads and sometimes newly produced in the Teutonic areas of Northern Europe) into the sixth and seventh centuries.[1] It follows that some of the many unassociated beads listed in these Schedules may prove, on further evidence, to belong to a period later than the terms of reference for this study.

(B) OPAQUE BLUE ANNULAR OR GLOBULAR BEADS WITH BLUE OR PURPLE WAVE (Schedules, p. 134) (fig. 21, nos. 4 and 5)

For obvious reasons of lack of contrast these two tones of blue were rarely used in combination. Both the two known examples belong in all probability to the second or first century B.C., but this may be fortuitous, though at Meare there was also a bead with light blue spirals on dark blue, likely to belong to the same approximate date.

The concentration of the three examples in the south-west is in agreement with that of many pre-Roman bead types in Britain.

(C) GREEN OR NATURAL TRANSLUCENT GREENISH GLASS ANNULAR BEADS WITH WHITE, YELLOW, OR BLUE WAVE (Schedules, pp. 134–5)

These cannot be regarded as other than a miscellaneous collection, each bead from which may be used for comparative purposes with others found in the future, so that one day classes may be distinguished amongst them. They were found at Arras, while the totally colourless glass example from Meare (see pp. 83 and 84) is separately classified (Class II). Meare also produced one translucent green bead with yellow wave (fig. 21, no. 3), and a related but bluer bead came from Almondbury (fig. 21, no. 2).

(D) VERY DARK GLASS, APPEARING BLACK

(i) *Annular beads with white wave.* See remarks in Schedules, pp. 135–7.

(ii) *Annular beads with irregular yellow scrawl* (Schedules, p. 136). A few undated examples come from Ireland and one from the Roman fort at *Segontium* in North Wales, where its date is uncertain but it is probably late Roman. It must be remembered that a 'black' annular bead with yellow streaks came from an apparently Roman background at Caerleon, though this is suspect as it came from old excavations and might be a Teutonic intrusion. For more globular types see (iv) below.

(iii) *Annular beads with various coloured waves* (Schedules, pp. 136–7). Both terracotta red and light sky-blue were colours which were popularly used during the early migration period, and there is no reason to doubt that on historical grounds some of these Teutonic or Frankish beads began to reach the British Isles during the fourth century (or maybe before). This hypothesis is supported by the few examples from datable contexts likely to fall between A.D. 350–450 or so. A doubt, however, about the contemporaneity of the 'Northern Ireland' bead must be stressed; not only is it right outside the area in which these beads normally occur, but the wave is bright cobalt blue rather than the very characteristic sky blue of the Frankish beads.

(iv) *Globular beads with yellow wave* (Schedules, p. 137) (fig. 21, no. 6). These have been separated from the annular beads of similar type only because there is more doubt about the dating of that group. Though these have been claimed as Sarmatian beads of the Roman period there is an apparently slightly

<hr/>

[1] See for instance Lethbridge, T. C. (1931), 76 ff. It is interesting to note that an example from Cow Down near Buxton, Derbyshire, was described as 'A type common in 7th century graves, probably in this case a toggle for a belt'. (*MAr* vi–vii (1962–3), 28.)

pre-Roman glass armlet made in a comparable technique and colouring from Hamworthy in Dorset. More evidence is required. The two British examples come from Chesters Fort in Northumberland and Mildenhall in Wiltshire, and according to Sulimirski they may have been Sarmatian imports.[1]

(E) OPAQUE YELLOW ANNULAR BEADS WITH COLOURED WAVE (Schedules, p. 138)

The frequent use of opaque yellow glass in pre-Roman times has been demonstrated for various classes of beads and armlets, and in fact several of the beads in this group are very closely related to the beads of Class 8 and appear to be identical with them but for the addition of a wave design in another colour, green or blue. In fact they are probably of British manufacture. One came from Meare itself and one from Burton Fleming in Yorkshire, from an Iron Age cemetery. Another (rather more globular and with a slaty blue wave, dated about 100 B.C.) has recently been found at Danebury, Hants. The date of these probably falls between the third and first century B.C. The rather thicker and more globular bead from Beckford in Worcestershire (associated with stamped wares) and one from All Cannings Cross in Wiltshire with a brown wave are slightly different (perhaps marginally earlier), as the latter is closely paralleled from a late Hallstatt period grave (no. 72) at Les Jogasses.[2] Care should be taken not to confuse these Iron Age beads with some rather similar but rare beads of the Migration period.

(F) Information in Schedules, p. 138.

(G) Information in Schedules, pp. 138–9.

(H) TRANSLUCENT COLOURLESS BEADS WITH YELLOW WAVE (see Class 11 (G))

(I) TRANSLUCENT GREENISH-GOLD WITH YELLOW WAVE (see p. 13, above, for example from Carrawburgh)

GROUP 6

Undecorated annular beads

For convenience, the sizes are divided as follows: *Large* over 30 mm. in diameter; *Medium*, from 15 – 30 mm. in diameter; *Small*, under 15 mm.

(i) Large beads of various colours.

(iia) Medium, and (iib) small natural greenish translucent glass.

(iiia) Medium translucent green, greenish-gold or greenish-brown, and (iiib) small translucent yellow or greenish-gold.

(iva) Medium and (ivb) small blue, translucent or opaque.

(v) Small translucent 'amber' (reddish-brown).

(vi) Small opaque terracotta-coloured.

(vii) Small opaque or translucent sky blue.

(viii) Small opaque. Other colours, but note that yellow beads of this type are separately discussed as Class 8, below.

(ix) Very dark ('black') glass.

(x) Colourless (not scheduled).

[1] Sulimirski, T. (1970).   [2] *RA* xxvi (1927), 113.

(i) LARGE BEADS OF VARIOUS COLOURS (German, *Ringperlen*) (Schedules, pp. 139–40)

These were never either made in, or imported on a large scale into, Britain. Those from such Iron Age sites as Worthy Down (Hants), Breedon-on-the-Hill (Leics.), Glastonbury (Somerset) and Congresbury (Somerset) (the last found with a La Tène III brooch) all point to a date within the third to first centuries B.C. In the light of our present knowledge of the type, which is a rare one, they seem to have died out after the Roman conquest, and this suggests that they were imported from the Continent and that the trade was discontinued after that event. Nearly all of them are blue, and they are mostly confined to the southern part of Britain. It seems probable that they belong with the many other large (but undecorated) beads of Continental Celtic origin.

(iia) MEDIUM ANNULAR NATURAL GREENISH TRANSLUCENT GLASS (Schedules, pp. 140–3) (pl. II, no. 11) AND (iib) SMALL ANNULAR OF SIMILAR GLASS (Schedules, pp. 143–5)

These should be considered together with undecorated globular beads (Group 7 (ii), p. 69).

The overwhelming proportion of these beads come from Roman sites and run right through the Roman period. Only a very few are earlier than the conquest, after which a number could have been made from Roman bottle-glass waste or vases imported from Continental sites. The earliest examples come from Glastonbury and Meare in Somerset (? third to first centuries B.C.); from Bury Wood Camp, Colerne in Wiltshire, and Moel Trigarn in Pembrokeshire (of about the same date) and from Trevelgue in Cornwall where the occupation began in the Iron Age but continued through the Roman period. By the first century B.C. or A.D. this glass was also used for probably locally produced cable beads. (See Class 9.)

Some very irregular beads were almost certainly made in hill-forts such as Traprain Law (East Lothian) and Coygan Camp (Carmarthenshire) and these are not easy to distinguish from the numerous and equally roughly made Anglo-Saxon beads from graves such as those at Stanton Harcourt (Oxon.) and Harwell (Berks.) cemeteries of about A.D. 450–550. Both of these are in the Ashmolean Museum in Oxford.

(iiia) MEDIUM TRANSLUCENT GREEN, GREENISH-GOLD OR GREENISH-BROWN AND (iiib) SMALL TRANSLUCENT YELLOW OR GREENISH-GOLD (see below for 'amber' (reddish-brown)) (Schedules, pp. 145–52)

It has already been pointed out (p. 13) that a concentration of greenish-yellow glass beads in the south from such sites as Worthy Down (Hants) and Bulbury Camp (Dorset), etc., suggests that they may have been made from one or more imported glass ingots of this glass in about the second or first century B.C. None is known to have been associated with Iron Age 'A' wares.

The rest of the beads in this group, where the varieties of greens and yellows are very marked, were also probably imports of around the first century B.C. to first century A.D., but they lingered on sporadically through most of the Roman period. Their pre-Roman distribution is mostly confined to that part of Britain lying to the south of a line from Chester to the Wash; two examples of approximately this date reached Western Scotland (Castle Hill, Dalry, Ayrshire, and Dunagoil Fort, Rothesay, Bute).

(iva) MEDIUM ANNULAR BLUE BEADS TRANSLUCENT OR OPAQUE (Schedules, pp. 152–5) AND (ivb) SMALL ANNULAR BLUE BEADS (Schedules, pp. 155–62) (pl. II, no. 11 and fig. 22)

These two groups can be considered together as their history appears to be similar. They began to be imported in about the sixth century B.C. and are present at several Iron Age 'A' sites of about that date. These are Gussage All Saints, Dorset; All Cannings Cross, Wilts.; Swallowcliffe, Wilts.; Chalbury Camp, Dorset; Chinnor, Oxon.; and possibly Crickley Hill, Gloucestershire. Their importation continued throughout the Iron Age, and their distribution in sites of that period strongly suggests

IRON AGE BLUE ANNULAR AND GLOBULAR BEADS   approx. 6th. c. B.C.– 1st. c. A.D.

■ *Large Annular*   ▲ *Medium Annular*   ● *Small Annular*

◉ *Concentration*   ○ *Globular*   - - - - - - *Jurassic Way*

Fig. 22: Distribution of beads of Groups 6 and 7 of known Iron Age date.

a south and south-western entry, possibly up the Bristol Channel and the Irish Sea (and possibly that they were made at or distributed from Meare and Glastonbury once these factories had begun production in about the third century B.C.). One or two examples even reached the extreme west of Scotland. In this respect they somewhat resemble the small opaque yellow annular beads of Class 8 which, however, differ from the blue beads in having consistent characteristics which enable them to be considered as a Class rather than a Group, and their period of popularity consequently lasted for a shorter time.

On Roman sites blue annular beads of small and medium size are far from uncommon, but it is noticeable that where they occur a native British element is apparent from the culture. In Ireland[1] most of these beads appear to belong to the seventh to tenth centuries A.D. (e.g., many from Lagore), but they are common from undated sites; they reached the Kintyre peninsula and a little further into Scotland, and they may perhaps have been worn by the Scotti in the Dalriadic territory of Ulster and Argyllshire. Unfortunately most of the Irish examples come from collections. Fig. 22 shows the distribution of the pre-Roman examples, covering roughly the last five or six centuries B.C. Its significance is

[1] See pp. 39–42, above.

therefore of limited value—the more so as we do not yet know which were of British and which of Continental manufacture.

In England, too, the type certainly persisted into post-Roman times, but from the dated examples at our disposal it seems possible that these blue beads were in use from about the sixth or fifth centuries B.C. to at least the eighth century A.D.

The Saxon beads of this group, though very common in the seventh-century pagan graves, are generally badly made, rough, and uneven, often with striations around the surface. There are also large quantities of annular blue (but generally opaque) beads from Viking sites such as Bïrka and Helgö.

These blue beads offer, therefore, very little help for dating purposes.

(v) SMALL TRANSLUCENT 'AMBER' (REDDISH-BROWN) COLOURED ANNULAR BEADS (Schedules, pp. 162–3)

Small annular beads appear to have been almost the only form in which this glass was made up, and it clearly pre-dated the Roman conquest on certain sites: Hunsbury (Northants.), probably first century B.C.; King Harry's Lane, Verulamium (Herts.), stratified 10 B.C. to A.D. 40; High Rocks Camp, Tunbridge Wells (Kent), ? first century B.C. Some lasted into the early Roman period, but none, it seems, very late. This glass was also used for a streaky annular bead of La Tène III Celtic type from Hamworthy in Dorset (first century B.C. to first century A.D.) but was evidently never very popular, or else was difficult to obtain, and it was not made into globular or other forms of bead. A small bead of this type but with an abnormally small perforation was found at Mousewold (Dumfriesshire) and this may in every probability be of Irish origin and post-Roman date.

(vi) SMALL OPAQUE TERRACOTTA-COLOURED BEADS (Schedules, p. 163)

Very rarely made into this shape. Two examples, both pre-Roman, from Croft Ambrey (Herefordshire) and Meare (Somerset), respectively, had this glass applied as a second layer over a yellow or cobalt core, implying that the terracotta glass was not easy to acquire.

(vii) SMALL OPAQUE OR TRANSLUCENT SKY BLUE ANNULAR BEADS (Schedules, p. 163)

These are not a common form and none of them appears to be pre-first century A.D. The Newstead bead is so far the earliest (about A.D. 80–200). For other forms in which this glass was used, see p. 18. On the whole they seem to be early rather than late in the Roman period.

(viii) SMALL OPAQUE ANNULAR BEADS OF OTHER COLOURS (Schedules, p. 164)

Very rare. Note that yellow beads of this type are British in origin. See Class 8.

(ix) SMALL 'BLACK' ANNULAR BEADS (Schedules, p. 164)

As mentioned above it is not always easy to say what is the true colour of this very dark glass. Small annular 'black' beads were certainly known before the Roman conquest, for instance, at Meare (Somerset) perhaps second or first century B.C., and a fragmentary one on a Belgic road at the east entrance of Maiden Castle (Dorset); this had a white marvered decoration and is not therefore truly characteristic. A small number of 'black' annular beads of this size have come from Roman sites of long duration and have not, unfortunately, been stratified. Two others, from Scotland, may well be considerably later and be of Irish origin, since in Ireland, again unassociated, there are large numbers from collections. Probably their main *floruit* in Britain (excluding Ireland) was limited from about the first century B.C. to some time in the Roman period, and their scarcity both on pre-Roman and Roman sites must reflect a very limited attraction for this colour. (It must be remembered that both shale and jet were made into beads in the Roman period.) Teutonic beads of this form are fairly common.

(x) COLOURLESS GLASS BEADS

An annular half-bead (diam. 2·3 mm.; ht. 0·6 mm.; perf. diam. 1·5 mm.) came from what appear to have been Iron Age 'B' (? second to first century B.C.) associations at Bury Wood Camp, Colerne, Wiltshire.[1] It was probably made at Meare. This glass is very rare except at Meare in Somerset. (See pp. 9–11.)

GROUP 7

Undecorated globular beads (here the term 'globular' applies to beads whose height is more than half their diameter)

The sizes into which the globular beads have been divided are as follows: *Large*, over 15 mm. in diameter; *Medium and Small*, under 15 mm. in diameter. (See Pl. II, no. 12.)

  (i) Large globular beads in various colours.
  (ii) Medium and small globular beads in natural greenish translucent glass.
  (iii) Medium and small globular beads in translucent or opaque green glass.
  (iv) Medium and small globular beads in cobalt blue translucent or opaque glass.
  (v) Medium and small globular beads in sky blue glass, both opaque and translucent.
  (vi) Medium and small globular beads in yellow or 'amber' (reddish-brown) translucent or opaque glass.
  (vii) Medium and small globular beads in terracotta-coloured, opaque glass (not scheduled).
  (viii) Medium and small globular beads in 'black' opaque glass.
  (ix) Small beads in bright red opaque glass (not scheduled).

(i) LARGE GLOBULAR BEADS IN VARIOUS COLOURS (Schedules, pp. 165–6)

A few globular beads of large size evidently reached the British Isles in the last century or so B.C. but they are only approximately dated from the sites in which they were found. The type was never popular either during the Iron Age or in Roman times. Blue beads of this size were discovered at Glastonbury (? first century B.C.), Bury Wood Camp, Colerne, Wiltshire, with Iron Age 'B' pottery, and from an Iron Age enclosure at Skipton in Yorkshire. A brownish-yellow translucent bead came from Meare (? second to first century B.C.) and others from two undated sites in Scotland. Others have been found unstratified on Roman sites. Nothing can really be said either culturally or chronologically on such little evidence, except that some of them came to Britain before the conquest. They do not represent a coherent group and should be considered together with globular beads of smaller sizes.

(ii) MEDIUM AND SMALL GLOBULAR BEADS IN NATURAL GREENISH TRANSLUCENT GLASS
  (Schedules, pp. 166–7)

All examples listed here point to a Roman date and none of them is definitely pre-Roman. About seven examples are vaguely Roman (unstratified) and the more closely dated ones are: Colchester A.D. 150–200; Castle Hill, Whitton, Suffolk (from villa occupied about A.D. 130–290); Barnsley Park Roman villa at Cirencester (occupation second to fourth century); Coygan Camp, Laugharne, Carmarthenshire (late third century). Badly made examples could easily have been made from Roman waste glass in Roman and post-Roman times. As might be expected, they appear to be rare in Ireland though present at Grannack, Ardrahan in Co. Galway.[2] These are very like those from St. David's Head in Pembrokeshire and probably reflect connexions across the Irish Sea during the early post-Roman period in the south.

[1] *WAM* lviii, lxii and lxiv.   [2] See pp. 39–42, above

(iii) MEDIUM AND SMALL TRANSLUCENT OR OPAQUE GREEN GLOBULAR BEADS
(Schedules, pp. 168–9)

The earliest bead of this type seems to be a dark semi-translucent bottle green one from a just pre- or post-conquest context at Bagendon in Gloucestershire. The remaining ones are only very vaguely dated and probably Roman. A dark green translucent bead came from the Rath of the Synods at Tara in Co. Meath, and this same site produced Roman pottery of the first to third centuries A.D. A pale green translucent bead was found in the aisled round-house of Clettraval in North Uist and was regarded as intrusive from a higher level than that in which it was found: it is probably Roman or even post-Roman, and may possibly belong to (ii) above. Many opaque green beads of this form come from post-Roman contexts and can generally be recognized by their bad workmanship. On the whole opaque green beads tend to be third century or later.

(iv) MEDIUM AND SMALL BLUE TRANSLUCENT AND OPAQUE GLOBULAR BEADS (Schedules, pp. 169–72).

A common form of bead which not unexpectedly had a very long life. It is possible that some of those listed in the Schedules will one day prove to be later than the Roman period. At present it is difficult to see how such featureless and common beads can be dated unless by some analytical method as yet unknown. They are known from a few native sites of Iron Age date: Bagendon, Gloucestershire (just pre- or post-conquest); Bredon (Gloucestershire–Worcestershire borders)—probably early first century A.D.; Meare, Somerset (second to first century B.C.); Dowles' Brickyard, Worcestershire, from what Miss L. F. Chitty thinks may have been an Iron Age urnfield; Loughey, Donaghadee, Co. Down, from the first-century B.C.–first-century A.D. necklace (see p. 80); and from a galleried wall-fort at Dun Ardtreck in Skye (first century B.C. to first century A.D.). The rest are probably Roman, and the type continued to be made for many centuries.

(v) MEDIUM AND SMALL OPAQUE AND TRANSLUCENT SKY BLUE GLOBULAR BEADS (Schedules, pp. 172–4)

Here there are very few examples which are not Roman, and this colour of glass was commoner in earlier Roman times. Castle Dore in Cornwall (occupied in the second and first centuries B.C.) produced one such bead, and a roughly contemporary one came from Meare as well.

As mentioned before, dating of stray examples cannot be attempted without analysis since what appears to be this kind of glass is still in use today for toys, and was much used in lace bobbins.

(vi) MEDIUM AND SMALL YELLOW OR 'AMBER' (REDDISH-BROWN) TRANSLUCENT CR OPAQUE GLOBULAR BEADS [1] (Schedules, p. 174)

Very few examples. A few are Roman (amber, translucent yellow). Two earlier beads came from Meare (second to first century B.C.) and one of these is made of the same glass as the opaque annular yellow beads of Class 8. All that can be said is that like other globular beads they were rare on pre-Roman sites, and continued occasionally throughout the Roman occupation into post-Roman times.

(vii) OPAQUE TERRACOTTA-COLOURED GLOBULAR BEADS (not scheduled)

Several from Meare. Two globular beads fused together, G109, and G133 (1·5 diam.); G134 is another. Perhaps made at Meare.[2]

(viii) MEDIUM AND SMALL 'BLACK' OPAQUE GLOBULAR BEADS (Schedules, p. 175)

Here the evidence is equally unsatisfactory as the form was very rarely used. The earliest example so far known from Britain is probably of pre-Roman date (Hunsbury, Northants.), the rest are either

---

[1] See pp. 12 and 16–17, above for the glass.　　　　[2] Bulleid, A. and Gray, H. St. George (1967).

Roman or post-Roman. The colour of these beads may be any very dark colour, appearing black. A small late Roman example came from Lankhills Cemetery, Winchester (Necklace 315, Grave 333, a foreign grave dated A.D. 390–410).

(ix) SMALL BRIGHT RED OPAQUE GLOBULAR BEADS (not scheduled)

These are almost unknown in Britain, but recently a number have come from the Roman villa at Kingscote, Glos., with many finds of the first century A.D. In colour they are a bright sealing-wax red.

GROUP 8

Exotic beads of Iron Age date (Schedules, pp. 176–8 and fig. 23). See also Groups 1–7

Each one of these beads is an original design which may one day be found to have analogies either on the Continent or from one of the British glass-working centres. For the present they are described in the Schedules only, and any known comparable beads are there cited.

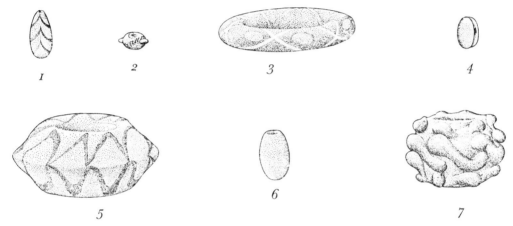

FIG. 23: Group 8—Examples of exotic beads of Iron Age date: *upper row*, 1. All Cannings Cross, Wilts. 2. Loughey, Donaghadee, Co. Down (see Group 3). 3. Trevelgue, Cornwall. 4. Badsey, Worcs.; *lower row*, 5. Hunsbury, Northants. 6. Clevedon, Somerset. 7. Boxford, Berks. Scale 1/1.

PART IV

IRON AGE BEADS OF BRITISH DESIGN AND ORIGIN

THERE are a number of beads which are thought on present evidence (see pp. 31–7) to have originated in the British Isles, worked from imported glass by craftsmen who almost certainly came from overseas and who had learnt their complicated and skilled methods of decorating glass beads in Celtic areas of the Continent. It is impossible to establish that this hypothesis is a valid one whilst such large areas of Europe—particularly the south-west—remain unstudied; all we can say is that in the light of present knowledge this seems to be true.

The following Classes of beads are therefore regarded as being of British design and manufacture, and the same must hold good for numbers of other plain or decorated glass beads already discussed but whose origins are as yet uncertain. Note particularly South Harting (Class 3) beads, and the opaque yellow annular beads with coloured waves (Group 5 (E)).

CLASS 8

Small opaque yellow annular beads (Schedules, pp. 179–82) (pl. II, no. 13, and figs. 24 and 25)

Unlike the small annular beads of other colours, there are certain features present in these yellow ones which allow them to be regarded as a Class rather than as a Group. Sometimes extremely fine

Fig. 24: Class 8—small opaque
yellow annular beads. Scale 1/1.

and thin, perhaps when the glass was difficult to acquire, they seldom exceed 12 mm. in diameter and were in all probability graded on necklaces, and sometimes also worn interspersed with other Classes of beads, so providing a useful chronological overlap, even if not complete contemporaneity of life-span. The main characteristics of this Class are the flattened upper and lower surfaces so often present around the perforation (a feature sometimes also noted on Iron Age blue annular beads and due, no doubt, to their method of manufacture) and an almost identical rather dull egg-yellow colour, perhaps imitating yellow amber, definitely less lemon-yellow than the superficially somewhat similar annular beads of the post-Roman period.

The initial date for these beads depends on the dating of the following sites, for which the approximate present day dates are in brackets, though these may be altered as more precise methods of dating become available.

In England, Wales, and the Isle of Man dated beads of this Class come from an early Iron Age fort, Twyn-y-Gaer (Cwmyoy, Monmouthshire), where one example was stratified with 'stamped ware' characteristic of the Welsh marches from about 300–150 B.C., and another from the same fort is thought to be a century or more later.[1] Others come from Castle Dore, Cornwall (c. 200–100 B.C.); Ballacagen A, Isle of Man (with Continental La Tène III armlets); Huckhoe Fort, Northumberland (in soil reused in an early Roman hut); Clevedon, Somerset (from a cist burial, on a necklace alternating with barrel-shaped crimson beads), and a 'Meare variant' bead (Class 11) also ascribed for other reasons to the second century or so B.C. Over fifty examples (including one of two segments) came from Meare,[2] from Mr. Michael Avery's Phase 2 which is discussed on p. 33. At Conderton Camp, Bredon, Worcs., one was found in a fort with 'stamped pottery'.[3] Taken together with those from Cwmyoy this emphasizes the evident trade up the Welsh marches. A third to first century B.C. date would also fit the bead of 'stud' type made of this same glass which was found with late Iron Age 'A' wares at Lidbury Camp (Wilts.), though a little second- to first-century B.C. pottery of Glastonbury type and Roman ware also came from this fort (see pp. 84–5). Note that a few small annular beads of this glass, with wave or swag decoration of a colour now lost, have been found in several Iron Age sites and are listed under Group 5 (E).[4]

From Scotland the pre-Roman examples come from a number of brochs, in Iona, Skye, Inverness-shire, etc., and from a wheelhouse in South Uist,[5] and a souterrain and house of late first to early second century A.D. Others came from Aitnock Fort, Dalry, Ayrshire (first to second century A.D.), and eight examples from Howrat Castle Hill, Dalry, nearby, as well as from Arrieolland Crannog in the same district. Here some glass-working may have taken place, and it is interesting to note that all the last three sites are near to the Stevenston Sands, a good source for suitable glass sand. A galleried wall-fort at Dun Ardtreck in Skye (thought to have been built in the early first century B.C.) produced a necklace including two decorated annular Scottish beads of Class 14 (ascribed—see pp. 87–9—to the late first century B.C. or first century A.D.). At Inverkeilor, Angus, a bead of the class under discussion was found with a Type I glass armlet (see p. 78) thought to be of Scottish first-century B.C. or A.D. manufacture.

In the Culbin Sands area around the mouth of the river Findhorn in Moray some 250 beads of this class have been discovered in the sand-dunes, as well as a group of eighty-five other beads. Such a quantity as this, together with other evidence (see pp. 34–5) supports the theory that there was a bead-making industry there: some also came from the Glenluce Sands in Wigtownshire, but not very many.

One of the most important discoveries for dating purposes is the well-known burial from Loughey, Donaghadee, Co. Down,[6] in Ireland. The bead here came from a group of objects including among

---

[1] For the latest discussion of this ware see Stanford, S. C. (1970 and 1974). The dating of both the stamped ware and the forts along the Welsh marches is still far from being clearly established.

[2] They are conspicuously absent from nearby Glastonbury where the occupation overlapped but started later than that at Meare.

[3] This excavation is still not published. I am grateful to Mr. Nicholas Thomas for information.

[4] See p. 65.

[5] Note that estimated radio-carbon dates now suggest that the semi-brochs and brochs and related buildings may, in some cases, go back to the second century B.C. See MacKie, Euan (1965 a, 1965 b, 1969 and 1975).

[6] Jope, E. M. (1957), 74–95 and (1960), 40. See footnote 2, p. 80.

YELLOW ANNULARS

● *Small Opaque Yellow Annular*   ◉ *Concentration*

○ *Similar Glass Stud Bead*   _ _ _ _ *Hadrian's Wall*

Fig. 25: Distribution of Class 8 beads.

other things a necklace with a number of these yellow beads and a 'Meare spiral' bead of Class 10, a small bead with cable decoration mentioned below and a fibula regarded, on Continental evidence, as belonging to the mid-first century B.C. So together all the evidence points to an initial date for these beads in the third to second century B.C. Concentration in both the Meare, Somerset, district and the Culbin Sands area in Moray is very noticeable, but the two centres need not have been strictly contemporary.

As already mentioned above, the Loughey beads include a small annular blue bead decorated with little coloured horns or knobs and a two-colour cable (fig. 23, no. 2) akin to the cable beads of Class 9, and it is impossible to say whether this bead (for which I have not been able to find any analogies) was produced in Britain, or whether it was imported. The whole necklace could belong to the later first century B.C. on the evidence of the brooch, with the yellow beads and the 'Meare spiral' bead as late survivals.

With regard to the chronology of this class of yellow bead, it seems probable that they were distributed from Meare in the third to second centuries B.C., and the hypothesis, which will again be put forward in discussing 'Meare spiral' beads (Class 10) and the North Scottish beads (Classes 13 and 14) is that, after initially working in the south, some glass craftsmen later migrated northwards and started making similar or related glass beads in the Culbin Sands until the expedition under Agricola put an end to their work, not so much perhaps by violence as by effectively cutting them off from their earlier trade contacts and reducing their living to more backward conditions. *Pace* D. V. Clarke (in *PPS* xxxvi, 214–32) the bone dice present in south-west England and again in west Scotland, may reflect the same trade.

A few of these beads come from Roman contexts, mostly first- or second-century as might be expected (e.g., Traprain Law and Castle Hill, Dalry), and one very battered example, perhaps even locally made, came from Coygan Camp in Carmarthenshire, stratified in a late third-century context but thought, surely rightly, by the excavator to have been derived from an earlier phase.

Were the northern beads of this Class made in the Culbin Sands in around the first century B.C. to early first century A.D., or did they come up before this from the southern Iron Age cultures? As we have seen from the evidence, there is nothing to refute MacKie's hypothesis that the broch and wheel-house complex began earlier than was once thought likely. On bead evidence alone they could have begun around the third or second century B.C. (if the beads came from Meare), or the first century B.C. to first century A.D. if they came from Culbin.[1] The distribution map must be studied with care, for we may be dealing with two centres of production, a southern earlier one at Meare, and a northern one beginning a century or even more later.

At all events, to summarize the chronology, these beads began around 250 B.C. and continued to be produced until about A.D. 50.

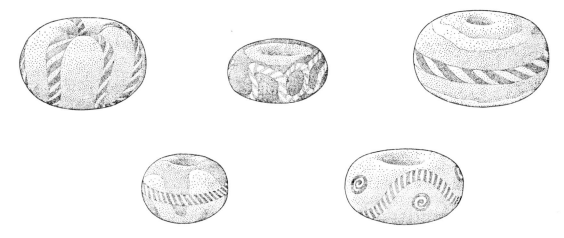

Fig. 26: Class 9—annular beads with two-coloured cables: *upper row,* 1. Tripontium, Warks. Natural greenish glass with red and yellow cable. 2. Moel-y-Gaer, Flints. Natural greenish glass overlaid with inky blue glass and marvered blue and white cable. 3. Wilderspool, Ches. Natural greenish glass. Two white bands and blue and white cable; *lower row,* 4. Newstead, Roxburghshire. Natural greenish glass with white wave and yellow and white cable 5. Traprain Law, E. Lothian. Natural greenish glass with blue and white cables and white spirals in blue roundels. Scale 1/1.

[1] The necklace from Dun Ardtreck in Skye included a very small North Scottish decorated annular bead (Class 14). The site, according to radio-carbon dating, might have belonged to the first century B.C., but see footnote 1, p. 83 below.

CLASS 9

Annular beads decorated with two-colour twisted cables (Schedules, pp. 182–7) (pls. II, nos. 14 a–c, and III, top right and figs. 26 and 27)

For convenience of study these have been sub-divided according to the ground colour, as follows: (A) natural glass; (B) cobalt blue or purple; (C) brown or golden brown.

All these cable-decorated beads are annular in shape and vary usually between 20 to 30 mm. in diameter, and 10 to 15 mm. in height; the rather wide perforation is almost always cylindrical. In the majority of cases the cable is at least 2 mm. wide and consists of a two-colour twist, rather loosely twisted, and in this respect differing from the somewhat similar but more globular beads with narrow tight twists which are sometimes found on sites of post-Roman date. This, however, is not invariable, for a large Irish toggle bead of unknown date has a wide cable, and can be seen in the Pitt-Rivers Museum in Oxford, and Irish beads of the early Christian period may have twisted cables at each end of long beads.

(A) NATURAL TRANSLUCENT GREENISH GLASS BEADS WITH COLOURED CABLES
    (Schedules, pp. 182–5)

The earliest examples so far discovered in England appear to be those from the Hembury hill-fort in Devon and Meare in Somerset, both thought to belong to about the first century B.C. Of the other stratified or associated examples one was mid-first century A.D., one is A.D. 10–50 and several are vaguely attributed to the Roman period, or sites which begin early; one is Claudian, one Neronian, and one, perhaps the latest, is second-century A.D. In Scotland several come from Roman or Romano-British sites, and one comes from a broch, which in all probability points to a first-century A.D. context. In Wales the only dated bead of this type came from Pen Llystyn fort in Caernarvonshire, a fort occupied apparently only from about A.D. 80 to 100.

(B) COBALT BLUE WITH COLOURED CABLES (Schedules, pp. 185–6)

Here the dates range from Glastonbury, Somerset (probably first century B.C.), and Hembury, Devon (about the same date), to Bagendon, Gloucestershire (stratified A.D. 10–50 or marginally later), and a mainly first- or early second-century A.D. scatter at Windmill Hill, Avebury, Wiltshire. In Scotland the only fairly closely dated example is from an A.D. 80–200 context.

(C) BROWN OR GOLDEN BROWN WITH COLOURED CABLES (Schedules, p. 187)

Here again the evidence is consistent, although this ground colour was never so popular as the natural glass or cobalt blue. In England the Leicester bead is probably of the first century A.D.; two were surface finds, and one (Willingham, Cambridgeshire) was associated with a bronze sceptre bearing a portrait thought to represent Antoninus Pius (A.D. 138–61). None of this Class has been recorded from Scotland and the only Welsh bead of the type came from Caerwent where it was associated with first-century pottery and a coin of Nero.

The dating evidence is therefore entirely consistent for these three types, as well as for the related beads. All began to be made in the first century B.C. and died out soon after the end of the first century A.D.

All types are absent from Ireland (see fig. 25) except for a possible example from a collection. There are noticeably few from Scotland north of the Lowlands, and in fact in this respect they contrast strongly with the related Newstead type armlets. The main concentration of cable beads is to the south of a line from Chester to Lincolnshire, and the concentration around the Somerset and Bristol Channel area makes one suspect that there was either a factory or an entrepôt in those parts. It is interesting to note that in four beads (from Meare, Lansdown near Bath, Charterhouse-on-Mendip and Cirencester) the true twisted cable has been imitated by nicking (and perhaps originally filling with colour?) a marvered trail. These I have called 'tentative' cables, and it may not only be fortuitous that all lie

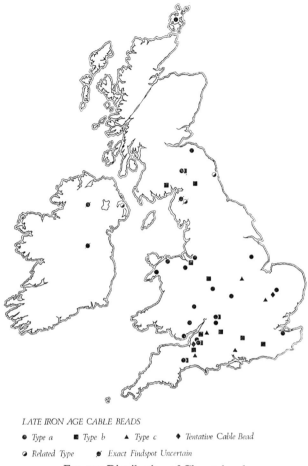

LATE IRON AGE CABLE BEADS

● Type a   ■ Type b   ▲ Type c   ♦ Tentative Cable Bead

◑ Related Type   ⬗ Exact Findspot Uncertain

FIG. 27: Distribution of Class 9 beads.

within easy range of the Somerset glass factories of Meare and Glastonbury. Since Glastonbury (rather later to start production of beads than was Meare) produced a true cable twist, it may be that production began there only shortly before the glass-makers moved to the north around the time of the Roman conquest. An increasing number of cable armlets, some quite early in the series, have been discovered in south Britain since Kilbride-Jones regarded them as a Scottish product centred perhaps on Traprain Law. Now we must not only recognize that they began before the late first century A.D. as he suggested, for Harden and Price have recognized a pre-Agricolan one from the Roman palace at Fishbourne, Sussex,[1] but we must also envisage more than one centre of production. Here a note of warning should be sounded, for it cannot be claimed that all British glass armlets are of local manufacture: a number certainly came in from the Continent, but it is not yet certain how many. The cabled types are different in design, and some of the British monochrome or bichrome ones may be Continental in origin [2] just like so many bead types; but the cable-decorated ones seem to be native.

The cable decoration is apparently an original one, but it is not impossible that it was inspired from

[1] Recently discovered armlets of Class II include one from Cirencester (*TBGAS* (1971), and one from Bisley, Tunley, Gloucestershire, in the Stroud Museum (*AR* (1969)). Others are listed *GAJ* iv (1976), 53–4.

[2] e.g., *HH* and Castle Dore, Cornwall (Radford, C. A. R. (1951), 68–9), and Hamworthy, Dorset (*PDNHAS* lvi, pl. iii).

variegated mosaic or millefiori glass patterns which are known from various sites in Britain such as Newstead, Richborough and the Brecon Gaer, and which were common on the Rhine in the early first century A.D. or before. Very much earlier than that a twist decoration had been used in the New Kingdom in Egypt, and in Mesopotamia at several periods. It was also destined to be commonly used in the later Irish string beads of post-fifth-century date.

As a working hypothesis it can be supposed that first the cable beads and some of the armlets were made or distributed in the south of Britain late in the first century B.C. After an interval of half a century or so they were also produced in Scotland, perhaps by people who had learnt their craft in the south and migrated northwards. The cable motif was imperfectly copied in North Scottish beads of Class 14.

Beads from near the Welsh borders were sometimes coated in a second colour before the cable was applied (fig. 26, centre).

CLASS 10

'*Meare spiral*' beads (Schedules, pp. 187–9) (pl. II, no. 15, and figs. 28 and 29)

These beads are translucent and colourless, usually globular in shape, but some of the spirals were slightly flattened by marvering into a sub-triangular shape. The dimensions of these beads vary from about 9 to 14 mm. in height, and 11 to 18 mm. in diameter. The perforations are small

FIG. 28: Class 10—Meare
spiral-decorated beads. Scale 1/1.

and neatly made. The decoration consists of three carefully wound spirals in opaque yellow glass, occupying almost the whole surface of the bead. These spirals, which are marvered into the body of the bead while warm, are made in the majority of cases with such exquisite precision that one is tempted to think that the very fine examples may have been the product of one man, and most of the rest from the same workshop.

Continental analogies, in spite of a fairly extensive search, have not been identified, and it is considered likely that, as such large numbers of them were found at the Iron Age village of Meare in Somerset, they may have been manufactured in that neighbourhood.[1]

The earliest examples of these 'Meare spiral' beads may be those from Meare itself where they were perhaps made during the second phase of the village, antedating the decorated Glastonbury type pottery and La Tène III brooches but contemporary either with the La Tène I or the La Tène II brooches—i.e., in about the third century B.C. From the same cultural context came the chevron beads (Class 11 (a)) and the small opaque yellow annular beads (Class 8). At Maiden Castle, Dorset,[2] a spiral-decorated bead was stratified late second or early first century B.C. with what Wheeler has called Bii pottery; with decorated Glastonbury ware (? late second to first century B.C.) from the hill-fort at South Cadbury in Somerset; from the hill-forts of Pen Dinas and Moel Trigarn in West Wales (? third to first centuries B.C.) and from the Culbin Sands in Moray (fused to and presumably therefore

[1] See pp. 32–3, above.　　　　[2] *MC*, 291–3 and fig. 98. For revised dating see Frere, S. (1958), 84–92.

MEARE SPIRALS

● *Meare Spiral*   ◉ *Concentration*   ○ *Exact Findspot Uncertain*

FIG. 29: Distribution of Class 10 beads.

contemporary with an armlet of the first century B.C. or first century A.D.[1] At Loughey, Donaghadee in Ireland (see p. 75), a bead of 'Meare spiral' type was on a necklace with seventy-one beads of Class 8, a small horned bead with cable, and sixty-five small blue beads, together with a brooch thought by Jope to be of the mid-first century A.D.—though possibly a century earlier.[2]

It is interesting to note the long survival of these beads in some instances, and these can only be explained at present as treasured heirlooms perhaps accidentally found and kept. For example, one roughly made example came from South Shields Roman fort,[3] perhaps not occupied before about

[1] This, apparently a true Meare type bead, though possibly a particularly colourless example of a Scottish spiral bead, was fused with part of an armlet of natural greenish glass with longitudinal cables in various colours. (N.M.A., BIB 62.) Note that BIB 6y in the same museum is a clear, colourless blob of molten glass from the same provenance.

[2] Jope, E. M. (1957), 73 ff. and (1960), 40 (note that an unpublished necklace from Meare East also comprised some yellow opaque beads (Class 8) and some spiral decorated

ones (Class 10)). The Nauheim type brooch is now considered to belong to the first half of the first century B.C. See Ralston, I. and Buchsenschutz, O. (1975), 11 and Müller Beck, H. and Ettlinger, E. (1962–3), 43–4.

[3] Perhaps an heirloom or a very rough imitation. Note that this site also produced a British coin and the tombstone of a Catuvellaunian girl who had married a Palmyrene soldier.

A.D. 122, and in Ireland one came from the seventh-century A.D. house at Lagore Crannog in Co. Meath,[1] and another from the habitation site of the early Christian period at Garryduff, Co. Cork.

One can argue tentatively that the heyday of these beads lies within the approximate date bracket 250 B.C.–A.D. 50 (or they may have finished rather earlier if Belgic domination of Dobunnic territory put an end to native bead production in the first century B.C.). They survived in rare instances into later contexts. At least some of the later craftsmen making these spiral beads may have migrated northwards around the end of the first century B.C. or only a little later, and started production of closely similar but technically inferior beads in the Culbin Sands district. (See North Scottish spiral beads, Class 13, and pp. 34–5.)

At their best these exquisite beads show 'the peculiar refinement, delicacy and equilibrium' which 'are not altogether what one would expect of men who, though courageous, were also savage, cruel, and often disgusting: for the archaeological refuse, as well as the reports of Classical antiquity, agree in this verdict'.[2]

CLASS 11

'*Meare variant*' *beads* (Schedules, pp. 189–92) (pl. II, a–h, and figs. 30 and 31)

These beads, like those of the previous class and those of Class 5 comprise the bulk of the colourless glass beads decorated with opaque yellow designs. Although the decoration of these 'Meare variant' beads is dissimilar, it is clear that they are all closely related among themselves, and were in all probability produced in the same workshops. Their dating may, however, not be exactly contemporary in the sense that, although they may overlap, they may have begun rather earlier or more probably later than the classic type with spirals.

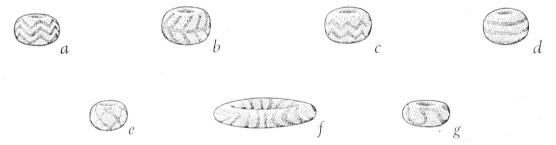

FIG. 30: Class 11—Meare variant beads (see also stud beads, fig. 32). Scale 1/1.

For ease of study they have been divided into several types, based on their decoration.

Type (*a*) has multiple chevron lines in opaque yellow, running round the bead at right angles to the perforation in such a way that the whole surface is covered.

Type (*b*) has a yellow band round the circumference with herring-bone lines radiating from it.

Type (*c*) has two circumferential chevrons.

Type (*d*) has several bands running round the bead at right angles to the perforation.

Type (*e*) has a yellow trellis over the whole bead.

Type (*f*) has yellow bands down the bead roughly parallel with the perforation.

---

[1] There were several other early-looking beads from Lagore, as well as from the site of Dunshaughlin. See Wilde,

W. R. (1857), 165, 167 and fig. 123, no. 21.

[2] Sandars, N. K. (1968), 226, discussing Celtic art.

Type (g) has a single wave round the centre.

Type (h) has lines round the bead, overlaid by a looped design running up and down the surface of the bead; with the exception of a few outliers, these beads are almost all grouped round Meare which has produced a number of them.

Type (i) possibly whirl beads of Class 7, Type (c) (pp. 58–9).

Type (j) possibly Irish finds of sub-Oldbury type beads (pp. 56–7).

Type (k) one example only. Decorated with opaque yellow spots.

TYPE (a)

Is the commonest variety, and Meare itself has produced at least twenty-four examples. One comes from Glastonbury, one from a burial at Clevedon (Somerset) on a necklace with small yellow annular beads of Class 8 and some so far unique crimson barrel-shaped beads (see p. 74, fig. 23, no. 6). Others come from not closely dated Iron Age camps at Ham Hill (Somerset) and Caynham (Shropshire). An outlier at Risby Warren (Lincs.) cannot be closely dated.[1] Michael Avery regards these chevron-decorated beads as contemporary with the spiral-decorated ones of Class 10. We must therefore postulate for the present a range of date for the chevron beads from approximately 250 B.C. to about the first century B.C. or so, for there was one example from Glastonbury. If this was a later stray or survival their *floruit* can be shortened. A note of warning should be given here, for very similar beads also occur in later contexts.[2]

TYPE (b)

These are rarer and their date is less easy to establish. One example came from Meare, and two from Ireland. The Lagore one is too damaged for certain diagnosis, but the site did produce beads which were earlier than the main occupation of the crannog in the seventh century A.D., and may have been discovered at that time on an earlier site nearby; the other one came from a cist-burial in a cemetery with an undated bronze ring at Carrowmore in Co. Sligo. As an example of Type (a) has also been found in a cist-burial, it is probable that the two variants, as might be expected, are related. Evidently Type (b) was rare and cannot be dated precisely, though these and Types (c), (d), and (f), when they occurred at Meare, were regarded by Avery as contemporary with his Phases 3 and 4 of that village (first century B.C. to early first century A.D.). Not all need be so late.

TYPE (c)

Has two circumferential chevrons only. It may or may not be related to the other types. An undated example came from Penzance in Cornwall. The glass is, however, very slightly coloured—not quite as colourless as the Meare ones, and it is not impossible that it may have been an import from Brittany.

TYPE (d)

Only one example, from Meare.

---

[1] The Belgic site at Dragonby is nearby. *AnJ* xxxviii, 43 and refs.

[2] Somewhat similar beads, but sometimes with a slightly greenish ground colour, include some from White Fort, Drumarood, Co. Down (latter part of the first millennium A.D.), one large bead from 'Ireland' (Belfast, Benn Collection, 1912–172), and Kilmartin, Argyllshire (from top soil of Iron Age and post-Roman fort). Some very similar beads of Dark Age date are made of not quite clear glass, and have the chevrons running parallel to the perforation; two of these come from Co. Antrim (B.M., nos. 92, 4–21, 17 and 18) and another from 'Ireland' (National Museum, Dublin, 1920–63). Seven related beads came from Garryduff I, Co. Cork, a seventh- to eighth-century site with glass-working evidence. See O'Kelly, M. J. (1962), 69. In rare cases these Irish beads have raised (i.e., unmarvered) decoration. Note a bead from Northern Ireland (B.M., 71.12–10, 34) and one with a trellis pattern like Type (h) (B.M., 1920, 11–9, 45). Unmarvered examples also come from Lagore and from Dun Beag, Skye (N.M.A., GA 1.105). See *PSAS* lv (1920–1), 125–6 and fig. 9.

MEARE VARIANTS : *Colourless glass with opaque yellow designs*

● *Type a*　　■ *Type b*　　▲ *Type c*　　▼ *Type d*　　▽ *Type e*

□ *Type f*　　◆ *Type g*　　◇ *Type h*　　◉ *Concentration*

FIG. 31: Distribution of Class 11 beads.

TYPE (e)

One example only, from an Iron Age site, 'from the top of an Iron Age "A" pit' at Overton Down in Wiltshire; not very closely datable but probably second to first century B.C.

TYPE (f)

Half a large annular bead with stripes roughly parallel to the perforation. One example only, from Meare.

TYPE (g), WITH YELLOW WAVE (Schedules, pp. 191–2)

This type is possibly earlier in origin than the miscellaneous patterns of Types (b), (d) and (f) and the earlier ones are probably the smaller beads about 10 to 12 mm. in diameter, of which the prototypes (noticeably very slightly coloured whereas the Meare examples are quite colourless) may be those from the Queen's Barrow at Arras in Yorkshire for which a date in about the fourth to third century B.C. has been postulated (see pp. 45–8). It is not yet possible to say whether they were produced in Britain or imported from the Continent. At Meare the several beads decorated with a wave design are annular and of varying sizes, and they fall within the groups tentatively dated by Michael Avery to the first century B.C. to first century A.D., though a very damaged one from Ham Hill may be a little earlier. In agreement with the later dating would be both the bead from Newstead, Roxburghshire (the site was occupied in the first to second century A.D. though this bead was a stray found in the area), and the one from Great Chesterford, Cambridgeshire, where the occupation began in the first century B.C. A unique stud-shaped bead decorated on both its elements in this manner may be later than a similar shaped bead found at Lidbury Camp, Enford, Wiltshire, made of the same opaque yellow glass as the small annular beads of Class 8. At present therefore we can only suggest that the Arras beads are not identical and may be earlier imports, and that the production of beads of truly colourless glass, decorated with yellow waves, only began in Meare Phases 2 to 3 (about the first centuries B.C. or A.D.).

In Northern Ireland there are a number of probably unrelated larger beads, mostly from Co. Antrim and likely to be of later date. It is not yet possible to place these chronologically.[1]

TYPE (h)
Is so far confined to Meare where there was one example only.

TYPES (i) AND (j)
Perhaps restricted to Ireland and made either there at an unknown date, or possibly at Meare in the last two centuries B.C.

TYPE (k)
Only one example of type (k) is known.[2]

CLASS 12

Stud beads (Schedules, p. 192) (pl. II, no. 17, and fig. 32)

These beads consist of two elements, one larger than the other like a modern collar stud. Two examples only are as yet known from Britain and I know of none on the Continent. One is made of clear

FIG. 32: Class 12—stud beads: *left*, Meare, Somerset; *right*, Lidbury Camp, Wilts. Scale 1/1.

colourless glass decorated with opaque yellow waves (as in Class 11 (g), see p. 83). It came from Meare in Somerset where both examples may have been manufactured. The second example made of opaque yellow glass, apparently identical with the glass used for Class 8 annular beads, came from Lidbury Camp, Enford (Wiltshire). It is possible that, as Professor Hawkes has mentioned to me,[3] 'the published material from Lidbury may contain two separate occupations, the later with the re-cut ditch and La Tène III brooch'. The pit in which this stud bead was found could belong to a later occupation than the fairly late 'A' pottery found in it, but on the whole this is improbable, though modern research has

---

[1] It is also worth noting that rather similar annular beads with opaque yellow trails are sometimes found in North European Migration Period contexts, but the ground colour is noticeably bluish, and not completely colourless.

[2] 'Found in Derbyshire' in about 1790. Now strung with other perhaps unassociated beads. (Dept. of Prehistoric and Romano-British Antiquities, B.M.). This is a large annular bead with wide perforation, and five oval spots of opaque yellow around the perimeter. It may belong to a later date.

[3] In a letter of about 1954.

done much to point to the danger of trying to draw too much evidence from old and very limited excavation of hill-forts and settlement sites.

The evidence points to both these beads belonging to approximately the third (or second) to first century B.C., and their apparent absence on the Continent need hardly surprise us if we are right in regarding both of them, on their own separate grounds, as of native British manufacture.

CLASS 13

North Scottish spiral-decorated beads (Schedules, pp. 193–7) (pl. III bottom left, and figs. 33 and 34)

These beads are similar in size (11–22 mm. in diameter and 10–18 mm. in height), shape, and pattern to the so-called 'Meare spiral' beads of Class 10 (pp. 79–81), but they differ in two main aspects: they more generally show a slightly angular shape, probably brought about when the spirals were rather roughly marvered into the bead, and the bead is never colourless but, probably as a result of chance impurities in the sand, may be greenish, brown, dark blue or some other dark colour. The spirals are invariably yellow and the perforations small.

FIG. 33: Class 13—North Scottish spiral-decorated beads:
left, Bedlam, Aberdeenshire; *centre*, Fouhlin, Sutherland;
right, 'Aberdeenshire'. Scale 1/1.

Continental beads, which are superficially similar, are more triangular in shape and nearly always on a blue ground. They are known from both north and south of the Alps,[1] and belong to a period several hundred years earlier than the Scottish ones. Although some derivatives of the Continental series may have found their way to Britain in the last few centuries B.C., the Scottish group seem clearly to be later and to have derived from the 'Meare spiral' beads of Class 10 which reached Scotland up the Irish Sea, and which, with the exception of their distinctively colourless ground and greater precision and competence of craftsmanship, resemble the North Scottish beads so closely.

The discovery of a 'Meare spiral' bead fused with a first-century A.D. armlet from Scotland [2] shows that the Meare beads (even though perhaps mostly belonging to the third- to second-century B.C. phases of that site) were available for local imitation in Scotland in the late first century B.C. or the early first century A.D., and this seems to be the most convincing explanation for the North Scottish group (see pp. 79–80, above). As the map shows (fig. 34), all are concentrated in Aberdeenshire and the neighbouring counties by the Moray Firth,[3] with the exception of a few outliers which may have been carried by individuals or reached their destinations in the course of trade. This map should be studied in conjunction with fig. 36 showing the distribution of the North Scottish decorated annular beads (Class 14, pp. 87–9), for that group, too, as well perhaps as some of the small opaque yellow annular beads of Class 8 (pp. 73–6), may have been made in the same area. There is little doubt that had the Scottish tribesmen known how to obtain a clear colourless glass like that used for the Meare beads, they might have preferred it, but faced with technical inexperience they seem to have used their

[1] Ebert, M. (ed.) (1924–9) xi, Taf. 135.
[2] No. BIB 62 in the N.M.A. in Edinburgh. See Schedules of Meare spiral beads, pp. 187–9.
[3] Overlapping the northern part of the area of the souterrains. See Rivet, A. L. F. (ed.) (1966), 33.

own methods in manufacturing beads with local sand, perhaps the Culbin Sands, containing a variety of impurities. At least eight beads of this type come from the area of the Sands. It is, however, possible that they were sufficiently able craftsmen to obtain the darker colours and to make what suited their own tastes. It is also worth noting that, as noted above (p. 34), a quantity of glass slag, blue, yellow, and green, was found in the Culbin Sands.[1]

The first Scottish imitations were presumably made in the early first century A.D. or only shortly before, and we cannot yet say whether they continued to be made after the Agricolan invasion later in the century. At Castle Newe a bead of this class came from an earth-house but was not necessarily associated with the bronze armlet of Castle Newe type[2] of the first century A.D. and with a coin of Nerva (A.D. 96–8) from the same site; two other earth-houses have produced these beads, one at Coldstone (Aberdeenshire) and the other at Fouhlin, Lake Eriboll (Sutherland). Yet others come from brochs at Bowermadden (Caithness) and Dun Iardhard, Dunvegan (Skye). Occasionally they have been

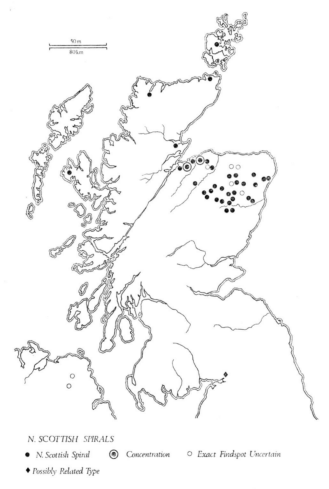

N. SCOTTISH SPIRALS

● N. Scottish Spiral   ◉ Concentration   ○ Exact Findspot Uncertain

◆ Possibly Related Type

FIG. 34: Distribution of Class 13 beads.

[1] *PSAS* xxv (1890–1) and iv (1862), 55, refers to a stone encrusted with glass from a place known as the Old Glass Kiln at Shoggle Burn, Moray. This need not, however, necessarily be ancient glass. See also *ibid.* ix (1871).

[2] *AnJ* xxxix (1959), 31.

associated with beads of North Scottish decorated annular type (see Class 14) which are thought to be contemporary and from the same production centre.

With the few outliers in the broch area and in the northern part of Ireland and one find from Netherby (perhaps from the Hadrianic fort there), the overwhelming majority come from Aberdeenshire, Moray, Nairn, and Banffshire, occupied at that time by tribes who were ancestors of the Picts. (See map, fig. 3.)[1]

When these beads ceased to be produced is unclear but it was probably after the Roman victory at *Mons Graupius* in the late first century A.D. The beads very rarely survived till the late second century, but not, probably, later.

CLASS 14

North Scottish decorated annular beads (Schedules, pp. 197–200) (pl. III, bottom right and figs. 35 and 36)

Beads belonging to this class differ widely in size, decoration, and colouring, and in fact it was only as a result of close study and an immediately apparent localized distribution that one was able to recognize them as coming from the same workshops. Their sole consistent feature (and even this is not invariable) is their annular form. Otherwise no two beads are identical, and it is only by a certain generic resemblance which they share that they can be isolated as a class, recognizably derived from known antecedents in the Celtic bead repertoire.

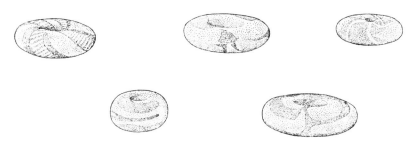

FIG. 35: Class 14—North Scottish decorated annular beads: *upper row*, 1. Aberdeenshire. 2. Clerkley Mill, Morayshire. 3. Culbin Sands, Morayshire; *lower row*, 4. Kennethmont, Aberdeenshire. 5. Dun Mor Vaul, Tiree. Scale 1/1.

The colours are nearly always opaque and include mostly blues, mauves, and browns; an opaque yellow element is present in almost every example. In size they vary from over 30 mm. in diameter to a few mm., and perforation is sometimes of rounded hour-glass form. A closer look at the patterns with which they are decorated shows that these are derived from two elements: whirls or rays as in the Celtic beads of Class 7, and ladder patterns which are in effect imitation cables (see Class 9).

It has already been made clear that both these prototypes were available to the glass-workers in north Scotland (see p. 35).

The beads now under discussion will be seen from the map to come from just the same region as the North Scottish spiral decorated beads, and there is little doubt that the annular ones, with their decoration inspired almost certainly from a mixture of two elements, whirl or ray and cables, were being made

---

[1] The bead from Croy (ninth-century) recently cited for dating these beads, in *PSAS* cv (1972–4), 197–8, is probably of earlier date but re-used, just as Iron Age beads are sometimes found in Saxon contexts.

at the same time and in the same area of Moray, a hypothesis substantiated by the absence of known parallels for these beads on the Continent. It is interesting to observe that, as in the case of many glass armlets of British origin, the bead-makers showed a strong propensity for the use of opaque yellow glass.

The evidence for dating the North Scottish spiral beads is satisfactory, and points to the first and second century A.D. The same dating fits the present class. At Cawdor (Nairn) and—less definitely— at Kennethmont (Aberdeenshire) these beads were found in association with North Scottish spiral beads. At Monquhitter (Aberdeenshire) a rather exceptional bead belonging to the first or second century A.D. was found with a Roman intaglio, a native armlet, etc. Necklaces both from the Culbin Sands and from the galleried wall-fort of Dun Ardtreck (Skye)[1] include beads of the annular decorated type associated with small annular opaque yellow beads of Class 8 which have been recognized from the same chronological context. At Dun Iardhard (Skye) and at Dun Mor Vaul (Tiree) the decorated class is contemporary with the brochs. It is also worth noting that the far northern Irish examples,

N. SCOTTISH ANNULARS

● N. Scottish Decorated Annular   ○ Exact Findspot Uncertain

FIG. 36: Distribution of Class 14 beads.

[1] It must be remembered that Dun Ardtreck, according to radio-carbon dating may go back to the early first century B.C. but, though possible, it is improbable that the necklace was so early, as nothing else yet supports the beginning of bead production in the Culbin area before the late first century B.C. This assumption may prove to be mistaken.

some of which make use of an opaque mauve coloured glass like one from Clerkley Hill (Moray), also include what may either be a true imported Celtic whirl bead from Cloughwater, Co. Antrim, or a Scottish imitation of apparently identical glass to that of another bead from the same county, which is definitely of Scottish type (Dublin, nos. 1907.97 and 1908.347, respectively). The few Irish examples certainly do not warrant the suggestion that they were manufactured there, and the notable concentration around northern Aberdeenshire and the Moray Firth should point clearly to their origin. What we do not yet know is from where the Scottish tribesmen obtained their glass. It seems that it can hardly have been imported as waste glass (p. 11) as sometimes must have happened further south, closer to established Roman frontier posts.

It is possible that during the early Roman period, the native tribesmen may have satisfied their desire for bright-coloured annular beads by using imported marbled stone or steatite from which to make streaky reddish annular beads. Such beads come from Romano-British sites at Fortingall and Carpow in Perthshire (the latter dated A.D. 209–11), Camelon in Stirlingshire, Newstead in Roxburghshire, Inverness, Parc-croc-rioch in Oronsay, an unidentified site in the Lothians, Rainton near Gatehouse-of-Fleet in Kirkcudbrightshire, and Housesteads and Corbridge in Northumberland and elsewhere.[1]

But where the production of lithomarge beads began and ended is still unknown; it is only suggested here that stone beads of this kind may have locally replaced the glass ones, beginning perhaps soon after Agricola's victory in the north in the late first century.

---

[1] Listed in *GAJ* iv (1976), 55–6. Both lithomarge and grey-veined creamy steatite were used. The former probably came from Europe and the latter from Banffshire. Both the Newstead bead and the 'egg' stone from Monquhitter (see p. 88) may belong to the first or second century A.D.

PART V

ROMAN PERIOD BEADS[1]

(pl. IV and fig. 37)

Small segmented beads

(a) VARIOUS COLOURS, GENERALLY BUT NOT INVARIABLY OPAQUE (Schedules, pp. 201–4)
    (fig. 37, nos. 1 and 2)

Although there are good fossil bone, bone or faience prototypes for this form of bead,[2] the origin for the glass ones is more probably simply the result of crimping a hollow rod which could then be broken up into as many segments as required. They did not become popular until Roman times, or shortly before, in Northern Europe and their popularity grew during the late Roman and post-Roman periods.

Several different methods were employed for achieving the required result, and the beads, varying from two to five or six segments, are sometimes only about 0·3 or 0·4 cm. in diameter. The basic requirement was a tube of glass, drawn from a 'gathering' of glass into which a bubble of air had deliberately been introduced; by drawing this out the result was not a solid rod, but a tube which could then be pinched or crimped at roughly regular intervals. Alternatively a thin rod of glass could be wound round and round a wire which was then withdrawn, leaving a tapering bead resulting from the

---

[1] See also Part III, Groups 6 and 7.   [2] See pp. 37–9, above.

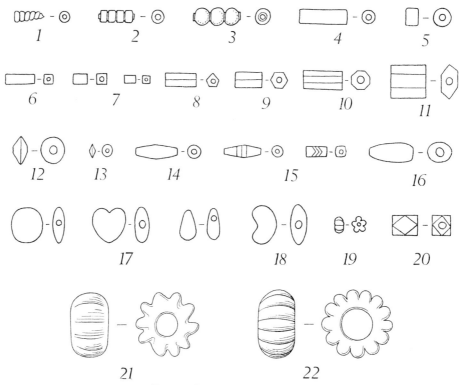

FIG. 37: Forms of Roman beads.

pulling out and consequent thinning of the glass. Such thin rods have been found on a number of British and Continental sites, but it is not always possible to distinguish between those intended for wound segmented beads and those which were designed to form part of an assemblage of rods of different colours to be sliced for millefiori or mosaic glass. Rather larger, hollow segmented beads may have been moulded, or blown, and a fairly common variety (see section (b)) was made with two layers of colourless or amber-coloured glass, often enclosing either gold or white metal foil.

There are very large numbers of these little beads in the Roman world, and they should not be confused with the much larger segmented beads (see below), each globule of which sometimes measures a centimetre or more in diameter; these occur in Viking and other post-Roman contexts.

The commonest colours employed for making the small segmented beads include very dark glass appearing black, opaque terracotta red, yellow, green or blue, and they are often, though not invariably, opaque.

Although they are known from Gallo-Roman contexts in the first century B.C. no such early bead has so far been recognized in Britain. A vast quantity of them come from unstratified Roman sites. One of the earliest is from a second-century context at Godmanchester (Huntingdonshire), and late third- or fourth-century examples are common: e.g., to mention only a few, from a late fourth-century necklace at Verulamium (St. Albans, Herts.); late third- to fourth-century from the Roman villa at Frocester (Gloucestershire); from late Roman graves at Cirencester (Gloucestershire), Lankhills, near Winchester (Hampshire), and Poundbury, Dorchester (Dorset); and from a late Romano-Celtic temple at Lamyatt Beacon (Somerset), where a narrow cane 2 cm. in length, ready perhaps for twisting round a wire, was also identified.[1] The fact that over 400 beads of this type came from Cold Kitchen Hill, Brixton Deverill (Wiltshire), which has also produced an opaque brown rod 1·8 cm. in length, makes one wonder whether the beads may have been manufactured near the site of such Romano-Celtic temples. (See p. 38, above.)

This small type of segmented bead, which, not surprisingly, is conspicuously absent from Ireland, did not die out after the Roman withdrawal, but continued to be made well into post-Roman times. Among post-Roman examples there are some from Yeavering (Northumberland)[2] and from Dalmeny in West Lothian, and they also occur in Teutonic necklaces (sometimes perhaps reused Roman beads), and sixth- and seventh-century examples, often with rather rectangular segments, are frequently discovered in Frankish graves: these are usually made by pinching rather than winding. Noticeably rectangular segments are also present at Lankhills, Winchester, from a fourth-century grave (Grave 336).

The large examples to which attention was drawn above, sometimes 1 or even 1·5 cm. in diameter and with several segments, are known from Early Christian sites in Ireland, where they are relatively common,[3] Lundy, etc., and are a common feature in fifth- to eighth-century France, as well as during the Viking period.[4] Their size and wide perforation distinguish them from Roman examples, and it is also noticeable that many Teutonic and Viking ones have a slight 'collar' where the globular segments were broken off[5] (also common but less visible on the smaller beads). These large beads may continue, at least in Ireland, into the tenth to eleventh centuries, e.g., at Ballymacash, Co. Antrim.[6]

(b) SEGMENTED BEADS SOMETIMES ENCLOSING GOLD OR WHITE-METAL FOIL (Schedules, pp. 205–6) (fig. 37, no. 3)

These beads are made with colourless transparent fibrous glass which may enclose either gold or white-metal foil which glows through the glass to give a pale golden or white colour. In the case of white-metal, it may be sandwiched between two layers of amber-coloured glass which may have been cheaper to produce but which gives a harsher and more glittering result. These beads have already been the subject of a study by G. C. Boon in recent years: it is therefore only necessary to summarize his conclusions and to add any relevant material which has come to light since his paper was published.[7]

As Boon says 'the working procedure was evidently to draw out a tube of glass over a wire core; metal foil was wrapped round this tube and coated with a thin protective layer of glass. The completed ensemble was then threaded upon a narrower wire to be crimped at intervals into the segments which could be broken apart for use as single or multiple units.' As a result of this process it is only to be expected that the broken globules of segments which once belonged to such beads, generally show a thin broken 'collar' at the point of easiest fracture.

There are large quantities of these colourless or amber-coloured segmented beads from Egypt and the Sudan (e.g., Meroe and Faras), and recently a factory of Hellenistic date producing these beads as well as many other varieties has been identified in Rhodes.[8] Their production began early.

---

[1] For similar rods see also Castle Hill and Howrat, Dalry (Ayrshire), in *PSAS* liii (1918), 123. The recent recognition at Caerwent (no. 1899–1912 Ho. V. North) of a long rod intended for this purpose, was published by G. C. Boon in *MAn* iii, pt. 2 (1972–3), 123, no. 49 and fig. 4. A long 'natural' glass rod, over 5 cm. long, came from Lyons Court Farm, Whitchurch, Somerset, dated to the second or third century A.D. See *ArJ* cxxii (1965), 25.

[2] Information from Dr. Brian Hope-Taylor.

[3] See *JRSAI* lxiv (1934), 268, and pl. xxix. There are also many from collections. At Garryduff I (Co. Cork) one bead

of seventh–eighth-century date measured about 1.6 cm. in diameter; O'Kelly, M. (1963). There was evidence for glass-working on this site. Still larger is a triple example from Letterkeen (Co. Mayo); *PRIA* liv, 113.

[4] See, e.g., Arbman, H. (1940 and 1943).

[5] e.g., a sixth-century bead from Winterbourne Gunner, near Salisbury, *WAM* lix (1964), 94.

[6] Information from Professor E. M. Jope. See also *JRSAI* lxiv (1934), 268.

[7] Boon, G. C. (1966) and (1977).

[8] Weinberg, G. Davidson (1969).

In Britain and the Continent they are mainly found in late Roman or post-Roman graves, and, especially in Eastern Europe, in medieval times, but whether these later ones were Roman survivals or were newly manufactured is as yet unsure; the latter hypothesis is more acceptable.

As has been mentioned above their place of origin seems to have been the Near East and Egypt,[1] but factories producing local imitations may eventually turn up in a variety of other countries. Boon has drawn attention to the fact that colourless glass and gold casing were employed as early as the XVIII Dynasty for decorative purposes, in the tomb of Tutankhamun for example.[2] How late it continued is at present unknown.

A few beads additional to those published by Boon will be found in the Schedules. Their chronological contexts substantiate his contention that Roman examples in the British Isles fall mainly in the second to fourth centuries and lingered into the seventh century at least (e.g., in the Ashmolean Museum there are fifth- to seventh-century examples from Abingdon, West Stow Heath, and Haslingfield cemeteries).

The few examples in which translucent reddish- or yellow-coloured glass has been used to encase gold foil came from the fourth-century burials at Lankhills, Winchester, and are suspected of having come into the country from east-central Europe: but this theory must be examined in relation to the other finds from the cemetery (publication forthcoming). Certainly non-Roman beads do appear in late Roman burials in Britain (cf. the recently discovered examples from fourth- to fifth-century graves outside Cirencester). There are examples from Roman Egypt in the British Museum.[3] In view of the very mixed population in Europe around the fourth to fifth centuries these beads (of both types) might arrive in Britain from various Continental sources. They probably continued to be made in Coptic Egypt and were exported along with the other Coptic material found in Germanic, etc., graves (bronze bowls, amethyst beads, etc.), and lingered even into the Viking period.[4]

A warning note about dating and the filling used in these beads results from recent technological analysis. Not all may be comparable and results will have to be awaited. In some instances the filling may not be metal but yellow imitation material.

Cylinder beads

(a) BLUE (Schedules, pp. 207–8) (fig. 37, no. 4)

These are simple tubular rod beads which may be made either of opaque or translucent glass. The average length—though this varies a lot—is about 15 mm., the width about 4 mm., and the perforation is usually small. (Late Roman examples may be wound beads, smoothed to hide signs of segmentation.)

From the Schedules it can be seen that in Britain they range throughout the Roman period but become commoner after the second century. The later Roman ones often show minute longitudinal striations on

---

[1] Although the type is fairly rare in Syria and Palestine, some came from probably Roman tombs at Gerasa. See V. C. Baur in Kraeling, C. H. (ed.) (1938), 546. Dan Barag has excavated one from a second- to fourth-century burial in south Phoenicia (now in Israel), and three others of third- to fourth-century date came from Hanita in the same region. See also Brunton, G. (1937) (B.M., Egyptian Dept., 62586 of the Roman period and 62592 of Roman or Coptic date; no. 51393 is a Ptolemaic example). Boon, G. C. (1966) has also reported examples from South Russia and Bucharest.

Some comparative analyses have been carried out by the Instytut Historii Kultury Materialnej (Polska Akademia Nauk, Warsaw).

[2] Lucas, A. (1959), 218.

[3] Dept. of Greek Antiquities, 1903, 8.13, 16 and 17. See also beads from Faras in the Sudan and in the Ashmolean Museum, Oxford (*Liverpool Annals Arch.* xii (1925), 98.) For mid-Roman dating see *ibid.* xi (1924), 144 ff.

[4] One example came from a late Saxon or Viking context in York; *A* xcvii (1959), 96. Here Arbman is quoted as writing, 'Some details of the constriction of the ends and centre look very like those of our gold foil beads of the 10th century; those of the 9th were often thicker and generally more regular. . . .' See Arbman, H. (1940 and 1943).

the surface caused by the drawing out, but not the polishing, of the glass. So far they have not been recorded from pre-Roman sites in Britain, but they clearly last into the post-Roman period and are common, for instance, in sixth- and seventh-century Frankish cemeteries on the Continent.

Apart from one isolated example from the Isle of Man at Close-ny-Chollagh, Scarlett,[1] all the beads of this type have a very noticeably southern distribution, and it can only be supposed that they were imported from across the Channel, or that they were made in the southern counties at some yet unidentified site.

It is interesting to observe that these beads do not seem to have habitually been cut into short segments as were the comparable opaque green ones described below. An unusual example of clear blue glass with bevelled ends, where it had been knocked off the next bead, seems to be unique in Britain and is thought to have been Coptic or Mediterranean in origin rather than Teutonic. It came from the hill-fort of Dinas Powys near Cardiff (Glamorganshire) occupied into the post-Roman period.[2]

Recently large numbers of small translucent blue cylindrical beads have been recovered from fourth- to fifth-century graves at Lankhills cemetery, Winchester, where a mixed Roman and Teutonic population is suspected.[3]

(b) GREEN CYLINDER OR CYLINDER SEGMENTS (NEARLY ALWAYS OPAQUE) (Schedules, pp. 208–12) (fig. 57, no. 5)

Everything listed in the Schedules is apparently of the Roman period or immediately before, but it must be noted that the type is not uncommon in Jutish and Anglo-Saxon cemeteries in England, e.g., Chessel Down (Isle of Wight), Stodmarsh (Kent), Sleaford (Lincs.) and Burwell (Cambridgeshire) just to mention a few.[4] In France they come from a Romano-Belgic cemetery at Villées, as well as from Frankish cemeteries at Samson, Bioul, Éprave, etc., dating from about the fifth to sixth centuries (now in the museums at Namur and St. Germain). Between the third and eighth centuries these beads were widespread and can be seen in Copenhagen and Oslo museums among a great many others.

The earliest examples so far recognized in Britain are perhaps those from a first-century burial at Santon Downham, Suffolk,[5] and from a 'Belgic' level of the first century B.C. or A.D. at Maiden Castle in Dorset [6]; they then carry on right through into post-Roman times, reaching their maximum popularity in Britain after the third century.

The same chronology applies to the cut segments, cut at various widths from cylinders of opaque green glass. These are very common in late Roman necklaces from such sites as Lankhills (Winchester), Poundbury near Dorchester (Dorset), Cirencester, etc. A very characteristic late Roman form is about 4 mm. long and 2–3 mm. in diameter.

A necklace largely composed of these came from a fourth-century burial at Cirencester [7] where the graves are still being excavated on the edge of the town.

---

[1] This site also produced two unpierced dumb-bell toggles of post-Roman type, common in Ireland, and one wonders if all three of these beads did not work down from a higher level of occupation. The blue cylinder bead is atypical both in its glass and in the fact that its provenance lies far to the north of the rest of the group. But it is said to have come from a level dated by a La Tène III brooch of Colchester type (current until about A.D. 80). See *PPS* xxiv (1958), 85 ff. I do not know of other dumb-bell beads or toggles of such an early date, and suspect that the majority of them are post-Roman.

[2] Alcock, L. (1964).

[3] For preliminary report see Biddle, M. (1972), 94–8. Full report forthcoming.

[4] For a discussion of these beads see Hencken, H. O'N. (1950–1), 136.

[5] Fox, Cyril (1923).

[6] *MC*, 291–3 and fig. 98. For redating, see Frere, S. (1958), 84–92.

[7] Report forthcoming.

(c) CYLINDERS IN OTHER COLOURS (not scheduled)

Cylinder beads which are in colours other than blue or green are rare in Britain. Attention has already been drawn to the long bottle-glass rod of second- to third-century date from Whitchurch (Somerset),[1] and 'black' glass examples have been found at the Keiss Broch, Caithness [2] (probably of Roman date), the Roman period site at Cold Kitchen Hill, Brixton Deverill (Wiltshire), now in the Devizes Museum, and Lankhills Cemetery, Winchester.

An opaque terracotta-coloured bead, evidently associated with the Roman site, came from Sea Mills (Somerset) [3] and another from Ospringe in Kent (with Group 9) on a necklace of late third-century date, now in the Maison Dieu Museum at Ospringe.

A necklace of melon-shaped beads mixed with small cylindrical beads came from a Roman villa at Wiggonholt (Sussex),[4] but no colour was specified in the report.

Square-sectioned beads (long or cube-shaped) (Schedules, pp. 212–15) (fig. 37, nos. 6 and 7)

The long beads are usually made of bright opaque turquoise blues and greens and appear to be mostly rather late in the Roman period, though it is possible that one example from Templebrough, Rotherham (Yorks.), may be earlier. For the most part they date from the third to fourth centuries.

Another type of smaller section and one slightly tapering end appears to be less common but belongs to the same date. Small cube-shaped beads in translucent blue were found at Lankhills on necklaces which can be dated to the fourth century (Grave 438, later than a coin of A.D. 361). Small green opaque beads of square section, but rather longer than cube-shaped, also came from the same grave. They appear to be rare and may have been brought from South Bavaria as they occur in the last third of the fourth century there.[5] But note that some came from Camerton (Somerset) on a necklace stratified 'before A.D. 284'.[6] So the late third to late fourth centuries may be the usual date.

Long polygonal beads (hexagonal, pentagonal or octagonal) (Schedules, pp. 215–18) (fig. 37, nos. 8, 9 and 10)

Almost invariably these are light green in colour, and most of them are opaque, and appear to have been made from the same glass as the opaque green cylinder and cut cylinder segments described above. Both types may have been cheap imitations of emeralds. Blue ones are less common and may prove to be mostly post-Roman in date.

From the Schedules it can be seen that the earliest recorded example from Britain—though not on the other side of the Channel—came from the Belgic burial in Essex at Mount Bures,[7] found with fire-dogs and other objects of 10 B.C.—A.D. 50, and two wooden beads of this type from Dorset seem to be only a little later.[8] From the Conquest onwards the green beads of this type last through the Roman period and were common throughout the Roman world. One very complex example [9] has a bright yellow core which radiates to each of the five angles and is then covered with translucent green glass: this bead may have been imported from Egypt or some sophisticated area of bead-making, and reached Whitton between the first century B.C. and about A.D. 300.

It can also be seen from the Schedules that the few rich blue examples, all hexagonal, came from sites with a late or post-Roman occupation: two from the Broch of Dun Beag in Skye, and one from

---

[1] *AnJ* cxxii (1965), 25.

[2] *PSAS* xliii (1909), 12.

[3] This site, *Portus Abonae*, dates from the first century and may have survived into the early fourth (Bristol Museum 2220). See Boon, G. C. (1945), 258–95 and (1949) 184–8.

[4] *SAC* lxxviii (1937), 35.

[5] Keller, E. (1971), Abb. 27, no. 19 and pp. 86 and 92.

[6] Information from Mr. W. J. Wedlake.

[7] Smith, C. Roach (1852) and Stead, I. M. (1967), 1–62.

[8] From Whitcombe, with blue annular beads with a white wave and Samian ware of A.D. 96–110. Information from Mrs. G. Aitken.

[9] From the Whitton Roman villa, near Barry, Glamorganshire.

Jarlshof in Shetland. One came from an evidently Teutonic necklace of the mid- or second half of the fourth century from Lankhills, Winchester, and may be an import from South Bavaria.

Whereas the green beads of these polygonal forms have a long duration, becoming more popular in the later Roman period, the blue ones may have been confined to the late Roman period and have entered Britain with non-Roman people. Only time and more closely dated examples will prove how true this hypothesis may be.

Prism-shaped beads (Hungarian *prisma formiga* beads) (See schedules of exotic beads of the Roman period below) (fig. 37, no. 11)

These are six-sided with two long sides, flat in section and with angular ends. They are a rare type but have come from Richborough (Kent),[1] Chesters Fort (Northumberland) and Verulamium (Hertfordshire), the latter being of mixed green and white rather than plain green glass. They are regarded by Professor Sulimirski as being of Sarmatian origin.[2] I am grateful to Dr. Grace Simpson for the reference to similar *prisma formiga* beads from Hungary.[3] The horsemen who introduced these beads are known to have been among the Roman troops sent to this country; over 5,000 of them were brought into Britain in the late second century.

Small biconical beads (Schedules, pp. 218–21) (fig. 37, nos. 12 and 13)

(a) BLUE

These beads are translucent, medium to dark blue in colour and fall into two main sizes, one slightly larger (measuring between about 5 to 7 mm. in diameter and about the same width or slightly more, and having a small perforation) and another very small and uniform variety.

The Schedules show that those of the first variety are for the most part of late Roman date but they are also known from earlier contexts. At Maiden Castle (Dorset) an example was stratified in a level of A.D. 25–70 and this is less surprising when another comes from the Holcombe villa in Devon, stratified late second century. These beads are also fairly common on the Continent, for instance, on Sarmatian sites,[4] and in the museum in Mainz there are some from South Russia of the second to third century A.D. Those on another necklace of first- to fourth-century date from Redel (Pomerania) are so sharply cut that they may have been segments from a longer row of beads broken into required lengths. It is clearly impossible to date the rather larger variety of biconical blue bead on its own grounds within the Roman period; this type probably continued into post-Roman times.

On the other hand the very small variety of translucent light blue, among several colours, seems to be consistently late as far as our limited knowledge extends at present. These only measure about 3 mm. in diameter and 2 mm., or even less, thick. They have recently been found at the fourth-century cemetery at Lankhills, Winchester, and can be paralleled from numerous Continental sites.[5] Like all Roman period beads, we do not yet know where they were made. We can only say that present evidence points to a fourth- to fifth-century date for these very small biconical blue beads.[6]

(b) AND (c) OTHER COLOURS (MOSTLY VERY SMALL)

These appear to be common in the very small form only and are found in quantities from fourth- to fifth-century graves at Lankhills and Cirencester. Most typical are the opaque green ones made of

---

[1] *Rich* iv (1949), 239. This site also produced a chalcedony bead (Richborough Museum, no. 28), rather like one from Chesters, Northumberland, thought by Prof. Sulimirski to be Sarmatian.

[2] Sulimirski, T. (1970).

[3] See Párduez, in *AH* xxv (1941), Taf. 24 and 25, and pp. 56 ff.

[4] Sulimirski, T. (1970).

[5] See, for instance, Keller, E. (1971): Sjorold, T., *The Early Iron Age Settlements of Arctic Norway* (Tromso, 1962). For Gaul and the Danubian provinces see Eck, T. (1891), 20, 6. For Hungary see Sagrar, B. in *Acta Arch.* xviii (1966), 204 ff.

[6] There is also a necklace largely composed of these small beads from Icklingham, Suffolk, in the Ashmolean Museum in Oxford.

the same glass as the green cylinder beads (see above, p. 95). The translucent yellow ones, some of which may be as early as A.D. 300–40 at Lankhills (Grave 188), are so far rare—but a few very dark ('black') or amber-coloured ones are also known. We may here be dealing with imports from the Germanic world of the Rhineland (? Alamannic products) but the evidence is too scanty to be certain. Both translucent yellow and opaque green beads of the type, as well as blue ones are dated there by Keller [1] to the last third of the fourth century in South Bavaria, and they are probably prolific in Northern Germany, Belgium, etc. In Hungary these very small biconical beads come from first- to second-century A.D. Sarmatian graves.

Long biconical beads (Schedules, pp. 221–2) (fig. 37, no. 14)

These are generally about 10 mm. in length and 3–4 mm. in maximum width, and are most commonly made of opaque blue glass though other colours, terracotta, turquoise, and bottle green (not yellow) have been recorded from the Continent, and two colourless translucent ones came from a late Roman burial at Poundbury, Dorchester.

Once again the dating is consistently Roman; only one (Bagendon, Gloucestershire) may have slightly antedated the occupation,[2] but was almost certainly obtained from an area under Roman influence, and in any case the bead is somewhat indeterminate in form. Within the Roman period it is impossible to narrow down the date of their popularity. They were already current by the second century and probably before, and they continued into the third century at least, though their conspicuous absence from the large numbers of fourth-century beads from Lankhills and Cirencester suggests that by that date they had gone out of fashion.

These beads reached Northumberland in a few instances but are largely confined to the southern and midland counties. It is not known where they were produced. The majority may prove to belong to the second and third centuries.

Long blue biconical or square-sectioned beads with bands or chevrons in opaque white with a red line in the centre (Schedules, pp. 222–3) (pl. II, bottom row, no. , and fig. 37, no. 15)

These beads are usually rather carelessly made and may sometimes be squarish in section. There may be one or more bands or chevrons. It is improbable that these were made in Britain and they may have been imported from North Africa or the Eastern Mediterranean. The British examples, when stratified, point to a late Roman date, third to fourth century, though it is impossible to be precise about this, as many came from unstratified contexts and may have been earlier. Somewhat similar beads, but larger, and with a straight band rather than a chevron, are occasionally found among Teutonic beads, e.g., Stouting, Sussex.[3] At least some of these were made by the folding method, as a straight join is visible down one side and the red and white bands do not meet correctly. Possibly some of these are reused Roman beads, but their manufacture persisted well into the post-Roman period. It is interesting to note that a bead similar to the English Roman period beads of this type was found with a possible Libyan burial,[4] accompanied by a coin of Constantine (A.D. 306–37), a date which accords well with British evidence.[5]

The post-Roman beads tend to be larger than the Roman ones.

[1] Keller, E. (1971).

[2] See *Brit* vi (1975), 36–61 (V. G. Swan, 'Oare reconsidered'), where it is suggested that the phase previously dated A.D. 50–60 may be A.D. 60–70.

[3] These are also rounded in section. There are two from a necklace of about A.D. 600 from Canterbury (Ashmolean Museum, no. 1909-215). The same types come from the Danubian site of Schretzheim, near Dillingen (sixth- to seventh-century) and will be published shortly, probably as vol. 13 of the *GDV* by Ursula Koch.

[4] Information from Dr. Cabot Briggs of Harvard University in about 1950. No further information.

[5] Note, however, that their manufacture began earlier in Nubia. A necklace of Ptolemaic date (approx. 304–30 B.C.) including both a little square-sectioned bead of this type and two larger round-sectioned ones came from Faras. See *Liverpool Annals Arch.*, viii-xii (1921–5) (Dept. Egyptian Antiquities, B.M., no. 51393, referred to on p. 23 above).

Oblong beads with round section (Schedules, p. 224) (fig. 37, no. 16)

Very few of these are known so far, all opaque sky blue in colour and varying in length from 1·1 to 1·8 cm. On such slender evidence we can only recognize them as being an uncommon type vaguely belonging to the Roman period in Britain.

Miscellaneous undecorated heart- or pear-shaped beads and oval or round beads with flat sections (Schedules, pp. 224–7) (fig. 37, no. 17)

The Schedules show that these vary so much in colour and shape that it is at present impossible to quote useful analogies for them: they are generally, in Britain, of Roman date though some drop- or pear-shaped beads come occasionally from earlier sites.[1] A rigid classification based on shape would be meaningless as they are often so worn round the perforation or carelessly made that the original shape has been lost. There is a tendency for flat-sectioned round or oval beads to be late Roman in date, and some were present at the big fourth-century cemetery (with Germanic graves also) at Oudenburg.[2]

Boat-shaped beads (German, *Perlen in Kahnform*) (fig. 37, no. 18) (not scheduled)

These boat- or 'kidney'-shaped beads are not at all common in Britain but one came from a late Roman necklace from Ham Hill, Montacute (Somerset), and another from Grave 199 at Lankhills, Winchester (Hants). The Ham Hill example was made of translucent natural greenish glass, and the Lankhills one of translucent light blue. Both of these were probably imported. The Lankhills grave in question was dated from other contents to *c.* A.D. 310–30 and similar beads came from graves of the first half of the fourth century at Krefeld-Gellep and other South Bavarian, North Rhenish and Westphalian sites.[3] Recently another has been identified on a fourth(?)-century necklace in the Colchester and Essex Museum. The find is an old one and the beads may be a miscellaneous collection strung together.

Small gadrooned beads (German, *gerippte*) (fig. 37, no. 19) (not scheduled)

Only one example of this variety is known to be from Britain, from an unstratified level at Winchester. These are known from South Bavaria and according to Keller[4] belong to the middle third of the fourth century. Perhaps rather later in date are three small opaque blue examples from Miss Young's Collection in Edinburgh from the Culbin Sands which are like some from Chamberlain's Barn, Leighton Buzzard.[5]

Diamond-faceted beads (Schedules, pp. 227–8) (fig. 37, no. 20)

There are a large variety of faceted beads in Europe but only one type appears to be recognizable as a class in Britain during the period at present under review: a cube-shaped translucent blue glass bead, measuring about 6 mm. by 4 mm. with a diamond-shaped facet on the two long sides. These come from late Roman burials at Cirencester (Gloucestershire), Lankhills, near Winchester (Hants), Lufton and Lamyatt Beacon in Somerset (the last from the same level as a coin of Constantine II as Caesar (A.D. 330–5)). At Lankhills a date of about A.D. 350–90 seems likely, and this would accord well with Continental dates quoted by Keller.[6] At Oudenburg in Belgium beads of this type came from

---

[1] Note that heart-shaped beads were made in Hellenistic Rhodes, so that the type was long-lived, but not, apparently, in Britain, where the earliest (more drop-shaped than heart-shaped) appear to be G131A and B from Meare in the Taunton Museum.

[2] *AB* (1971), 135.

[3] See Keller, E. (1971), Abb. 27, no. 13. There are two

such beads from late Roman necklaces from Boulogne in the Ashmolean Museum (Evans Collection, nos. 1927.1346 and 1347).

[4] Keller, E. (1971).

[5] *ArJ* cxx (1954). These are of late sixth- or seventh-century A.D. date.

[6] Keller, E. (1971), 88.

Grave 67, dated around A.D. 370–400. It is interesting to note that both at Lankhills and at Oudenburg Germanic elements were present.[1]

There is good reason to suppose that these particular beads reached Britain from the Rhineland, Poland or the Low Countries, together with other Germanic beads and metal objects. The type was widespread. Moreau[2] makes it clear that faceted beads of this character were common in fifth- to sixth-century Gallo-Roman graves in the Aisne district, and they are common too in late Sarmatian graves in Hungary. Their overall dates seem, therefore, to range from the third or fourth century until about the sixth. It should be noted, however, that somewhat similar beads made of opaque blue glass or terra-cotta paste also appear in Viking graves of A.D. 800–1000 but there should be no confusion between these and the late Roman ones.

Glass melon beads (Schedules, pp. 228–30, excluding Ireland) (fig. 35, nos. 21 and 22)

It was not my original intention to include glass melon beads in this study for it is well known that, in faience or paste, and perhaps glass too, they were so long-lived that it seemed improbable that extensive work in museums and publications would yield valuable chronological evidence. The Schedules, albeit far from complete, are nevertheless worthy of careful study and give surprising results.

When Hencken[3] gave his detailed description of beads coming from one site in Britain (in this case Lagore in Ireland), he wrote, 'Melon beads are a long-lived and widespread type that began in pre-Roman times and continued to be common among the Germanic peoples in West and Northern Europe to the Viking Age. They are also fairly common in Ireland.' As an overall picture for Europe this statement is true, but it proves to be misleading if applied to glass melon beads in Britain.

Although these beads do begin early on the Continent (for instance they came from a third- to second-century B.C. cart burial at St. Etienne-au-Temple, and from the Beaulieu cemetery at Nogent-sur-Aube),[4] as yet no pre-Roman example can be recognized from Britain.

The earliest are Roman, and a study of the Schedules reveals that mostly blue or green glass melon beads come from many Flavian and Antonine sites. But then they die out and do not reappear until post-Roman times. As Hencken pointed out, they were popular again among Germanic peoples in the sixth century and later, when they were often made in a rather slap-dash way with nicks rather than true gadroons like the Roman ones. Many of the Germanic ones are made from smoky yellow translucent glass.

So they continue right through into Viking times. One came from a Viking house at Birksay, Orkney,[5] and they were common at Birka.[6] Sometimes they were twisted so that the fluting is S-shaped.

A few come from Ireland, some certainly of post fifth-century date, and others perhaps imported from the Roman world. By the tenth-eleventh centuries very small examples were common and numbers of that date have been found at York.

To sum up: the true Roman glass melon beads were imported into Britain from Claudian to Antonine times. They may have been imitated in local factories here, e.g. Castleford (see p. 37), but their chronological range is almost entirely restricted to the first and second centuries. They reappear in numbers in post-Roman times but are less well made and can generally be distinguished from the earlier ones.

One unusual example, decorated with horizontal bands, came from Caerlon and will be found in the Schedules of exotic Roman beads.

[1] *AB* (1971), 135.
[2] Moreau, F. (1892).
[3] Hencken, H. O'Neil (1950).
[4] Now in the St. Germain Museum, nos. 12720 and 24516, respectively.
[5] N.M.A., IL 505.
[6] Arbman, H. (1940).

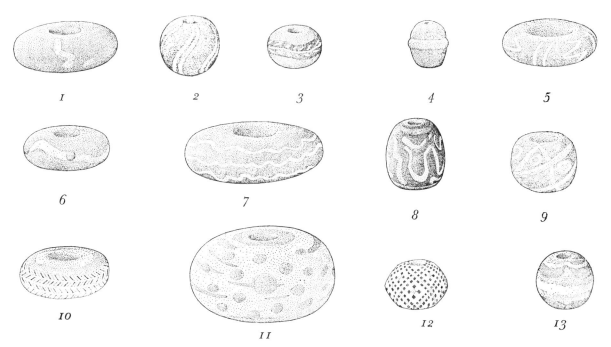

FIG. 38: Examples of exotic beads of the Roman period: *upper row,* 1. Colchester, Essex. 2, 3. Newstead, Roxburghshire. 4. Kenchester, Herefordshire. 5. Colchester, Essex; *centre row,* 6. Caernarvon (Segontium). 7. Willingham, Cambs. 8. Aldborough, Yorks. 9. Barnsley, Gloucs.; *lower row,* 10. South Shields, Durham. 11. Caerleon, Mon. 12. Colchester, Essex. 13. Bromham, Wilts. Scale 1/1.

Exotic beads of the Roman period (Schedules, pp. 231–7) (pl. II, 1–5 and fig. 38)

Very roughly these beads, which for the most part do not resemble either each other or anything else in the recorded repertoire of the British Isles, fall into two main groups. First are the beads which are variations on a native pre-Roman idiom, generally annular beads with free designs, very non-Roman in character; these appear to linger into the Roman period but to die out after about the second century or soon afterwards. Then comes a short period in the third century when only the unimaginative designs of the little standard Roman beads, current in so many districts in or contiguous to the Continental Roman world, predominate. By the early fourth century the native Celtic world was beginning to make itself felt again. Once more decorated and often large beads begin to reach Britain from the European mainland. This time the delight in curvilinear design has been lost, and the very different taste, albeit sometimes derived from the Celtic origin of the Central European tribes, is reflected in the heavy Germanic beads, many of which may have reached first Europe and then Britain from Egypt, exotic treasures carried in the course of trade or of troop movements from one part of the Empire to another by auxiliaries drawn from all over the Empire, and brought to Britain first perhaps by *numeri* (regiments raised from outside the Empire) and then increasingly by craftsmen and *foederati* in the fourth century. After this century we are in the dark about the classification of glass beads; Irish glass-working seems to have begun quickly, the true Anglo-Saxon settlement of South and East England intensified, and after that, there was first sporadic raiding and then more extensive settlement by the Vikings. The bridging century, the fifth, is still archaeologically difficult to define.[1]

[1] See, for instance, a report on continuing excavations at Mucking, Essex. Here the question is asked, 'Were the original Saxon immigrants soldiers or settlers?', *EAH* v (1973).

The beads in the Schedules draw attention to some of the non-Roman objects reaching Britain from overseas. As more knowledge accrues, it should be possible before long to identify their places of origin, even if the search will need to be very wide. British auxiliaries were sent to Thracia, Dacia and North Africa; the Roman inscriptions mention soldiers from Spain, Tungria, Pannonia, Raetia, and Batavia. We know that Sarmatian cavalry were serving in Britain in the second century, that Thracians were at Colchester and Cirencester (and Brigantian tribesmen served with the *Cohors II Thracum*), that the fifth Cohort of Gauls was at South Shields (Durham) in about A.D. 222, and that in 277–8 defeated Burgundian and Vandal tribesmen were sent to Britain. At times Usipii from Germany and contingents from Spain joined the medley as well as a detachment of Tigris boatmen and Alamanni from the Rhineland, large numbers of whose near neighbours, the Marcomanni from Bohemia, had been sent to Britain by Marcus Aurelius. Syrians, too (*Cohors I Hamiorum sagittariorum*) served on the Wall.

Some of the principal sources of information are listed below, and there the matter must rest.[1]

Among recognizably foreign beads in Britain in the early centuries are the segmented clear glass beads with gold or metal foil enclosed (? Syria and Egypt),[2] a little gadrooned bead which appears to be Central European, some 'black' globular beads with yellow waves (Sarmatian), boat-shaped beads (? Rhenish), cube-shaped faceted beads (Gallo-Roman and North European), large long 'black' or dark brown slightly biconical beads decorated with roughly applied unmarvered decoration in yellow, white, sky blue or sealing-wax red bands, eyes or chevrons (? Central Europe) acquired perhaps over a century or more from Syria or Egypt by Teutonic peoples, and early (? Teutonic) examples of 'black' annular beads decorated with red or yellow or blue scrabble designs, single or double, swags, etc., which became more common after about A.D. 400 and are noticeably common in Ireland. About all these we know very little, but study of them might throw much light on the archaeology of the sub- and post-Roman periods.[3]

[1] See, *inter alios*, Collingwood, R. G. and Wright, R. P. (1965); Frere, S. (1967) especially Chapters 11 and 14; Boisserain, U. P. (ed.) (1955); Ammianus Marcellinus, see *Incerti Auctoris: Epitome de Caesaribus* xli; Simpson, G. (1964); Birley, E. (1953); Webster, Graham (1969); Cheesman, G. L. (1915); Richmond, I. A. and Thompson, E. A. (1944 and 1956); Sulimirski, T. (1970); Starr, C. G., *Roman Imperial Navy 31 B.C.–A.D. 324* (Illinois, 2nd ed., 1960); Wacher, J. (1974). For late Roman sites on the Continent see *inter alios* Diaconu, G. (1965) and Párduez, M.

[2] For Roman glass from Syria, etc., see Harden, D. B. (1969), and refs. Also *Iraq* xi, 2 (1949), 151–9.

[3] The most recent general historical and archaeological surveys of the period between A.D. 367 and 634 include Alcock, L. (1973), Thomas, C. (1971), and Morris, J., *The Age of Arthur . . .* (1973). See also Laing, L. (1975).

PLATE I

1, Class 1: Arras types I and II. 2, Class 2: Welwyn Garden City type 3, Class 3: South Harting type. 4, Class 4: Findon type. 5, Class 5: Hanging Langford type. 6, Class 6: Oldbury type (*a*), Colchester type (*b*), and related type (*c*). 7, Class 7: whirl (*a*) and ray (*b*) beads. 8, Group 2: Miscellaneous spiral-decorated beads. 9, Group 4: Garrow Tor type. 10 (*a–d*.), Group 5: wave-decorated beads.

Scale 1/1

(N.B. Many of these beads have been 'idealised' to show their shape and decoration).

PLATE II

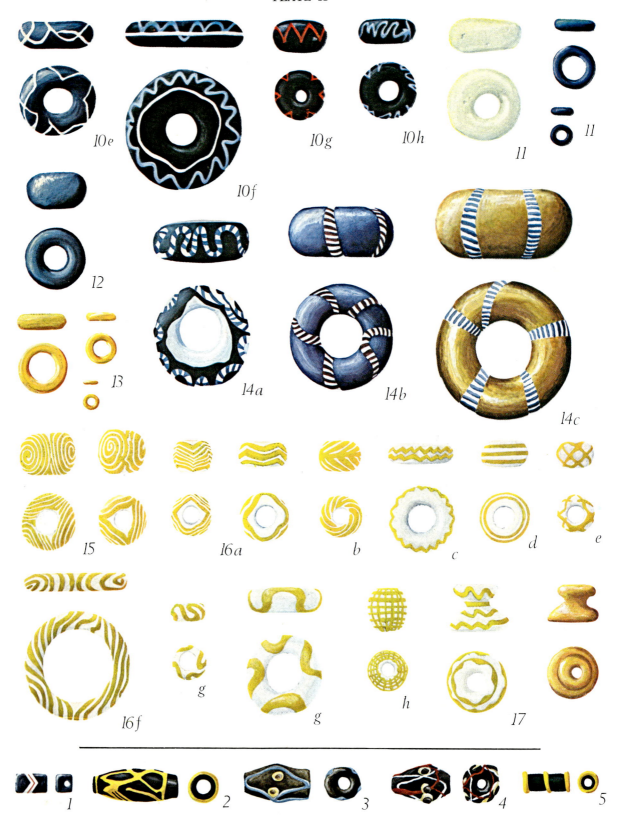

10 (e–h), Group 5: wave-decorated beads. 11, Group 6: undecorated annular beads. 12, Group 7: undecorated globular bead. 13, Class 8: small opaque yellow annular beads. 14, Class 9 (a–c): annular beads with two-coloured cables. 15, Class 10: Meare spiral beads. 16, Class 11 (a–h), Meare variant beads. 17, Class 12: stud beads. Bottom row, 1–5: exotic beads of the Roman period (for no. 1, see p. 98).

Scale 1/1

(N.B. Many of these beads have been 'idealised' to show their shape and decoration).

PLATE III

b. Above, Class 9: cable bead (*l.*) and Class 7: Celtic whirl (*r.*).
Below, Class 7: Celtic ray

a. Above, Class 6: Oldbury type. *Below,* Class 3: South Harting type.

d. Class 14: North Scottish decorated annular beads.

c. Class 13: North Scottish spiral beads.

Scale approximately 1/1.

PLATE IV

a. Late Roman period necklace from Lankhills cemetery, Winchester
(Scale approximately 2/3).

(Photograph: Winchester Research Unit).

b. Late Roman necklace from Fordington, Dorchester, Dorset (scale 2/3).

(by courtesy of Dorset County Museum)

THE SCHEDULES

NOTES

(i) Most of the references under the column COUNTY refer to the position before the local government reorganisation of 1974.

(ii) *Museums*. Certain frequently cited museums in the column MUSEUM AND NO. are abbreviated as follows:

A.M.   Ashmolean Museum, Oxford

B.M.   British Museum

C.M.   Cambridge Museum of Archaeology and Ethnology

N.M.A.   National Museum of Antiquities, Edinburgh

N.M.W.   National Museum of Wales, Cardiff

It should also be noted that the Guildhall Museum collections (cited as 'Formerly Guildhall Museum') have now been merged in the Museum of London.

(iii) *Publication references*. For the identification of references cited under the column PUBLICATION, see Abbreviations on pp. xix–xxi.

BEADS OF CONTINENTAL ORIGIN OR INSPIRATION
DECORATED CLASSES OF THE IRON AGE

CLASS 1

ARRAS TYPE I

(Grooved Circles filled with White)

SITE AND PARISH	COUNTY	MUSEUM & NO.	DESCRIPTION AND APPROX. DIMENSIONS	ASSOCIATIONS AND REMARKS	PUBLICATION
			ENGLAND		
London	Middlesex	Collection of the Marquis Mayeda	Beck's notes say 'Probably the largest bead of this sort known'. No dimensions	Probably this type to judge from sketch. 'Dug up near London'	Beck's notes, Cambridge
Lake or Winterbourne Stoke	Wiltshire	Lost	Dimensions approx. 1·3 cm. diam. and 1·2 cm. high. Inaccurate drawing	Not clear from text if associated with another bead illustrated—of Type II	Smith, A. C. (1884), p. 19
Arras, Queen's Barrow	Yorkshire	Originally 100 beads of various types. Remainder as follows. Yorkshire Museum beads not individually numbered. The B.M. ones of Type I are: 73.12–19.176 and 177; 80.8–2.142; 91.3–27.1 and 2; 92.4–21.78	White filling mostly gone, 3 eyes. Diam. 1·5 cm. Ht. 1·3 cm. 27 others similar	From Queen's Barrow with 18 examples of Type II, and many other beads now scattered with 15 natural greenish beads with yellow wave and 5 blue beads with white wave	Davis, J. B. and Thurnam, J. (1865); PAI (1846–published 1848), 26–32. For full details, see Stead, I. M. (1965), p. 59
Cowlam	Yorkshire	B.M. 79.12–9.536	One example. Diam. 2 cm. Ht. 1·5 cm.	From Barrow L. with 69 blue with white wave	Greenwell, W. (1877), 208–9, fig. 112. See also Stead, I. M. (1965), p. 59

ARRAS TYPE II

(Stratified Eyes)

ENGLAND

SITE AND PARISH	COUNTY	MUSEUM & NO.	DESCRIPTION AND APPROX. DIMENSIONS	ASSOCIATIONS AND REMARKS	PUBLICATION
Hatford	Berkshire	A.M. 1942.205	Diam. 1·9 cm. Ht. 1·1 cm. Straight perforation 7 mm. wide. Opaque ground	Near Iron Age A2 sherds, carinated bowl of Wessex A type, and sherd of B type. But not necessarily associated	O vii (1941–2), 103n.

SITE AND PARISH	COUNTY	MUSEUM & NO.	DESCRIPTION AND APPROX. DIMENSIONS	ASSOCIATIONS AND REMARKS	PUBLICATION
? East Anglia		Norwich Fitch Colln. 641–2. 427 and 649.76.94	Characteristic of this class. Diam. 1·3 cm. Ht. 8 mm.	This comes from a collection and may not even have been found locally	Not published
Maiden Castle, Winterbourne Monkton	Dorset	Dorchester, Dorset	Diam. 1·8 cm. Ht. 1·3 cm. Straight perforation 8 mm. wide	Regarded as probably an earlier stray in a deposit including Bii pottery of 2nd to early 1st c. B.C.	*MC*, fig. 98, no. 10, fragment no. 11
Hunsbury, Hardingstone	Northampton-shire	Lost	'A blue glass bead with white inlaid dots. Cf. Queen's Barrow & Swallowcliffe'	Not stratified. Occupation until 1st c. B.C. Initial date perhaps 4th–3rd c. B.C. till 1st c. A.D.	Fell, C. (1936), p. 69
Meare, Lake Village (West)	Somerset	Taunton G8 and G65	G8, diam. 1·7 cm. Ht. 1·2 cm. Perf. diam. 6 mm. (3 rows of eyes). G65, diam. 1·3 cm. Ht. 9 mm. Perf. diam. 4 mm. (2 rows of eyes)	Occupation probably began 3rd c. B.C.	*Me* iii
Wookey Hole	Somerset	Wells	Appears to be a carelessly made example of this type. Diam. 13 mm. Ht. 9 mm. Perf. diam. 3 mm.	From Hole Ground above the cave	
Swallowcliffe	Wiltshire	Devizes	Diam. 1·4 cm. Ht. 9 mm. Perf. diam. 5 mm.	From Iron Age settlement ? 5th to 4th c. B.C.	*WAM* xlii (1925–7),88–9
No exact provenance	'Wiltshire'		Globular, *c.* 1.2 cm. high and 1.3 cm. diam.	Old find	Smith, A. C. (1884), p. 19. Inaccurate drawing
Conderton Camp, Conderton	Gloucestershire –Worcestershire borders	Birmingham	Diam. 1·4 cm. Ht. 8 mm. Perf. diam. 5 mm. Opaque ground	With 'duck' pottery from 2nd main phase of the camp	Expected to be published by N. Thomas
Arras, Queen's Barrow	Yorkshire	Originally a necklace of 100 varied beads of several types, the remainder are in the Yorkshire Museum and the B.M. and their registration numbers are given under Type I	18 beads of this class	With a number of beads including 28 of Arras Type I	*A* lx (1906), 296. See also Stead, I. M. (1965)

SITE AND PARISH	COUNTY	MUSEUM & NO.	DESCRIPTION AND APPROX. DIMENSIONS	ASSOCIATIONS AND REMARKS	PUBLICATION
Garton Slack	Yorkshire		35 beads described as 'of Arras type' (? Type II)	With an inhumation etc., in area of the chariot burials	Preliminary note in *An* xlv (1971), 289

WALES

SITE AND PARISH	COUNTY	MUSEUM & NO.	DESCRIPTION AND APPROX. DIMENSIONS	ASSOCIATIONS AND REMARKS	PUBLICATION
Whitton, nr. Barry	Glamorgan-shire	N.M.W.	Nearly half bead. Diam. 1·6 cm. Ht. 1·2 cm. Perf. diam. 9 mm.	Site occupied 1st c. B.C. to about A.D. 300	Information from Dr. Michael Jarrett

CLASS 2

WELWYN GARDEN CITY TYPE

ENGLAND

SITE AND PARISH	COUNTY	MUSEUM & NO.	DESCRIPTION AND APPROX. DIMENSIONS	ASSOCIATIONS AND REMARKS	PUBLICATION
Welwyn Garden City	Hertfordshire	B.M.	Fragment with parts of 2 rings only. Original diam. *c.* 2·9 cm. Ht. *c.* 2·8 cm. Perf. diam. *c.* 8 mm. (see fig. 7)	With rich grave goods of last 20 years of 1st c. B.C. This bead is very fragmentary but I do not think the form restored in the publication is correct. It appears to be globular not annular	*A* ci (1967), 18, fig. 10. I think incorrectly restored to an annular shape instead of globular
Wiggonholt, Pulborough	Sussex	Worthing Museum, Wig. 64–65 A186.2.	Fragment, globular —broken remains of 4 eyes. Original height and diameter both about 3 cm. Perf. diam. 1 cm.	From large pit full of Romano-British pottery of 1st–2nd c. A.D., coin of Vespasian etc.	*SAC* cxii (1974), fig. 7, no. 28

CLASS 3

SOUTH HARTING TYPE

ENGLAND

SITE AND PARISH	COUNTY	MUSEUM & NO.	DESCRIPTION AND APPROX. DIMENSIONS	ASSOCIATIONS AND REMARKS	PUBLICATION
Willingham	Cambridge-shire	C.M. 1918.160.9–15	Dark blue translucent with white rings round blue eyes. Diam. *c.* 3·5 cm. Ht. 1·9 cm.	Found with a club bearing portrait of Antoninus Pius, and a cable bead, etc.	*AnJ* vi (1926), 178; *JRS* xiii (1923), 91 and xxxix (1949), 19
Taddington (Old Woman's House)	Derbyshire	Buxton	Four eyes all blue. Diam. 3·1 cm. Ht. 1·7 cm.	Not stratified	*JDANHS* xxxiii (1911)

SITE AND PARISH	COUNTY	MUSEUM & NO.	DESCRIPTION AND APPROX. DIMENSIONS	ASSOCIATIONS AND REMARKS	PUBLICATION
Gussage Down	Dorset	Dorchester 1889.1.21	Blue with one green and two yellow eyes ringed with white. Ht. 1·4 cm. Diam. 2 cm.	Wake Smart Colln.	
Wimborne?	Dorset	Dorchester	Blue with white rings round 3 red eyes. Diam. c. 2 cm.	Site called 'Vindogladia' on label probably Badbury Rings	
Chester-le-Street	Durham	B.M. 83.7–5.107	Almost opaque dark blue with five cobalt eyes ringed with white. Diam. 3·5 cm. Ht. 2·3 cm.		
Chedworth	Gloucester-shire	Chedworth Roman Villa Museum	Dark blue with several blue eyes	Said to be 'Early Iron Age' and possibly found in a barrow near the villa	For villa, see TBGAS lxxviii (1959), 5
Chatham Lines	Kent	?	Diam. about 2·8 cm. Blue with white rings round orange centres	Almost certainly an earlier bead reused in Saxon Barrow IV	Douglas, J. Nenia Britannica (1767), pl. 4, no. 2
Corbridge	Northumber-land	Corstopitum Museum	Very large amber brown with 3 rows of blue eyes ringed in white. Fragmentary. Diam. c. 4·5 cm. Ht. c. 3·5 cm.	Early find from Corstopitum	
Priddy, East Harptree	Somerset		4 beads with white around brown eyes on a blue ground	St. Cuthbert's lead mines ? mid-1st c. A.D.	A lxxii (1911), 567
Wookey Hole	Somerset	Wells	Blue with white around brown eyes. 4 others from woman's skeleton	From so-called 'Celtic' levels with Glastonbury pottery (2nd–1st c. B.C.?)	A lxii (1911), 579
Lewes	Sussex	Lewes	Atypical. Four depressions for eyes, now weathered out	From Caburn hill-fort. This may have been a post-Roman bead as suggested in the report	SAC lxviii (1927), 19
South Harting	Sussex	c/o National Trust, Uppark	Dark blue with white rings round 2 green eyes. Diam. 2·3 cm. Ht. 1·1 cm.	From Romano-British site near Harting Beacon	Unpublished
Atworth	Wiltshire	Devizes	Half a translucent cobalt bead with 2 green eyes and a third missing. Diam. 2·1 cm. Ht. 11 mm. Perf. diam. 6 mm.	Unstratified	Probably to be published in WAM about 1977

SITE AND PARISH	COUNTY	MUSEUM & NO.	DESCRIPTION AND APPROX. DIMENSIONS	ASSOCIATIONS AND REMARKS	PUBLICATION
Below Barbury Castle, Wroughton	Wiltshire	Devizes 479	Badly made cobalt blue with 2 irregular green eyes and 1 brown eye ringed in white. Diam. 2·1 cm. Ht. irreg. 1·4 cm. Perf. diam. 8 mm.	From Romano-British settlement near the hill-fort, occupied 1st or 2nd c. to 4th c. A.D.	*WAM* xxiii (1887), 183–4

SCOTLAND

SITE AND PARISH	COUNTY	MUSEUM & NO.	DESCRIPTION AND APPROX. DIMENSIONS	ASSOCIATIONS AND REMARKS	PUBLICATION
'Probably Scotland'		N.M.A. FJ82	Cobalt with 3 reddish eyes ringed in white. Diam. 2·5 cm. Ht. 1 cm.		
Wick	Caithness	C.M., E. A. B. Barnard Gift	Opaque greenish-black with 3 bright azure eyes	This is not like the rest of this Class and may belong to a later date	
Newstead	Roxburgh-shire	N.M.A. FRA896	Part of cobalt bead with blue eyes ringed in white. Diam. 3·0 cm. Ht. 1·7 cm.	Probably early Roman occupation *c.* A.D. 80–200	*Ne*, pl. xci, no. 16
Newstead	Roxburgh-shire	N.M.A.	Natural translucent greenish glass with one eye striped in yellow and blue, surrounded with ring of yellow. The other eye blue. Diam. *c.* 3 cm. Ht. 1·1 cm.	Probably early Roman occupation *c.* A.D. 80–200	*Ne*, pl. xci, no. 12
Camelon Fort, Falkirk	Stirlingshire	N.M.A. F340	Cobalt blue. Of the 4 eyes in white rings, 2 are missing and 2 are blue. Diam. 2·2 cm. Ht. 1·2 cm.	This site produced native glass armlets of 1st–2nd c. A.D.	*PSAS* xxxv (1900–1), 329
Camelon Fort, Falkirk	Stirlingshire	N.M.A. F164	Bright cobalt with 3 blue eyes ringed in white	This site produced native glass armlets of 1st–2nd c. A.D.	*PSAS* xxxv (1900–1), 329

WALES

SITE AND PARISH	COUNTY	MUSEUM & NO.	DESCRIPTION AND APPROX. DIMENSIONS	ASSOCIATIONS AND REMARKS	PUBLICATION
Nevin	Caernarvon-shire	Lost	Described as an ox-eyed bead	Almost certainly this type. From big fort at Garn Boduan	*ArJ* cxvii (1962), 1 ff.

SITE AND PARISH	COUNTY	MUSEUM & NO.	DESCRIPTION AND APPROX. DIMENSIONS	ASSOCIATIONS AND REMARKS	PUBLICATION
Whitton, nr. Barry	Glamorgan-shire	?N.M.W.	Dark blue, white rings round bright blue eyes. Half another, translucent cobalt with one remaining green eye. Diam. 1·9 cm. Ht. 9 mm. Perf. diam. 8 mm.	From Roman villa excavation no. 65 IX. Site occupied about 1st c. B.C. to A.D. 300	Information frm Dr. Jarrett, Univ. College of S. Wales, Cardiff
Llanuwchllyn	Merioneth-shire	Once on loan to Carmarthenshire Antiquarian Soc. Museum	Opaque blue with 3 eyes (red, dark green and light green) in white rings	Found near Castell Carn Dochan	*AC* lxxviii (1923), 311
Abergavenny	Monmouth-shire	Abergavenny	One-third of blue semi-translucent bead. One eye only remains, yellowish-green. Orig. diam. 1·7 cm. Ht. 8 mm. Perf. diam. 7 mm.	From Flannel Street (no. F166). 1st c. finds from this Roman site	To be published in *MAn*
Caerleon	Monmouth-shire	N.M.W.	Fragment of large royal blue bead with one remaining blue eye. Diam. 3·9 cm. Ht. 2·4 cm. Perf. diam. 1·3 cm.	Roman period, almost certainly late 1st–early 2nd c. A.D.	*AC* cxix (1970)

CLASS 4

OPAQUE YELLOW BEADS WITH PAIRS OF SUPERIMPOSED BLUE AND WHITE EYES ('FINDON TYPE')

Woodeaton	Oxfordshire	A.M. 1896–1908, R159	Small bead. Diam. 1 cm. Ht. 7 mm. Perf. diam. 3 mm. Two tiers of blue and white eyes	Definitely from Wood-eaton, possibly Gordon Collection	Harding, D. W. (1972)
Findon (Muntham Court)	Sussex	Worthing	Diam. 1·3 cm. Ht. 9 mm. Perf. diam. 6 mm. Two tiers of eyes (fig. 10)	From Iron Age A ritual site, culturally related to Park Brow	*ANL* v, no. 10 (March 1955), 204–5 and vi, no. 4 (1957). *SNQ* xiv (1954–7), 196–8, 232–3. See also Frere, S. (ed.) (1958), 20

Nightingale Collection. A larger one is illustrated in drawings of 1850 in the Society of Antiquaries of London library, Burlington House, Piccadilly. It has no location but was probably found in England

SITE AND PARISH	COUNTY	MUSEUM & NO.	DESCRIPTION AND APPROX. DIMENSIONS	ASSOCIATIONS AND REMARKS	PUBLICATION

CLASS 5
THE HANGING LANGFORD TYPE

ENGLAND

SITE AND PARISH	COUNTY	MUSEUM & NO.	DESCRIPTION AND APPROX. DIMENSIONS	ASSOCIATIONS AND REMARKS	PUBLICATION
Castle Dore fort (Fowey)	Cornwall	Truro	No bead of this type but part of armlet in identical technique	Occupation from early 2nd c. B.C. to c. 100 B.C.	*JRIC* n.s. i (1951), 68
Nor'nour, Scilly	Cornwall	St. Mary's, Scilly	Clear glass with faint yellow traces inside. Half only. Diam. 2·2 cm. Ht. 6 mm.	Site 1, Room 2. Site may begin in pre-Roman period with *floruit* in 2nd c. A.D. Lasted till late Roman times	*ArJ* cxxiv (1967)
Maumbury Rings, Dorchester	Dorset	Dorchester 273	Yellow unevenly applied. Diam. 2 cm. Ht. 5 mm.	With early Romano-British material. Incorrectly republished in *A* (1975)	H. St. George Gray, *Excavations of Maumbury Rings, Dorchester* (1912)
? Colchester	Essex	Colchester	No details	Among collection of miscellaneous beads	
Cirencester	Gloucester-shire	Cirencester C908	Half bead. Diam. 2·2 cm. Ht. 6 mm. Perf. diam. 1·1 cm.	From Roman town	
Faversham	Kent	C.M., Beck Colln. 1659	Diam. 2·3 cm. Ht. 7 mm.	Grave XX A 1a. Said to be from Anglo-Saxon context. If so it is almost surely an earlier bead reused	
Hunsbury Iron Age fort, Hardingstone	Northamp-tonshire	Northampton	Diam. 2·3 cm. Ht. 5 mm.	Unlikely to be later than early 1st c. B.C. Occupation may have begun in 4th c. B.C.	Fell C. (1936), p. 69
Meare Lake Village (West Village)	Somerset	Taunton G3 and G74	Two beads. Diams. 25 and 19 mm.	Mound VII in pre-Roman village of 3rd–1st c. B.C.	*Me* iii, 289
Hanging Langford Camp, Steeple Langford	Wiltshire	Salisbury 139/39	Half bead only. Diam. 2·2 cm. Ht. 0·7 cm. (fig. 11)	Almost all the pottery is Belgic and the finds c. 1st B.C.–1st c. A.D. except for one La Tène I bronze fibula	Unpublished
No provenance		A.M. 1836.70	Diam. 2·3 cm. Ht. 8 mm. Perf. diam. 11 mm.	This comes from a miscellaneous collection of beads, some probably early Iron Age and some Irish	*ArJ* iii (1846), 355

SITE AND PARISH	COUNTY	MUSEUM & NO.	DESCRIPTION AND APPROX. DIMENSIONS	ASSOCIATIONS AND REMARKS	PUBLICATION
			IRELAND		
Newcastle	Co. Down	N.M. Dublin P842 or 843	Battered example. Diam. 2·5 cm. Ht. 7 mm.	Found on shore	Unpublished

CLASS 6

OLDBURY AND COLCHESTER TYPES

ENGLAND

SITE AND PARISH	COUNTY	MUSEUM & NO.	DESCRIPTION AND APPROX. DIMENSIONS	ASSOCIATIONS AND REMARKS	PUBLICATION
Yewden, Hambledon	Buckingham-shire	Aylesbury		Romano-British villa with pre-Roman occupation	*A* lxxi (1920–1), 141 ff.
Nr. Great Kimble	Buckingham-shire	A.M.	Fragment only	Found in 1866	
Burnt Fen, Shippea Hill, nr. Ely	Cambridge-shire	C.M.	Two rows of spirals. Diam. 2·4 cm. Ht. 1·4 cm.	Found with a bead paralleled at Great Chesterford (probably 1st c. B.C. or A.D.)	
Haslingfield	Cambridge-shire	Hull	3 rows of spirals. Max. diam. 3 cm. Ht. 1·5 cm.	Fragment. Less than half	Drawing in Beck's notes in C.M.
Netherby	Cumberland		No details	Found in the 18th c. Probably from Roman fort. ? Hadrianic	Pennant, *Tour in Scotland and Voyage to the Hebrides* (1772), pl. vii
Dorchester (Colliton Park)	Dorset	Dorchester	Globular. Well marvered, finely drawn spirals. Diam. 2·9 cm. Ht. 2·3 cm. Perf. diam. 9 mm.	Found unstratified in Roman area in 1941	Information from Mr. R. A. H. Farrar. See R.C.H.M. *Dorset* ii S.E., pt. 3
Maiden Castle, Winterbourne Monkton	Dorset	Dorchester		Stratified early 1st c. B.C. in Iron Age camp	*MC*
Marnhull	Dorset	Gillingham Museum	Half bead, blue with white spirals. Diam. 2·6 cm.	Iron Age and Romano-British site	
Swanage	Dorset	City Museum Bristol F710	3 rows of spirals. Max. diam. 3·7 cm. Ht. 2 cm.	Given to the Museum in 1904	*PDNHAS* lxx (1949), 53
Colchester	Essex	Colchester	Bossed spirals and yellow swags	Period III–IV. Early to mid-1st c. A.D.	*Cam*, 306, no. 2

SITE AND PARISH	COUNTY	MUSEUM & NO.	DESCRIPTION AND APPROX. DIMENSIONS	ASSOCIATIONS AND REMARKS	PUBLICATION
Danebury Ring, Nether Wallop	Hampshire		Fragment with 3 spirals. Max. diam. 2·8 cm. Ht. 1·4 cm. Perf. diam. 9 mm.	From Iron Age fort. Pit 463, layer 2. ? Early 1st c. B.C.	Information from Barry Cunliffe
Winchester (Brook Street)	Hampshire	Winchester	Very abraded half bead with 3 very worn spirals. One on a slight boss. No filling colour remains. Diam. 2·4 cm. Ht. 1·5 cm. Perf. diam. 6 mm.	Evidently kept as a curiosity. From Roman or post-Roman pit 463. Found in 1972	Biddle, M. (forthcoming)
Hythe	Kent				*ACt* xlv (1933), pl. iv
Oldbury fort, Ightham	Kent	Sir Edward Harrison Colln., Maidstone	Diam. 3·4 cm. Ht. 1·4 cm.	From 2-period hill-fort. Period I early 1st c. B.C., Period II redefended about 100 years later. This bead came from a fox earth below the western rampart	*ACt* xlv (1933), 158, and pl. iv, li (1939), 162, 180; *A* xc (1944), 165 ff.
Romney Marsh	Kent		Yellow spirals. Diam. *c.* 2·5 cm.	From Haunted House Field. Now in hands of Mr. J. Sinden, Hope Farm, St. Mary in the Marsh, Romney Marsh, Kent	*ACt* l (1938), 153–4 with photograph
Westerham	Kent	B.M. 1928.11.5	3 rows slightly bossed spirals. Max. diam. 2·8 cm. Ht. 1·7 cm.		
Wilderspool, Warrington	Lancashire–Cheshire border	Warrington	Fragment. Ht. 1·4 cm.	Roman industrial site	Thompson, F. H. (1965), fig. 20, no. 22
Old Winteringham	Lincolnshire	Scunthorpe	3 rows spirals, slightly bossed. Max. diam. 3·2 cm. Ht. 2 cm.	Probably a Claudian fort, almost surely dating between A.D. 47–71	To be published shortly
Spilsby	Lincolnshire	Lincoln 270–209	Colchester type. Bossed spirals between yellow swags. Max. diam. 2·6 cm. Ht. 1·6 cm. (fig. 13, right)	Originally in Trollope Colln. and thought to be Saxon	*PSAL*, 2nd S., vi, 75; *ArJ* xci, 181
London	Middlesex	Formerly Guildhall Museum 17347	Badly made and fragmentary. Orig. diam. *c.* 2·6 cm. Ht. 1·5 cm.	Almost surely up-river from Brentford	

SITE AND PARISH	COUNTY	MUSEUM & NO.	DESCRIPTION AND APPROX. DIMENSIONS	ASSOCIATIONS AND REMARKS	PUBLICATION
Hunsbury fort, Hardingstone	Northampton-shire	Northampton	2 with strongly pro-jecting knobs. One has one row and slight collar at each end. Max. diam. 2·6 cm. Ht. 1·6 cm. The other 3 rows of spirals: Max. diam. 3 cm. Ht. 1·8 cm.	From Iron Age hill-fort. Unlikely to be much after 1st c. B.C. but occupation seems to have begun about 4th c. B.C.	Fell, C. (1936), p. 69. See also *JNNHSFC* xviii and xix
Weekley, Kettering	Northampton-shire	Northampton	3 rows bossed spirals. Less than half remains	Coins from this Roman villa range from Vespasian to Valentinian	*JNNHSFC* xviii and xix, pl. 10 and viii, 35
'Probably Northumberland'		University Museum Newcastle-upon-Tyne 652 (T. Stevens Colln.) no. 22	Fragment. Two slightly bossed spirals remain		
Broughton Poggs	Oxfordshire	A.M. 1909.489b	Diam. 1·8 cm. Ht. 1 cm.	Reused in grave with Saxon spearhead, 2 bronze small long brooches	
Ducklington	Oxfordshire	A.M. 1971.473	White spirals on slight bosses. Diam. 2·4 cm. Ht. 1·5 cm. Perf. diam. 7 mm.	Reused in Saxon grave (Grave 2)	*PSAL* i (1859–61), 100–1
Glastonbury Lake Village	Somerset	Glastonbury G1, G5, G9, and G11	Fragments. G9 has 2 rows spirals: Diam. 2·5 cm., ht. 1·6 cm. G1, one row spirals: Diam. 2·1 cm., ht. 1·1 cm. G5 and G11 fragments	From Lake Village	*Gl* ii, pl. lix
Meare Lake Village	Somerset	Taunton G45EV	Half only. Diam. 2·4 cm. Ht. 1·4 cm.	From Lake Village, 3rd–1st c. B.C.?	*Me* iii
South Cadbury	Somerset		Fragment with 3 yellow spirals and another smaller with white spiral	Pre-Roman Iron Age	Information from Prof. Leslie Alcock
Richmond	Surrey	Formerly Guildhall Museum 331	Colchester type. White spirals and opaque yellow swags. Diam. 3·1 cm.	No further details	
Bexley Hill, Eastbourne	Sussex	B.M. 67.12–17.1	3 rows slight bosses. Max. diam. 3 cm. Ht. 2 cm.	Given by T. O. Barlow 1867	

SITE AND PARISH	COUNTY	MUSEUM & NO.	DESCRIPTION AND APPROX. DIMENSIONS	ASSOCIATIONS AND REMARKS	PUBLICATION
Chichester	Sussex	Chichester	3 rows of spirals on bosses. Max. diam. 3 cm. Ht. 1·7 cm. Perf. diam. 1 cm.	With a burial dated by pottery and other objects to the Late Antonine period. (Group 228)	Down, A., and Rule, M. *Chichester Excavations*, i (1971) (Chichester Civic Society Excavations Committee)
Torberry, South Harting	Sussex		Small fragment only	Iron Age hill-fort	Cunliffe, B. (1976), fig. 14, no. 6 and p. 14
Brough-under-Stainmore	Westmorland	A.M. 1927.881	Related type. Single row of spirals. Max. diam. 2·2 cm. Ht. 1·6 cm.	Stray find 1888. This site was probably Flavian in origin. It was restored in *c.* 200 A.D. and by the 4th c. a *vicus* had grown up outside	
Beckford	Worcester-shire		Damaged. Half bead. 3 rows spirals on bosses. Diam. 21 mm. Ht. 1·4 cm. Perf. diam. 1 cm.	Iron Age site in course of excavation	Information from Mr. Britnell
'Probably Wiltshire'		Once at Stourhead	Two beads		Thurnam, *Ancient British Barrows*, p. 212, n. 6. One may be the bead referred to in Hoare, R. Colt (1812), i, p. 176
Fulwood, nr. Sheffield	Yorkshire	Sheffield	Very dark, almost opaque. 2 or 3 tiers of badly made spirals. Diam. 2·1 cm. Ht. 1·8 cm. Perf. diam. 1 cm.	Stray find in same area as Roman pottery	Information from Mr. Butterworth, Sheffield Museum
'Probably East England'		Salisbury 18a	3 slightly knobbed rows of spirals. Max. diam. 2·2 cm. Ht. 1·5 cm.	This has no proven-ance and could perhaps be one of the Wilts. beads men-tioned above	

IRELAND

SITE AND PARISH	COUNTY	MUSEUM & NO.	DESCRIPTION AND APPROX. DIMENSIONS	ASSOCIATIONS AND REMARKS	PUBLICATION
Sandy Braes	Antrim	Belfast, Knowles Colln. 638 (1924)	3 rows of spirals (not bossed). Max. diam. 3·5 cm. Ht. 2·2 cm.	Site is 8 miles S.E. of Ballymena	
'Northern Ireland'		Dublin 1907.85	Max. diam. 2·4 cm. Ht. 1·6 cm.		

SITE AND PARISH	COUNTY	MUSEUM & NO.	DESCRIPTION AND APPROX. DIMENSIONS	ASSOCIATIONS AND REMARKS	PUBLICATION
'Northern Ireland'		Dublin 1920.63			
'Northern Ireland'		Belfast, Grainger Colln. 2414	2 rows only flat spirals		
'Northern Ireland'		Belfast 2416	3 rows of flat spirals. Diam. 2·6 cm. Ht. 1·6 cm.		
Dun-na-mana	Tyrone	B.M. 90.2.15.11	Very dark blue. Well made spirals. Diam. 2·7 cm. Ht. 1·7 cm.	Found in 1890	*JRSAI*, 4th s., vi (1883–4), 70, fig. 5

SCOTLAND

SITE AND PARISH	COUNTY	MUSEUM & NO.	DESCRIPTION AND APPROX. DIMENSIONS	ASSOCIATIONS AND REMARKS	PUBLICATION
Earlston	Berwickshire	N.M.A. FJ103	Fragmentary. One remaining spiral on pronounced boss. Max. diam. 2·6 cm. Ht. 1·7 cm.	'Near Earlston'	
	Berwickshire (probably)	N.M.A. FJ112	Single row of spirals. Diam. 2·3 cm. Ht. 1·2 cm.	From Lady John Scott's Colln.	
Arinabost, Isle of Coll	Argyllshire	N.M.A. FJ94	Rather squat. Max. diam. 2·5 cm. Ht. 2·0 cm. (fig. 13, left)	From an earth house 2 miles NW. of Arinagour (1896). Said to have been found with a large bronze pin with fluted head, etc. Also part of a twisted gold bracelet	Beveridge, *Coll and Tiree*, 1–3 and *PSAS* xxxvii (1903), 68
Kilmany	Fife	N.M.A. FJ21	Max. diam. 2·4 cm. Ht. 1·6 cm.	Brighouse Farm, Logie	*PSAS* xix (1884–5), 133
Gilmerton	Midlothian	N.M.A. FJ99	Max. diam. 2·8 cm. Ht. 1·6 cm.	Ploughed up in about 1909	*PSAS* xliv (1909–10), 9

WALES

SITE AND PARISH	COUNTY	MUSEUM & NO.	DESCRIPTION AND APPROX. DIMENSIONS	ASSOCIATIONS AND REMARKS	PUBLICATION
The Breiddin	Montgomery-shire		Blue-black fragment with bossed spiral. Max. diam. 2·5 cm. Ht. 1·4 cm.	From hill-fort	Information from Mr. Christopher Musson
Gronant, nr. Prestatyn	Flintshire	Not yet placed	Very fine example without bosses. Diam. 2·7 cm. Ht. 1·8 cm. Perf. diam. 9 mm.	Near a dewpond at SJo845	Found 1975 and awaiting publication

SITE AND PARISH	COUNTY	MUSEUM & NO.	DESCRIPTION AND APPROX. DIMENSIONS	ASSOCIATIONS AND REMARKS	PUBLICATION
			OLDBURY CLASS EXOTIC TYPE		
No location		Slade Colln., B.M. 71.12–10.35	Except for colour it resembles the Old-bury Class. It is made of clear colourless glass and the spirals are in opaque yellow. Diam. 2·7 cm. Ht. 1·7 cm.	Found in 1871	
'Ireland'		Bell Colln., N.M.A. FK20	Clear glass. 3 tiers of protuberances with white spirals round amber coloured eyes	No details known	
North Bersted, nr. Felpham	Sussex	Sussex	Half bead. Large yellow spirals alter-nating with vertically placed pairs of white spirals. Diam. 2·4 cm. Ht. 1·4 cm. Perf. diam. 9 mm.	Unstratified but almost certainly derived from ditch with 'saucepan' type pottery or a Romano-British ditch	Information from Michael Pitts, Oving, Chichester, 1975

CLASS 7

LARGE ANNULAR CELTIC BEADS: WHIRL OR RAY TYPE

TYPE (A), BLUE OR PURPLE GROUND WITH WHITE OR YELLOW WHIRLS OR RAYS

ENGLAND

SITE AND PARISH	COUNTY	MUSEUM & NO.	DESCRIPTION AND APPROX. DIMENSIONS	ASSOCIATIONS AND REMARKS	PUBLICATION
Nor 'nour, Scilly	Cornwall	St. Mary's, Scilly	Almost opaque cobalt with signs of white rays. Less than half remains. Diam. 4·1 cm. Ht. 1·9 cm.	Site perhaps pre-Roman in origin but perhaps lasting to 4th c. A.D.	*ArJ* cxxiv (1967)
Norsey Wood, Billericay	Essex	Chelmsford B18.513	Opaque blue with irregular yellow whirl. Diam. 3·5 cm. Ht. 9 mm. (fig. 15)	Found in the last century. Many Belgic and Roman finds from site	For the site see *JBAA*, 3rd s., iii (1938), 139, and iv (1939), 189
Kelvedon	Essex	Ipswich? Property M. R. Campen	Almost opaque with white whirl. Diam. 2·9 cm. Ht. 1·1 cm. Perf. diam. 1 cm. (fig. 15)	From an early Romano-British rubbish pit	
Glastonbury	Somerset	Glastonbury G14	Semi-translucent dark purple with opaque yellow whirl. Diam. 3 cm. Ht. 1·3 cm.	From Lake Village	*Gl.* ii

SITE AND PARISH	COUNTY	MUSEUM & NO.	DESCRIPTION AND APPROX. DIMENSIONS	ASSOCIATIONS AND REMARKS	PUBLICATION
Danebury Ring, Nether Wallop	Hampshire		Less than half. White whirls overlaid partly with blue lines. Diam. 2·5 cm. Ht. 9 mm. Perf. diam. 1·3 cm.	From hill-fort. Pit 313. Level thought to belong to ? late 2nd c. B.C.	Information from Barry Cunliffe
Meare	Somerset	Taunton G73	Half. Blue with white whirl. Diam. 2·6 cm. Ht. 9 mm. Perf. diam. 1·1 c.m.	From Iron Age village site, 2nd–1st c. B.C.?	Me iii
Salisbury Plain	Wiltshire	A.M.	Very dark blue or black with yellow rays. Diam. 3·5 cm. Ht. 1·5 cm. (fig. 15)	Once described as 'from Dr. Stukeley's collection'	Douglas, J., Nenia Britannica (1767), pl. xxi, no. 2, fig. 3
Wick Wood, Nettleton	Wiltshire	c/o Bath and Camerton Archaeological Society	Fragment. Rounded section. Dark, purplish blue with white whirls. Diam. 2·9 cm. Ht. 1·1 cm. Perf. diam. 7 mm.	From fort defences of 1st to early 2nd c. A.D. date	Information from Mr. W. J. Wedlake

IRELAND

'Ireland'		Belfast	Rich cobalt blue with white whirl. Diam. 3·2 cm. Ht. 1·2 cm.		
Cloughwater, nr. Lisnacrogher	Co. Antrim	Dublin 1907.97	Dark ground, uncertain colour with yellow whirls. Diam. 2·7 cm. Ht. 8 mm. Perf. diam. 1·3 cm.	No details of discovery	JRSAI cii, Pt. 1 (1972), 14–18
'Northern Ireland'		Belfast 1912.172 Benn Colln.	Rich cobalt blue with white whirl. Diam. 2·7 cm. Ht. 1·4 cm.		
'Probably Ireland'		N.M.A. FK41 Bell Colln.	Rich cobalt blue with white whirl. Diam. 4·0 cm. Ht. 1·9 cm.		
Edenderry (Drumcooley Hill)	Co. Offaly	C.M.	Purplish-blue with yellow whirl. Diam. 3·5 cm. Ht. 1·3 cm.	This must be a stray found with earlier bronze implements	

SCOTLAND

Kirkmaiden	Wigtownshire	N.M.A. FJ24	Appears black but really bright cobalt with yellow rays and concentric bands of cobalt. Diam. 4·5 cm. Ht. 2·2 cm. (fig. 15)	Presented by Sir H. Maxwell in 1889. Probably a poor imitation of the Continental type	AANHSC (1885), 46 and PSAS xxii (1889), 151

SITE AND PARISH	COUNTY	MUSEUM & NO.	DESCRIPTION AND APPROX. DIMENSIONS	ASSOCIATIONS AND REMARKS	PUBLICATION
			WALES		
Caerleon	Monmouth-shire	N.M.W.	Fragment. Diam. 2·9 cm. Ht. 1·3 cm.	Stratified A.D. 130–230 in excavation to S.W. of legionary fortress, in 1962.	See Boon, G. C., *Isca* (1972)
Walesland Rath	Pembroke-shire		Fragment. Blue with remains of white whirls	Dated from associations and radio-carbon to 3rd–2nd c. B.C. (210 ± 90 B.C. (NPL 245))	Wainwright, G. J., 'The excavation of a fortified settlement at Walesland Rath, Pembrokeshire', in *Brit* ii (1971), 48 ff.

TYPE (B), BROWN OR YELLOWISH-BROWN WITH YELLOW WHIRL

ENGLAND

SITE AND PARISH	COUNTY	MUSEUM & NO.	DESCRIPTION AND APPROX. DIMENSIONS	ASSOCIATIONS AND REMARKS	PUBLICATION
Hengistbury Head	Dorset	Christchurch	Part only. Diam. 3·7 cm. Ht. 1·5 cm.	From Site 33. Occupation lasted from early 1st c. B.C. to Antoninus Pius to judge from coins only. Iron Age entrepôt	*HH*, pl. xxx, no. 20
Welwyn Garden City	Hertfordshire	B.M.	Rich bright brown with yellow inlay. Fragment only. Diam. 3·2 cm. Ht. 1·4 cm.	Probably belongs to this Class. It came from a rich grave with gaming pieces and imported Italian objects of the late 1st c. B.C.	*A* ci (1967), 1 ff.
Glastonbury	Somerset	Glastonbury G21	Dark brown with yellow whirl. Diam. 3·4 cm.	From Lake Village	*Ge* ii

SCOTLAND

Two related beads from 'Scotland' are in the N.M.A.: no. FJ27, dark brownish glass with circumferential bands in yellow and green, diam. 3·5 cm., ht. 1·8 cm. perf. diam. 8 mm.; the other is smaller and paler pinkish-brown (FJ134) and may not belong to this Class.

SITE AND PARISH	COUNTY	MUSEUM & NO.	DESCRIPTION AND APPROX. DIMENSIONS	ASSOCIATIONS AND REMARKS	PUBLICATION
			TYPE (C), MISCELLANEOUS COLOURS		
			ENGLAND		
Colchester	Essex	Colchester Group 94	Finely made opaque white with pale blue circumferential bands overlaid by purple rays. Diam. 2·8 cm. Perf. diam. 7 mm. (fig. 15)	Group 94 is post A.D. 54 as it contained a coin of Nero and other objects. The groups are not regarded as reliable as some are muddled	May, T., *Catalogue of the Colchester and Essex Museum*
Seamills	Gloucester-shire	N.M.W.	About one-third bead. Opaque yellow core covered in milky white glass overlaid with rays and bands in purple. Diam. *c.* 3·2 cm. Ht. 1·3 cm. Perf. diam. *c.* 9 mm. Hour-glass perforation.	From a Flavian context.	Information from Miss J. Price, Cardiff University
			IRELAND		
? Ireland		A.M.	Whitish glass with circumferential bands and purple rays. Diam. 2·9 cm. Ht. 1·3 cm. Perf. diam. 4 mm.	From a miscellaneous collection	*ArJ* iii (1846), 355 and (1836), 123
Probably Ireland		N.M.A. FK21, 22, 23 (Bell Colln.)	Ground colour is green	This and the Den-hamstown bead must be from the same workshop. 'Dug up in a gravel-pit with human bones'	
Hawkhill, Kildare	Co. Offaly	Dublin 1945.323	Almost colourless ground. Finely made whirls in yellow. Diam. over 3 cm. Slightly hour-glass perforation	'Found in a quarry in hole among débris and ashes'	*JRSAI* cii, Pt. I (1972), 14–18
Denhamstown, Ardcath	Co. Meath	Dublin 1907.79	Almost colourless ground. Finely made whirls in yellow. Diam. over 3 cm. Slightly hour-glass perforation		*Ibid.* 14–18

DECORATED OR UNDECORATED GROUPS
(BOTH IRON AGE AND ROMAN IN DATE)

GROUP I
LARGE OR MEDIUM ANNULAR BEADS WITH STREAKY OR MOTTLED DESIGN

SITE AND PARISH	COUNTY	MUSEUM & NO.	DESCRIPTION AND APPROX. DIMENSIONS	ASSOCIATIONS AND REMARKS	PUBLICATION
			ENGLAND		
Hamworthy	Dorset	Poole	Fragment of large translucent amber glass bead with opaque yellow streaks. Diam. 2·9 cm. Perf. diam. 9 mm.	Other imported late pre-Roman and Roman beads and a glass armlet from this site	H. P. Smith, *History of Poole*, pl. 1, nos. 46 and 47
Hengistbury Head	Dorset	Christchurch	Bright translucent cobalt with opaque fawn streaks	Stray find. From hill-fort of pre-Roman date, probably 2nd–1st c. B.C. entrepôt	Found by Mr. Sidney Pester
Colchester	Essex	Colchester 99–105	Large dark translucent cobalt bead with white streaks mostly confined to outer edges. Diam. 3·6 cm. Ht. 1·1 cm. Perf. diam. 1·2 cm. (fig. 17)	Now thought to have come from Grave 53 (c. A.D. 25–50). These groups are not completely reliable	May, T. (1930)
Twyford and Owslebury	Hampshire		Dark blue with yellow streaks. Diam. c. 3·1 cm. No other details	Colden Common	
Sittingbourne	Kent	Way Colln. Drawings (S.A.L.)	Large blue streaks with yellow. No details		Dunkins, *Canterbury Congress*, 336
Leicester	Leicestershire	Leicester	Dark blue with yellow streaks. Diam. 2·7 cm. Ht. 1·4 cm. Perf. diam. 1 cm.	From level VI (A.D. 220) of Roman site	Kenyon, K. M. (1948), p. 269, fig. 93, no. 2
Charterhouse-on-Mendip	Somerset	A. C. Pass Colln. Bristol F2083	Dark greenish-brown	From early Roman lead mines (until around A.D. 170 imperially controlled)	*VCH Somerset* i, 334
Haughley	Suffolk	A.M. 1909.417	Brown with yellow streaks. Diam. c. 3 cm.		

SITE AND PARISH	COUNTY	MUSEUM & NO.	DESCRIPTION AND APPROX. DIMENSIONS	ASSOCIATIONS AND REMARKS	PUBLICATION
Wick Wood, Nettleton	Wiltshire	c/o Bath and Camerton Archaeological Society	Fragment, dark blue semi-translucent with opaque streaks. Diam. 2 cm. Ht. 1 cm. Perf. diam. 9 mm.	Stratified 'post-Constantinian'	Information from Mr. W. J. Wedlake

IRELAND

Several unassociated examples. One dark blue with white speckled decoration (diam. 2·3 cm. N.M.A. Bell Colln. FK44) is probably from Ireland. Another comes from Shanganagh, Dublin, light green translucent with yellow speckles (diam. 2·2 cm.) and is in C.M. There is nothing to suggest a date for these and they may well be post-6th c. in date.

SCOTLAND

SITE AND PARISH	COUNTY	MUSEUM & NO.	DESCRIPTION AND APPROX. DIMENSIONS	ASSOCIATIONS AND REMARKS	PUBLICATION
'Stirlingshire ?'		Falkirk Museum	Translucent bottle glass with yellow streaks. Diam. 3·3 cm. Ht. 9 mm. Perf. diam. 8 mm.	Thought to come from a site producing Roman pottery. Given by A. Craig	Unpublished

GROUP 2

MISCELLANEOUS SPIRAL-DECORATED BEADS

(See also Oldbury Class and North Scottish 'Spirals' and Horned Eye with Spirals (Classes 6 and 13 and Group 3))

ENGLAND

SITE AND PARISH	COUNTY	MUSEUM & NO.	DESCRIPTION AND APPROX. DIMENSIONS	ASSOCIATIONS AND REMARKS	PUBLICATION
Hengistbury Head	Dorset	B.M.	Globular blue with design in white related to spirals. Diam. 1·7 cm. Ht. 1·1 cm. Perf. diam. 5 mm.	From fort with Late Iron Age finds	*HH*, pl. xxx, 21; cf. Reinecke, S. (1911), v, pl. xiv, figs. 233 and 238
Ashley Camp, Ashley	Hampshire	Winchester	Half annular bead. Blue with one line of yellow spirals. Related to Oldbury type beads of Class 6	This seems to be an Iron Age stray from a site mostly producing later Roman material	
Kingscote	Gloucestershire		Fragment of small annular bead in blue glass with one white marvered spiral (originally there may have been 3 spirals). Diam. 1·2 cm. Ht. 5 mm. Perf. diam. 6 mm.	Surface find in the 1st c. A.D. area of the Roman villa.	Information from Mr. Graham Walker

SITE AND PARISH	COUNTY	MUSEUM & NO.	DESCRIPTION AND APPROX. DIMENSIONS	ASSOCIATIONS AND REMARKS	PUBLICATION
Weston-under-Penyard, Bollitree	Herefordshire	Gloucester 1734	Small dark blue with 3 white spirals—related to Oldbury Class. Diam. 1 cm. Ht. 7 mm. Perf. diam. 5 mm.	Early Roman site and some Belgic coins from the site as well	*JBAA* xxvii (1871), 211 ff.
Westerham	Kent		One row large yellow spirals. Diam. 2·3 cm. Ht. 1·4 cm. Perf. diam. 1 cm.	From an Iron Age hill-fort	Publication forthcoming after 1971. Information from W. Kent Border Archaeological Society
Corbridge (near)	Northumberland		Annular bottle-glass bead 'ornamented with spots of opaque blue and white paste each forming a small spiral on its surface'	Probably a stray find. Date unknown.	*ArJ* vii (1850), 192
Meare	Somerset	Taunton G15	Small globular bead with light blue spirals on dark blue. Diam. 6 mm. Ht. 5 mm. Perf. diam. 2 mm.	Occupation mostly 3rd to 1st c. B.C.	*Me* iii (1967)
Meare	Somerset	Taunton G46	Globular blue with opaque yellow running spiral. Diam. 1·6 cm. Ht. 1·1 cm. Perf. diam. very small (fig. 18, left)	Occupation mostly in 3rd–1st c. B.C.	*Me* iii (1967)
Meare	Somerset	Taunton G68EV	On necklace with 39 small yellow opaque annular beads and 4 Meare spiral beads. Light green triangular with opaque yellow spirals. Diam. *c.* 8 mm. Ht. 6 mm. Perf. diam. 3 mm.	Evidently contemporary with Meare spiral beads. See Class 10	*Me* iii (1967)
Worthing	Sussex	Worthing 4547	Annular, semi-translucent bright cobalt with 4 opaque yellow spirals. ? Related to Oldbury Class. Diam. *c.* 2 cm. Ht. irregular *c.* 8 mm. Perf. diam. 1 cm. (fig. 18, right)	Stray find from Heene Court, Bath Road, Worthing in 1913. A not uncommon type on the Continent, this can be dated from 2nd–1st c. B.C. sites at Ludwigshafen, Worms, Manching, etc.	Mentioned only in *SAC* xcviii (1960), 18

SITE AND PARISH	COUNTY	MUSEUM & NO.	DESCRIPTION AND APPROX. DIMENSIONS	ASSOCIATIONS AND REMARKS	PUBLICATION
Castle Bromwich	Warwickshire	Birmingham City Museum and Art Gallery	Annular natural glass with opaque yellow spirals. Slightly flattened upper and lower surfaces. Diam. 2·4 cm. Ht. irregular *c.* 7 mm. Perf. diam. 1·1 cm.	Stray find	Information from Mr. Nicholas Thomas

IRELAND

'Ireland'		Belfast 623.1924	Small annular dark cobalt with 3 white spirals like Weston-under-Penyard above. Diam. 1·1 cm. Ht. 6 mm. Perf. diam. 4 mm.	From a collection	

SCOTLAND

Traprain Law, Prestonkirk	East Lothian	N.M.A. 111.20–376	Rather square globular. Dark blue with four inset lime green roundels containing yellow spirals flattened where spirals. Diam. 1·5 cm. Ht. 1·4 cm. Uneven perforation.	Lowest level. Thought to be Late Iron Age or early Roman. (Reminiscent of gaming pieces from Welwyn Garden City (end 1st c. B.C.). See Stead, I. M. (1967))	*PSAS* liv (1919–20), 70, fig. 8, no. 10
Traprain Law, Prestonkirk	East Lothian	N.M.A. 1922.204	Opaque dark blue globular with 3 inlaid white spirals. Diam. 1·4 cm. Ht. 1 cm. Perf. diam. 8 mm.	Probably relates to Oldbury Class	*PSAS* lvi (1921–2), 227, fig. 24.1
Traprain Law, Prestonkirk	East Lothian	N.M.A. 1924.171	See cable beads		
Castle Island, Mochrum	Wigtownshire	Lord David Stuart, Old Place of Mochrum, Port William, Wigtown-shire	Globular translucent green with small blue spirals in white roundels. Diam. 1·6 cm. Ht. 1·5 cm. Perf. diam. 2 mm.	Found with other beads in N.E. building in 1910. Undated but cf. Welwyn Garden City gaming pieces quoted above and also marbles from Monquhitter (*PSAS* lxvi, 295)	*TDGNHAS* xxviii (1949–50)

SITE AND PARISH	COUNTY	MUSEUM & NO.	DESCRIPTION AND APPROX. DIMENSIONS	ASSOCIATIONS AND REMARKS	PUBLICATION

GROUP 3

MISCELLANEOUS HORNED BEADS (SOME WITH EYES OR SPIRALS)

(See also Classes 6 and 13 and Group 2)

ENGLAND

SITE AND PARISH	COUNTY	MUSEUM & NO.	DESCRIPTION AND APPROX. DIMENSIONS	ASSOCIATIONS AND REMARKS	PUBLICATION
Tarporley	Cheshire	C.M.	Translucent light bottle glass with 4 blue horns with white spirals. Diam. 3·3 cm. Ht. 1·2 cm. Perf. diam. 1·1 cm. (fig. 19, left)	Found in 1775. Identical to the bead from Newstead below	
Silchester	Hampshire	Reading	Fragment. Dark blue semi-translucent with yellow and brown horn. Diam. 2·4 cm. Ht. 1·2 cm. Perf. diam. 8 mm.	Occupation 1st–5th c. A.D.	For refs., see Collingwood and Richmond, *The Archaeology of Roman Britain* (revised ed., 1969). See also Boon, G. C. (1957)
Cooling	Kent	Rochester	Large blue bead, drum-shaped with large very projecting horns surrounded by opaque white rings. Diam. 2·5 cm. Ht. 2·3 cm. Perf. diam. 8mm. (fig. 19, right)	This is a Continental La Tène II import from a later Romano-British salt panning site in an Antonine level. Exact parallels from Berne and Zollikofen. See Viollier, D. (1916), pl. 32, nos. 11 and 12	Information from Mr. M. Syddell. To be published in *ACt*
Skeffington	Leicestershire	Leicester	Translucent bottle glass white swags and 4 opaque white eyes with spirals in light brown translucent glass. Diam. 3 cm. Ht. 1·4 cm.	Stray find 1966. Date uncertain	
Hunsbury, Hardingstone	Northampton-shire		One 'blue with white knobs' (lost)	Iron Age hill-fort ? 4th–1st c. B.C.	Fell, C. (1936) with refs. to earlier publications
Chesters Fort	Northumber-land	Chesters	Very dark blue. Two horned eyes, in blue and yellow. Diam. 3 cm. Ht. 1·6 cm. Perf. diam. 1·1 cm.	Site occupied about A.D. 122–383	
Icklingham	Suffolk	Bury St. Edmunds	Black ground with green or yellow horns	With a hoard of about A.D. 400	Clarke, R., *East Anglia* (1960)

SITE AND PARISH	COUNTY	MUSEUM & NO.	DESCRIPTION AND APPROX. DIMENSIONS	ASSOCIATIONS AND REMARKS	PUBLICATION
			IRELAND		
Loughey, Donaghadee	Co. Down	B.M. 62.7–1.19	Small blue bead with yellow and blue cable and three tiny opaque yellow horns (fig. 23, 2)	On necklace including Meare spirals of Class 6. Dated by Nauheim type brooch, 1st c. B.C.–1st c. A.D.	*ArJ* xiii (1856), 407, and Jope, E. M. (1957) and (1960)
Lagore Crannog	Co. Meath	Dublin 1498	Fragment of blue bead with bottle glass eyes with white opaque spirals	There are some early beads (1st c.) from a mainly 7th c. occupation	*PRIA* liii, Section C (1950–1)
	'Ireland'	Benn Colln., Belfast, 1912:172	Bottle glass bead with 4 eyes in opaque white and translucent blue. Diam. 2·3 cm. Ht. 1 cm. Perf. diam. 6 mm.	No information	
			SCOTLAND		
Newstead	Roxburghshire	N.M.A. FRA895	Half natural green glass bead, blue and white spirals, Diam. 3.3 cm. Ht. 1·4 cm. Perf. diam. 1·6 cm.	Site occupied about A.D. 80–200	*Ne*, 336–7
Newstead	Roxburghshire	N.M.A. FRA398	Opaque grey green with two horned eyes in yellow in white. Diam. 2·5 cm.		
			WALES		
Caerleon	Monmouth-shire	N.M.W.	Crimson glass with blue-green clear glass knobs. Diam. *c.* 2·3 cm. Ht. 12 mm. Perf. diam. 9 mm.	Among miscellaneous beads. No date. From Castle Villa	Lee, *Catalogue Museum Caerleon* (1862), pl. xxviii. See also *ArJ* viii (1851), 160
Whitton, nr. Barry	Glamorgan-shire	?N.M.W.	Half of big irregular yellow bead with large translucent brown horns (originally four). Diam. irregular. Ht. 1·8 cm.	Roman villa site occupied earlier *c.* 1st c. B.C. to A.D. 300	Information from Dr. M. Jarrett

SITE AND PARISH	COUNTY	MUSEUM & NO.	DESCRIPTION AND APPROX. DIMENSIONS	ASSOCIATIONS AND REMARKS	PUBLICATION

GROUP 4
MULTI-EYED WITH SMALL EYES SET IN ROUNDELS ('GARROW TOR' TYPE)

ENGLAND

SITE AND PARISH	COUNTY	MUSEUM & NO.	DESCRIPTION AND APPROX. DIMENSIONS	ASSOCIATIONS AND REMARKS	PUBLICATION
Garrow Tor (Bodmin Moor)	Cornwall		Blue ground, orange background to small eyes. Diam. 1·5 cm. Ht. 1·1 cm. Perf. diam. about 6 mm. (fig. 20)	Hut on Bodmin Moor with pottery not closely datable but perhaps 4th–3rd c. B.C.	See Hencken, H. O'N., *Archaeology of Cornwall and Scilly* (Methuen, 1932)
Cirencester	Gloucestershire	Cirencester A273	Dark blue ground with brighter blue and white eyes, in mustard-coloured roundels. Diam. 1·4 cm. Ht. 1 cm.	Unstratified in Roman town	
Silchester	Hampshire	Reading	Turquoise ground mustard background to eyes. Diam. 1·7 cm. Ht. 9 mm. Perf. diam. 6 mm.	Unstratified. Occupation from *c*. 80 B.C. to early 5th c. A.D. but a La Tène I brooch also came from the site and this may also be the date of this bead	Boon, 'Belgic and Roman Silchester: Excavations of 1954–8', *A* cii (1969), 53. The Silchester glass is to be published by Boon for the Reading Museum
No provenance	? Britain	B.M. Slade Colln. etc.	Several examples	For information see footnote 4, p. 62	

IRELAND

SITE AND PARISH	COUNTY	MUSEUM & NO.	DESCRIPTION AND APPROX. DIMENSIONS	ASSOCIATIONS AND REMARKS	PUBLICATION
'Antrim'		N.M. Ireland, Dublin, 1908–299	Opaque turquoise ground with eyes on same coloured background. Globular. Diam. 1·5 cm. Ht. 1·3 cm. Perf. diam. 2 mm.	No details. Probably found with bead below	
'Antrim'		N.M. Ireland 1908–300	Ground similar. Eyes on yellowish background. Diam. 1·6 cm. Ht. 1·6 cm.	No details	

Related but dissimilar beads with eyes in roundels are also in Irish collections. Two annular examples—both with roundels containing 'eyes' are nos. Belfast 1912:173 and (from Antrim). The ground colour of both of them is greenish; they are also differently coloured in the roundels.

SITE AND PARISH	COUNTY	MUSEUM & NO.	DESCRIPTION AND APPROX. DIMENSIONS	ASSOCIATIONS AND REMARKS	PUBLICATION

GROUP 5

WAVE BEADS

(A) TRANSLUCENT BLUE ANNULAR AND GLOBULAR BEADS WITH OPAQUE WHITE OR YELLOW WAVE

ENGLAND

SITE AND PARISH	COUNTY	MUSEUM & NO.	DESCRIPTION AND APPROX. DIMENSIONS	ASSOCIATIONS AND REMARKS	PUBLICATION
Pangbourne	Berkshire	C.M., Beck Colln. 1697	Semi-translucent blue with angular upright wave. Diam. 2 cm. Ht. 8 mm.	Stray find. (? Dark Ages)	
Yewden, Hambledon	Buckingham-shire	Hambledon Villa Museum	Irregular wave of more than one strand on translucent blue. Diam. 1·5 cm. Ht. 8 mm.	Villa occupied shortly before Roman Conquest, approx. A.D. 40–400	*A* lxxi (1921), 141 ff.
Lakenheath	Cambridge-shire	C.M., Beck Colln. 1715 XLVII A3a	Irregular wave bright cobalt ground semi-translucent. Diam. 1·8 cm. Ht. 6 mm.	From collection	
Lakenheath	Cambridge-shire	? C.M.	Small with regular angular wave. Diam. 1·4 cm. Ht. 9 mm.	From mainly Iron Age A site (? 3rd c. B.C.) but with little later scatter	*PCAS* xlii (1949), 110
Wilderspool, Warrington	Cheshire–Lancashire borders	Warrington 1298	Opaque blue with wide 2-strand wave. Diam. 1·8 cm. Ht. 1 cm.	Roman site, ? earlier occupation	May, T. (1904); Thompson, F. H. (1965)
Ashton	Cheshire	Chester 9R61	Semi-translucent blue with irregular rather flat wave. Diam. 1·8 cm. Ht. 8 mm.	Surface find 5 miles from Chester on line of Watling Street	*JCNWAAHS* xxxv, Pt. 1 (1942) 58
Nor' nour, Scilly	Cornwall	St. Mary's, Scilly	2-strand irregular wave or translucent light blue. Diam. 1·4 cm. Ht. 6 mm.	Site mainly 2nd c. A.D. but began earlier and lasted till 4th c.	*ArJ* cxxiv (1967)
Probus	Cornwall	Truro	White rather angular wave. Fragment. Diam. 2·1 cm. Ht. 1 cm. Perf. diam. 8 mm.	From Romano-British camp of Carvossa. Occupation into late Roman or ? early 5th c.	Information from Mr. H. L. Douch
Glassonby (Grayson Lands Tumulus)	Cumberland	Carlisle 262	Irregular wave on light blue semi-translucent glass. Diam. 1·8 cm. Ht. 9 mm.	Secondary stray in earlier tumulus. ? Dark Ages	*TCW*, n.s. i (1901), 295

SITE AND PARISH	COUNTY	MUSEUM & NO.	DESCRIPTION AND APPROX. DIMENSIONS	ASSOCIATIONS AND REMARKS	PUBLICATION
No location	Derbyshire	B.M.	Bright cobalt with irregular wave. Diam. 2 cm. Ht. 7 mm.	Found in 1790 and now strung with others from Derbyshire	
Whitcombe	Dorset	Dorchester	6 beads. Diams. about 1·8 cm. and perf. diams. 8 mm.	On necklace with burial accompanied by Samian ware of A.D. 96–110 and 2 wooden beads among others	Information from Mrs. Gertrude Aitken
Cirencester	Gloucester-shire	Cirencester C922	Light blue with ? white wave. Diam. 2·2 cm. Ht. 1·1 cm. Perf. diam. 1 cm.	Unstratified in Roman town	
Fairford	Gloucester-shire			Stray find. c/o Mrs. Llewellyn Jones, Manor Farm	
Micheldever	Hampshire	B.M. 63.1–20, 5	Regular wave. Diam. 1·6 cm. Ht. 1 cm.	Unstratified from site producing much Roman and some post-Roman material	*ArJ* vi (1849), 399
Silchester	Hampshire	Reading	Rich dark cobalt with regular wave. Diam. 1·5 cm. Ht. 8 mm.	Belgic-Roman site occupied *c.* 1st–5th c. A.D.	Boon, G. C. (1957)
Weston-under-Penyard, Bollitree	Hereford-shire	Hereford 7630	Dark blue with rather irregular wave. Diam. 1·6 cm. Ht. 6 mm.	Coin of Cunobelin	G. H. Jack, 'Excavations on the site of Ariconium', *TWNFC* (1923), pl. 12, fig. 2
Weston-under-Penyard, Bollitree	Hereford-shire	Gloucester 1760	Semi-translucent blue with very small angular wave. Diam. 1·1 cm. Ht. 6 mm.	With many other early Roman beads from early Roman (perhaps pre-Roman) lead-mining site	*JBAA* xxvii (1871), 211 ff.
Northchurch	Hertfordshire	B.M. 93.4–7	Translucent light blue with irregular wave. Diam. 1·7 cm. Ht. 6 mm.	This site also produced Dark Ages pin and brooch but not necessarily associated	
Verulamium	Hertfordshire	Verulamium (St. Albans)	Blue with white wave. Diam. 1·6 cm. Ht. 9 mm. Perf. diam. 3 mm.	Stratified A.D. 155–60	Frere, S. (1972), fig. 79, no. 71
Richborough	Kent		Very irregular and angular wave. Diam. 2 cm. Ht. 9 mm.	Pit 54. 21 feet down *c.* A.D. 400. Threaded on bronze wire	*Rich* iii, 80, no. 25 and pl. XI, no. 25

SITE AND PARISH	COUNTY	MUSEUM & NO.	DESCRIPTION AND APPROX. DIMENSIONS	ASSOCIATIONS AND REMARKS	PUBLICATION
Leicester (Jewry Wall)	Leicester-shire	Leicester	Dark blue with yellow rather irregular wave. Diam. 1·7 cm. Ht. 8 mm.	Stratified A.D. 150–60. Another stratified c. A.D. 400	Kenyon, K. M. (1948), fig. 93, no. 3 and p. 269
Risby Warren (Sandyheath)	Lincolnshire	Scunthorpe, R104	Half, semi-opaque cobalt with yellow wave. Diam. 1·8 cm. Ht. 6 mm. Perf. diam. 8 mm.	Found in silt of late 1st c. A.D.	
Walbrook, London	London	Formerly Guildhall Museum 18.642	Half light blue bead with irregular wave. Diam. 1·7 cm. Ht. 7 mm.	? Dark Ages	
Irchester	Northampton-shire		Thin yellow trail. Diam. 2·4 cm. Ht. 1·2 cm. Perf. diam. 1 cm.	Unstratified but probably Roman period	*ArJ* cxxiv (1967), 119, fig. 7, no. 2
Great Chesters	Northumber-land	Chesters Museum 2506	Cobalt blue with irregular wave. Diam. 1·7 cm. Ht. 8 mm.	Roman	
Probably from Chesters fort	Northumber-land	Chesters Museum 1361	Very dark ground with greyish white wave. Diam. 2·1 cm. Ht. 1 cm.	Probably between A.D. 122–383 (19th c. find)	
Milking Gap Romano-British homestead	Northumber-land	Newcastle-upon-Tyne	Part of blue bead with irregular wave. Diam. 1·7 cm. Ht. 7 mm.	Occupation suggested from A.D. 122–80. Now thought to antedate the middle of Hadrian's reign	*AA*, 4th s. xv (1938), 345; see Richmond, I. A. (ed.) (1956), p. 63
Wroxeter	Shropshire	Rowley's House Museum, Shrewsbury	Bright cobalt. Diam. 1·5 cm. Ht. 6 mm. Perf. diam. 5 mm.	From topsoil of Roman town	Information from Dr. John Houghton, Shrewsbury
Camerton	Somerset	Bristol, Skinner Colln. F2313	Blue with rather irregular white wave. Diam. 1·7 cm. Ht. 8 mm.	Site produced Saxon and earlier finds	*VCH Somerset* and Wedlake, W. J. (1958)
Charterhouse-on-Mendip	Somerset	? Beck Colln. C.M.		From Roman lead mines, probably mid-1st c. A.D.	See *VCH Somerset* for this site
Meare Lake Village	Somerset	Taunton G38 and another	One dark opaque with flattened surfaces.: diam. 1·5 cm.; ht. 7 mm.; perf. diam. 4 mm. Half another: diam. 1·7 cm.; ht. 4 mm. Perf. diam. 1 cm.	From Lake Village. (At least G38 resembles the Arras variety rather than the Roman period beads)	*Me* iii

SITE AND PARISH	COUNTY	MUSEUM & NO.	DESCRIPTION AND APPROX. DIMENSIONS	ASSOCIATIONS AND REMARKS	PUBLICATION
Monkton Combe	Somerset		Very battered and perhaps opaque. Diam. 1·7 cm.		
Coddenham	Suffolk	Ipswich	Battered. Irregular wave. Diam. 1·4 cm. Ht. 7 mm. Perf. diam. 6 mm.	Roman site, perhaps Combretonium	
Martlesham Heath	Suffolk	Ipswich	Identical to one from Whitton Roman villa (see below)	Chance find	Information from Ipswich Museum
Whitton Roman villa	Suffolk	Ipswich	Translucent with rather irregular wave. Diam. 1·5 cm. Ht. 8 mm. And another	Villa reputedly occupied 2nd–4th c. A.D.	*PSIA* xxi (1931–3), 240, 249 and figs. 16, 17
Bagshot Heath	Surrey		No details	Early find	*A* vii (1785)
Farley Heath, Albury	Surrey	Guildford	3 examples	Romano-Celtic temple site	*AnJ* xviii (1938) and *A* xxxiv (1852)
Nr. Rugby	Warwickshire		Slightly flattened around perforation. Irregular wave on light blue translucent ground. Diam. 2 cm. Ht. 1·3 cm. Perf. diam. 5 mm.	Unstratified in Roman *Tripontium*	*TPBAS* (Nov. 1971)
Bokerly Dyke, Woodyates	Wiltshire–Dorset borders	Salisbury	Translucent light blue with yellow wave. Diam. 1·7 cm. Ht. 1 cm. Perf. diam. 6 mm.		Pitt-Rivers, A. H. L. F. (1888), p. 171
Kennet	Wiltshire	Devizes 135	Opaque slaty blue with regular wave	Associated with small schist hone	
Longbridge Deverill Cow Down	Wiltshire	Devizes	Semi-translucent with irregular scrabble. Diam. 1·35 cm. Ht. 7 mm. Smaller than usual	Ditch of enclosure. Probably from Iron Age 'B', ? 3rd c. B.C.	Forthcoming. Information from Mrs. Sonia Hawkes
Mildenhall	Wiltshire	c/o Adams, Landulph Rectory, Saltash, Cornwall	Half of light translucent blue bead. Diam. 1·7 cm. Ht. 8 mm.	Blackfields Roman site. This bead found near site of Saxon burial	
Almondbury Camp, Huddersfield	Yorkshire	Tolson Memorial Museum, Huddersfield	Squarish, globular, dark greenish-blue with cream wave. Diam. 1·3 cm. Ht. 1 cm. (fig. 21, no. 2)	From Iron Age camp	Information from the late Dr. W. J. Varley

SITE AND PARISH	COUNTY	MUSEUM & NO.	DESCRIPTION AND APPROX. DIMENSIONS	ASSOCIATIONS AND REMARKS	PUBLICATION
Arras	Yorkshire	B.M. 80.8.2. 142–144. For full reference to museum numbers see Stead, I. M. (1965)	Small with regular wave. Diam. 1·2 cm. Ht. 7 mm.	From Arras culture barrow. Found in 1817	Stead, I. M. (1965), pp. 59–60
Whitby	Yorkshire	Whitby	Semi-translucent with irregular wave. Diam. 1·6 cm. Ht. 6 mm.	Found in Knipe Howe tumulus	

SCOTLAND

SITE AND PARISH	COUNTY	MUSEUM & NO.	DESCRIPTION AND APPROX. DIMENSIONS	ASSOCIATIONS AND REMARKS	PUBLICATION
Haughton-Alford	Aberdeenshire	N.M.A. FJ22	Bright, translucent with rather irregular wave. Diam. 2·0 cm. Ht. 8 mm.		
Castle O'er	Dumfries-shire	Dumfries	Fragment with irregular wave. Diam. 1·3 cm. Ht. 6 mm.	Near the fort. Many others from this locality, mostly melon beads	
Traprain Law, Prestonkirk	E. Lothian	N.M.A. V21.342	Light, translucent with irregular wave. Diam. 1·9 cm. Ht. 8 mm.	From 4th level	PSAS lv (1920–1), 172
Traprain Law, Prestonkirk	E. Lothian	N.M.A. 1923.143	Almost opaque. Flat facets around perforation. Diam. 1·3 cm. Ht. 7 mm.		PSAS lvii (1922–3), 195
Castle Haven Fort, Borgue	Kirkcud-brightshire	Robertson House, Castlehaven	Irregular wave. Diam. 2·0 cm.	This fort is not closely datable but a brooch of Elizabeth Fowler's 'D7' type suggests a slightly post-Roman date for one phase	PSAS xli (1906–7), 79
Covesea	Morayshire	N.M.A. HM209	Bright, semi-translucent	Various finds from the site include fragments of imported glass of the 2nd c. A.D.	PSAS lxv (1930–1), 177
Newstead	Roxburgh-shire	N.M.A. FRA897, 899, 901, 902 and from Mr. Mason's Colln., Selkirk	5 examples. Diams. 2·1, 2·0, 1·9, 1·6, and 1·4 cm.	Occupation about A.D. 80–200	Some in Ne, pl. xcli, 17, 19, 23, 26
'Scotland'		N.M.A., Duns Colln. FJ95	Opaque grey-blue. Half only. Perforation small. Diam. 1·5 cm. Ht. 9 mm.		

SITE AND PARISH	COUNTY	MUSEUM & NO.	DESCRIPTION AND APPROX. DIMENSIONS	ASSOCIATIONS AND REMARKS	PUBLICATION
			WALES		
Bryn-yr-Hen-Bobl	Anglesey	N.M.W. 37/7/46	Translucent dark blue. Diam. 1·7 cm. Ht. 7 mm.	Secondary in megalithic tomb	Grimes, W. F., *Prehistory of Wales*, p. 156 and refs. p. 38
Nevin	Caernarvonshire		Two examples. One lighter than the other, very irregular scrabble. Diams. 2·0 and 1·7 cm. Hts. 8 and 5 mm.	From Garn Boduan fort. Thought to be about A.D. 600, but could be earlier	*ArJ* cxvii (1962), pl. VI, 8
Prestatyn	Flintshire	c/o Prestatyn Council	Light blue with irregular wave. Diam. 1·8 cm. Ht. 1·1 cm. Perf. diam. 5 mm.	From Roman site. Many melon beads but also one thought to be post-Roman	Ellis Davies, *Prehistoric and Roman Remains of Flintshire* (1949), p. 303, is very similar to this bead. See also *AC* (1937)
Whitton, nr. Barry	Glamorganshire	N.M.W.	2 examples. Diams. 1·7 and 1·6 cm.	From Roman villa. Topsoil occupation 1st c. B.C.–A.D. 300	Information from Dr. Jarrett, University College of S. Wales, Cardiff
Caerleon	Monmouthshire	N.M.W.	Irregular 2-strand scrabble on translucent ground. Diam. 1·9 cm. Ht. 7 mm.	'Near the Castle mound'	Lee, *Catalogue of the Antiquities of Caerleon*, pl. XXVIII, fig. 8
Caerleon	Monmouthshire	N.M.W.	Translucent with 2-strand irregular scrabble. Diam. 1·7 cm. Ht. 8 mm. (fig. 21, no. 1)	Seems to be unrecorded. Probably from 1909 excavation	
Caerleon	Monmouthshire	N.M.W.	Dark with irregular wave. Diam. 1·9 cm. Ht. 9 mm.	From Broadway drain near legionary fortress stratified A.D. 230–96	Ellis Davies, *Prehistoric and Roman Remains of Flintshire* (1949), p. 310, fig. 127, 5, is an almost similar bead. See also *AC* xcii (1937), 208–32
Usk	Monmouthshire	N.M.W.	Globular with irregular angular wave. Diam. 1·3 cm. Ht. 1·3 cm. Perf. diam. 4 mm. Slight flattening above and below perforation	Found in 1968 excavation in Roman fort occupied A.D. 55–60 and again later	Information from excavator

SITE AND PARISH	COUNTY	MUSEUM & NO.	DESCRIPTION AND APPROX. DIMENSIONS	ASSOCIATIONS AND REMARKS	PUBLICATION
(B) OPAQUE BLUE ANNULAR OR GLOBULAR BEADS WITH BLUE OR PURPLE WAVE					
ENGLAND					
Hamworthy	Dorset	Poole	2 opaque blue globular beads with opaque purplish black angular wave. Diam. 1·8 cm. Ht. 1·6 cm. Perf. diam. 7 mm. (fig. 21, no. 5)	From pre-Roman and early Roman site with imported Celtic bracelet, etc.	Smith, H. P., *History of Poole*, Pt. 1, pp. 46–7
Glastonbury	Somerset	Glastonbury G18	Slaty blue opaque annular with blue-black wave. Diam. 1·7 cm. Ht. 8 mm. Perf. diam. 7 mm. (fig. 21, no. 6)	Pre-Roman site, 3rd to 1st c. B.C. or early 1st c. A.D.	*Gl* ii
(C) GREEN OR NATURAL GREENISH TRANSLUCENT GLASS ANNULAR BEADS WITH WHITE, YELLOW OR BLUE WAVE					
ENGLAND					
Carrawburgh	Northumberland	Chesters	Greenish-gold with yellow scrabble design. Diam. 1·7 cm. Ht. 8 mm. Perf. irregular small	The site was occupied from *c.* A.D. 122–383. This bead may belong to the very end of the occupation and be of early Teutonic origin	
Woodeaton	Oxfordshire	A.M., Gordon Colln. 1900:R108	Large annular natural glass bead with opaque yellow rather crowded wave. Diam. 2·6 cm., Ht. 1·1 cm. Perf. diam. 2 mm.	Roman site but occupation runs from Iron Age to post-Roman	*O* xix (1954), 15–37, for Romano-Celtic temple. (Note this bead comes from old excavations in the area)
Meare	Somerset	Taunton G78	Fragment large natural glass with blue wave. Diam. 3·2 cm. Ht. 1·5 cm. Perf. diam. 1·5 cm.	From settlement of 3rd to 1st c. B.C.	*Me* iii
Meare	Somerset	Taunton G83	More globular light green with opaque yellow inlay. Diam. 7 mm. Ht. 7 mm. Perf. diam. 5 mm. (fig. 21, no. 3)	Belongs to this group though barrel-shaped	*Me* iii
Farley Heath, Albury	Surrey	? B.M.	Fragment translucent grass green with white wave. Diam. 2 cm. Perf. diam. 1 cm.	Found in 1847 in Romano-Celtic temple site. Cf. Newstead, below	*A* xxxiv (1852), pl. V, no. 11. See also *AnJ* xviii (1938), 371

SITE AND PARISH	COUNTY	MUSEUM & NO.	DESCRIPTION AND APPROX. DIMENSIONS	ASSOCIATIONS AND REMARKS	PUBLICATION
Queen's Barrow, Arras	Yorkshire	York	Annular beads of almost colourless clear glass and opaque yellow wave. Diam. 1·2 cm. Ht. 4 mm. Perf. diam. 6 mm.	Iron Age burial, ? 4th–3rd c. B.C. Note the glass is not so colourless as the Meare series. See Arras beads (Class 1) for relevant discussion	*A* lx (1906), and see Stead, I. M. (1965)

SCOTLAND

SITE AND PARISH	COUNTY	MUSEUM & NO.	DESCRIPTION AND APPROX. DIMENSIONS	ASSOCIATIONS AND REMARKS	PUBLICATION
Newstead	Roxburgh-shire	N.M.A. FRA903	Translucent grass green with white wave. Diam. 1·8 cm. Ht. 8 mm. Perf. diam. 7 mm.	Roman fort occupied *c*. A.D. 80–200	*Ne*, pl. xci
No provenance	'Wigtonshire'	N.M.A. FJ80	Part of translucent greenish-yellow with slightly raised yellow opaque wave. Diam. 2·1 cm. Ht. 6 mm. Perf. diam. 7 mm.	Galloway Collns. 1898. Possibly post-Roman	

WALES

SITE AND PARISH	COUNTY	MUSEUM & NO.	DESCRIPTION AND APPROX. DIMENSIONS	ASSOCIATIONS AND REMARKS	PUBLICATION
Caerhun	Caernarvon-shire	Llandudno, Rapallo House	Light greeny-blue with yellow wave. Diam. 1·8 cm. Ht. 9 mm. Perf. diam. 6 mm.	Flavian period fort	*AC* xci (1936)

(D) 'BLACK' (VERY DARK COLOURS APPEARING BLACK)

(i) *Annular with White Wave*

Several come from England, Ireland, and Scotland, e.g., N.M.A., Bell Colln. nos. FK37, 38, 39 and 42. FK45, 'perhaps Ireland', and in Stranraer Museum, Wigtown (no. 1945.326A) is an example perhaps from the Glenluce Sands. From the Beck Colln. in Cambridge, nos. 1320 J and H and others are said to have come from Co. Antrim. From England 2 examples are from a Saxon necklace from Mildenhall, Wilts. (Devizes Museum S30 and 31 with saucer brooches) and a similar one, undated, from Cheverell, Wilts. (Devizes Museum S3). Another from Faversham, Kent, is in the Beck Colln. at C.M. (no. 1677) and is probably Saxon, as are also one example from Lakenheath in the same collection and one from Ling Hill, Whitby, in the Whitby Museum. The general impression is that these black and white examples may be slightly later than the late 4th c. A.D. when the annular beads with coloured waves seem to have first reached England from Frankish areas.

SITE AND PARISH	COUNTY	MUSEUM & NO.	DESCRIPTION AND APPROX. DIMENSIONS	ASSOCIATIONS AND REMARKS	PUBLICATION
			(ii) *Annular with Irregular Yellow Scrawl*		
			IRELAND		
'Northern Ireland'		B.M. 71.2–10.54	Half bead. Opaque black with irregular yellow wavy scrawls. Diam. 2·5 cm. Ht. 1·1 cm.		
Several others from Ireland in the British Museum					
			WALES		
Caernarvon	Caernarvon-shire	Caernarvon, Segontium Museum	Opaque black with irregular yellow wavy scrawls. Diam. *c.* 2·5 cm.	From fort erected in late 1st c. A.D. but unstratified and probably later	Wheeler, R. E. M. *Segontium and the Roman Occupation of Wales* (1924), p. 169
Caerleon	Monmouth-shire	N.M.W. CY50	Large black bead with irregular yellow scrabble. Diam. 3·1 cm. Ht. 1·2 cm. Perf. diam. 1·2 cm.	From Roman legionary bath-house (described in old catalogue as 'Castle Villa'). This may be Roman or a later stray	Lee, *Catalogue of the Museum at Caerleon*, pl. XXVIII, fig. 6. See *AC* (1929)
			(iii) *Annular with Various Coloured Waves*		
			ENGLAND		
Silchester	Hampshire	Reading	Half a large flat bead decorated with white concentric bands and light blue wave between. Diam. 3·2 cm. Ht. 7 mm. Perf. diam. 9 mm.	From Atrebatic town occupied before the conquest and throughout Roman period. Related to a very similar dark green bead decorated in green from Richborough, Kent	See Boon, G. C. (1957) and in *A* cii (1969)
Silchester	Hampshire	Reading	Several other smaller annular bead decorated with waves in light blue, or yellow or grey	From town occupied throughout Roman period	See Boon, G. C. (1957) and in *A* cii (1969)
Richborough	Kent	Richborough	Several black beads with red wave, double white swag with blue dots, etc.	Probably these begin to appear around A.D. 400 and may be Frankish	Some illustrated in *Rich* iv, 149 pl. iv
London	London	Formerly Guildhall Museum 3961	Sharp angled blue wave. Diam. 1·5 cm. Ht. 9 mm. Slightly hour-glass perforation		

SITE AND PARISH	COUNTY	MUSEUM & NO.	DESCRIPTION AND APPROX. DIMENSIONS	ASSOCIATIONS AND REMARKS	PUBLICATION
Wolstonbury Hill, Pycombe	Sussex	Lewes	Azure blue scrabble cm. Ht. 6 mm. Perf. diam. 5 mm.	From floor of hut with late 4th c. A.D. pottery. This bead was compared by Kendrick to some from a hoard at Icklingham dated c. A.D. 400	*SAC* lxxvi (1935), 38, and *ibid.* xciv (1956), 70
Monkton Downs	Wiltshire	Devizes 131	Bead comparable to Wolstonbury, Sussex	With other beads, not closely datable and not necessarily associated	
Wick Wood, Nettleton	Wiltshire		Badly made with bright azure wave. Diam. 1·3 cm. Ht. 6 mm. Perf. diam. 4 mm.	Stratified late 4th c. A.D.	Information from Mr. W. J. Wedlake
Wick Wood, Nettleton	Wiltshire		Another of dark green with yellow wave and wide perforation	Romano-British and later site	Information from Mr. W. J. Wedlake

IRELAND

'Northern Ireland'		B.M. 71.12.10.48	Rather like Wolstonbury but wave is bright cobalt blue	No details	

(iv) *Globular Beads with Yellow Wave*

ENGLAND

Chesters Fort	Northumberland	Chesters	Wide pear-shaped shiny black. Max. diam. 1·6 cm. Ht. 1·5 cm. Very small perforation	May date from A.D. 122–383; found in 19th c. (An armlet from a Roman context at Hamworthy (in Poole Museum) is made in identical manner)	
Mildenhall	Wiltshire	Devizes 129	Badly burnt. Max. diam. 1·5 cm. Ht. 1·3 cm. Small perforation (fig. 21, no. 6)	Probably from Roman site. Very similar to Chesters example above	

SITE AND PARISH	COUNTY	MUSEUM & NO.	DESCRIPTION AND APPROX. DIMENSIONS	ASSOCIATIONS AND REMARKS	PUBLICATION
(E) OPAQUE YELLOW ANNULAR BEADS WITH COLOURED WAVE					
ENGLAND					
Danebury Rings, Nether Wallop	Hampshire		More globular than normally. Very abraded and now grey. Originally yellow. Rather straight-sided. Irregular slaty-blue wave. Diam. 1·5 cm. Ht. 1·1 cm. Perf. diam. 6 mm.	Hill-fort. From layer thought to date from about 100 B.C.	Information from Barry Cunliffe
Meare	Somerset	Taunton G135, G39, G20	2 examples (1 about 1·5 cm. diam.) and have wide perforations and green waves. Ht. c. 5 mm. Another half-bead, smaller, may have had brown wave	From Meare pre-Roman site of 3rd–1st c. B.C.	Me iii
All Cannings Cross	Wiltshire	Devizes	Yellow ground with brown wave. Diam. 1·2 cm. Ht. 7 mm. Perf. diam. 2 mm.	Iron Age A site with long occupation	Cunnington, M. E. (1923), pl. 18, no. 15 and p. 120
Beckford	Worcester-shire		Diam. 1·4 cm. Ht. 8 mm. Perf. diam. 5 mm. (off-centre). Irregular wave or swag. Filling lost	Found with duck-stamped and linear-tooled wares	Information from W. J. Britnell, Dept. Archaeology, University College, Cardiff
Burton Fleming	Yorkshire		Small fragment of bead similar to Meare example above. Double wave or swag filling now lost	From an Iron Age cemetery	Information from T. C. M. Brewster
(F) OPAQUE WHITE ANNULAR BEADS WITH YELLOW WAVE					
ENGLAND					
Madmarston Camp, Swalcliffe	Oxfordshire	A.M.		Near top of rampart of Middle Iron Age hill-fort reoccupied during 4th c.	O xxv (1960), 38 and 46; fig. 19, no. 17
(G) TRANSLUCENT 'AMBER' (REDDISH-BROWN) BEADS WITH YELLOW WAVE					
ENGLAND					
Nor' nour, Scilly	Cornwall	St. Mary's, Scilly	Rust colour probably originally translucent. The wave is double in some parts. Diam. 8 mm. Ht. 3 mm. Perf. diam. 4 mm.	From a house occupied into late Roman period. It was a brooch factory in the 2nd c. A.D.	ArJ cxxiv (1967)

SITE AND PARISH	COUNTY	MUSEUM & NO.	DESCRIPTION AND APPROX. DIMENSIONS	ASSOCIATIONS AND REMARKS	PUBLICATION
			SCOTLAND		
Lochspouts Crannog, Maybole	Ayrshire	N.M.A. HW20	Diam. 1·9 cm. Ht. 1 cm. Perf. diam. 8 mm.	Early Roman period. Probably 1st–2nd c. A.D.	*PSAS* xv (1880–1), 110

GROUP 6

ANNULAR BEADS

(i) LARGE BEADS OF VARIOUS COLOURS

ENGLAND

SITE AND PARISH	COUNTY	MUSEUM & NO.	DESCRIPTION AND APPROX. DIMENSIONS	ASSOCIATIONS AND REMARKS	PUBLICATION
Santon Downham	Cambridge-shire	C.M.	Half only. Blue. Diam. 3·2 cm. Ht. 9 mm. Perf. diam. 1·4 cm.	With 1st c. A.D. finds	Fox, C. (1923) p. 104
Nor' nour, Scilly	Cornwall	St. Mary's, Scilly	Blue. ? fragment of ring bead. Diam. *c.* 3 cm.	Site occupied throughout Roman period	*ArJ* cxxiv (1967)
Gussage All Saints	Dorset		Fragment. Opaque green, almost turquoise, ring-bead, rounded section. Diam. 3·4 cm. Ht. 4 mm. Perf. diam. 2·7 cm.	This is almost surely a ring bead for hanging on a torc. Found with early Iron Age A pottery and socketed bone chisels of All Cannings Cross type. ? 5th–4th c. B.C.	Information (in advance of publication) from Dr. Geoffrey Wainwright
Worthy Down, Winchester	Hampshire	Winchester	Fragment. Blue. Slight internal nicking probably due to weathering. Diam. 4 cm. Ht. 1·1 cm. Perf. diam. 2 cm.	Pre-Roman site. Possible analogy in Déchelette, J. (1914) 1321	*PHFCAS* x (1929), 184
Corbridge	Northumber-land	Corbridge	Blue. About 1/3 remains. Diam. 3·4 cm. Ht. 1·7 cm. Perf. diam. 1·2 cm.	This could possibly be part of a South Harting Class bead	
Glastonbury	Somerset	Glastonbury Museum G10	Blue. Diam. 3·1 cm. Ht. 1·3 cm. Perf. diam. 8 mm. centre of rounded section	Pre-Roman site	*Gl* ii, G10
Nyland (Cheddar Moor)	Somerset	Wells	Blue. Less than half remains. Diam. 3·7 cm. Ht. 1·3 cm. Perf. diam. 1·2 cm.	With 1st–2nd c. A.D. Samian, etc.	

SITE AND PARISH	COUNTY	MUSEUM & NO.	DESCRIPTION AND APPROX. DIMENSIONS	ASSOCIATIONS AND REMARKS	PUBLICATION
Temple-brough	Yorkshire	Rotherham	Half opaque yellow. Diam. 3 cm.	Fort of probably Flavian and Hadrianic date. Unscientific excavations	May, T. (1922)

(iia) NATURAL GREENISH TRANSLUCENT GLASS (MEDIUM SIZE)
ENGLAND

SITE AND PARISH	COUNTY	MUSEUM & NO.	DESCRIPTION AND APPROX. DIMENSIONS	ASSOCIATIONS AND REMARKS	PUBLICATION
Hambledon, Yewden	Buckingham-shire	Hambledon	Half only. Diam. 2 cm. Ht. 1 cm. Perf. diam. 8 mm.	Roman villa with rather earlier Belgic occupation on site, *c.* A.D. 40–end 4th c.	*A* lxx (1921), 71
Nor' nour, Scilly	Cornwall	St. Mary's, Scilly	Half. Rather striated. Diam. 1·8 cm. Ht. 7 mm. Perf. diam. 9 mm.	Occupation of this site was mainly 2nd c. A.D. but also later	Found after the original report in *ArJ* cxxiv (1967)
Porthmeor, Zennor	Cornwall		Diam. 1·7 cm. Ht. 6 mm. Perf. diam. 4 mm.	With another similar but olive green bead and small blue biconical bead of Roman type from Romano-British village	Information from the late Miss F. Patchett
Porth Cressa, Hughtown, Scilly	Cornwall		Irregularly made. Diam. 1·7 cm. Ht. 1 cm. or less. Perf. diam. 5 mm.	From cist with brooch and pot probably early Romano-British	*ArJ* cxi (1954), 17
Colchester	Essex	Colchester	2 examples. One: diam. 1·7 cm.; perf. diam. 7 mm. The other slightly smaller	From Group 94, dated A.D. 150–200	May, T. (1930), p. 279
Ongar	Essex	Hazzledine Warren Colln.	Diam. 1·7 cm. Ht. 1·3 cm. Perf. diam. 5 mm.	Hallsford brickfields. Unassociated	Information from the late Mr. S. H. Warren
Cirencester	Gloucester-shire	Cirencester B893	Diam. 1·7 cm. Ht. 8 mm. Perf. diam. 7 mm.	From Roman town	
Barnwood	Gloucester-shire	Cheltenham	Diam. 1·5 cm. Ht. 1 cm. Perf. diam. 6 mm.	Roman villa	*TBGAS* lii (1930), 207 ff.
Frocester	Gloucester-shire		Badly made with perforation off-centre. Diam. 2 cm. Ht. 1 cm. Perf. diam. 4 mm.	From Frocester Court Roman villa. Stratified late 4th c. A.D.	*TBGAS* lxxxix (1970)
Gloucester	Gloucester-shire	Gloucester 348	Fragment. Diam. 2·6 cm. Ht. 1·6 cm. Perf. diam. 1·1 cm.	With Roman and post-Roman material	Information from Mrs. Bonner

SITE AND PARISH	COUNTY	MUSEUM & NO.	DESCRIPTION AND APPROX. DIMENSIONS	ASSOCIATIONS AND REMARKS	PUBLICATION
Silchester	Hampshire	Reading	2 examples. One complete: diam. 2 cm.; ht. 8 mm.; irregular; perf. diam. 8 mm. Another half slightly larger	Most of the occupation belongs to the Roman period	For site, see Boon, G. C. (1957)
Weston-under-Penyard, Bollitree	Herefordshire	Gloucester A1754 and 1074	One: diam. 1·8 cm.; ht. 8 mm.; perf. diam. 8 mm. Another similar but smaller perforation	Roman	*JBAA* xxvii (1871), 211
King's Langley	Hertfordshire	B.M.	Diam. 1·7 cm. Ht. 8 mm. Irregular. Perf. diam. 6 mm.	Given by Mr. James Nantes. Stray find from Chipperfield	
Faversham	Kent	C.M., Beck Colln. 1660	Diam. 1·9 cm. Ht. 6 mm. Perf. diam. 8 mm.	? Anglo-Saxon from Group XX.A.1.a	H. C. Beck's notes, Cambridge
Richborough	Kent	Richborough 1330	Series of nicks radiating from surface. Diam. 1·5 cm. Ht. 6 mm. Perf. diam. 6 mm.	Unstratified in Roman and Saxon fort	*Rich* iv, p. 258
Richborough	Kent	Richborough 3919	Slightly pitted with bubble marks. Diam. 2·3 cm. Ht. 1·3 cm. Perf. diam. 8 mm.	From inner stone fort ditch middle layer. Probably 3rd or 4th c. A.D.	*Rich* iv, p. 235
Normanby	Lincolnshire	Scunthorpe R74	Diam. 1·8 cm. Ht. 8 mm. Perf. diam. 8 mm.	The same site produced early 4th c. A.D. ware	Dudley, H., *Early Days in N.W. Lincolnshire*
Chesters Fort	Northumberland	Chesters	Flattened surface. Diam. 1·9 cm. Ht. 9 mm. irregular. Perf. diam. 5 mm.	Found in 19th c. Probably the site dates between A.D. 122 and 383	
Corbridge	Northumberland	Corstopitum	Almost opaque. Diam. 1·7 cm. Ht. 7 mm. Perf. diam. 5 mm.	Stray find. Occupation 1st–5th c. A.D.	
Housesteads	Northumberland	Blackgate Museum, Newcastle-upon-Tyne	About: Diam. 2·5 cm.; ht. 1 cm.	On a necklace with cylinder beads and other Roman types	
Brough, South Collingham	Nottinghamshire	Newark	Diam. 1·6 cm. Ht. 5 mm. Perf. diam. 7 mm.	Stray find. Roman site	
Ditchley	Oxfordshire	A.M. 1936.367	Rather irregular. Diam. 1·7 cm. Ht. about 8 mm. Perf. diam. 6 mm.	Roman villa	*O* i (1936), 57

SITE AND PARISH	COUNTY	MUSEUM & NO.	DESCRIPTION AND APPROX. DIMENSIONS	ASSOCIATIONS AND REMARKS	PUBLICATION
Wroxeter	Shropshire	Rowley's House Museum, Shrewsbury	Irregular. Diam. 1·8 cm. Ht. 8 mm. Perf. diam. 5 mm.	Not stratified	
Kingsdown Camp, Bath	Somerset		Incomplete. Diam. 2 cm. Ht. 8 mm. Perf. diam. 6 mm.	With late Iron Age and 1st–2nd c. A.D. Roman finds	Information from excavator
Glastonbury	Somerset	Glastonbury G3	Half bead. Diam. 2 cm. Ht. 4 mm. Perf. diam. 1·2 cm.	Late Iron Age site	Gl ii
Meare	Somerset	Taunton	Irregular. Diam. 1·9 cm. Ht. 7 mm. to 1 cm. Perf. diam. 6 mm. to 8 mm.	From Iron Age site. ? 3rd to 1st c. B.C.	Me iii
'Mendip'	Somerset	Bristol, A. C. Pass Colln. F2076 and F2074	2 beads. Diam. 1·6 cm. and diam. 1·8 cm. Rather thick	Both stray finds	
Bury Wood Camp, Colerne	Wiltshire		Diam. 2·2 cm. Ht. 8 mm. Perf. diam. 1·1 cm.	Associated with Iron Age B ware	Interim reports in WAM lvii, lxii and lxiv
Broadtown, Broad Hinton	Wiltshire	Devizes S16	Diam. 2·2 cm. Ht. 1 cm. Perf. diam. 5 mm. off-centre	Secondary inhumation in a barrow with amber bead and socketed iron arrowhead. ? Roman or Saxon. There is a Romano-British cemetery near by	WAM xl (1918–19), 353
Catterick	Yorkshire		Diam. 1·8 cm. Ht. 7 mm. Perf. diam. 6 mm.	(Bead 15) Roman	Information from Mr. J. Wacher
Scarborough	Yorkshire	Scarborough 1009.38	Diam. 2 cm. Ht. 8 mm. Perf. diam. 8 mm.	From Roman signal station occupied about A.D. 370–400	

SCOTLAND

SITE AND PARISH	COUNTY	MUSEUM & NO.	DESCRIPTION AND APPROX. DIMENSIONS	ASSOCIATIONS AND REMARKS	PUBLICATION
	Dunbartonshire	N.M.A. FJ37	Diam. 2 cm. Ht. 1·1 cm. Perf. diam. 7 mm.	Found by J. Johnstone, 1849	
Mosspebble	Dumfriesshire	N.M.A. FJ39	Roughly made. Diam. 2 cm. Ht. 9 mm. Perf. diam. 8 mm.	Found by A. H. Borthwick in 1869	
Newstead	Roxburghshire	N.M.A. FRA905 and 906	One: Diam. 2·3 cm.; ht. 4 mm.; perf. diam. 1·1 cm. Another, half only, rather smaller and thicker	The occupation of this site lasted from about A.D. 80–200	Ne, pp. 336–7 and PSAS lxxxiv (1949–50), 1 ff.

SITE AND PARISH	COUNTY	MUSEUM & NO.	DESCRIPTION AND APPROX. DIMENSIONS	ASSOCIATIONS AND REMARKS	PUBLICATION
			WALES		
Penmaenmawr	Caernarvonshire		Diam. 2·1 cm. Perf. diam. 7 mm.	Found with late 1st to early 2nd c. Samian	*AC* lxxviii (1923), 253
Llandegai	Caernarvonshire		Half-bead. Flattened surfaces. Diam. 1·8 cm. Ht. 8 mm. Perf. diam. 7 mm.	Found in ditch silting of henge monument	*An* xlii (1968), 220
Whitton, nr. Barry	Glamorganshire		Diam. 1·9 cm. Ht. 9 mm. Perf. diam. 6 mm.	Topsoil of Roman villa. Site occupied 1st c. B.C. to about A.D. 300	Information from Dr. Michael Jarrett
Caerleon	Monmouthshire	Caerleon	Diam. 1·7 cm. Ht. 7 mm. Perf. diam. 8 mm.	Roman site not stratified	
Usk	Monmouthshire		2 almost identical beads. Diam. *c.* 1·8 cm. Ht. 8 mm. Perf. diam. 5 mm. Another more globular	Found in 1969 and 1970 in Roman fort occupied A.D. 55–60 and again in late Roman period	Report forthcoming

(iib) NATURAL GREENISH TRANSLUCENT GLASS (SMALL)

SITE AND PARISH	COUNTY	MUSEUM & NO.	DESCRIPTION AND APPROX. DIMENSIONS	ASSOCIATIONS AND REMARKS	PUBLICATION
			ENGLAND		
Trevelgue, St. Columb Minor	Cornwall	Truro	Rather globular. Diam. 1·5 cm. Ht. 1 cm. Perf. diam. 4 mm.	From fort—probably 1st c. B.C.	See note in Thomas, C. (ed.) (1966), pp. 77–8
Nor' nour, Scilly	Cornwall	St. Mary's, Scilly	Small ring bead. Diam. 9 mm. Ht. 2 mm. Perf. diam. 6 mm.	On dump on Roman site, occupied about 1st–4th c. A.D. Mostly 2nd c. finds	*ArJ* cxxiv (1967), 1 ff.
Probus	Cornwall	Truro	Almost opaque. Ice-coloured, ? whipped glass. Diam. 9 mm. Ht. 3 mm.	Atypical for quality of glass. From Romano-British camp, Carvossa. Occupied in late Roman times (? Gallo-Roman)	Information from Mr. H. L. Douch
No location	Cumberland	Carlisle	Irregular. Diam. 1·4 cm. Ht. 6 mm. Perf. diam. 4 mm.		
Portland (The Verne)	Dorset	Dorchester 1932.9.5	Small ring bead. Diam. 1·1 cm. Ht. 3 mm. Perf. diam. 6 mm.	From Romano-British cemetery	
Owslebury	Hampshire	Winchester ?	Irregular. Diam. 1 cm. Ht. irregular, about 2 mm. Perf. diam. 6 mm.	Roman period	*AnJ* xlviii (1968) and l (1970)

SITE AND PARISH	COUNTY	MUSEUM & NO.	DESCRIPTION AND APPROX. DIMENSIONS	ASSOCIATIONS AND REMARKS	PUBLICATION
Silchester	Hampshire	Reading	2 examples. One: diam. 1·4 cm.; ht. 5 mm. irregular; perf. diam. 1·6 cm. Another: diam. 1·3 cm.; ht. 6 mm.; perf. diam. 5 mm.	Site occupied 1st c. B.C.–5th c. A.D.	
Kenchester	Hereford-shire	Hereford 4436	Upper surface slightly dished. Diam. 8 mm. Ht. 4 mm. Perf. diam. 1 mm.	Occupation until late 4th c. A.D.	*TWNFC* 1916 and 1936
Weston-under-Penyard, Bollitree	Hereford-shire	Gloucester A1752	Diam. 1·2 cm. Ht. 5 mm. Perf. diam. 5 mm.	Roman	*JBAA* xxvii (1871), 211 ff.
Verulamium (King Harry's Lane)	Hertfordshire	Verulamium (St. Albans)	2 beads. Diams. 1·3 and 1·5 cm. Ht. 4 mm. Perf. diam. 8 mm.	Necklace on Burial 29 of pre-Roman Aylesford type. About 10 B.C.–A.D. 40	Information from Dr. I. M. Stead, F.S.A.
Godman-chester	Huntingdon-shire		Rather irregular and almost colourless. Diam. 1·1 cm.	c. A.D. 150–200	*PCAS* liv (1960), 83–4
Risby Warren	Lincolnshire	Scunthorpe R18	Several examples	Mixed Romano-British and Saxon occupation material	
Great Chesters	Northumber-land	University Museum, Newcastle-upon-Tyne	2 small examples. Diam. about 1·2 cm.	On necklace with other Roman beads	
Bath	Somerset	Bath Pump Room Museum	Several small ring beads about 8 mm. to 1 cm. in diam.	Roman period	Cunliffe, B., *Roman Bath Discovered* (1971) and refs.
Ham Hill, Montacute	Somerset	Taunton	Diam. 1·1 cm. Ht. 4 mm. irregular. Perf. diam. 6 mm.	Hill-fort with pre-Roman and Roman occupation	*VCH Somerset* i, 295 and *A* xlviii
Ham Hill, Montacute	Somerset	Taunton	Another rather larger	No details of position of finds	*VCH Somerset* i, 295 and *A* xlviii
Hartfield	Sussex		Diam. 1 cm. Ht. irregular 3 mm. Perf. diam. 6 mm.	From Garden Hill Romano-British iron working site	Information from Mr. J. H. Money
Rotherly	Wiltshire	Salisbury	Rather globular. Diam. 1·4 cm. Ht. 9 mm. Perf. diam. 4 mm.	Romano-British village	Pitt-Rivers, A. H. L. F. (1888) and *ArJ* civ (1947)
Stockton Earthworks	Wiltshire	Salisbury	2 examples. One has diam. 1·4 cm.; ht. 4 mm.; perf. diam. 7 mm. Another (half): diam. 8 mm.; perf. diam. 6 mm.	Belgic and Roman site	*WAM* xliii (1897), 389

SITE AND PARISH	COUNTY	MUSEUM & NO.	DESCRIPTION AND APPROX. DIMENSIONS	ASSOCIATIONS AND REMARKS	PUBLICATION
Catterick	Yorkshire		Irregular. Diam. 1·3 cm. Ht. 4 mm. Perf. diam. 5 mm. Two others very similar	Beads 41, 50, 13 from Roman town	Information from Mr. J. Wacher

SCOTLAND

SITE AND PARISH	COUNTY	MUSEUM & NO.	DESCRIPTION AND APPROX. DIMENSIONS	ASSOCIATIONS AND REMARKS	PUBLICATION
Traprain Law, Prestonkirk	East Lothian	N.M.A.	Three clumsily made examples. Diam. 8 mm. or smaller	Roman period	For references to Traprain Law, see Rivet, A. L. F. (ed.) (1966)
Covesea	Morayshire	N.M.A. HM214	Rather yellower green than usual	Occupation in early Roman period. Fragment of 2nd c. A.D. imported glass from this site	PSAS lxv (1931), 177

WALES

SITE AND PARISH	COUNTY	MUSEUM & NO.	DESCRIPTION AND APPROX. DIMENSIONS	ASSOCIATIONS AND REMARKS	PUBLICATION
Plas Bach	Angelsey	Bangor	Diam. 1·3 to 1·4 cm. Ht. 5 mm. irregular. Perf. diam. 6 mm. Hole worn on thinner side of bead		AC, 5th s., ix (1892), 243
Coygan Camp Laugharne	Carmarthen-shire		2, badly made with irregular perforation, diam. about 1 cm.	Late 3rd c. A.D.	Wainwright, G. J. (1967)
Whitton, nr. Barry	Glamorgan-shire		Diam. 1·5 cm. Ht. 9 mm. Perf. diam. 5 mm.	Surface soil in Roman villa occu-pied about 1st c. B.C. to A.D. 300	Information from Dr. M. Jarrett
Moel Trigarn Fort	Pembroke-shire	Tenby	Several examples, one: Diam. 1·4 cm.	One came from same hut as a Meare spiral bead (Class ?)	AC lv (1900), 206

(iiia) MEDIUM GREEN, GREENISH-GOLD OR GREENISH-BROWN
(TRANSLUCENT IF NOT STATED)

(Note: For natural glass, see Group 6 (iia) and (iib), and, for smaller beads, see Group 6 (v))

ENGLAND

SITE AND PARISH	COUNTY	MUSEUM & NO.	DESCRIPTION AND APPROX. DIMENSIONS	ASSOCIATIONS AND REMARKS	PUBLICATION
Yewden, Hambledon	Buckingham-shire	Reading	Part of ring bead, rich yellowish-green. Diam. 1·9 cm. Ht. 5 mm. Perf. diam. 1·2 c.m.	Roman villa with some earlier occupa-tion of about A.D. 30–400	A lxxi (1920–21), 141 ff.
Porthmeor, Zennor	Cornwall		Light greenish-gold. Diam. 2·2 cm. Ht. 7 mm. Perf. diam. 7 mm.	Romano-British village	Information from Miss F. Patchett

SITE AND PARISH	COUNTY	MUSEUM & NO.	DESCRIPTION AND APPROX. DIMENSIONS	ASSOCIATIONS AND REMARKS	PUBLICATION
St. Mawgan-in-Pyder	Cornwall	Truro	Greenish-gold. Diam. 2·5 cm. Ht. 7 mm. Perf. diam. 1·2 cm.	This site (Carloggas) occupied from the 1st c. B.C. into the Roman period	*ArJ* cxiii (1956)
Trevelgue, St. Columb Minor	Cornwall	Truro	Yellow-green. Very irregular. Diam. 1·6 cm. Perf. diam. 9 mm.	From hill-fort, perhaps 1st c. B.C. or earlier	Awaiting publication. See notes in Thomas, C. (ed.) (1966), 77–8
Cadbury Castle, Bickleigh Bridge	Devonshire		Dark blue-green. Diam. 1·4 cm. Ht. 9 mm. Perf. diam. 4 mm.	With 3rd c. A.D. Roman objects in a well	*PDAS* lxxxiv (1952), 105–14
Bulbury Camp (or Belbury), Lytchett Minster	Dorset	Dorchester 1884.9.113	8 beads in bright greenish-gold varying in diam. from 1·2 to 2·3 cm.	Pre-Roman site with associated objects. These beads were found with a mirror, etc., of early 1st c. A.D. The camp produced an iron anchor of early Roman type. For this variety of glass, see p. 13	*A* xlviii (1884), 116, and pl. vi, 10; illustrated in *AnJ* lii (1972), pl. liv
Hengistbury Head	Dorset	Southampton ?	Bright greenish-gold Diam. 2·6 cm. Ht. 8 mm. Perf. diam. 1·3 cm.	Apparently the same glass as Bulbury (Dorset), above. Associated with Dressel Type IA amphorae of 2nd to mid-1st c. B.C.	Information in advance of publication from Dr. D. Peacock
Maiden Castle, Winterbourne Monkton	Dorset	Dorchester	Thick annular 'green vitreous paste'. Diam. 1·9 cm. Ht. 1·4 cm. Perf. diam. 8 mm.	With pottery thought to belong to early 1st c. B.C. (redated since the report)	*MC*, 292, no. 4
Portland (The Verne)	Dorset	Dorchester 1932.9.4	Light green. Diam. 1·5 cm. Ht. 4 mm. Perf. diam. 9 mm.	From Romano-British cemetery	
Studland	Dorset		Said to be similar to Maiden Castle	From Romano-British settlement	*PDNHAS* lxxxvii (1965), 193
Colchester	Essex	Colchester	2 examples. One greenish-brown: diam. 2·2 cm.; ht. 1 cm.; perf. diam. 8 mm. Another about half this size	Found with burial group 94 on Roman site. Dated from associations *c.* A.D. 54–68. Perhaps made of 'Bulbury' glass (see p. 13). (These groups are entirely reliable)	May, T. (1930), p. 279

SITE AND PARISH	COUNTY	MUSEUM & NO.	DESCRIPTION AND APPROX. DIMENSIONS	ASSOCIATIONS AND REMARKS	PUBLICATION
Birdlip	Gloucester-shire	Cheltenham	'Bulbury' glass, greenish gold. Diam. 2·4 cm. Ht. irreg. 7 mm. Perf. diam. 1·4 cm.	Stray find on slopes of Birdlip hill	
Bagendon	Gloucester-shire		Almost clear but slightly greenish. About 1/3 missing. Diam. 2·7 cm. Perf. diam. 1·6 cm.	Stratified A.D. 10–50 on Belgic site	Clifford, E. M. (1961)
Salmonsbury, Bourton-on-the-Water	Gloucester-shire	Cheltenham	Translucent greenish-gold like Bulbury, Dorset. Diam. 1·7 cm. Ht. 6 mm. Perf. diam. 8 mm.	From 2nd to 1st c. B.C. settlement. 'Period 1: not earlier than 150 B.C.'	Dunning, G. C., 'Salmonsbury, Bourton-on-the-Water, Glou-cestershire', in Harding, D. W. (ed.), *Hillforts* (1976), p. 110 and fig. 24, 6
Cirencester	Gloucester-shire	Cirencester B908	Bright green. Diam. 1·8 cm. Ht. 6 mm. Perf. diam. 7 mm.	Collection from Roman town	
Kingscote	Gloucester-shire		Half bead, bright greenish-gold. Diam. c. 1·9 cm. Ht. irreg. 5 mm. Perf. diam. 1·1 cm.	Surface find from area with 1st c. A.D. objects (? Bulbury type glass)	Information from Mr. R. Wichard
Silchester	Hampshire	Reading	Yellowish-green. Diam. 1·8 cm. Ht. 9 mm. Perf. diam. 7 mm.	Occupation from late Iron Age to Roman period	For site see Boon, G. C. (1957)
Silchester	Hampshire	Reading	Yellowish-green radiating nicks from the perforation in one side. Diam. 1·9 cm. Ht. 6 mm. Perf. diam. 4 mm.	As above	As above
Silchester	Hampshire	Reading	Dark blue-green with swirls of iridescence. Diam. 2 cm. Ht. 9 mm. Perf. diam. 8 mm.	As above	As above
Worthy Down	Hampshire	Winchester	Bright greenish-gold. Diam. 2·4 cm. Ht. 7 mm. Perf. diam. 1·3 cm.	Upcast from pit in Iron Age settlement	*PHFCAS* x (1926–30), 178 ff. and fig. 87
Kenchester	Herefordshire	Hereford	Half. Translucent greenish. Diam. 1·6 cm. Ht. 6 mm. Perf. diam. 6 mm.	From Roman town occupied until end of 4th c. A.D.	For site see *TWNFC* 1916 and 1926

SITE AND PARISH	COUNTY	MUSEUM & NO.	DESCRIPTION AND APPROX. DIMENSIONS	ASSOCIATIONS AND REMARKS	PUBLICATION
St. Albans	Hertfordshire	Verulamium 141	Half bead, medium green and rather globular. Diam. 1·5 cm. Ht. 1 cm. Perf. diam. 6 mm.	From site of *Verulamium*	*Ver*
St. Albans	Hertfordshire	Verulamium 1633. 360	Greenish-gold. Diam. 2·2 cm. Ht. irregular 8 mm. Perf. diam. 1·1 cm.		
St. Albans	Hertfordshire	Verulamium 33.767	Lighter green. Diam. 1·8 cm. Ht. 8 mm. Perf. diam. 9 mm.		*Ver*, 113–20
St. Albans	Hertfordshire	Verulamium	Green, accidentally streaked with purple. Diam. 1·7 cm. Ht. 8 mm. Irregular perforation.	Stratified A.D. 105–15	Frere, S. (1972)
Richborough	Kent	Richborough 1294 & 3920	Both about 1·7 cm. in diam. and 5 mm. high. Perf. diam. 9 and 5 mm.	Unstratified in Roman and Saxon fort	*Rich* iv, 259
Dowgate Hill, London	London	Formley Guildhall Museum 3964	2 examples	Old sporadic finds	Unpublished
Wallbrook	London	Formerly Guildhall Museum 18643	Semi-translucent. Diam. 2 cm. Ht. 7 mm. Perf. diam. 7 mm.	Dated late 1st c. A.D.	
Wallbrook	London	Formerly Guildhall Museum 18643	Pale yellowish-green. Diam. 1·8 cm. Ht. 1 cm. Perf. diam. 7 mm.	No details. Could be classified 'as bottle glass'	
Hunsbury, Harding-stone	Northampton-shire	Northampton	2 large, light green. Diams. 2·5 and 2·8 cm. Ht. 6 mm. Perf. diam. 1·4 and 1·7 cm. Two larger and yellow	From Iron Age fort. Not stratified. Prob-ably 1st c. B.C. (Occupation *c.* 4th c.–1st c. B.C. or early 1st c. A.D.)	Fell, C. (1936), p. 69
Hunsbury, Harding-stone	Northampton-shire	Northampton	Clear yellowish-brown. Diam. 2·5 cm. Ht. 6 mm. Perf. diam. 1·4 cm.	From pre-Roman fort perhaps 1st c. B.C. (Fort occupied *c.* 300 B.C.–early 1st c. A.D.)	Fell, C. (1936), p. 69
Irchester	Northampton-shire	c/o Dept. of Environment	Striated round perimeter. Semi-translucent. Diam. 2 cm. Ht. 8 mm. Perf. diam. 8 mm.	Probably Iron Age B or early Belgic. 'Bulbury' type glass	*ArJ* cxxiv (1967), 65

SITE AND PARISH	COUNTY	MUSEUM & NO.	DESCRIPTION AND APPROX. DIMENSIONS	ASSOCIATIONS AND REMARKS	PUBLICATION
Corbridge	Northumberland	Corstopitum	Almost opaque greenish-brown. Diam. 1·6 cm. Ht. 6 mm. Perf. diam. 7 mm.	Roman site occupied 1st–5th c. A.D.	
'Rochester and Alnham'	Northumberland	Chesters Museum	Greenish-gold. Diam. 2 cm. Ht. 9 mm. Perf. diam. 7 mm.	Almost surely Roman and same glass as a bead with yellow scrabble from Carrawburgh dated c. A.D. 122–383	
Newark	Nottinghamshire	Newark	Light green. Diam. about 1·8 cm. Ht. not seen. Perf. diam. 6 mm.	Presented by R. Woolley	
Clungunford, Brand Hill	Shropshire	Clun	Olive green. Hourglass perforation. Diam. 2·5 cm. Perf. diam. on surface 8 mm.	On Clun-Clee Ridgeway. Surface find	Information from Miss L. F. Chitty
Glastonbury	Somerset	Glastonbury Lake Village Museum G4	Bright yellowish-brown. Diam. 2·2 cm. Ht. 6 mm. Perf. diam. 1·4 cm.	From Lake Village of pre-Roman Iron Age	*Gl* ii
Meare	Somerset	Taunton G6EV	Attached to bronze ring. Translucent brownish-yellow. Diam. 1·9 cm. Ht. 6 mm. Perf. diam. 9 mm.	From East village of Iron Age site occupied c. 3rd–1st c. B.C.	*Me* iii
Meare	Somerset	Taunton G9	Dark greenish-gold. Diam. 2 cm. Ht. 1 cm. Perf. diam. 9 mm.	From East village of Iron Age site occupied c. 3rd–1st c. B.C.	*Me* iii
'Mendip'	Somerset	Bristol F2073, A. C. Pass Colln.	Rather light green. Diam. 2·1 cm. Ht. 7 mm. Perf. diam. 8 mm.	A number of Roman beads from here	
Wetton	Staffordshire	Derby 178.12.'29	Diam. 1·6 cm. Ht. 6 mm. Perf. diam. 5 mm.	From 'Thor's Cave' with Roman objects of 2nd c. A.D.	
Mildenhall	Wiltshire	Devizes 126	Opaque grey-green ring-bead. Diam. 2·1 cm. Perf. diam. 1·3 cm.	Roman and Saxon finds from this site	
Brough	Yorkshire	Hull	Badly made opaque greenish-brown. Diam. 1·7 cm. Ht. 7 mm. Perf. diam. 6 mm.	Roman and Anglian finds from this site	

SITE AND PARISH	COUNTY	MUSEUM & NO.	DESCRIPTION AND APPROX. DIMENSIONS	ASSOCIATIONS AND REMARKS	PUBLICATION
Scarborough	Yorkshire	Scarborough 1008.38	Yellowish-green. Small hour-glass perforation. Diam. 1·8 cm. Ht. 5 mm. Perf. diam. 2 mm.	Roman signal station occupation A.D. 270–400	Information from the late Mr. F. G. Simpson

SCOTLAND

SITE AND PARISH	COUNTY	MUSEUM & NO.	DESCRIPTION AND APPROX. DIMENSIONS	ASSOCIATIONS AND REMARKS	PUBLICATION
Castle Hill, Dalry	Ayrshire	N.M.A. HH364	Irregular brownish-yellow. Diam. 1·7 cm. Ht. 6 mm. Perf. diam. 6 mm.	Finds from this site thought to date from 1st c. B.C. to early Roman period	*PSAS* liii (1918–19), 123
Dunagoil	Bute	Rothesay	Fragment opaque honey-coloured ring-bead. Diam. 2·6 cm. Ht. 4 mm. Perf. diam. 1·7 cm.	From Iron Age fort with other objects of about 1st c. B.C.–1st c. A.D.	*TBNHS* viii (1914–15), 42–9 and 68–86

WALES

SITE AND PARISH	COUNTY	MUSEUM & NO.	DESCRIPTION AND APPROX. DIMENSIONS	ASSOCIATIONS AND REMARKS	PUBLICATION
'Aber-fawr'	Anglesey	Lost	'An adder bead or Glain Neidr, of green glass'. Diam. about 1·7 cm.	Could be any date	Camden, *Britannia* (Gibson's edit., 1695), p. 697, fig. a
Prestatyn	Flintshire	c/o Prestatyn Council	Greenish-gold. Asymmetrical. Diam. 2·5 cm. Ht. 1·3 cm. Perf. diam. 7 mm.	Almost certainly from Roman site	Ellis Davies, *Prehistoric and Roman Remains in Flintshire*, p. 309
Usk	Monmouth-shire		Dirty greenish-yellow. Diam. 1·5 cm. Ht. 5 mm. Perf. diam. 8 mm. Another slightly larger	Roman fort. Occupation A.D. 55–60 and again in late Roman period	Report forthcoming

(iiib) SMALL TRANSLUCENT YELLOW AND GREENISH-GOLD

ENGLAND

SITE AND PARISH	COUNTY	MUSEUM & NO.	DESCRIPTION AND APPROX. DIMENSIONS	ASSOCIATIONS AND REMARKS	PUBLICATION
Trevelgue, St. Columb Minor	Cornwall	Truro	Bright translucent, yellow. Diam. 1·2 cm. Ht. about 3 mm. variable. Perf. diam. about 7 mm.	Site not yet published. Perhaps 1st c. B.C.	Unpublished. See notes in Thomas, C. (ed.) (1966)
Newton Abbot	Devonshire		Translucent yellow. Diam. 1 cm.	From modern cutting through the defences of Berry's Wood Fort	*PDAS* lxxxiv (1952), 246
Dorchester	Dorset	Dorchester, Hogg Collns. 1886.9, 110	Greenish-gold Rather irregular. Diam. 1·3 cm. Ht. 3 mm. Perf. diam. 7 mm.	'From Roman stratum'. Glass as Bulbury above (see pp. 13 and 145-150)	

SITE AND PARISH	COUNTY	MUSEUM & NO.	DESCRIPTION AND APPROX. DIMENSIONS	ASSOCIATIONS AND REMARKS	PUBLICATION
The Verne, Portland	Dorset	Dorchester 1932.5, 6, 7	Three beads. Greenish-gold. Diam. 9 mm. Ht. 3 mm. Perf. diam. about 4 mm.	From a Romano-British cemetery. Glass appears to be similar to Bulbury Camp (see above and p. 13)	
Bredon, Bredon's Norton	Gloucester-shire– Worcester-shire border	Private museum at Overbury Court	Yellowish. Diam. 1 cm. Ht. 4 mm. Perf. diam. 3 mm.	Last period of inner entrance of pre-Roman hill-fort. Suggested date early or mid-1st c. A.D.	*ArJ* xcv (1938), 86
Winchester, Lankhills Cemetery	Hampshire		Yellow translucent. Diam. 4 mm.	From necklace 353 (foreign) in Grave 336. Dated *c.* 350–70 A.D.	Guido, M. (forthcoming) in Biddle, M. (forthcoming)
Weston-under-Penyard, Bollitree	Herefordshire	Gloucester 1756	Yellowish-green slightly biconical. Diam. 1·2 cm. Ht. 3 mm. Perf. diam. 6 mm.	From Roman context	*JBAA* xxvii (1871), 211 ff.
St. Albans, King Harry's Lane	Hertfordshire	Verulamium	2 greenish-gold beads about 1·4 cm. diam. Wide perforations	From necklace on Burial 29 of Aylesford type cemetery dated *c.* 10 B.C.–A.D. 40. This glass is like that from Bulbury Camp, Dorset (p. 13)	Information from Dr. I. M. Stead
Dowgate Hill	London	Formerly Guildhall Museum 3964	Greenish-yellow. Diam. 1·4 cm. Ht. 4 mm. Perf. diam. 5 mm.	Stray find	Unpublished
Corbridge	Northumber-land	Corstopitum Museum	Translucent yellowish-brown. Diam. 8 mm. Ht. 2 mm. Perf. diam. 4 mm.	Roman site occupied from 1st–5th c. A.D.	
Mendip	Somerset	A. C. Pass Colln. Bristol F2075	Shiny yellowish. Roughly made, perhaps coiled. Diam. 1·2 cm. Ht. irregular. Small perforation	Stray find with other Roman beads	
Baginton	Warwickshire	Coventry, Herbert Art Gallery and Museum	Yellowish-green. Slightly flattened around perforation. Diam. 1·4 cm. Ht. 5 mm. Perf. diam. 8 mm.	From The Lunt Roman fort. (Lower fill of pit II)	*PCNHHS* ii, no. 5 (1951)

SITE AND PARISH	COUNTY	MUSEUM & NO.	DESCRIPTION AND APPROX. DIMENSIONS	ASSOCIATIONS AND REMARKS	PUBLICATION
			SCOTLAND		
Mousewald	Dumfries-shire	N.M.A. FJ44	Rather globular. Reddish-yellow. Diam. 1·3 cm. Ht. 6 mm. irregular. Small perforation	Stray find perhaps unrelated to this series	
Covesea	Morayshire	N.M.A. HM214	Light yellowish-green. Diam. 1·2 cm. Ht. 4 mm. Perf. diam. 6 mm.	2nd c. A.D. imported glass from here	*PSAS* lxv (1931), 177
			WALES		
Whitton, nr. Barry	Glamorgan-shire		Pale greenish-yellow. Diam. 9 mm. Ht. 2 mm. Perf. diam. 5 mm.	Unstratified in pre-Roman and Roman site	Report by Dr. M. Jarrett (forthcoming)
The Breiddin hill-fort	Montgomery-shire		Very pale translucent yellow. Diam. 7 mm. Ht. 3 mm. Perf. diam. 3 mm. One flattened surface	Unstratified in hill-fort occupied from mid-Iron Age to 4th c. A.D.	Information from Mr. Chris Musson

(iva) MEDIUM SIZED BLUE (TRANSLUCENT IF NOT STATED)

SITE AND PARISH	COUNTY	MUSEUM & NO.	DESCRIPTION AND APPROX. DIMENSIONS	ASSOCIATIONS AND REMARKS	PUBLICATION
			ENGLAND		
Yewden, Hambledon	Buckingham-shire	Aylesbury	Medium blue. Striation in the glass around the circumference on the sides. Diam. 1·8 cm. Ht. 6 mm. Perf. diam. 8 mm.	From Roman villa occupied throughout the Roman period	*A* lxxi (1921)
Trelan Bahow, and St. Keverne	Cornwall	B.M.	One bright cobalt, and another greyer. Both diams. about 2·2 cm. Perf. diam. 1 cm.	With a mirror, etc., of 1st c. A.D.	Hencken, H.O'N., *Archaeology of Cornwall*, p. 120 and *ArJ* xxx (1873), 267
Burnt Fen	Cambridge-shire	C.M.	Mixed grey-blue and greenish-blue, opaque. Diam. 2·2 cm. Ht. 8 mm. Perf. diam. 8 mm.	For similar glass see Great Chesterford (below). The same site produced a bead of Oldbury type (Class 6)	
Great Chesterford	Cambridge-shire	C.M.	Glass as Burnt Fen above. Diam. 2 cm. Ht. 8 mm. Perf. diam. 7 mm.	Probably pre-Roman or early Roman	
	Cumberland	Carlisle	Medium cobalt. Diam. 1·7 cm. Ht. 5 mm. Perf. diam. 9 mm. irregular	No evidence of association	

SITE AND PARISH	COUNTY	MUSEUM & NO.	DESCRIPTION AND APPROX. DIMENSIONS	ASSOCIATIONS AND REMARKS	PUBLICATION
Somerleigh	Dorset	Dorchester 1893.2.11	Drab grey-blue. Diam. 2 cm. Ht. 1·3 cm. Perf. diam. 9 mm.	The rather globular form of this bead suggests that it may belong to the Dark Ages	
South Shields	Durham	University Museum, Newcastle-upon-Tyne	Rather light blue. Diam. 1·8 cm. Perf. diam. 7 mm.	From Roman fort occupied about A.D. 122–369	
Cirencester	Gloucestershire	Cirencester B908	Diam. about 1·8 cm. Ht. 8 mm. Perf. diam. 7 mm.	Roman occupation 1st–5th c. A.D.	
Micheldever	Hampshire	B.M. 63. 1-20. 6	Light blue with bubbly surface. Diam. 2 cm. Ht. 9 mm. irregular. Perf. diam. 6 mm.	Rather globular in form. The bead came from a site which also produced a Dark Age bead and may be of the same period	
Silchester	Hampshire	Reading	Light blue. Diam. 1·7 cm. Ht. 4 mm. Perf. diam. 9 mm.	Roman occupation 1st–5th c. A.D.	For site see Boon, G. C. (1957)
Weston-under-Penyard, Bollitree	Herefordshire	Gloucester A1757	Bright dark cobalt. Diam. 1·9 cm. Ht. 5 mm. Perf. diam. 8 mm.	With many other Roman beads	*JBAA* xxvii (1871), 211 ff.
St. Albans	Hertfordshire	Verulamium Museum 33.275	Medium blue. Diam. 1·8 cm. Ht. 8 mm. irregular. Perf. diam. 9 mm.		
Breedon-on-the-Hill	Leicestershire	Leicester	Opaque dark blue. Straight perforation. Diam. c. 2·5 cm. Ht. 1 cm. Perf. diam. 1·2 cm.	With Iron Age pottery in a pit	*TLAHS* xxvi (1950), 39 and fig. 7, no. 3
Leicester (Jewry Wall)	Leicestershire	Leicester	Pale blue. Diam. 2 cm. Ht. 7 mm. Perf. diam. 8 mm.	From disturbed levels but a similar bead was stratified c. A.D. 180	Kenyon, K. M. (1948), p. 269, fig. 93.1
Risby Warren	Lincolnshire	Scunthorpe 106	Half only. Rather light cobalt. Diam. 1·8 cm. Ht. 7 mm. Perf. diam. 1 cm.	Site produced mostly Romano-British finds	
Corbridge	Northumberland	Corstopitum P501	Rather light cobalt. Diam. 2 cm. Ht. 8 mm. irregular. Perf. diam. 7 mm.	Occupation throughout the Roman period	
Alchester (Wendlebury)	Oxfordshire	A.M. 1930.603	Light translucent cobalt with striated surface. Diam. 1·6 cm. Ht. 4 mm. Perf. diam. 7 mm.	Roman town occupied throughout Roman period	For site see *AnJ* vii (1927), 155–84

SITE AND PARISH	COUNTY	MUSEUM & NO.	DESCRIPTION AND APPROX. DIMENSIONS	ASSOCIATIONS AND REMARKS	PUBLICATION
Newcastle, Whitcott	Shropshire		Diam. 1·4 cm. Ht. 8 mm. Perf. diam. 6 mm. irregular	Found in drain-cutting	Information from Miss L. F. Chitty
Glastonbury	Somerset	Glastonbury G2	Fragment. Rich cobalt. Original diam. 2·1 cm. Perf. diam. 1 cm.	From Lake Village, probably 2nd–1st c. B.C. or early 1st c. A.D.	*Gl* ii, frontispiece
Ham Hill (Montacute)	Somerset	Taunton	Smoky grey-blue. Diam. 2 cm. Perf. diam. 1·2 cm.	From Iron Age hill-fort with some Roman occupation	*A* xlviii (1884),116. See also *ArJ* cvii (1950), 90
Shepton Mallet	Somerset	Shepton Mallet	Light cobalt. Half only. Diam. 1·9 cm. Ht. 7 mm. irregular. Perf. diam. 9 mm.	With Roman objects	
All Cannings Cross	Wiltshire	Devizes	Brilliant dark cobalt. Diam. 1·8 cm. Ht. 6 mm. Perf. diam. 9 mm.	From Iron Age site with long occupation	Cunnington, M. E. (1923), p. 120 and pl. 18, fig. 16
Bury Wood Camp, Colerne	Wiltshire		Almost opaque. Irregular. Diam. 1·3 cm. Ht. 6 mm. Perf. diam. 7 mm.	Associated with Iron Age 'B' pottery. ? 2nd–1st c. B.C.	Interim reports in *WAM* lvii, lxii and lxiv
Stockton Earthworks	Wiltshire	Salisbury	Diam. 1·7 cm. Ht. 9 mm. Perf. diam. 6 mm.	Probably a Belgic site in origin	*WAM* xliii (1897), 389
Woodcuts	Wiltshire	Salisbury	Fragment of ring bead. Diam. 2 cm. Ht. 2 mm. Perf. diam. 1·6 cm.	Surface trenching in Romano-British village	Pitt-Rivers, A. H. L. F. (1887), pp. xliv, 20. See also *ArJ* civ (1947)
Briggswath Whitby	Yorkshire	Whitby	Diam. 2·2 cm. Ht. 1 cm. Perf. diam. 6 mm.	With Romano-British ware of the late Roman period found at the 'Riverside Tea Gardens'	
Skipton	Yorkshire	Skipton	Diam. 1·7 cm. Ht. 1·1 cm. Perf. diam. 6 mm.	From an Iron Age enclosure	Forthcoming, perhaps in *YAJ*

IRELAND

There are some examples from collections. Mostly about 2 cm. diameter and undated

SCOTLAND

Traprain Law, Prestonkirk	East Lothian	N.M.A.	Bright dark cobalt. Diam. 1·6 cm. Ht. 4 mm. Perf. diam. 3 mm.	From hill-fort occupied throughout Roman period	For references see Rivet, A. L. F. (ed.) (1966)

SITE AND PARISH	COUNTY	MUSEUM & NO.	DESCRIPTION AND APPROX. DIMENSIONS	ASSOCIATIONS AND REMARKS	PUBLICATION
Covesea Cave	Morayshire	N.M.A. HM213.	Almost opaque. Diam. 1·8 cm. Ht. 9 mm. Perf. diam. 7 mm.	Probably Roman period	*PSAS* lxv (1931), 177
Newstead	Roxburgh-shire	Mr. Mason's Colln., Selkirk	Rather globular. Diam. 1·7 cm. Ht. 1·1 cm. Perf. diam. 8 mm.	Roman site occupied approx. A.D. 80–200	*Ne* (for site)

WALES

SITE AND PARISH	COUNTY	MUSEUM & NO.	DESCRIPTION AND APPROX. DIMENSIONS	ASSOCIATIONS AND REMARKS	PUBLICATION
Tythegston	Glamorgan-shire		Very irregular and perhaps locally made. Translucent. Diam. about 2 cm.	From defended en-closure of Cae Somerhouse. Topsoil. Site occupied from late Iron Age to 4th c. A.D.	Information from Jeffrey Davies, University Col-lege, Aberystwyth
Caerleon	Monmouth-shire	Caerleon	Scratched lines round surface. Diam. 1·8 cm. Ht. 1·1 cm. Perf. diam. 8 mm.	No details known. Probably Roman	*AC* lxxxiv (1929), lxxxv (1930), lxxxvi (1931), lxxxvii (1932) and *A* lxxviii (1928), 191
Sudbrook	Monmouth-shire		Diam. 1·8 cm. Ht. 7 mm. Perf. diam. 9 mm.	Probably 1st c. B.C.–1st c. A.D.	*AC* xciv (1939), 75

(ivb) SMALL BLUE ANNULAR BEADS (TRANSLUCENT OR OPAQUE)

(under 1·5 cm. diam. and translucent if not stated)

ENGLAND

SITE AND PARISH	COUNTY	MUSEUM & NO.	DESCRIPTION AND APPROX. DIMENSIONS	ASSOCIATIONS AND REMARKS	PUBLICATION
Wilderspool, Warrington	Cheshire–Lancashire borders	Warrington 118.08	Rather more globular than most. Diam. 1 cm.	From Roman site	For site see May, T. (1904) and Thompson, F. H. (1965)
Castle Dore, Fowey	Cornwall	Truro	2 small beads. Diams. 6 mm. and 8 mm. and one lighter in colour. Diam. 1·1 cm.	From Iron Age fort, unstratified, occupied about 200 B.C.–1st c. A.D.	*JRIC* n.s. i (1946–52), 70, fig. 8, no. 5
Kynance Gate, Lizard	Cornwall	c/o Lizard Field Club, Helston	Diam. 7 mm. Another smaller and greener	From hut in a settle-ment which produced Iron Age A and South-Western B pottery and con-tinued into Roman period	

SITE AND PARISH	COUNTY	MUSEUM & NO.	DESCRIPTION AND APPROX. DIMENSIONS	ASSOCIATIONS AND REMARKS	PUBLICATION
Nor' nour, Scilly	Cornwall	St. Mary's, Scilly	Diam. 4 mm.	Roman and just pre-Roman site. Site I, Room I.	*ArJ* cxxiv (1967), 1 ff.
Cadbury Castle, Bickleigh Bridge	Devonshire		Dark greenish-blue. Diam. 1·3 cm. Ht. 9 mm. Perf. diam. 5 mm.	Not closely dated in camp—Iron Age to Roman occupation	*PDAS* lxxxiv (1952), 109–12
'Derbyshire'		B.M.	Diam. 9 mm.	Strung together with other beads found in Derbyshire in about 1790 and probably not associated	
Chalbury Camp, Bincombe	Dorset	Dorchester	Diam. 5 mm. Ht. 2 mm. Perf. diam. 2 mm.	From hut in Iron Age A fort associated with Iron Age A wares. ? 6th c. B.C. or little later	*AnJ* xxiii (1943), 118 and fig. 8, no. 53
Dorchester	Dorset	Dorchester 1886.9. 113 & 111 (B. A. Hogg Colln.)	Diam. 1 cm. Another: Diam. 7 mm.	'From Roman stratum'	
Colliton Park Villa, Dor-chester	Dorset	Dorchester	Thick annular. Diam. 1·1 cm. Ht. 7 mm. Perf. diam. 3 mm.	From Roman villa (mostly late). Begun late 2nd c. A.D.	R.C.H.M. *Dorset* ii
Gussage All Saints	Dorset	Uncertain	1 whole and 1 half bead. Translucent. Rather irregular. Both diam. 1·2 or 1·3 cm. Ht. 5 or 6 mm. Perf. diam. 4 or 5 mm.	From an early Iron Age A site with socketed bone chisels of All Cannings Cross type. 5th–4th c. B.C. ?	Information in advance of publication by Dr. Geoffrey Wainwright
Portland	Dorset	Dorchester 1932.9.2	Opaque very worn and rather slaty blue. Diam. 9 mm.	From 'The Verne' Romano-British cemetery	
Dorchester (Poundbury Camp cemetery)	Dorset	Dorchester	Slightly striated surface. Diam. 9 mm. Ht. 4 mm. Perf. diam. 3 mm.	Late Roman. Stray find in cemetery	Information from Mr. Christopher Green, 1973
Waddon Hill, Stoke Abbott	Dorset	Bridport	Half a translucent blue bead and a turquoise greenish-blue about 1 cm. in diam.	From a Claudian fort	Preliminary reports in *PDNHAS* lxxxii (1960) and lxxxvi (1963)
Cirencester	Gloucester-shire		Very small. Diam. 3 mm.	Barnsley Park Roman villa, occupied 2nd–4th c. A.D.	Information from Dr. Graham Webster

SITE AND PARISH	COUNTY	MUSEUM & NO.	DESCRIPTION AND APPROX. DIMENSIONS	ASSOCIATIONS AND REMARKS	PUBLICATION
Bredon, Bredon's Norton	Gloucester-shire–Worces-tershire borders	Private museum at Overbury Court	Dark blue, opaque and rather globular. Diam. 1·3 cm. Ht. 1 cm.	Probably from the last period of the inner entrance. About mid-1st C. A.D.	*ArJ* xcv (1938)
Crickley Hill, Coberley	Gloucester-shire		Diam. *c.* 8 mm. Translucent. Another with flattened surface	Unstratified from hill-fort with occupation apparently before 450 B.C.	Information from Mr. Philip Dixon, 1972 and 1973
Portchester	Hampshire		Striated around cir-cumference. Diam. 9 mm. Ht. 3 mm. Perf. diam. 5 mm.	Stratified from late Roman deposits	Information from Prof. Barry Cunliffe
Silchester	Hampshire	Reading	Several examples of varying sizes and both opaque and translucent.	Probably pre-Roman or Roman period	
Winchester (Lankhills cemetery)	Hampshire		Diam. 8 mm.	From necklace 436 in Grave 323. A foreign grave dated *c.* A.D. 350–70	Clark, G. (forthcoming) fig. 86, g
Croft Ambrey hill-fort, Lucton	Herefordshire	c/o S.C. Stanford, Dept. Extra Mural Studies, Birmingham	One, smaller, has flattened top and bottom surfaces. Diam. 5 mm. The larger has less flattening on surfaces. Diam. 8 mm.	The smaller example provisionally dated late 3rd c. B.C. and the larger 1st c. A.D.	Stanford, S. C. (1974)
Weston-under-Penyard, Bollitree	Herefordshire	Gloucester 1759, 1763, 1764, 1765, 1766, 1767	Almost all small and about 7 mm. diam. One (1763) is almost opaque. One (1767) is slightly biconical and one (1759) is larger, opaque with diam. 1·2 cm.; ht. 9 mm.	Probably 1st c. A.D.	*JBAA* xxvii (1871), 211 ff.
Poston Camp, Vowchurch	Herefordshire	Hereford	Diam. about 8 mm.	From Iron Age camp occupied 1st c. B.C.–2nd c. A.D.	I. E. Anthony, *The Iron Age Camp at Poston, Hereford-shire* (Woolhope Club, 1958), and R.C.H.M. *Herefords.* i (1931), 245 and ii (1934), pp. xlvii–ix
St. Albans	Hertfordshire	Verulamium Museum	Diam. 6 mm.	Found in 1944 in Room V of Roman villa	

SITE AND PARISH	COUNTY	MUSEUM & NO.	DESCRIPTION AND APPROX. DIMENSIONS	ASSOCIATIONS AND REMARKS	PUBLICATION
Ballacagen A	Isle of Man	Douglas, I.o.M.	Diam. 6 mm. Another larger, diam. 1 cm.	One from Phase I of round-house. Probably 2nd or 1st c. B.C. Larger one unstratified	Bersu, G., *Three Iron Age Round Houses in the Isle of Man* (1977)
London	London	Formerly Guildhall Museum 3964	Diam. 1·2 cm., irregular shape, slightly biconical	From Dowgate Hill	
London	London	Formerly Guildhall Museum 2604	Diam. 1·2 cm. Wide perforation	No exact location	
Chinnor	Oxfordshire	A.M. 167 and the other in Aylesbury Museum on loan	Diam. 6 mm. Another: Diam. 8 mm.	From Iron Age A settlement. ? 5th c. B.C.	*AnJ* xxxi (1951), 146, fig. 10, no. 5
Bath	Somerset	Pump Room and Museum, Bath	Clear cobalt. Diam. 9 mm. Ht. 2 mm. Perf. diam. 5 mm.	From Roman town founded late 1st c. A.D.	
Glastonbury	Somerset	Glastonbury G6, G15	Various sizes	From Lake Village. Occupation beginning 2nd c. B.C. and ending in early 1st c. A.D.	*Gl* ii, frontispiece
Meare	Somerset	Taunton	A number of various sizes both translucent and opaque	From Iron Age village. 3rd–1st c. B.C. ?	*Me* iii
'Mendip'	Somerset	Bristol F2072 (A. C. Pass Colln.)	Opaque light blue-grey. Diam. 1·2 cm.	Stray find from site producing many Roman finds	
Worlebury hill-fort (Weston-super-Mare)	Somerset	(Not in Weston-super-Mare)	Diam. 9 mm. Ht. 5 mm. Perf. diam. 3 mm.	From a pit in the hill-fort	Dymond, C.W., *Worlebury* (1902), pl. x, no. 15
Farley Heath, Albury	Surrey		Diam. 1·1 cm.	Found in 1847 on site of a Romano-Celtic temple	*A* xxxiv (1851), pl. v, no. 12
Fishbourne	Sussex	Fishbourne Roman palace	Half-bead. About 1 cm. diam.	1st c. A.D.	*Fi* ii, fig. 69, no. 2
Baginton	Warwickshire		Diam. 1·1 cm. Ht. irregular 2–3 mm.	From Romano-British site	*PCNHSS* ii, no. 5 (1951)
Ryton-on-Dunsmore	Warwickshire	Coventry	Very thin. Diam. 6 mm. Large perforation	Iron Age context	*ArJ* cxxi (1965), 1–22
All Cannings Cross	Wiltshire	Devizes	Very worn and grey. Slight peripheral groove. Diam. 8 mm. Perf. diam. 5 mm.	Iron Age settlement with long occupation	Cunnington, M. E. (1923), p. 120, pl. 18, xvi
Cold Kitchen Hill, Brixton Deverill	Wiltshire	Salisbury	Diam. *c.* 7 mm.	Mostly Roman period finds from this site	*WAM* xliii (1925–7), 180 ff. and 327 ff., and xlviii (1937–9), 185–8

SITE AND PARISH	COUNTY	MUSEUM & NO.	DESCRIPTION AND APPROX. DIMENSIONS	ASSOCIATIONS AND REMARKS	PUBLICATION
Mancombe Down, Warminster	Wiltshire	Salisbury	Diam. 1·3 cm. Ht. 6 mm. Perf. diam. 4 mm.	Pre-Roman settlement	*WAM* lx (1965), 53
Swallowcliffe	Wiltshire	Devizes F3	Rather globular. Diam. 1 cm.	From Iron Age settlement *c.* 4th–3rd c. B.C.	*WAM* xliii (1925–7), 88–9, 546 and pl. vii
Swallowcliffe	Wiltshire	Devizes F4	Another lighter in colour very slightly smaller	Probably 4th–3rd c. B.C.	*Ibid.*
Swallowcliffe	Wiltshire	Devizes F2 & F5	Diams. about 1·2 cm.	Probably 4th–3rd c. B.C.	*Ibid.*
Wick Wood, Nettleton	Wiltshire	c/o Bath and Camerton Arch. Soc.	No. 620 has diam. 3 mm. No. 1311 is badly made and irregular: Diam. 1·1 cm. (Half only)	Romano-British and later. No. 1311 was post-Roman and No. 620 'after 330 A.D.'	Wedlake, W. J. (forthcoming)
Wick Wood, Nettleton	Wiltshire	c/o Bath and Camerton Arch. Soc.	Another light blue: Diam. 9 mm.; ht. 2 mm.; perf. diam. 6 mm.	Stratified in post-Constantinian level	Wedlake, W. J. (forthcoming)
Ogbourne St. George	Wiltshire	Devizes 132	Opaque dark. Irregular and rather globular. Diam. 1·1 cm. Small perforation	Stray find	
Rotherley	Wiltshire	Salisbury	Diam. 6 mm.	Romano-British	Pitt-Rivers, A. H. L. F. (1888) and *ArJ* civ (1947)
Teffont Evias	Wiltshire	Salisbury 4/49	Opaque and very worn. Diam. 1·3 cm.	From a quarry. Stray find	
Beckford	Worcestershire		Half bead. Translucent. Diam. 1·3 cm. Ht. 6 mm. Perf. diam. 6 mm.	Associated with 'duck' stamped and linear tooled wares	Information from W. J. Britnell, University College, Cardiff
Bredon (Conderton Camp)	Worcestershire	Birmingham	2 examples. About 6 and 7 mm. in diam. 2 others very fine in section	Site contemporary with Meare and Glastonbury earlier phase	Forthcoming. Information from Mr. N. Thomas
Burton Fleming	Yorkshire		Pale translucent blue. Diam. 6 mm. Ht. 2 mm. Perf. diam. 3 mm.	From Iron Age cemetery. ? 3rd–2nd c. B.C.	Information from Dr. Ian Stead
Doncaster	Yorkshire		Dark blue. Diam. 6 mm. Ht. 3 mm.	From Roman site at Edlington Wood	Grimes, W. F. (ed.) (1951), pp. 90–1

SITE AND PARISH	COUNTY	MUSEUM & NO.	DESCRIPTION AND APPROX. DIMENSIONS	ASSOCIATIONS AND REMARKS	PUBLICATION
			IRELAND		
Dunshaughlin crannog, Lagore	Co. Meath		Diam. 8 mm. (no. 813)	Óne example from period Ia. This must be either early like the Meare spiral bead from the same site, or 7th c. A.D.	*PRIA* liii C (1950–1), 134
Tara	Co. Meath	Dublin	Bright translucent cobalt. Diam. 5 mm. Ht. 2 mm. Perf. diam. 3 mm.	From the Rath of the Synods which produced Roman 1st–3rd c. A.D. pottery	Ó Ríordáin, S. P. (1964)
			SCOTLAND		
Dunadd	Argyllshire		Irregularly made and rather globular. Diam. 1 cm.	Stronghold of the Dalriadic Scots, 7th–8th c. A.D. or a little earlier perhaps initially	*PSAS* xxxix (1904–5), 315
Kildonan Fort	Argyllshire		Diam. 8 mm. half only	Not very closely datable but between 2nd–7th c. A.D. and perhaps Scottic	*PSAS* lxxiii (1938–9) and lxxvii (1942–3)
Ugadale Fort, Kintyre	Argyllshire	? Glasgow		Probably 8th c. A.D.	*PSAS* lxxxviii (1954–6), 19
Siccar Point, Cockburnspath	Berwickshire	N.M.A. FJ126	Diam. 7 mm.	From middle of Iron Age fort	*PSAS* lxix (1935), 158
Dunagoil Fort	Bute	Rothesay Museum	3 examples all under 1 cm. in diam. 2 at least are opaque	Probably 1st c. B.C.– 1st c. A.D. native fort with some Roman period occupation	*TBNHS* viii (1914–15), 42–9 and 68–86
Traprain Law	East Lothian	N.M.A. nos. 1922.245; 23.172; 260, III 20.382, etc.	Various examples all small and some opaque	Native fort occupied through Roman period	For site, see refs. in Rivet, A. L. F. (ed.) (1966)
Nr. Coulter	Lanarkshire	N.M.A. FJ33, Sim Colln.	Rather light blue. Diam. 1·5 cm., wide perforation	Stray find	
Fendom Sands	Ross-shire		About ¾ of bead. Diam. 1·1 cm., wide perforation		
Bonchester	Roxburghshire	N.M.A.	Diam. 8 mm.	Probably Roman period or later. (The remarks then published need not now hold good for dating)	*PSAS* lxxxiv (1949–50), 128
Yair	Selkirkshire	Mr. Mason's Colln., Selkirk	Diam. 1·2 cm., wide perforation	Stray find by river bank	
Culbin Sands	Morayshire	N.M.A.	About 8 examples various sizes and blues		

SITE AND PARISH	COUNTY	MUSEUM & NO.	DESCRIPTION AND APPROX. DIMENSIONS	ASSOCIATIONS AND REMARKS	PUBLICATION
Culbin Sands	Morayshire	Miss Young's Colln., Edinburgh 1954	About 10 examples		
Nr. Selkirk	Selkirkshire	Mr. Mason's Colln., Selkirk	One very fine section. Diam. 8 mm. and another more globular. Diam. 4 mm.		
Dun Ardtreck, Skye	Inverness-shire	Hunterian Museum, Glasgow	Several very small examples	Probably early 1st c. B.C. From galleried wall-fort. Small annular opaque yellow beads from the same archaeological horizon	*An* xxxix (1965) for preliminary report and *ibid*. xliii (1969) for more accurate dating
Glenluce Sands	Wigtownshire	N.M.A.	Several examples		
Castle Island, Mochrum	Wigtownshire	c/o Lord David Stuart, Old Place of Mochrum, Port William	2 examples, one diam. 6 mm., another diam. 8 mm.	With other beads including Roman melon beads and finds of later date as well	*TDGNHAS* xxviii (1949–50)
		WALES			
Coygan Camp, Lougharne	Carmarthen-shire		2 examples, one flattened surface. Diam. 1 cm. One Diam. 4 mm.	Stratified late 3rd c. A.D.	Wainwright, G. J. (1967)
Moel Hiraddug, Dyserth	Flintshire		Broken. Diam. 1 cm. Ht. 5 mm. Perf. diam. 6 mm.	Topsoil behind inner rampart of Iron Age hill-fort	Information from Jeffrey Davies, University College, Aberystwyth
Twyn-y-Gaer hill-fort, Cwmyoy	Monmouth-shire	To be either in N.M.W. or Abergavenny	2 examples, 7 mm. and half one of 1 cm. diameter. The smaller has flattened upper and lower surfaces. The half-bead is badly made and irregular	The smaller example came from under the revetment wall of the second stone phase of the east gate. ? 3rd to 1st c. B.C.; the half-bead, not closely dated within the same bracket, came from the annex fence of the ? first phase	Information from excavator, L. A. Probert (see Boon, G. C. and Lewis J. M. (eds.), *Welsh Antiquity* (1976), pp. 105–19)
Sudbrook	Monmouth-shire		2 examples. One small, diam. 1·2 cm., ht. 6 mm., perf. diam. 4 mm., and one medium size came from this site	One at least should be native and of 1st c. B.C.–1st c. A.D.	*AC* xciv (1939), 75
Caldy Island (Nanna's Cave)	Pembroke-shire			Small blue bead with Romano-British pottery	*AC*, 6th s., xvii (1917), 73

SITE AND PARISH	COUNTY	MUSEUM & NO.	DESCRIPTION AND APPROX. DIMENSIONS	ASSOCIATIONS AND REMARKS	PUBLICATION
Caldy Island (Potter's Cave)	Pembroke-shire		48 beads of various sizes and blues. Most have flattened surfaces	Found in a midden sealed by blown sand layer of Roman or post-Roman date	Information from Brother James, The Abbey, Caldy Island
Moel Trigarn	Pembroke-shire	Tenby	Flattened upper and lower surface like many small annular beads of opaque yellow type—diam. 1·1 cm.	From hill-fort. The same fort produced a bead of Meare spiral type Class 6 3rd–2nd c. B.C.	*AC*, 5th s., xvii (1900), 189–211

(v) SMALL TRANSLUCENT 'AMBER' (REDDISH-BROWN)

ENGLAND

SITE AND PARISH	COUNTY	MUSEUM & NO.	DESCRIPTION AND APPROX. DIMENSIONS	ASSOCIATIONS AND REMARKS	PUBLICATION
Whitcombe	Dorset	Dorchester	Irregular 'amber' coloured. Diam. 1·5 cm. Ht. 3 mm. Perf. diam. 8 mm. 3 others. Also fragments of a very light yellow one, and two wooden beads	From 1st c. A.D. burial On necklace dated A.D. 96–110 from associated Samian	Information from Mrs. Aitken Information from Mrs. Aitken
Silchester	Hampshire	Reading	Pinkish-brown. Diam. 1·1 cm. Ht. 5 mm. Perf. diam. 5 mm.	Site occupied *c.* 1st–5th c. A.D.	
Kenchester	Herefordshire	Hereford 165L	'Amber'. Diam. about 9 mm. Ht. irregular about 2 or 3 mm. and another similar	Roman town occupied till about A.D. 390	*TWNFC* 1916 and 1926
St. Albans (King Harry's Lane)	Hertfordshire	Verulamium	One reddish-brown. Diam. 1·4 cm. Ht. 4 mm. Perf. diam. 7 mm.	From necklace on Burial 29 of Aylesford type cemetery dated *c.* 10 B.C.–A.D. 40	Information from Dr. I. M. Stead
Richborough	Kent	Richborough 39, 31	Several badly shaped light brownish-yellow. Diam. about 1 cm.	From Roman and Saxon site	Information from Mr. G. C. Dunning
Tunbridge Wells	Kent		Reddish-brown. Diam. 1 cm. Ht. 5 mm. Perf. diam. 5 mm.	From High Rocks Camp (late Iron Age) 2nd c. B.C. to Roman conquest	*SAC* cvi (1968)
Bath	Somerset	Bath, Roman Baths Museum	3 similar, reddish-brown, varying between diams. 6 and 9 mm. All are small ring-beads with wide perforation	From Roman Bath site	Cunliffe, B. *Roman Bath Discovered* (1971) and refs.

SITE AND PARISH	COUNTY	MUSEUM & NO.	DESCRIPTION AND APPROX. DIMENSIONS	ASSOCIATIONS AND REMARKS	PUBLICATION
			SCOTLAND		
Culbin Sands	Morayshire		Reddish. Appears very new. Diam. 1·2 cm.		
			WALES		
Caerwent	Monmouth-shire	Newport D.2.353	Brownish-yellow. Diam. 1·1 cm. Perf. diam. 6 mm.	From Roman site	
		(VI) SMALL OPAQUE TERRACOTTA COLOURED			
			ENGLAND		
Croft Ambry, Lucton	Herefordshire	Hereford 223	Over a cobalt core. Diam. 1·4 cm. Ht. 8 mm. Perf. diam. 3 mm.	From hill-fort ? 1st c. A.D.	Stanford, S. C. (1974)
Meare	Somerset	Taunton G73	Over a ? yellow core. Diam. 8 mm. Ht. 3 mm. Perf. diam. 4 mm.	From mound XXVIII ? 3rd–1st c. B.C.	Me iii
		(VII) SMALL OPAQUE OR TRANSLUCENT SKY BLUE			
			ENGLAND		
Cople	Bedfordshire	c/o James Dyer, 45 Ashcroft Rd., Luton, Beds.	Light blue. Diam. 8 mm. Ht. 5 mm. Perf. diam. 3 mm.	Unstratified mixed site. Ring ditch of Iron Age A date with subsequent building inside. The bead almost certainly belongs to the later (undated) phase	Information (1962) from excavator
South Shields	Durham	From University Museum, Newcastle-upon-Tyne	Diam. 7 mm. Ht. 3 mm. Perf. diam. very small	Fort occupied c. A.D. 122-369	See Richmond, I.A. (1953)
			IRELAND		
Tara	Co. Meath	Dublin (Tara, no. 132)	Opaque turquoise	Rath of the Synods which produced Roman pottery of 1st–3rd c. A.D.	ÓRíordáin, S. P. (1964)
			SCOTLAND		
Newstead	Roxburgh-shire	Private hands (Mr. Mason, Selkirk)	Diam. 7 mm. Ht. 2 mm. Perf. diam. very small	Site occupied c. A.D. 80-200. Stray find	For site see Ne
Selkirk (Nr.)	Selkirkshire	Private hands	Diam. 5 mm. Ht. 3 mm. Perf. diam. 2 mm.	From Mr. Mason's Colln., Selkirk. Stray find	

SITE AND PARISH	COUNTY	MUSEUM & NO.	DESCRIPTION AND APPROX. DIMENSIONS	ASSOCIATIONS AND REMARKS	PUBLICATION
			(viii) SMALL OPAQUE BEADS, OTHER COLOURS		
			(Note that yellow beads of this type are separately discussed as Class 8, below)		
			SCOTLAND		
Glenskirdie	Aberdeenshire	N.M.A. FN 174	? glass yellow-brown. Diam. 1·2 cm. Ht. 4 mm. Perf. diam. 5 mm.	Presented by Hugh Lumsden in 1937	
Traprain Law, Prestonkirk	East Lothian	N.M.A.	Half opaque bottle-green. Diam. 1·0 cm. Ht. 5 mm. Perf. diam. 5 mm.	From hill-fort occupied in Roman period	Richmond, I. A. (ed.) (1958)
			(ix) SMALL, VERY DARK ('BLACK') BEADS		
			ENGLAND		
Worth Matravers	Dorset		Dull black. Diam. 1 cm. Ht. 2 mm. Perf. diam. 6 mm.	Surface find west of road to Kingston	Information from Mr. R. A. H. Farrar
South Shields	Durham	University Museum, Newcastle-upon-Tyne	Glossy. Diam. 1 cm. Ht. 2 mm. Perf. diam. 5 mm.	Roman fort occupied c. A.D. 122–369	Richmond, I. A. (1953)
Weston-under-Penyard, Bollitree	Hereford-shire	Gloucester 1751	Glossy. Diam. 1·3 cm. Ht. 3 mm. Perf. diam. 7 mm.	From site of Roman *Ariconium*	Information from Mr. T. G. Barnett
Corbridge	Northumber-land	Corstopitum Museum	Glossy and slightly irregular. Diam. 1·2 cm. Ht. 3 mm. Perf. diam. 7 mm.	From Roman *Corstopitum* occupied 1st–5th c. A.D. Old excavations	
Meare	Somerset	Taunton G49EV	Jet black. Diam. 1·2 cm. Ht. 6 mm. Perf. diam. 3 mm.	From the East Village of Iron Age site occupied ? 3rd–1st c. B.C.	*Me* iii
			IRELAND		
'Ireland'		Belfast, Benn Colln. 1912.183	About 26 beads both glossy and opaque. Diam. c. 1·7 cm.		
			SCOTLAND		
Culbin Sands	Morayshire	N.M.A.	Glossy. Diam. 1·3 cm. Ht. 4 mm. Perf. diam. 5 mm. Another slightly smaller	Chance finds	
Dykeside	Harray, Orkney	N.M.A. FJ122	Glossy. Diam. 1·2 cm. Ht. 3 mm. Perf. diam. 6 mm.		Information from Mr. John Fraser, 1930

SITE AND PARISH	COUNTY	MUSEUM & NO.	DESCRIPTION AND APPROX. DIMENSIONS	ASSOCIATIONS AND REMARKS	PUBLICATION

GROUP 7

UNDECORATED GLOBULAR BEADS

(i) LARGE GLOBULAR BEADS IN VARIOUS COLOURS

ENGLAND

SITE AND PARISH	COUNTY	MUSEUM & NO.	DESCRIPTION AND APPROX. DIMENSIONS	ASSOCIATIONS AND REMARKS	PUBLICATION
Hamworthy	Dorset	Poole	Semi-translucent bright cobalt. Diam. 1·7 cm. Ht. 1·5 cm. Perf. diam. 6 mm.	From pre-Roman and Roman site	H. P. Smith, *History of Poole*, Pt. i, pp. 46–7
Tuffley	Gloucester-shire	Gloucester Museum, no. 1028	Bright translucent cobalt. Diam. 1·7 cm. Ht. 1·5 cm. Perf. diam. 5 mm.	Stray find from Roman and post-Roman site	
Wilderspool, Warrington	Lancashire-Cheshire-border	Warrington, no. 51	Bright green. Diam. 1·7 cm. Ht. 1·6 cm.	From Roman site	For site, see May, T. (1904) and Thompson, F. H. (1965)
Rainsborough Camp, Newbottle	Northampton-shire	A.M.	Fragment only. Diam. 2·5 cm. Ht. 2·3 cm. Perf. diam. 5 mm.	From late Iron Age level, ? 2nd–1st c. B.C., in Iron Age fort	*PPS* xxxiii (1967), fig. 28, no. 121
Glastonbury	Somerset	Glastonbury G8	Greeny blue opaque but probably origin-ally translucent. Diam. 1·6 cm. Ht. 1·2 cm. Perf. diam. 7 mm.	Pre-Roman	*Gl* ii
Meare	Somerset	Taunton G9	Translucent brownish-yellow. Diam. 2 cm. Ht. 1 cm. Perf. diam. 7 mm.	From East Village of pre-Roman site	*Me* iii
Bury Wood Camp, Colerne	Wiltshire		Half bead. Translu-cent. Striated. Diam. 2·2 cm. Ht. 1·5 cm. Perf. diam. 9 mm.	From what seem clearly Iron Age B associations (2nd–1st century B.C. ?)	For interim reports on this site see *WAM* lviii (1961), 40–7 and 185–208; lxii (1967), 1–5, and lxiv (1969), 21–50
Skipton	Yorkshire	Skipton	Opaque. Blue. Diam. 1·8 cm. Ht. irregular 1·1 cm. Perf. diam. 6 mm.	From an Iron Age enclosure	To be published in *YAJ*

IRELAND

Some beads of this form are known from Ireland but from collections

SITE AND PARISH	COUNTY	MUSEUM & NO.	DESCRIPTION AND APPROX. DIMENSIONS	ASSOCIATIONS AND REMARKS	PUBLICATION

SCOTLAND

Two yellowish-brown examples are in the N.M.A. in Edinburgh. They are both translucent and about 23 mm. in diameter. They come from Craigsford Mains, Earlston, Berwickshire (N.M.A. FJ142) and from Birrens, Dumfries (N.M.A. FP254). See for the latter *PSAS* xxx (1896), 81 ff.

WALES

SITE AND PARISH	COUNTY	MUSEUM & NO.	DESCRIPTION AND APPROX. DIMENSIONS	ASSOCIATIONS AND REMARKS	PUBLICATION
Moel Trigarn Fort	Pembroke-shire	Tenby	Natural glass. 7 half-beads about 1·8 cm. diam. Ht. 1·3 cm. Some of these had been repaired in antiquity	Iron Age fort. With a Meare spiral bead (Class 10) about 3rd to 1st c. B.C.	*AC*, 5th s., xvii (1900)

(ii) MEDIUM AND SMALL GLOBULAR BEADS IN NATURAL GREENISH TRANSLUCENT GLASS

ENGLAND

SITE AND PARISH	COUNTY	MUSEUM & NO.	DESCRIPTION AND APPROX. DIMENSIONS	ASSOCIATIONS AND REMARKS	PUBLICATION
Nor' nour, Scilly	Cornwall	St. Mary's, Scilly, nos. 114, 65	2 small beads about diam. 7 mm.	Most of the occupation of this site was 1st–4th c. A.D.	*AC*, 5th s., xvii (1900)
Holcombe Roman Villa	Devonshire	Sidmouth	Irregularly made. Diam. 8 mm. Ht. 9 mm.	Unstratified from Roman villa. The bronze mirror from this villa is in the B.M.	*PDAS* xxxii (1974)
Woodyates	Dorset	Salisbury	2 or 3 small examples	Early Romano-British	Pitt-Rivers, A. H. L. F. (1888)
Colchester	Essex	Colchester	Rather darker than normal. Diam. 1·5 cm. Ht. 1·4 cm.	From burial group 94. Apparently with other beads but the group has been confused	May, T. (1930), 279
Cirencester	Gloucester-shire		Half-bead. Diam. 7 mm. Ht. 5 mm. Perf. diam. 2 mm.	From the Roman villa at Barnsley Park. Occupation 2nd–4th c. A.D.	Information from Dr. G. Webster
Silchester	Hampshire	Reading	Small beads (several)	On necklace. Site occupied throughout Roman period	For refs. see Collingwood and Richmond, *The Archaeology of Roman Britain* (rev. ed. 1969) and Boon, G. C. (1957)
Kenchester	Herefordshire	Hereford	Diam. 6 mm. Ht. 7 mm. Very small perforation	From Roman town occupied till *c.* A.D. 390	*TWNFC* 1916 and 1926

SITE AND PARISH	COUNTY	MUSEUM & NO.	DESCRIPTION AND APPROX. DIMENSIONS	ASSOCIATIONS AND REMARKS	PUBLICATION
Weston-under-Penyard, Bollitree	Herefordshire	Gloucester, nos. 1755, 1753	Almost opaque now through weathering. Diam. 1·4 cm. Ht. 1 cm. Perf. diam. 5 mm. Another smaller	With many early Roman objects	*JBAA* xxvii (1871), 211 ff.
Great Chesters	Northumberland	University Museum, Newcastle-upon-Tyne	2 examples about 1 cm. in diam.	On Roman necklace. Early excavations	
Castle Hill, Whitton	Suffolk	Ipswich	A number of small beads strung on wire with a flat pendant of same glass	Roman villa occupied *c.* A.D. 130–290	*PSAI* xxi (1931–3), 249 ff.

IRELAND

Grannagh, Ardrahan	Co. Galway	Galway ?	Diameter and height 1·7 cm. ? reused Roman bottle glass	Very like the St. David's beads. Probably first four centuries A.D. Perhaps pillaged Roman glass	*PRIA* xxxiii (1916–17), 508

WALES

Coygan Camp, Lougharne	Carmarthenshire	c/o G. Wainwright	Rather large irregular and perhaps made of reused Roman glass	Late 3rd c. A.D.	Wainwright, G. J. (1967)
Merthyr, Mawr Warren	Glamorganshire	N.M.W. 50.466/37	Diam. 9 mm. Ht. 6 mm. Perf. diam. 4 mm.	Mixed pre-Roman and Roman finds	*BBCS* xiv (1952), 170–1
Whitton, nr. Barry	Glamorganshire	N.M.W.	Diam. 7 mm. Ht. 6 mm. Very small perforation	Site of Roman villa. Occupied 1st c. B.C.– *c.* A.D. 300	Information from Dr. M. Jarrett
Caerwent	Monmouthshire	Newport D2.351	Diam. 9 mm. Ht. 1·1 cm. Very small perforation	From House 13 of Roman town	Information from Dr. G. C. Dunning
Usk	Monmouthshire		Diam. 6 mm. Ht. 6 mm. Very small perforation	Roman fort. Main occupation A.D. 55–60 but sporadic later Roman occupation	Information from excavator
Moel Trigarn	Pembrokeshire	Tenby	Several examples of varying sizes	From huts in hill-fort with Iron Age and later occupation	*AC,* 5th s., xvii (1900)
St. David's Head	Pembrokeshire	Tenby	Several examples	The beads from this site look sub- or post-Roman	

SITE AND PARISH	COUNTY	MUSEUM & NO.	DESCRIPTION AND APPROX. DIMENSIONS	ASSOCIATIONS AND REMARKS	PUBLICATION
			(iii) MEDIUM AND SMALL GLOBULAR BEADS TRANSLUCENT OR OPAQUE GREEN GLASS		
			ENGLAND		
Nor' nour, Scilly	Cornwall	St. Mary's, Scilly	Mixed opaque green and yellowish glass. Diam. 8 mm. Ht. 8 mm. Small perforation	This site produced many Roman finds	*ArJ* cxxiv (1967)
Woolley Barrow, Morwenstow	Cornwall		Bright bottle green. Concave boring. Diam. 6 mm.	In passage dug by tomb robbers in about the late 5th c. A.D., but perhaps not Roman	Information from Miss D. Dudley
Dorchester	Dorset	Dorchester	Light green opaque. Diam. 1·2 cm. Ht. 1·2 cm. Small perforation	From Roman stratum	R.C.H.M. *Dorset*
Dorchester	Dorset	Dorchester, Hogg's Colln.	Opaque. Diam. 1 cm. Ht. 1·1 cm. Perf. diam. 3 mm.	Probably from the town	R.C.H.M. *Dorset*
Bagendon	Gloucestershire		Dark bottle green almost opaque. Diam. 5 mm.	Mid-1st c. A.D.	Clifford, E. M. (1961)
Tuffley	Gloucestershire	Gloucester 1030	Almost opaque. Diam. 6 mm.	Stray find on site producing Roman and post-Roman objects	
Winchester (Lankhills Cemetery)	Hampshire		Several beads, green or greenish-yellow, diam. approx. 3 mm.	Necklaces 85, 182, 215, 424, and 425, all in grave variously dated with the period A.D. 310–70	Clarke, G. (forthcoming), figs. 73, a, 79, a, 80, l, 87, a, 90, c
Lincoln (Flaxengate)	Lincolnshire	Lincoln City and County Museum	2 examples	Both could be stratigraphically either Roman or medieval	*JRS* xxxviii(1948), 88
London	London	Formerly Guildhall Museum 17215	Dark translucent. Diam. 7 mm.	Chance find	
'Mendip'	Somerset	A. C. Pass Colln., Bristol F2090	Translucent squarish. Diam. 5 mm.	Probably Roman	*VCH Somerset*
Shepton Mallet	Somerset	Shepton Mallet	Translucent. Diam. 8 mm. Ht. 8 mm. Very small perforation		

SITE AND PARISH	COUNTY	MUSEUM & NO.	DESCRIPTION AND APPROX. DIMENSIONS	ASSOCIATIONS AND REMARKS	PUBLICATION
			IRELAND		
Tara	Co. Meath	Dublin	Well made, translucent dark greenish. Diam. 9 mm. Ht. 8 mm. Perf. diam. 2 mm.	From the Rath of the Synods which produced 1st–3rd c. Roman pottery (excav. no. 204). The bead is probably Roman	ÓRíordáin, S. P. (1964)
Tara	Co. Meath	Dublin	Smaller and bluer green	Excav. no. 182	

SCOTLAND

Two examples from the Culbin Sands (Moray) in N.M.A. in Edinburgh are undated

| Clettraval | North Uist Inverness-shire | N.M.A. | Half bead, described as pale green translucent. Diam. 1·4 cm. Ht. 1·4 cm. Perf. diam. 3 mm. | This was found below the level of the floor in an aisled round-house but is thought to have worked down from a higher level. It is probably of early Roman date | PPS xiv (1948), 66 |

WALES

Two very small ones from Laugharne (Coygan Camp) in Wales belong to the late 3rd c. A.D. (Wainwright, G. J. (1967))

(iv) MEDIUM AND SMALL BLUE, TRANSLUCENT OR OPAQUE GLOBULAR BEADS

ENGLAND

Thatcham	Berkshire	Newbury	Translucent light blue. Diam. 9 mm. Ht. 8 mm. Perf. diam. 2 mm.	Romano-British settlement	TNDFC vii (1937), 219 ff.
Santon Downham	Cambridgeshire	C.M.	Blue swirled glass. Diam. 1·4 cm. Ht. 9 mm. Perf. diam. 3 mm.	With 1st c. A.D. hoard	Fox, C. (1923), 104
Nor' nour, Scilly	Cornwall	St. Mary's, Scilly	Light cobalt blue translucent and badly made possibly part of segmented bead about 3 mm. diam.	Mostly 2nd c. A.D. finds but others of Roman period generally	ArJ cxxiv (1967)
St. Mawgan-in-Pyder	Cornwall	Truro	Rich cobalt, semi-translucent. Diam. 1·1 cm. Ht. 9 mm. Small perforation	Unstratified in pre-Roman and early Roman period settlement (Carloggas)	ArJ cxiii (1956)
Fordington, Dorchester	Dorset	Dorchester	A number of small examples	From cemetery mostly 4th c. A.D.	Smith, C. Roach (1852), iii and R.C.H.M. Dorset ii

SITE AND PARISH	COUNTY	MUSEUM & NO.	DESCRIPTION AND APPROX. DIMENSIONS	ASSOCIATIONS AND REMARKS	PUBLICATION
Woodcuts	Dorset	Salisbury	2 examples. Diam. 1 cm. Diam. 1·4 cm.	Surface trenching in Romano-British site	Pitt-Rivers, A. H. L. F. (1887), pl. xliv, nos. 11 and 12 and *ArJ* civ (1947)
Colchester	Essex	Colchester	Bright translucent cobalt. Diam. 1·4 cm. Ht. 1·1 cm.	From group 94 dated A.D. 150–200. Group possibly confused).	May, T. (1930), 279
Bagendon	Gloucester-shire		Semi-translucent fragment. Diam. 1·1 cm. Ht. 9 mm. Perf. diam. 3 mm.	Pre-Roman Belgic of 1st c. A.D.	Clifford, E. M. (1961)
Bredon, Bredon's Norton	Gloucester-shire–Worces-tershire borders	Private museum at Overbury Court	Dark opaque. Diam. 8 mm. Ht. 7 mm.	Probably last period of inner entrance of hill-fort. 1st c. ? B.C.	*ArJ* xcv (1938), 86 and fig. 12
Winchester (Lankhills Cemetery)	Hampshire		Blue, diam. 6–3 mm.	Necklaces 85, 215, 248, 353, 425, all variously dated within the period A.D. 310–70	Clarke, G. (forthcoming)
Weston-under-Penyard, Bollitree	Herefordshire	Gloucester 1758	Opaque rich cobalt. Diam. 1 cm. Ht. 9 mm. Perf. diam. 2 mm.	Probably early Romano-British. (The site produced an Oldbury type bead)	*JBAA* xxvii (1871), 211 ff.
Weston-under-Penyard, Bollitree	Herefordshire	Gloucester 1749, 1747	2 others slightly smaller	Probably early Romano-British. (The site produced an Oldbury type bead)	*JBAA* xxvii (1871), 211 ff.
Weston-under-Penyard, Bollitree	Herefordshire	Gloucester 1770	Opaque dull blue. Diam. 5 mm. Ht. 5 mm. Very small perforation	Probably early Romano-British. (The site produced an Oldbury type bead)	*JBAA* xxvii (1871), 211 ff.
St. Albans	Hertfordshire	Verulamium	One or two on neck-lace	Dated 'probably 4th c.' A.D.	*Ve*, p. 214 and fig. 47
London	London	Formerly Guildhall Museum 17217/17216, 3964	Three examples, all translucent	All chance finds	
Great Chesters	Northumber-land	University Museum, Newcastle-upon-Tyne	Several	Roman necklace. Old excavations	
Chesters Fort	Northumber-land	Chesters Museum 614	Several examples	Clayton excavation. Likely date between A.D. 122–383	
Brislington	Somerset	Bristol F2318	Slightly translucent. Diam. 9 mm.	Roman villa, occu-pied late 3rd to mid-4th c. A.D.	*TBGAS* xxiii (1900) and xxiv (1901)
Ham Hill (Montacute)	Somerset	Taunton	Rich dark trans-lucent. Diam. 8 mm. Ht. 8 mm. Very small perforation	Iron Age hill-fort with later occupation. Mostly late Iron Age and Roman	*VCH Somerset* i, p. 295 and *ArJ* cvii (1950), 90

SITE AND PARISH	COUNTY	MUSEUM & NO.	DESCRIPTION AND APPROX. DIMENSIONS	ASSOCIATIONS AND REMARKS	PUBLICATION
Meare	Somerset	Taunton G1	Rich dark cobalt. Slightly mottled and opaque. Diam. 9 mm. Ht. 8 mm. Perf. diam. 3 mm.	From pre-Roman settlement. ? 3rd–1st. c. B.C.	*Me* iii
Whitton	Suffolk	Ipswich	Several mounted on bronze rings. Diam. 6 mm.	Roman villa (Castle Hill) occupied *c.* A.D. 130–290	*PSIA* xxi (1931–3), 249 ff.
Cold Kitchen Hill, Brixton Deverill	Wiltshire	Devizes	Almost opaque. Diam. 1 cm. Ht. 8 mm.	Hundreds of late Roman period beads came from this hill. ? Romano-Celtic temple here. Site probably deserted by mid-4th c. A.D.	*WAM* xliii (1925–7), 183 ff.
Stockton Earthworks	Wiltshire	Salisbury	Light cobalt, translucent. Diam. 4 mm.	Belgic-Roman	*WAM* xliii (1925–7)
Wick Wood, Nettleton	Wiltshire	c/o Bath and Camerton Arch. Soc.	Several small beads	Roman necklace 'before A.D. 284'	Information from Mr. W. J. Wedlake
Dowles Brickyard	Worcestershire	Once in Bewdley Institute		Two beads from what seems to have been an early Iron Age urnfield. Sherds in Kidderminster Museum	Information from Miss L. F. Chitty
Catterick	Yorkshire		Small cobalt blue, opaque	Roman site	Information from Mr. J. Wacher
Seamer	Yorkshire	Scarborough	Deep translucent cobalt. Diam. 1·5 cm. Ht. 9 mm. Perf. diam. 4 mm.	From Roman site. Found with rusticated ware of *c.* A.D. 90–110 in ditch of enclosure	For site see *JRS* xxxviii (1948), 86 and *YAJ* xxxvii (1950), 420–8

IRELAND

SITE AND PARISH	COUNTY	MUSEUM & NO.	DESCRIPTION AND APPROX. DIMENSIONS	ASSOCIATIONS AND REMARKS	PUBLICATION
Loughey, Donaghadee	Co. Down	B.M. 62. 7–1.19	A number of small globular beads	Necklace including Meare spiral beads, etc., dated by brooch to 1st c. B.C. or A.D.	*UJA* xx (1957), 74–95 and *ArJ* xiii (1856), 407

A number come from the Lagore Crannog and several from the Rath of the Synods, Tara. 1st–3rd c. A.D. A number of milky-blue opalescent beads from the Benn Colln., Belfast. Date unknown. The type persisted throughout the post-Roman period and is found on Teutonic necklaces—generally rather striated on the surfaces (unpolished).

SCOTLAND

SITE AND PARISH	COUNTY	MUSEUM & NO.	DESCRIPTION AND APPROX. DIMENSIONS	ASSOCIATIONS AND REMARKS	PUBLICATION
Coulter	Lanarkshire	N.M.A. FJ34	Roughly made. Diam. 9 mm. Ht. 9 mm. Perforation irregular	A number of post-Roman beads come from this locality	

SITE AND PARISH	COUNTY	MUSEUM & NO.	DESCRIPTION AND APPROX. DIMENSIONS	ASSOCIATIONS AND REMARKS	PUBLICATION
Covesea	Morayshire	N.M.A. HM211	Opaque, slightly biconical. Diam. 9 mm. Ht. 6 mm. Perf. diam. 5 mm.	Site produced some 2nd c. A.D. Roman imported glass	*PSAS* lxv (1930–1), 177
Dun Ardtreck	Skye	Glasgow		From a necklace. From galleried wall-fort of 1st c. B.C.–1st c. A.D. date	*An* xxxix (1965)

A number of small beads from Glenluce and Culbin Sands in the N.M.A., Edinburgh.

WALES

SITE AND PARISH	COUNTY	MUSEUM & NO.	DESCRIPTION AND APPROX. DIMENSIONS	ASSOCIATIONS AND REMARKS	PUBLICATION
Caerwent	Monmouth-shire	Monmouth	Several small, pale blue, translucent and opaque	With pottery of late 1st to early 2nd c. A.D.	Information from Mr. G. C. Dunning
Usk	Monmouth-shire		Slight flattening around perforation. Diam. 7 mm. Ht. 7 mm. Perf. diam. 2 mm.	Roman fort occupied from A.D. 55–60 and again in late Roman times	Awaiting publication

One or two badly made tiny examples, perhaps locally made, from Coygan Camp, Laugharne (Carmarthenshire), and several large beads from huts on St. David's Head, Pembrokeshire. These are in Tenby Museum and are probably post-Roman or Irish. For the site, see *AC*, 5th s., xvi (1899), 105 ff. and, for Coygan, see Wainwright, G. J. (1967)

(v) MEDIUM AND SMALL OPAQUE AND TRANSLUCENT SKY BLUE GLOBULAR BEADS

ENGLAND

SITE AND PARISH	COUNTY	MUSEUM & NO.	DESCRIPTION AND APPROX. DIMENSIONS	ASSOCIATIONS AND REMARKS	PUBLICATION
Bottisham Milford	Cambridge-shire	C.M., Beck Colln. 47, 560, 1739	A number of examples	All from collns.	
Wilderspool, Warrington	Cheshire–Lancashire border	Warrington 570.06	Diam. 9 mm. Ht. 8 mm. Perf. diam. 2 mm.	From Roman industrial site	May, T. (1904) and Thompson F. H. (1965)
Castle Dore, Fowey	Cornwall	? Lost	? Opaque or translucent. Diam. 8 mm. Ht. 8 mm. Perf. diam. 2 mm.	Fort occupied about 200 B.C. to 1st c. A.D. and again in the 5th c. A.D.	*JRIC*, n.s., i (1946–52), fig. 8, no. 7 (wrongly illustrated in report)
West Ham	London	Passmore-Edwards Museum, Newham	Half opaque. Sky blue. Diam. 6 mm.	Found with Roman material in Prince Regent Lane in 1918	
Dorchester	Dorset	Dorchester 1886.9.112	Slightly translucent. Diam. 8 mm. Ht. 8 mm. Perf. diam. 2 mm.	From Roman stratum	See R.C.H.M. *Dorset* ii
Somerleigh	Dorset	Dorchester	Very light in colour. Diam. 7 mm. Ht. 6 mm.		

SITE AND PARISH	COUNTY	MUSEUM & NO.	DESCRIPTION AND APPROX. DIMENSIONS	ASSOCIATIONS AND REMARKS	PUBLICATION
Sydling	Dorset	Dorchester	Slightly translucent. Diam. 8 mm. Ht. 8 mm. Perf. diam. 2 mm.		
South Shields	Durham	University Museum, Newcastle-upon-Tyne	Diam. 1 cm. Ht. 6 mm. Perf. diam. 2 mm.	From Roman site occupied c. A.D. 122–369	Richmond, I. A. (1954) and *JRS* lvii (1967)
Cirencester	Gloucester-shire	Cirencester	Many examples	Unstratified in Roman town occupied from 1st to 5th c. A.D. or later	*AnJ* xlix (1969), 222 and earlier reports
Kingscote	Gloucestershire		A number of pale opaque or bright translucent beads about 1 cm. diam.	From surface of area of Roman site producing 1st c. A.D. finds	Information from Messrs. Graham Walker and Ted Swain
Silchester	Hampshire	Reading	Half only. Diam. 1·1 cm. Ht. 8 mm. Perf. diam. 3 mm.	Occupation throughout Roman period	For refs. see Collingwood and Richmond, *The Archaeology of Roman Britain* (rev. ed. 1969)
Kenchester	Herefordshire	Hereford	Diam. 8 mm. Ht. 6 mm. Very small perforation	Site occupied almost throughout Roman period	*TWNFC* 1916 and 1926
Weston-under-Penyard, Bollitree	Herefordshire	Gloucester 1740-1748	Various examples	From Roman site of *Ariconium*	*JBAA* xxvii (1871), 211 ff.
Richborough	Kent	Richborough 2140	Diam. 9 mm. Ht. 9 mm. Perf. diam. 2 mm.	Topsoil in Roman fort road	*Rich* iv, p. 242
High Rocks Camp, Tunbridge Wells	Kent		Diam. 8 mm. Ht. 7 mm. Perf. diam. 4 mm.	Surface find in High Rocks Iron Age Camp. Originally Iron Age B, refortified later with flat-bottomed ditch of Fécamp type	*SAC* cvi (1968), 158
Hampstead	London	C.M., Beck Colln.	About 1 cm. diam.		
Meare	Somerset	Taunton G24	Pale sky blue. Diam. and ht. 8 mm. Small perforation	From Iron Age settlement, 3rd c. B.C. to 1st c. A.D. occupation	*Me* iii
Lakenheath	Suffolk	C.M., Beck Colln.	A number of various sizes and shapes		
Amesbury	Wiltshire	C.M., Beck Colln. 2553	Diam. 1 cm. Ht. 8 mm. Perf. diam. 3 mm.	From 'Vespasian's' Camp. Iron Age but not verified by excavation	

SITE AND PARISH	COUNTY	MUSEUM & NO.	DESCRIPTION AND APPROX. DIMENSIONS	ASSOCIATIONS AND REMARKS	PUBLICATION
Salisbury Plain	Wiltshire	C.M., Beck Colln. 1738	Diam. 1 cm. Ht. 1 cm. Perf. diam. 3 mm.	Found '3 miles from Stonehenge towards Devizes'	
Templebrough	Yorkshire	Rotherham	A number, both translucent and opaque	Unstratified from fort thought to be Flavian and Hadrianic	See May, T. (1922)

SCOTLAND

Fragment from Glenluce, Wigton, in Stranraer Museum
(no. 343A) and another in N.M.A.

(vi) MEDIUM AND SMALL GLOBULAR BEADS: YELLOW OR 'AMBER' (REDDISH-BROWN)
TRANSLUCENT OR OPAQUE

(These do not yet constitute a group but are mostly sporadic finds some of which may not be ancient. They are as follows:)

ENGLAND

Nor' nour, Scilly	Cornwall	St. Mary's, Scilly	Translucent yellow-fawn. Diam. 5 mm. Ht. 5 mm. Perf. diam. 1 mm.	The site produced mainly Roman objects	*ArJ* cxxiv (1967)
Gloucester	Gloucester-shire	Gloucester Museum 1289	Yellow-green. Diam. 5 mm. Ht. 3 mm. Very small perforation		
Gloucester	Gloucester-shire	Gloucester Museum 1287	Bright orange. Diam. 9 mm. Ht. 6 mm. Perf. diam. 4 mm.		
St. Albans	Hertfordshire	Verulamium Museum 232		From late Roman necklace	See *Ve*, p. 214 and fig. 47
Wilderspool, Warrington	Lancashire–Cheshire border	Warrington Museum 1299	Bright, clear reddish-yellow. Diam. 1·4 cm. Ht. 1·3 cm. Perf. diam. 2 mm.	Probably Roman	May, T. (1904) and Thompson, F. H. (1965)
Meare	Somerset	Taunton G82	Like the small opaque yellow annular beads of Class 8. Diam. 1·1 cm. Ht. 8 mm. Perf. diam. 3 mm.	From Mound XIII in pre-Roman site	*Me* iii
Meare	Somerset	Taunton G44	Smaller. Opaque lemon yellow	From Mound XVII in pre-Roman site	*Me* iii

WALES

Dinas Powys	Glamorgan-shire	N.M.W.	One pale yellow fragment. Roman or ? Teutonic. Diam. 1·5 cm.		Alcock, L. (1964)

(vii) TERRACOTTA-COLOURED GLOBULAR BEADS (OPAQUE)
(Not Scheduled)

SITE AND PARISH	COUNTY	MUSEUM & NO.	DESCRIPTION AND APPROX. DIMESNIONS	ASSOCIATIONS AND REMARKS	PUBLICATION
			(viii) MEDIUM AND SMALL 'BLACK' OPAQUE BEADS		
			ENGLAND		
Weston-under-Penyard, Bollitree	Herefordshire	Gloucester 1750	Bright shiny 'black'. Diam. 1·3 cm. Ht. 1·2 cm. Perf. diam. 2 mm.	Site produced early Roman and later beads	*JBAA* xxvii (1871), 211 ff.
Hunsbury Hill-Fort, Hardingstone	Northamptonshire	Northampton	Dull blackish. Diam. 2·2 cm. Ht. 1·4 cm. Perf. diam. 6 mm.	From pre-Roman fort. ? 4th c. B.C. to early 1st c. A.D.	Fell, C. (1936), p. 68 and *JNNHSFC* xviii and xix
Yockleton	Worcestershire	c/o Miss L. F. Chitty, F.S.A.	Diam. 1·1 cm. Ht. 9 mm. Perf. diam. 2 mm.	Found in Moor Field with 18th c. pottery on line of probable Roman road	Information from Miss L. F. Chitty

IRELAND

Nothing from a definitely pre-Roman or early Christian period. A number of examples in the Dublin and Belfast museums from collections. It is clear that black glass was commonly made in Ireland but it is not possible yet to date the beads.

SCOTLAND

SITE AND PARISH	COUNTY	MUSEUM & NO.	DESCRIPTION AND APPROX. DIMESNIONS	ASSOCIATIONS AND REMARKS	PUBLICATION
Coulter Seat, Udney	Aberdeenshire	N.M.A. FJ40, 41	Two examples. Diams. 1·2 cm. approx.		
Birrens	Dumfriesshire	N.M.A. FP253	Diam. 1·1 cm. Ht. 8 mm.	Antonine fort. Constructed A.D. 158	*PSAS* xxx (1895–6), 81 and lxxii (1937–8), 270
Dun Beag	Skye		Glossy slightly barrel shaped. Diam. 1·3 cm. Ht. 1·3 cm. Perf. diam. 5 mm.	From brooch with post-Roman occupation	*PSAS* lv (1920–1), 110

WALES

One from a mixed R.B. and later site at Laugharne (Carmarthenshire) and two from hut sites on St. David's Head, (Pembrokeshire), probably Roman period or post-Roman, in Tenby Museum.

SITE AND PARISH	COUNTY	MUSEUM & NO.	DESCRIPTION AND APPROX. DIMENSIONS	ASSOCIATIONS AND REMARKS	PUBLICATION

GROUP 8

EXOTIC IRON AGE BEADS

ENGLAND

SITE AND PARISH	COUNTY	MUSEUM & NO.	DESCRIPTION AND APPROX. DIMENSIONS	ASSOCIATIONS AND REMARKS	PUBLICATION
Boxford	Berkshire	Newbury	Fragment of blue cobalt large annular bead with raised blobs and swags like continental armlets. Diam. 3 cm. Ht. 1·6 cm. Perf. diam. *c.* 1·1 cm. (fig. 23, no. 7)	From Iron Age habitation site. Exactly similar bead found at Vieux Passage, Brittany (1st c. B.C.). A glass bracelet came from Guervech (Brech) associated with La Tène III Gaulish coins (2nd half 1st c. B.C.) and from Castle Dore, Fowey, Cornwall. See also Wiedmer Stern, F., *Das gallische Gräberfeld bei Münsingen* (1908), p. 78, Taf. 24, 5. With fibulae of La Tène II type	*TNDFC* vi (1933), 211–17. See also *ArJ* c (1943), 140
St. Mawgan-in-Pyder, Carloggas	Cornwall	Truro	Part of damaged bead —perhaps thick annular. Translucent greeny blue glass with opaque yellow roughly parallel vertical bands	Could be imitation of Celtic whirl bead. Site occupied 1st c. B.C.–mid-Roman period	*ArJ* cxiii (1956), 33–81 and see *C.B.A. Research Report*, 7, p. 78
Trevelgue Head, Newquay	Cornwall	Truro	Translucent blue-green fragment of ring bead decorated with white double swag with opaque yellow spots between. Diam. 3·8 cm. Ht. 8 mm. Perf. diam. *c.* 2·4 cm. (fig. 23, no. 3)	From Trevelgue Head Iron Age promontory fort. It was probably occupied from *c.* 200 B.C. throughout the Roman period	Inadequately published. See note in Thomas, C. (ed.) (1966), 78 and footnote
Maiden Castle, Winterbourne Monkton	Dorset	Dorchester	Fragment of black glass bead with white blobs round circumference. Shape and decoration uncertain.	From Belgic road in E. entrance. Dated after mid-1st c. B.C. in recent revision	*MC*, p. 292, no. 11
Bagendon	Gloucester-shire	Cheltenham	Dark blue glass core fragment covered with reddish glass and white patches of in-crustation. Evidently damaged by fire	Stratified in Belgic *oppidum* A.D. 10–50	Clifford, E. M. (1961)

SITE AND PARISH	COUNTY	MUSEUM & NO.	DESCRIPTION AND APPROX. DIMENSIONS	ASSOCIATIONS AND REMARKS	PUBLICATION
Hunsbury, Hardingstone	Northamptonshire	Northampton	Large part of bottle glass biconical bead with raised running swags of translucent blue glass above and below carination. Diam. 4 cm. Ht. 1·9 cm. Perf. diam. 1·9 cm. (fig. 23, no. 5)	Unstratified in Roman hill-fort. Perhaps occupied 2nd–1st c. B.C.	Fell, C. (1936), pp. 68–9 and fig. 3, no. 7
Shakenoak, Wilcote	Oxfordshire		Large blue, white, green, red and yellow mixed glass annular bead fragment. Diam. 1·8 cm. Perf. diam. 8 mm.	Certainly native. Perhaps reusing Roman glass	Brodribb, A. C. C., Hands, A. R. and Walker, D. R., *Excavations at Shakenoak* ii (1971), 105
Clevedon	Somerset	Taunton	8 barrel-shaped very thin clear glass beads, coated in red glass. Hand moulded, and of varying sizes. About 1·3 cm. long and 7 mm. diam. at end and 1·1 cm. at centre (fig. 23, no. 6)	Necklace of these beads and 10 small annular beads of Class 8 and one of Meare Class 11 with a burial	*PSANHS* lxxxviii (1942), 73. A possibly similar bead was found at Shapwick, Dorset. See Warne, C. (1866), 39–40. Another necklace of these beads is said to have come from Meare
Meare	Somerset	Taunton G25	Small blue opaque pulley-shaped bead exactly like Badsey (Worcester) example below	From site occupied 3rd–1st c. B.C.	*Me* iii
All Cannings Cross	Wiltshire	Devizes	Long rather drop-shaped bead of yellowish-green translucent glass with dark blue chevrons. Or the dark blue may be the ground colour. Length 1·2 cm. Width 5 mm. Very small diameter perforation (fig. 23, no. 1)	From Iron Age settlement with long occupation	Cunnington, M. E. (1923), pl. 19, no. 9 and p. 122
Badsey	Worcestershire	c/o Miss L. F. Chitty or Worcester Museum	Small, pale blue opaque pulley-shaped bead (fig. 23, no. 4)	There is 'duck' stamped ware, etc., from Badsey but not associated. Exactly like Meare specimen G25	See for site *ANL* (October 1949), 88

SITE AND PARISH	COUNTY	MUSEUM & NO.	DESCRIPTION AND APPROX. DIMENSIONS	ASSOCIATIONS AND REMARKS	PUBLICATION
Burton Fleming	Yorkshire		Half annular yellow opaque glass, like Class 8 but with crossing swags (once coloured). Diam. 1 cm. Ht. 4 mm. Perf. diam. 5 mm.	With objects of ? 3rd–2nd c. B.C. in Iron Age cemetery	Information from Dr. Ian Stead
			IRELAND		
Loughey, Donaghadee	Co. Down		For details p. 126		

IRON AGE BEADS OF BRITISH DESIGN AND ORIGIN

CLASS 8

SMALL OPAQUE YELLOW ANNULAR BEADS

SITE AND PARISH	COUNTY	MUSEUM & NO.	DESCRIPTION AND APPROX. DIMENSIONS	ASSOCIATIONS AND REMARKS	PUBLICATION
			ENGLAND		
Castle Dore, Fowey	Cornwall	Truro	Diam. 9 mm.	From Iron Age camp, unstratified. Occupation *c.* 200–50 B.C. and post-Roman	*JRIC*, n.s., i (1946–52), 69, fig. 8, no. 3
Maiden Castle, Winterbourne Monkton	Dorset	Dorchester		From Iron Age A level of hill-fort	*MC*, p. 291 and fig. 98, no. 1
South Shields	Durham	University Museum, Newcastle-upon-Tyne	2 examples with flattened surface, one diam. 8 mm. and another smaller	Fort occupied *c.* A.D. 122 to 4th c.	
Silchester	Hampshire	Reading	Diam. 6 mm.	Site occupied 1st c. B.C.–5th c. A.D.	Boon, G. C. (1957) and *A* cii (1969)
Kenchester	Herefordshire			Unstratified in Roman town founded 2nd half of 1st c. A.D. and occupied till late Roman period	Jack, G. H. & Hayter, A. G. K. *Excavations on the site of the Romano-British Town of Magna (Kenchester)* (1916), pl. 45, no. 3 and *TWNHFC* 1958 and 1961
Ballacagen A	Isle of Man	Douglas	12 beads graduated. All characteristically flattened around perforation	From same horizon as armlets of 2nd–1st c. B.C. Continental type Phase I of Celtic round-house	Bersu, G., *Three Iron Age Round Houses in the Isle of Man* (1977)
Bolham (Huckhoe Fort)	Northumberland	c/o G. Jobey, F.S.A. Newcastle-upon-Tyne	Rather flattened surface. Diam. 3 mm.	From reused soil in wall of hut of early Roman date	*AA*, 4th s., xxxvii (1959)
Corbridge	Northumberland	Corstopitum Museum, 4325	Diam. 1 cm.	Occupation 1st–5th c. A.D.	
Halton Chesters	Northumberland	University Museum, Newcastle-upon-Tyne, 1956.202	Flattened surface. Diam. 1·1 cm. Ht. 3 mm. Perf. diam. 3 mm.	Fort on Hadrian's Wall	
Housesteads	Northumberland	University Museum, Newcastle-upon-Tyne	Diam. 8 mm.		

SITE AND PARISH	COUNTY	MUSEUM & NO.	DESCRIPTION AND APPROX. DIMENSIONS	ASSOCIATIONS AND REMARKS	PUBLICATION
'Rochester and Alnham'	Northumberland	Chesters Museum 1708 or 3801	Diam. 1 cm.	One of the two Roman sites, unstratified	
Wroxeter	Shropshire	Rowley's House Museum, Shrewsbury	No details	Not examined, but may belong to this Class. From Roman site	
Clevedon	Somerset	Taunton	Diam. 6 mm.	10 on a necklace with an inhumation burial in a cist. Some barrel-shaped, pink-covered beads and one Meare chevron type, (Class 11 a)	*PSANHS* lxxxviii (1942), 73
Meare (East)	Somerset		Necklace of these beads and Meare spirals of Class 10	Unpublished by H. St. George Gray	
Meare	Somerset	Taunton G68EV and others	Over 50 examples from West Village. Mostly under 1 cm. in diam. and with flattened surfaces. One necklace of 39 beads. One example of 2 segments	From pre-Roman site ? 2nd c. B.C.	*Me* iii, pp. 285–6
Conderton Camp, Conderton	Worcestershire	Birmingham	Slightly flattened surface. Diam. 9 mm.	From early phase of fort 3rd–2nd c. B.C. ?	Report forthcoming. Information from Mr. N. Thomas

IRELAND

SITE AND PARISH	COUNTY	MUSEUM & NO.	DESCRIPTION AND APPROX. DIMENSIONS	ASSOCIATIONS AND REMARKS	PUBLICATION
Loughey, Donaghadee	Co. Down	B.M. 62.7.1.19	Number of very small examples	Burial of 1st c. B.C. or A.D. together with fibula and Meare spiral beads and a bead of group 3 (see fig. 23, no. 2)	*UJA* xx (1957), 74–95

SCOTLAND

SITE AND PARISH	COUNTY	MUSEUM & NO.	DESCRIPTION AND APPROX. DIMENSIONS	ASSOCIATIONS AND REMARKS	PUBLICATION
Inverkeilor	Angus		Diam. 4 mm.	From promontory fort of West Mains of Ethie in same stratum as Type I glass armlet	Information from Abertay Arch. Soc.
Aitnock Fort, Dalry	Ayrshire			With objects of 1st or 2nd c. A.D.	*PSAS* liii (1919), 132
Arrieolland Crannog	Ayrshire	N.M.A.	Identical but reddish and perhaps burnt		*PSAS* xxiii (1888–9), 228 and *AGC* v (1885), 113
Howrat Castle Rock, Dalry	Ayrshire	N.M.A. HH366 to 373	8 beads of varying sizes	Greenish-yellow glass was cast in this fort	*PSAS* liii (1919), 123

SITE AND PARISH	COUNTY	MUSEUM & NO.	DESCRIPTION AND APPROX. DIMENSIONS	ASSOCIATIONS AND REMARKS	PUBLICATION
Lochspouts Crannog, Maybole	Ayrshire	N.M.A. HW19	Flattened surface. Diam. 1 cm.	Early Roman period crannog	*PSAS* xv (1880–1), 110 and *AGC* iii (1882), 15 and fig. 16
Allasdale	Barra	N.M.A.	3 examples of varying size	One from upper chamber of soutterain and others from a house of late 1st or early 2nd c. A.D.	*PSAS* lxxxviii (1952–3), 104
Freswick Links, Canisbay	Caithness	N.M.A. FJ141	Slightly flattened surface. Diam. 5 mm.		*PSAS* xxxv (1900–1), 143
Culbin Sands, Elgin	Morayshire	N.M.A. acquired about 85 beads	Slightly varied in size	Over 250 found at the base of one of the sandhills	*PSAS* xxv (1890–1), 510
Dun Troddan Broch, Glenelg	Inverness-shire	N.M.A. GA1125	Slightly flattened surface. Diam. 9 mm.	From the broch	*PSAS* lv (1920–1), 92
Dun Bhuirg, Iona	Argyllshire		2 examples not examined	From small dun with broch-type pottery	Noted in *PSAS* xxvi (1960), 348
Traprain Law, Prestonkirk	East Lothian	N.M.A.	Several examples of varying sizes	Mostly said to have come from earlier levels of native fort occupied through the Roman period	*PSAS* lv (1920–1), 198
Clickhimin	Shetland		Not seen	From pre-broch level	Hamilton, J. R. C. *Excavations at Clickhimin in Shetland* (H.M.S.O. 1968)
Fetlar	Shetland	N.M.A. FJ123	Slightly flattened surface. Diam. 8 mm.		
Dun an Iardhard Broch, Skye	Inverness-shire	N.M.A.	Diam. 1·1 cm.	Apparently in central hearth of broch	*PSAS* xlix (1914–15), 65–6 and fig. 10, 7
Dun Ardtreck, Skye	Inverness-shire	Hunterian Museum, Glasgow, SF76, 97	8 or 9 very small examples	Probably from a necklace in galleried wall fort with 2 small decorated Scottish annular beads (see Class 14)	*An* xxxix (1965)
Dun Mor Vaul, Tiree	Argyllshire	Hunterian Museum, Glasgow, nos. 409, 348, 390, 341, 250, 416, 278 of report	Several of varying sizes, from very small to diam. 9 mm.	From broch	MacKie, E. W. (1975)
Drimore, South Uist	Inverness-shire		2 examples, one diam. 1 cm.	In sand on floor of wheel-house at A Cheardach Mhor and another unstratified	*PSAS* xciii (1959–60), 150

SITE AND PARISH	COUNTY	MUSEUM & NO.	DESCRIPTION AND APPROX. DIMENSIONS	ASSOCIATIONS AND REMARKS	PUBLICATION
Glenluce Sands	Wigtownshire	Edinburgh and Stranraer	Mostly small. About 8–10 examples	Chance finds in sandhills	

WALES

Coygan Camp, Laugharne	Carmarthen-shire	Ministry of Works	Very battered. This may be a local imitation of the type	Stratified late 3rd c. A.D. but possibly earlier	Wainwright, G. J. (1967), fig. 49, no. 5
Ffestiniog	Merioneth-shire	c/o Gwynedd Arch. Trust	Slightly oval. Diam. c. 9 mm. Ht. 4 mm.	With piece of 2nd c. A.D. olla	Forthcoming
Twyn-y-gaer Fort, Cwmyoy	Monmouth-shire	Destined for N.M.W. Abergavenny	Two small examples, very finely made with flattened surfaces. Diams. 6 mm. and 5 mm. Large perforations	Smaller one was stratified with stamped pottery of about 3rd c. B.C. and and the other maybe 1st c. B.C.	Information from A. Probert, F.S.A.
The Breiddin	Montgomery-shire		Flattened surfaces. Diam. 9 mm. Ht. 3 mm. Perf. diam. 5 mm.	Found near bead of Oldbury type (Class 6) but not stratified in fort occupied into Roman period	Information from C. Musson

CLASS 9

ANNULAR BEADS DECORATED WITH TWO-COLOUR TWISTED CABLES

(a) NATURAL TRANSLUCENT GREENISH GLASS BEADS WITH COLOURED CABLES

ENGLAND

Wilderspool, Warrington	Cheshire–Lancashire border	Warrington 1294	Cable round maximum diam. and white girth-ring above and below (fig. 26, no. 3)	Roman site	May, T. (1904) and Thompson, F. H. (1965), fig. 20, no. 20
No provenance	'Cumberland'	Carlisle	Cable in yellow and natural glass. Diam. 2·6 cm. Ht. 1·1 cm. Perf. diam. 7 mm.		
Hembury Fort, Payhembury	Devonshire	Exeter 827	Fragment. Diam. 3·2 cm. Ht. 1·3 cm.	From the date of the fortification. Occupied 2nd and 1st c. B.C. until A.D. 65–70	PDAS ii, pt. 3, 164
South Shields	Durham	South Shields Museum	Very fine. White circumferential bands containing blue and red twists (see Roman exotic beads). (Perhaps an imported bead from the Near East)	Occupation about A.D. 122 to the 4th century A.D.	AA xi (1934), 81–102. See also JRS lvii (1967)

SITE AND PARISH	COUNTY	MUSEUM & NO.	DESCRIPTION AND APPROX. DIMENSIONS	ASSOCIATIONS AND REMARKS	PUBLICATION
Bagendon	Gloucester-shire		Fragment only	From Belgic site stratified A.D. 10–50	Clifford, E. M. (1961), p. 201
Cirencester	Gloucester-shire	Cirencester C909	Half bead. Indistinct, partly greenish cable. Diam. 2·8 cm. Ht. 1·4 cm. Perf. diam. 1 cm.	Unstratified in Roman town occupied from 1st c. A.D.	Information from excavator
Kingscote	Gloucestershire		3 examples, all with blue and white cables. Diam. c. 3 cm.	Surface finds from area mainly of 1st c. A.D. date	Awaiting publication
Silchester	Hampshire	Reading	Translucent light blue. Diam. 3 cm. Ht. 1·8 cm.	Occupation 1st c. B.C.–5th c. A.D.	Boon, G. C. (1957) and in *A* cii (1969)
Kenchester	Herefordshire	Hereford 6058	Fragment only. Diam. 3·3 cm. Ht. 1·4 cm.	Approximate date of this Roman town A.D. 69–392	Jack, G. H. & Hayter, A. G. K *Excavations on the Site of Magna (Kenchester)* (1916), fig. 26
Strood	Kent	Humphrey Wickham Colln.	Bottle glass ground with yellow and green cable	From Roman graves ranging in date from Claudius to Gratian	Roach Smith, C. (1848), i, pl. ii, pp. 17 ff.
Lincoln	Lincolnshire	City and County Museum, Lincoln	Armlet (not a bead) but in identical technique	Claudian	*ArJ* ciii (1946), 27
Charterhouse-on-Mendip	Somerset	Bristol F2084	Fragment. Blue and white cable. Diam. 2·9 cm. Ht. 1·8 cm. Perf. diam. 1·2 cm.	Lead mines beginning 1st c. A.D. A lead 'pig' of A.D. 49 was recovered. After A.D. 70 the mines ceased to be under Imperial control but continued in use	*VCH Somerset* i
Meare	Somerset	Taunton G. 78	Fragment of bead of 3 cm. diam. with blue-filled nicking to give cable effect	Meare village occupied c. 250 B.C.–A.D. 20	*Me* iii
Wall	Staffordshire	Birmingham	White and dark red cable	Neronian level	*TLSSAHS* viii, 13
Santon Downham	Suffolk	C.M.	Almost colourless fragment with blue and white cable. Diam. 3·2 cm. Ht. 9 mm. Perf. diam. 2 mm.	From Beck's note-books this bead was found with the important 1st c. A.D. hoard. This included much bronze-work and fragments of bluish-green glass—perhaps part of an armlet	*PCAS* xiii (1908–9), 156

SITE AND PARISH	COUNTY	MUSEUM & NO.	DESCRIPTION AND APPROX. DIMENSIONS	ASSOCIATIONS AND REMARKS	PUBLICATION
Nr. Rugby (Roman *Tripontium*)	Warwickshire		Opaque yellow and red cable. Diam. 3·4 cm. Ht. 2·2 cm. Perf. diam. 1·1 cm. (fig. 26, no. 1)	Stratified 2nd c. A.D.	*TPBAS* lxxxv (1972), 131

IRELAND

'Northern Ireland'		A.M. 1836 p. 123. 70	Blue and white cable round centre, over- lying opaque white wave	Miscellaneous collection	Unpublished. See Wilderspool and Newstead for comparable cable
'Ireland'		N.M. Dublin	Fragment. Blue and white cable. Diam. 2 cm. Ht. 1·4 cm.	Said to be one of 4 beads from collection, provenance unknown	

SCOTLAND

Traprain Law, Prestonkirk	E. Lothian	N.M.A. 1924–171	Fragment. Cables and also roundels with white spirals on blue. Diam. 2·9 cm. Ht. *c.* 1·6 cm. (fig. 26, no. 5)	From native hill-fort occupied during the Roman period and perhaps site of glass- working. Level 2. Romano-British	*PSAS* lviii (1924), 268
Aikerness Broch, Evie	Orkney	N.M.A. 360	Fused lump of part of a cabled bead or armlet	From a broch	*PSAS* lxvii (1932–3), 7
Newstead	Roxburgh- shire	N.M.A. FRA900	White wave and cir- cumferential cable in yellow and another colour now lost. Atypical (fig. 26, no. 4)	Fort occupied about A.D. 80–200	*Ne*, pl. xci, no. 20

WALES

Caerhun	Caernarvon- shire	Llandudno	Half bead. Royal blue and opaque red cable. Diam. 3·4 cm. Ht. 1·8 cm. Perf. diam. 8 mm.	Roman site	
Pen Llystyn	Caernarvon- shire	Caernarvon ?	Fragment with blue/ yellow cable. Diam. 3 cm. Ht. 1·7 cm.	Roman fort of about A.D. 80–100	*ArJ* cxxv (1968), 180
Moel y Gaer, Northop	Flintshire		Irregular band of dark blue round cir- cumference with blue and white cable. Diam. 2·7 cm. Ht. 1·3 cm. Perf. diam. 1·1 cm. (fig. 26, no. 2)	Pre-Roman native fort in course of excavation	Information from Mr. Graeme Guilbert

SITE AND PARISH	COUNTY	MUSEUM & NO.	DESCRIPTION AND APPROX. DIMENSIONS	ASSOCIATIONS AND REMARKS	PUBLICATION
Cardiff	Glamorgan-shire	N.M.W.	Wide opaque yellow band round circumference. Opaque red and white cable. Diam. 2·6 cm. Ht. 1 cm. Perf. diam. 9 mm.	Unassociated find behind Queen Street. Found about 1910	Information from Mr. George Boon
Caerleon	Monmouth-shire	Caerleon 63.228B G6	Greenish-blue ground with brown and yellow cable. Fragment. Diam. 3 cm. Ht. 1·5 cm.	Building in legionary fortress. Antonine	Boon, G. C. (1972)
Usk	Monmouth-shire		Fragment. Translucent blue and opaque white cable. Diam. 3·3 cm. Ht. 1·6 cm. Perf. diam. 1·6 cm.	Found in 1967 in Roman fort occupied in A.D. 55–60 and again in later Roman period	Information from the excavator

(b) COBALT BLUE WITH COLOURED CABLES

ENGLAND

SITE AND PARISH	COUNTY	MUSEUM & NO.	DESCRIPTION AND APPROX. DIMENSIONS	ASSOCIATIONS AND REMARKS	PUBLICATION
Fordham	Cambridge-shire	A.M. 1909–319	Purple/white cable. Diam. 2·2 cm. Ht. 1·4 cm.		
Hilbre Island	Cheshire		Yellow and green cable	Found in 1893. Surface find	Thompson Watkin, W. (1886) Roman Cheshire, p. 280
Hembury Fort, Payhembury	Devonshire	Exeter 497	Yellow-brown and white cable with patch of pale green blue glass. Fragment. Diam. 2·4 cm. Ht. 1·5 cm.	Hill-fort probably 2nd c. B.C. to c. A.D. 70	PDAS ii (1933–6), 167
Bagendon	Gloucester-shire		Blue/yellow cable. Fragment. Ht. 1·9 cm. Another fragment with green/yellow cable	Belgic oppidum. Stratified A.D. 10–50	Clifford, E. M. (1961), p. 201, fig. 42, no. 5
Silchester	Hampshire	Reading	Dark purple/white cable. Fragment. Diam. 2·9 cm. Ht. 1·3 cm. Another fragment with blue and white cable.	Occupation 1st c. B.C.–5th c. A.D.	Boon, G. C. (1957) and in A cii (1969)
Barcombe Hill, Chesterholm	Northumber-land	University Museum, Newcastle-upon-Tyne, 1947.1	White and brownish-mauve cable. Diam. 2·1 cm. Ht. 1 cm. Perf. diam. 9 mm.	No details. This hill overlooks the fort of Vindolanda on Hadrian's Wall	Information from Dr. D. J. Smith

SITE AND PARISH	COUNTY	MUSEUM & NO.	DESCRIPTION AND APPROX. DIMENSIONS	ASSOCIATIONS AND REMARKS	PUBLICATION
Camerton	Somerset		Blue with green cable. Diam. 1·6 cm. Smaller than most of this Class	Surface find, possibly unrelated to the rest of this Class	Wedlake, W. J. (1958), fig. 57, no. 8
Charterhouse-on-Mendip	Somerset	Bristol F2085 (A. C. Pass Colln.)	Cable is yellow with another colour not distinguishable. Fragment. Diam. 2·5 cm. Ht. 1·1 cm.	From Roman (and perhaps pre-Roman) lead mines in use around A.D. 40–50 and later	*VCH Somerset* i
Glastonbury	Somerset	Glastonbury G12	Fragment. Translucent blue and white cable	Iron Age village site begun about 150 B.C. abandoned before Roman period about 60 B.C.	*Gl* ii, pl. lix, G12. See also *PSANHS* cxii (1968), 21
Meare	Somerset	Taunton G78	Large fragment with tentative 'cable' incised. Diam. 2·8 cm. Ht. 1·1 cm. Perf. diam. 1·3 cm.	Occupation 3rd to 1st c. B.C.	*Me* iii
Seamills, nr. Bristol	Somerset	B.M. 91.3.276	Cable is yellow twisted with dark blue or brown. Diam. 3 cm.	From Roman port of *Portus Abonae*, of Claudian and later date	Not published. For site see *TBGAS* lxviii (1949), 184
Hales	Staffordshire	Newcastle-under-Lyme	Fragment. Mauve and white cable. Diam. 2·4 cm. Ht. 1·6 cm. Perf. diam. 9 mm.	Unstratified in Roman villa first occupied in 1st c. A.D.	Information from Mr. F. H. Goodyear. See *NSJFC* ix (1969), 115
Southwater	Sussex		Fragment. Cable of 2 yellow and 1 white twist. Diam. 2·4 cm. Perf. diam. 1 cm.	Casual find in ploughed field	Information from Miss D. Standing, Horsham
Avebury	Wiltshire	Avebury	Cable is white with another colour now indistinguishable. Fragment. Diam. 3·2 cm. Ht. 1·6 cm. Perf. diam. 1·1 cm.	From R.-B. scatter mostly late 1st–early 2nd c. A.D. from Neolithic site of Windmill Hill	Smith, I. (ed.), *Windmill Hill and Avebury* (Oxford 1965), p. 174

SCOTLAND

SITE AND PARISH	COUNTY	MUSEUM & NO.	DESCRIPTION AND APPROX. DIMENSIONS	ASSOCIATIONS AND REMARKS	PUBLICATION
Crossmichael	Kirkcudbrightshire	N.M.A. FJ124	Atypical. Imitation cable of two twisted yellow threads. Diam. 2 cm. Ht. 1·2 cm.	Found with a Roman melon bead	*PSAS* lxvii (1932–3), 314
Newstead	Roxburghshire	Mr. Mason's Colln., Selkirk	Fragment with yellow and green cable. Diam. 1·8 cm. Ht. 1·1 cm.	Unassociated find unrelated to main excavations. Roman site occupied *c.* A.D. 80–200	For site see *Ne*

SITE AND PARISH	COUNTY	MUSEUM & NO.	DESCRIPTION AND APPROX. DIMENSIONS	ASSOCIATIONS AND REMARKS	PUBLICATION

(c) BROWN OR GOLDEN BROWN WITH COLOURED CABLES

ENGLAND

SITE AND PARISH	COUNTY	MUSEUM & NO.	DESCRIPTION AND APPROX. DIMENSIONS	ASSOCIATIONS AND REMARKS	PUBLICATION
Willingham	Cambridge-shire	C.M. 1918. 160 (9–15)	Blue and white cables. Diam. 2·7 cm. Ht. 1·1 cm.	Found with beads, one of Class 3, and a bronze sceptre with a portrait thought to be Antoninus Pius	*AnJ* vi (1926), 178 and *JRS* xxiii (1923), 91 and xxxix (1949), 19
St. Giles' Hill, Winchester	Hampshire	Winchester	Blue/white cable, very broken. Diam. 3·6 cm. Ht. 2 cm.	Surface find	
Leicester	Leicestershire	Leicester 421.1965/50	Cable white and another colour not identifiable. Fragment only. Diam. 2·4 cm. Ht. 1·2 cm. Perf. diam. 1 cm.	Probably 1st c. A.D.	*B* iv (1973), 54
Lansdown, Bath	Somerset	Once in Victoria Art Gallery and Museum, Bath. Now lost	Blue cable with another unidentified colour. Fragment. Diam. 3·3 cm. Ht. 1·7 cm.	Upper Langridge Farm. Stray find	
Catsgore, Somerton and Kingsdon	Somerset		A third of a bead, almost black in appearance with blue and white cable. Approx. diam. 3·3 cm. Ht. 1·6 cm. Perf. diam. 1·6 cm. Slightly concave inside of perf.	Site dated A.D. 70–80 to A.D. 370. Romano-Celtic settlement	Preliminary report in C.B.A. (Groups XII and XIII) *A. R.* 7 (1972), 41. Information from Mr. Roger Leech

WALES

SITE AND PARISH	COUNTY	MUSEUM & NO.	DESCRIPTION AND APPROX. DIMENSIONS	ASSOCIATIONS AND REMARKS	PUBLICATION
Caerwent	Monmouth-shire	D.O.E.	Blue/white cable. Diam. 2·8 cm. Ht. 1·4 cm.	From Roman town with 1st c. A.D. pottery and coin of Nero	Forthcoming

CLASS 10

MEARE 'SPIRAL' BEADS

ENGLAND

SITE AND PARISH	COUNTY	MUSEUM & NO.	DESCRIPTION AND APPROX. DIMENSIONS	ASSOCIATIONS AND REMARKS	PUBLICATION
Chester	Cheshire	Chester 24.R.63	Max. diam. 1·2 cm. Ht. 9 mm.	Chance find, 1963, in 29 Argyll Avenue, Curzon Park	Unpublished
Maiden Castle, Winterbourne Monkton	Dorset	Dorchester	Diam. 1·1 cm. Ht. 8 mm.	Stratified with BII pottery, perhaps early 1st c. B.C. on revised dating	*MC*, p. 291, no. 8 and fig. 98

SITE AND PARISH	COUNTY	MUSEUM & NO.	DESCRIPTION AND APPROX. DIMENSIONS	ASSOCIATIONS AND REMARKS	PUBLICATION
South Shields Roman Fort	Durham	South Shields Fort Museum	Diam. 1·2 cm. Ht. 1·3 cm.	Occupation *c.* A.D. 122–369	*AA* 4th s., xi (1934), 81–102. See *JRS* lvii (1967)
Meare	Somerset		Necklace of these beads and small annular opaque (Class 8)	Unpublished by H. St. George Gray	Information from Mr. M. Avery
Meare	Somerset	Taunton	Large numbers	Pre-Roman Iron Age village. ? 3rd c. B.C.	See *Me* iii
South Cadbury	Somerset		One example about 1·5 cm. diameter	From a pit with decorated Glastonbury ware, in Iron Age fort	Information from Prof. Leslie Alcock
			IRELAND		
Garryduff	Co. Cork	Cork	Diam. 1·1 cm. Ht. 8 mm.	Found in habitation refuse in Dark Age site, it is probably an earlier stray	*PRIA* lxiii, C (1963)
Sheephaven (Campion Sands), Rosguil	Co. Donegal		Diam. 1·3 cm. 'A clear glass bead with raised yellow spiral ornament'	This seems to have later been used as a pin-head. The bead was evidently not properly marvered	*JRSAI* xxxii (1902), 228
Rosapenna Sandhills	Co. Donegal	Belfast 1–1908	Diam. 1·1 cm. Ht. 9 mm.	Given by R. Welch	*JRSAI* xxxii (1902), 228
Loughey, Donaghadee	Co. Down	Glass armlets and 152 beads in B.M. and bronzes in A.M.	8 examples of this type, all normal size	Almost surely a native of the S. English Iron Age, buried in 1st. c. B.C. or A.D., if this is the correct date of the Roman brooch, etc., with the burial	*ArJ* xiii (1856), 407 and Jope, E. M. (1957), 74–95 and (1960)
Lagore Crannog	Co. Meath	N.M. Dublin W27	2 examples, Diams. 1·5 and 1·8 cm. respectively	From Lagore Crannog. One unstratified from 7th c. A.D. Crannog and one from the nearby site of Dunshaughlin	Wilde, W.R. (1861), pp. 165, 167, fig. 123, no. 21, and *PRIA* liii, C (1950)
			SCOTLAND		
Culbin Sands	Morayshire	N.M.A. BIB62	Mass of fused glass originally a bead of clear glass with yellow spirals, and a section of an armlet of green glass with longitudinal cables in various colours	This shows the contemporaneity of the Meare spiral beads and 1st–2nd c. A.D. armlets, at least in Scotland, and suggests that the Culbin Sands were used for manufacturing beads at this date	*PSAS* lxxxviii (1954–6), 218

SITE AND PARISH	COUNTY	MUSEUM & NO.	DESCRIPTION AND APPROX. DIMENSIONS	ASSOCIATIONS AND REMARKS	PUBLICATION
'Orkney'	Orkney			Said to be identical to example from Caerwent. Both are atypical	Waring, J. B., *Rude Stone Monuments in Orkney* (1870), pl. 53, fig. 5a
Glenluce Sands	Wigtownshire	N.M.A.	2 examples both *c.* 1·3 cm. diam. Ht. 1·2 cm. One very fine. The other coarser with flattened facets	Stray finds	Unpublished

WALES

Anglesey	Anglesey	B.M.	Diam. 1·8 cm. Ht. 1·3 cm.	No information	Unpublished
Pen Dinas (native fort), Aberystwyth	Cardiganshire		Globular. Diam. 1·2 cm.	Occupation layer in native fort, perhaps colonized from Welsh marches	*AnJ* xv (1935), 66 and *AC* cxii (1963), 152
Caerwent	Monmouthshire	Caerwent Museum	More triangular and flatter than normal in section.	Said to be identical to one from Orkney	*A* lxxx (1930), 39, fig. 2 and 240
Moel Trigarn (Iron Age fort)	Pembrokeshire	Tenby	Diam. 1·8 cm. Ht. 2·4 cm.	With late Iron Age objects in Hut 21	*AC*, 5th s., xvii (1900), 189 ff. and 203, fig. 6

CLASS 11

'MEARE VARIANT' BEADS

(Clear glass with opaque yellow decoration)
See also Classes 5, 10, and 12

TYPE (a): MULTIPLE CHEVRONS

ENGLAND

Risby Warren	Lincolnshire	Scunthorpe R18	Diam. 1·2 cm. Ht. 7 mm. Perf. diam. 5 mm.	Site produced mixed finds mostly Roman-Saxon but Belgic site of Dragonby is very near	
Caynham Camp, nr. Ludlow	Shropshire		Diam. 1·2 cm. Ht. 6 mm. Perf. diam. 5 mm.	Iron Age hill-fort	*TSAS* lviii (1966), 99 and fig. 22
Clevedon	Somerset	Taunton	Rather straight sides. Diam. 1·1 cm. Ht. 9 mm. Perf. diam. 2 mm.	With red barrel-shaped beads and small opaque yellow annular beads of Class 8 from urn in inhumation burial in a cist	*PSANHS* lxxxviii (1942), 73 ff.

SITE AND PARISH	COUNTY	MUSEUM & NO.	DESCRIPTION AND APPROX. DIMENSIONS	ASSOCIATIONS AND REMARKS	PUBLICATION
Ham Hill, Montacute	Somerset	Taunton	Half a bead. Diam. 1·6 cm. Ht. 1·3 cm. Perf. diam. 5 mm. Another, very damaged, seems to be very similar but probably Type (g)	From late Iron Age hill-fort. Just below rampart and near the old turf line. The second is unstratified	*PSANHS* lxxxviii (1942), 73 ff. and *ArJ* cvii (1950), 90
Glastonbury	Somerset	Glastonbury Lake Village Museum G22	Diam. 1·1 cm. Ht. 1 cm.	From pre-Roman village site of about 150 B.C. Abandoned *c.* 60 B.C.	*Gl* ii
Meare	Somerset	Taunton	Over 2 dozen examples	From pre-Roman village site. 3rd–1st c. B.C. ?	*Me* iii

SCOTLAND

Glenluce Sands	Wigtownshire		No details	Two of these beads are referred to by Bulleid and Gray in *Gl* ii, 358, n. 2	

TYPE (b): YELLOW CIRCUMFERENTIAL BANDS WITH RADIATING HERRING-BONE LINE

ENGLAND

Meare	Somerset	Taunton G14	Diam. 1·1 cm. Ht. 8 mm. Perf. diam. 4 mm. One herring-bone design separated by circumferential type	Pre-Roman village site	*Me* iii

IRELAND

Carrowmore	Co. Sligo	Dublin WK450	Diam. 6 mm. Ht. 5 mm. Perf. diam. 3 mm. One herring-bone design separated by circumferential type	From cist burials in a cemetery with bronze ring	Wood-Martin, W. G., *The Lake Dwellings of Ireland* (Dublin, 1886)
Lagore Crannog	Co. Meath	Dublin 1202	Another somewhat similar but not identical and very damaged. The decoration is not herring-bone but parallel lines each side of central band	Mainly 7th c. A.D. but some much earlier beads. Note that this bead is atypical of the Iron Age series and is likely to be later	*PRIA* liii, C (1950–1)

SITE AND PARISH	COUNTY	MUSEUM & NO.	DESCRIPTION AND APPROX. DIMENSIONS	ASSOCIATIONS AND REMARKS	PUBLICATION
			TYPE (c) : TWO CIRCUMFERENTIAL CHEVRONS		
			ENGLAND		
St. Buryan	Cornwall	Penzance	Annular bead with almost clear glass with 2 yellow opaque chevrons. Diam. about 2 cm.	In neighbourhood of circle and [Bronze Age] barrows at Boscawen-un	
		TYPE (d) : SEVERAL CIRCUMFERENTIAL BANDS AT RIGHT-ANGLES TO PERFORATION			
			ENGLAND		
Meare	Somerset	Taunton G29EV and another	Diam. 1·1 cm. Ht. 9 mm. Perf. diam. 4 mm.	From mound XXI and another from recent excavations	*Me* iii and information from Mr. Michael Avery
			TYPE (e) : YELLOW OVERALL TRELLIS		
			ENGLAND		
West Overton Down	Wiltshire		Diam. 1 cm. Ht. 7 mm. Perf. diam. 5 mm.	From Iron Age site, Site XI, top of Iron Age A pit	*WAM* lxii (1967). Preliminary report in *CA* 16 (Sept. 1969)
		TYPE (f) : YELLOW BANDS ROUGHLY PARALLEL TO PERFORATION			
			ENGLAND		
Meare	Somerset	Taunton G84	Half of a flat large annular ring bead. Diam. 2·9 cm. Ht. 6 mm. Perf. diam. 2 cm.	From Meare East, XIII Iron Age village	*Me* iii
			TYPE (g) : SINGLE WAVE ROUND CENTRE		
			ENGLAND		
Great Chesterford	Cambridge-shire	C.M.	Diam. 2·1 cm. Ht. 9 mm. Perf. diam. 1·4 cm.	From a site producing finds from 1st c. B.C. to end of Roman period	
Madmarston Camp, Swalecliffe	Oxfordshire	A.M. 1969.165	Tinge of bluish-green in yellow waves. Diam. 2·5 cm. Ht. 6 mm. Perf. diam. 1 cm.	Iron Age camp with post-Roman occupation	*O* xxv (1960)
Ham Hill, Montacute	Somerset	Taunton HHG5	Fragment. Very damaged. Appears to be a wave rather than chevron	From near the turf line below late Iron Age rampart	*PSANHS* lxxxviii (1942), 73 ff.
Meare	Somerset	Taunton G4EV	A stud bead. For details, see p. 84	From Iron Age village site	*Me* iii

SITE AND PARISH	COUNTY	MUSEUM & NO.	DESCRIPTION AND APPROX. DIMENSIONS	ASSOCIATIONS AND REMARKS	PUBLICATION
Meare	Somerset	Taunton G33, 34, 52	Annular beads of various sizes	From Iron Age village site	*Me* iii

IRELAND

Note that a number of larger colourless glass annular beads with yellow wave come from Northern Ireland, particularly Co. Antrim. The date of these is still not yet known

SCOTLAND

Nr. Newstead	Roxburgh-shire	Mr. Mason's Colln., Selkirk	One chevron	In fields near New-stead occupied 1st–2nd c. A.D.	Information from Mr. R. B. K. Stevenson

TYPE (h): CIRCUMFERENTIAL BANDS OVERLAID BY LOOPED DESIGN

ENGLAND

Meare	Somerset	Taunton G69, G114, G120	Barrel-shaped about 1 cm. diam.	From Iron Age village	*Me* iii (1967)

TYPES (i)–(k)—NOT SCHEDULED, SEE p. 83.

CLASS 12

STUD BEADS

ENGLAND

Meare	Somerset	Taunton G4EV	Clear glass decorated with opaque yellow waves. Diam. of larger end 1·8 cm.; at smaller end 1·3 cm. Length 1·3 cm. Perf. diam. 6 mm. (fig. 32, no. 1)	From pre-Roman village. (For technical affinities, see Class 11)	*Me* iii (1966)
Lidbury Camp, Enford	Wiltshire	Devizes	Diam. at larger end 1·5 cm. and at smaller end 8 mm. The bead is made of opaque yellow glass and 1 cm. in height (fig. 32, no. 2)	This came from a pit associated with late Iron Age A pottery. On current dating this is thought to be 3rd to 2nd c. B.C. and it is improbable that the bead is later. The glass resembles small annular opaque yellow beads (see Class 8). (A bead of this glass in two segments also came from Meare. ? 3rd–2nd c. B.C.)	*WAM* xl (1917), 33–4 and pl. ix, no. 12

SITE AND PARISH	COUNTY	MUSEUM & NO.	DESCRIPTION AND APPROX. DIMENSIONS	ASSOCIATIONS AND REMARKS	PUBLICATION

CLASS 13

NORTH SCOTTISH SPIRAL-DECORATED BEADS

ENGLAND

Netherby	Cumberland	Probably lost	Evidently fairly large and faceted	The writer also mentions an Oldbury type bead but no association can be proved. Perhaps from the Hadrianic fort	Pennant, T., *Tour in Scotland and Voyage in the Hebrides* (1772), pl. vii

IRELAND

'N.E. Ireland'		Belfast 306–1913	Rich reddish-brown. Diam. 2·2 cm. Ht. 1·5 cm.	Both stray finds without information	
'? Antrim'		B.M. 92, 4–21, 16	Dark brown ground, wide spirals—faceted. Diam. 1·5 cm. Ht. 9 mm.		

SCOTLAND

Ballogie	Aberdeenshire	N.M.A. FJ68	Pale semi-translucent greenish-blue ground. Diam. 1·7 cm. Ht. 1·3 cm.	Rae Colln. 1892	
Bedlam?, nr. New Deer	Aberdeenshire	N.M.A. FJ14	Very dark blue and rather triangular. Diam. 1·6 cm. Ht. 1.6 cm. (fig. 33, no. 1)	'At a stone circle.' The name recorded as Beetloun is probably a scribal error for Bedlam	*PSAS* xxiv (1890), 11
Birse	Aberdeenshire	N.M.A. FJ64	Very dark blue. Diam. 1·6 cm. Ht. 1·1 cm.		
Blelack	Aberdeenshire	N.M.A. FJ9	Very dark blue. Diam. 1·6 cm. Ht. 1·1 cm.		
Buck of Carbrach	Aberdeenshire	N.M.A. FJ136	Translucent yellow. Diam. 2 cm. Ht. 1·2 cm.		
'Aberdeenshire'		Miss Young's Colln., Edinburgh	Bright brown. Diam. 1·8 cm. Ht. 1 cm.	Provenance unknown	
'Aberdeenshire'		N.M.A. FJ15	Dark purplish-brown, rather faceted. Uneven perforation. Diam. 1·9 cm. Ht. 1 cm. (fig. 33, no. 3)		

SITE AND PARISH	COUNTY	MUSEUM & NO.	DESCRIPTION AND APPROX. DIMENSIONS	ASSOCIATIONS AND REMARKS	PUBLICATION
Castle Newe	Aberdeenshire	Banff Institution Museum		From earth-house associated with hut. Finds included coin of Nerva (A.D. 96–8) and bronze armlet of Castle Newe type	*PSAS* xxii (1887–8), 369; Simpson, W. D., *Province of Mar* (1943), p. 74; Anderson, J. *Scotland in Pagan Times* (1886), pp. 141–3
Clova	Aberdeenshire	N.M.A. FJ13	Almost opaque yellowish-green. Diam. 1·6 cm. Ht. 1·2 cm.	Found with bronze implements, no details	*PSAS* xxiv (1890), 11
Coldstone	Aberdeenshire	N.M.A. FJ7, 8	One bright semi-translucent brown. Diam. 2 cm. Ht. 1·8 cm. One pale yellow, translucent. Diam. 1·5 cm. Ht. 1·1 cm.	'From near a Pict's house' (earth-house)	*PSAS* vii (1866–8), 385
Cromar	Aberdeenshire	N.M.A.	'A circular bead of vitreous paste enamelled on the sides with 3 sets of spiral convolutions'		*PSAS* vii (1866–8), 320
Callievar Hill, Cushie	Aberdeenshire	N.M.A. FJ138			Mentioned in *PSAS* cv (1972–4), 198
Ellon	Aberdeenshire	C.M. Given by Mr. Cosmo Gordon of Insch	Very dark opaque blue. Half only. Diam. 1·4 cm. Ht. 8 mm.	Stray find at Lady-mire Fen, 1¼ miles E.S.E. of Ellon (noted by Beck)	
Glenbuchat Hill	Aberdeenshire	N.M.A. FJ137	Very dark ground, slightly faceted. Diam. 1·6 cm. Ht. 1·3 cm.	Found by Captain Hugh Lumsden in 1937	
Kennethmont	Aberdeenshire	Broughton House, Kirkcudbright, on loan to N.M.A.	Dark cobalt ground. Diam. 1·5 cm. Ht. 1 cm.	Found in digging foundations for bridge over the Bogie. Apparently association with bead of Scottish decorated annular type	Unpublished
Kildrummy	Aberdeenshire	King's Coll. Museum, Aberdeen	'2 small beads of vitreous paste striped with yellow'		*PSAS* xxii (1888), 357
Kinnord	Aberdeenshire	N.M.A. FJ69	Dark blue ground, rather faceted. Diam. 1·5 cm. Ht. 1 cm.		
Midmar	Aberdeenshire	N.M.A. FJ67	Purplish-brown and rather triangular. Diam. 1·6 cm. Ht. 1 cm.		

SITE AND PARISH	COUNTY	MUSEUM & NO.	DESCRIPTION AND APPROX. DIMENSIONS	ASSOCIATIONS AND REMARKS	PUBLICATION
Rhynie	Aberdeenshire	c/o Mr. Alex. Shand, Longcroft, Rhynie	Very dark ground, slightly hexagonal. Diam. 1·7 cm.		*PSAS* lxix (1935), 454
Slains	Aberdeenshire	N.M.A. FJ10	Very dark opaque? with flattened facets. Diam. 1·5 cm. Ht. 1·4 cm.	Unassociated find	*PSAS* l (x873–4), 699
Strathdon	Aberdeenshire	N.M.A. FJ66, Rae Colln. 1892	Light yellow. Flattened spirals. Diam. 1·5 cm. Ht. 1 cm.	It is possible that this came from Castle Newe which is also in Strathdon	
Tough	Aberdeenshire	N.M.A. FJ65	Opaque brownish ground. Diam. 1·4 cm. Ht. 9 mm.		
Balmerion Farm, Glenrinnes	Banffshire	N.M.A. FJ16	Translucent yellowish-green. Diam. 1·3 cm. Ht. 9 mm.	This is almost as colourless as a Meare spiral bead but is more roughly made	
?	Banffshire	N.M.A.	'One round bead with yellow spirals'		*PSAS* xxv (1890), 8
?	Banffshire	Banff Institution Museum	'Two beads of vitreous paste striped with yellow'		*PSAS* xxii (1888), 369
Bowermadden	Caithness	N.M.A. GA92	'Blue vitreous paste enamelled with yellow spirals, triangularly compressed'	From the broch	Anderson, J., *Scotland in Pagan Times* (1886), p. 233 and *PSAS* ix (1873), 247
Croy	Inverness-shire	N.M.A.	Rather triangular. Blue core covered with opaque brown with yellow spirals	Probably a survival of this class found with 9th c. A.D. coins, etc.	*PSAS* xx (1886), 93 and 96
Dun an Iardhard, Dunvegan, Skye	Inverness-shire	N.M.A. GA1003	Fawn ground. Diam. 1·1 cm. Ht. 9 mm.	From the broch	*PSAS* xlix (1914–15), 65 and fig. 10, no. 1
Burghead	Morayshire	N.M.A. FJ5, 6	2 with dark blue ground. One, diam. 1·5 cm., ht. 5 mm. One, diam. 1·9 cm. ht. 1·2 cm.	Found in 1890 in the rampart material of the post-Roman fort	*PSAS* xxiv (1890), 379 and xxv (1890–1), 68 and Small, A., in *Scottish Arch. Forum* i (1969), 61–8
Culbin Sands	Morayshire		Half-bead of brown glass. Diam. 1·5 cm.		*PSAS* liv (1919–20), 15

SITE AND PARISH	COUNTY	MUSEUM & NO.	DESCRIPTION AND APPROX. DIMENSIONS	ASSOCIATIONS AND REMARKS	PUBLICATION
Culbin Sands	Morayshire	Miss Young's Colln., Edinburgh	2 half-beads, one dark translucent cobalt and the other darker and smaller		
Culbin Sands	Morayshire	N.M.A.	Remains of at least 5 or 6 specimens, all broken	One published in *PSAS* xxv (1890–91), 509, has translucent pale blue glass tips and may be later. All stray finds	
Keith	Morayshire	Elgin	Bluish ground		*PSAS* xxii (1888), 343
Orton	Morayshire	Elgin	Translucent blue-green. Diam. 1·7 cm. Ht. 1·2 cm. Perf. diam. 7 mm.	Found at Dykeside, Orton, in 1970	Unpublished
'Pitcroy' probably Pitchroy, nr. Ballindalloch	Morayshire		'Bead of bluish glass enamelled with yellow spirals'	'Found on the hill of Pitcroy'	*PSAS* xxviii (1893–4), 62
Cawdor	Nairnshire		2 blue beads. Diam. 1·5 cm. Ht. 1 cm.	One is rather more faceted than the other	*PSAS* xix (1885), 133
Cawdor	Nairnshire	N.M.A. FJ1–4 and others	2 dark blue ground, one green, one light greenish-yellow translucent, one blue-green bottle glass. All normal size	'Near Cawdor' in a ditch apparently with 2 beads of Scottish decorated annular type (Class 14)	Probably the beads referred to in *PSAS* v (1864), 300 and 313
Nairn (unprovenanced)	Nairnshire	N.M.A. FJ11	Dark brown semi-translucent. Diam. 1·6 cm. Ht. 1·1 cm.		
Evie	Orkney	J. W. Cursiter Colln., Kirkwall	Smaller but similar to bead from Slains		*PSAS* xix (1885), 139
?	Orkney		White with yellow spirals and plain ring round perforation	This may or may not belong to this Class	Waring, J. B., *Rude Stone Monuments in Orkney* (London, 1870), pl. 53, fig. 9; *A* lxxx (1930), 240
Eddertoun	Ross-shire	N.M.A. EQ45	Very dark opaque blue. The spirals are white and a yellow patch is over some and under others. Diam. 1·5 cm. Ht. 1 cm.	This is not typical and may not belong to this Class. It was found in a cist with a cremation and thought to be contemporary with a food vessel or cordoned urn of very degenerate type	*PSAS* v (1864), 311 ff.

SITE AND PARISH	COUNTY	MUSEUM & NO.	DESCRIPTION AND APPROX. DIMENSIONS	ASSOCIATIONS AND REMARKS	PUBLICATION
Loch Eriboll, Fouhlin	Sutherland	Hunterian Museum, Glasgow, NC405541	Translucent almost colourless with facets. Diam. 1·5 cm. Ht. 9 mm. (fig. 33, no. 2)	From a hut-circle associated with an earth-house	Forthcoming
'Scotland'		N.M.A. FJ12, 84	2 examples. One semi-translucent bluish and one dark opaque—almost black. Both are typical in size		

CLASS 14
NORTH SCOTTISH DECORATED ANNULAR BEADS

ENGLAND

'Derbyshire'		B.M.	Translucent blue ground with patches of translucent green and opaque yellow whirls. Diam. 2·1 cm. Perf. diam. 4 mm.	Found in 1790. Unlike the majority of beads in this Class the ground is translucent. It may not belong to this Class	

IRELAND

'Ireland' (probably the north)		Belfast 2412	Dark blue whirls on whitish ground or vice-versa. Purplish bands round circumference. Diam. 3·2 cm. Ht. 1·6 cm.	Probably belongs to this Class	
'Probably Ireland'		N.M.A., Bell Colln., FK40	Opaque greyish with opaque white whirls and a patch of greenish-yellow round interior of perforation. Diam. 2·5 cm. Ht. 1·4 cm. Perf. diam. 7 mm.	May well belong to this Class	
'Antrim'		N.M. Ireland, Dublin, 1908.347	Dark ground with yellow whirls alternating with yellow and brown ladder whirls. Diam. 2·7 cm. Ht. 1·1 cm. Perf. diam. 5 mm.	Similar glass, apparently, as the whirl bead from Cloughwater, Antrim (Dublin, 1907.97)	

SCOTLAND

'Aberdeenshire'		N.M.A., Rae Colln., FJ70	Badly made. Brown with yellow streaks. Diam. 1·7 cm. Ht. 5 mm. Small perforation	From colln. No details	

SITE AND PARISH	COUNTY	MUSEUM & NO.	DESCRIPTION AND APPROX. DIMENSIONS	ASSOCIATIONS AND REMARKS	PUBLICATION
'Aberdeenshire'		N.M.A. FJ72	Badly made. Dark opaque brownish with brown/white ladder and yellow bands. Diam. 1·8 cm. Ht. 7 mm. Small perforation	From colln. No details	
'Aberdeenshire'		N.M.A., Rae Colln., FJ73	Brown with wide yellow whirls. Diam. 2·5 cm. Ht. 9 mm. Perf. diam. 5 mm.		
'Aberdeenshire'		N.M.A., Rae Colln., FJ71	Opaque dark slaty blue with yellow and white whirls. Diam. 1·7 cm. Ht. 7 mm. Perf. diam. 4 mm. (fig. 35, no. 1)	No details	
'Aberdeenshire'		N.M.A. FJ118	Whirled bands in yellow edged with brown. Intervening whirls in dark and light blue ladder pattern. Diam. 2·4 cm. Ht. 8 mm. Perf. diam. 7 mm.	Purchased in 1925	
Kennethmont	Aberdeenshire	On loan to N.M.A. from Broughton House, Kirkcudbrights.	Clear glass with opaque yellow and brown bands. Diam. 1·6 cm. Ht. 1 cm. Perf. diam. 4 mm. (fig. 35, no. 4)	Found with a North Scottish spiral bead when digging bridge foundations at Smithston. Apparently associated	
Lickleyhead, Premnay	Aberdeenshire	N.M.A. FJ139	Opaque yellow with girth bands of dark brown bordering grey and white ladder. Diam. 2·3 cm. Ht. 8 mm. Perf. diam. 7 mm.	Presented in 1937	
Cairnhill, Monquhitter	Aberdeenshire	? colln., EQ330	Very large rich dark brown with superficial white streaks. Semi-translucent. One side flattened and smooth. Diam. 5·5 cm.	Found with a North Scottish spiral bead, armlet, etc. Probably 1st–2nd c. A.D. Found 1894	
Udney (Cloister Seat)	Aberdeenshire	N.M.A. FJ20	Dark brown whirled with yellow. Fragment only. Diam. 2·3 cm. Ht. 8 mm. Small perf.	Found with FJ19 and other beads, 2 black and one whitish. ? Associated	*PSAS* xxiv (1890), 11

SITE AND PARISH	COUNTY	MUSEUM & NO.	DESCRIPTION AND APPROX. DIMENSIONS	ASSOCIATIONS AND REMARKS	PUBLICATION
Udney	Aberdeenshire	N.M.A. FJ19	Grey opaque ground with slaty green whirls. Diam. 2·2 cm. Ht. 9 mm. Perf. diam. 5 mm.	Found with FJ20, above, and other beads. ? Associated	*PSAS* xxiv (1890), 11
Dun Mor Vaul, Tiree	Argyllshire	Hunterian Museum, Glasgow, SF167	Fragment only. Opaque blue with yellow inlay. Diam. *c.* 2·5 cm.	Could be part of a bead or armlet. From a broch	MacKie, E. W. (1975)
Dun Mor Vaul, Tiree	Argyllshire	Hunterian Museum, Glasgow, SF410	Brownish-purple with opaque yellow inlay. Diam. 2·5 cm. Ht. 1 cm. Perf. diam. 8 mm. (fig. 35, no. 5)	Probably dates from the construction of the broch or very soon after. Radio-carbon dating suggests second part of 1st c. B.C. for this phase	MacKie, E. W. (1975)
Clerkley Hill	Morayshire	Miss Young's Colln., Edinburgh	Opaque yellow with purplish-blue inlay. Diam. 2·2 cm. Ht. 9 mm. Irregular perforation (fig. 35, no. 2)	From a cairn	
Culbin Sands	Morayshire	N.M.A.	Half only. Opaque dark blue with streaks of yellow and green. Diam. 1·5 cm. Small perforation		
Culbin Sands	Morayshire	N.M.A.	Fragment. Opaque yellow with broad dark green and white ladder bordered in brown. Diam. 2·4 cm. Ht. 7 mm.		
Culbin Sands	Morayshire	N.M.A. B.1.424	Fragment. Translucent light blue-green with whirls in yellow and white. Diam. *c.* 2·7 cm. Ht. 7 mm.		
Culbin Sands	Morayshire	Miss Young's Colln., Edinburgh	Green ground streaked with yellow and white whirls. Diam. 1·8 cm. Ht. 6 mm. Very small perforation (fig. 35, no. 3)		
Culbin Sands	Morayshire		Amber brown with yellow and opaque white ladder design round part of circumference. Diam. 1·1 cm. Ht. 3 mm.	Found on a necklace with small annular opaque yellow beads of Class 8	

SITE AND PARISH	COUNTY	MUSEUM & NO.	DESCRIPTION AND APPROX. DIMENSIONS	ASSOCIATIONS AND REMARKS	PUBLICATION
Cawdor Castle	Nairnshire	N.M.A. FJ17	Opaque yellow whirled with blue and white ladders outlined in brown. Diam. 2·2 cm. Ht. 9 mm. Perf. diam. 4 mm.	Almost certainly one of the 6 beads exhibited in 1864. Found in digging a ditch. Some were North Scottish spiral beads of Class 13 (FJ 1–4)	*PSAS* v (1862–4), 313
Cawdor Castle	Nairnshire	N.M.A. FJ18	Large bead of opaque yellow whirled with blue and white ladders edged in darker blue. Diam. 3 cm. Ht. 1 cm. Perf. diam. 9 mm.	As above	As above
'Scotland'		N.M.A. FJ83	Dark brown with yellow streak and thin light blue line. Diam. 1·6 cm. Ht. 4 mm. Perf. diam. 5 mm.	Purchased in 1900	
Dun Ardtreck, Bracadale, Skye	Inverness-shire	Hunterian Museum, Glasgow	2 small annular beads with traces of yellow. Diam. 4 mm. Ht. 1 mm.	Probably related to this Class, though smaller. These beads were found with some small annular opaque yellow ones in a galleried wall-fort, thought to have been built in the early 1st c. B.C.	*An* xxxix (1965). For radio-carbon dating, see *An* xliii (1969), 23
Dun an Iardhard, Dunvegan, Skye	Inverness-shire	N.M.A. GA1007	Half. Dark opaque core with streaks of yellow and blue. Diam. 2·2 cm. Ht. 9 mm. Irregular perforation	This bead and a small opaque yellow annular bead were found separately from the Dark Ages beads from this broch	*PSAS* xlix (1914–15), 7–70
'Wigtownshire'		N.M.A. FJ26	Globular. Opaque yellow with circumferential ladder patterns in brown and yellow outlined in brown. Diam. 2·3 cm. Ht. 1·8 cm. Perf. diam. 0·6 cm.	Possibly not of this Class, as it is globular not annular. Given by Sir H. E. Maxwell in 1889	
Dowalton Loch	Wigtownshire	N.M.A. HU33	Blue and white coil on surface and blob of opaque yellow at perforation. Evidently related to this Class. Diam. 1·2 cm. Ht. 5 mm. Perf. diam. 5 mm.	From site of Roman period crannog	*PSAS* vi (1866), 114 ff.

ROMAN PERIOD BEADS
(SEE ALSO UNDECORATED ANNULAR AND GLOBULAR BEADS, GROUPS 6 and 7)
SMALL SEGMENTED BEADS

(a) VARIOUS COLOURS

ENGLAND

Nor' nour, Scilly	Cornwall	St. Mary's, Scilly	Several examples of different colours. Some appear black but really purplish-red or dark green glass	Site occupied through Roman period. Found after the original report was published	For site see *ArJ* cxxiv (1967), 1 ff.
Little Chester, Derby	Derbyshire	Derby	2 green beads. Both broken and 2 segments. One translucent, one opaque	One from filling of 4th c. A.D. ditch. One probably 3rd c.	Information from Mr. Christopher Green
Cadbury Castle, Bickleigh Bridge	Devonshire		5 examples, greeny blue or china blue. Wound	With 3rd c. objects from a Roman well	*TDA* lxxxiv (1952), 109–12
Newton Abbot	Devonshire		2 segments of one bead and one of another, both blue. Wound	From Berry's Wood Fort (modern cutting across defences). Roman period	Mentioned in *TDA* lxxxiv (1952), 109
Colliton Park, Dorchester	Dorset	Dorchester	8–9 examples, mostly green or blue and one black	From Roman villa with late Roman occupation	R.C.H.M. *Dorset* ii. The villa is not published
Dorchester	Dorset	Dorchester	Now in 2 parts (? blown). Probably originally part of a segmented light opaque sky blue bead	Roman site	Unpublished
Hengistbury Head	Dorset	Red House Museum, Christchurch, B50 3	Blue-green. Pinched. Two segments now remain	Found by Mr. Sidney Pester. Stray find from Iron Age hill-fort	
Wimborne St. Giles	Dorset	Dorchester	Several examples	From Roman barrow	*PDNHAS* lxxiii (1951), 103 and lxxv (1953), 36
Woodcuts	Dorset	Salisbury	Dark blue. Semi-translucent. 4 segments. ? pinched	Surface trenches on Romano-British site	Pitt-Rivers, A. H. L. F. (1887), pp. xliv, 18, and *ArJ* civ (1947)
South Shields	Durham	University Museum, Newcastle-upon-Tyne	3 segments opalescent and perhaps once gilded	Roman fort. Occupation *c.* A.D. 122–396	Richmond, I. A. (1954), and see *JRS* lvii (1967)
Wickford	Essex	? Southend-on-Sea	Small fragment of translucent bottle green segment	Roman site	Information from Mr. W. Rodwell

SITE AND PARISH	COUNTY	MUSEUM & NO.	DESCRIPTION AND APPROX. DIMENSIONS	ASSOCIATION AND REMARKS	PUBLICATION
Cirencester, Barnsley Park	Gloucester-shire	Cirencester	Four wound green examples and several others in blue, turquoise blue, etc.	From Roman villa mainly early 2nd to 4th c. A.D.	Information from Dr. G. Webster
Frocester	Gloucester-shire		Fragments of blue and green segments of about 8 beads	Stratified late 3rd and late 4th c. A.D. in Roman villa at Frocester Court	*TBGAS* lxxxix (1970)
Portchester	Hampshire		Remains of 5 or 6 beads green or greenish-blue	From late Roman strata	Information from Prof. Barry Cunliffe. See *AnJ* xlix (1969), 62
Lankhills Cemetery, Winchester	Hampshire		Over 100 rectangular sections of originally segmented beads, in green or blue glass	Necklace 364, from Grave 336, dated *c.* A.D. 350–70. The grave is intrusive, and the beads are unusual	Clarke, G. (forthcoming), fig. 90
Weston-under-Penyard, Bollitree	Herefordshire	Gloucester 1772	Several green and blue examples	From necklace of Roman period	*JBAA* xxvii (1871), 211 ff.
St. Albans	Hertfordshire	Verulamium 30.15	Greeny blue. 3 segments and others	Roman period	
St. Albans	Hertfordshire	Verulamium	2 small silvery segments	From late Roman necklace, probably 4th c. A.D.	*Ve*, p. 214, fig. 47
Godman-chester	Huntingdon-shire		2 segments	Second half of 2nd c. A.D.	*PCAS* liv (1960)
Lympne	Kent		Light blue. 4 segments	Roman	Smith, C. Roach, *Excavations on the Site of the Roman Castrum at Lymne* (London 1852), pl. viii, no. 10
Dowgate Hill, London	London	Formerly Guildhall Museum 3964	2 segments of clear glass		
Carrawburgh	Northumber-land	Chesters	Bottle green, irregular boring. 4 segments	19th c. find. Site dated A.D. 122–383	
Chesters Fort	Northumber-land	Chesters Museum 1362	One segment broken off and several others. Green wound	19th c. find. Site dated A.D. 122–383	
Great Chesters	Northumber-land	University Museum, Newcastle-upon-Tyne	2 segments of bottle green glass	Roman	
Housesteads	Northumber-land	University Museum, Newcastle-upon-Tyne	One greeny blue translucent	Roman Wall fort	

SITE AND PARISH	COUNTY	MUSEUM & NO.	DESCRIPTION AND APPROX. DIMENSIONS	ASSOCIATIONS AND REMARKS	PUBLICATION
Old Yeavering	Northumberland		2 examples blue-green glass probably pinched. Translucent	Post-Roman	Information from Dr. Brian Hope Taylor
East Markham	Nottinghamshire	Private hands	3 segments. Translucent bottle green. Pinched	Found in 1950 with Romano-British pottery	Information from finder
Brislington	Somerset	Bristol F2320–2325	Several examples, green, black and terracotta-coloured. One has iron wire through it. Wound	Roman villa	*TBGAS* xxiii (1900) and xxiv (1901)
Camerton	Somerset	Bristol F2317 (Skinner Colln.)	Opaque bright turquoise-coloured. 5 segments. Tapered		For site see *VCH Somerset* and Wedlake, W. J. (1958)
Ham Hill, Montacute	Somerset	Taunton	A number of examples, bottle green, light blue and black. Wound	Iron Age. Site occupied through Roman period	For site see *VCH Somerset* i, p. 295
Lamyatt Beacon, Lamyatt	Somerset	Mr. Jones's Colln.	Many small examples, pinched or wound. Mostly green but a few black. One fine rod ready for use	About 30–40 different coloured segments. From Romano-Celtic temple at Lamyatt Beacon, probably built about A.D. 300. (Beads may have been made here)	Information from Mrs. C. Bennett and Mr. Roger Leech
South Cadbury	Somerset		4 segments, translucent green, probably wound	Unstratified in Iron Age to post-Roman hill-fort	Information from Dr. Leslie Alcock
Whitchurch	Somerset		One very small blue bead of 2 segments	From Lyons Court Farm. Possibly 2nd–3rd c.	*ArJ* cxxii (1965), 25
Worlebury, Weston-super-Mare	Somerset	Weston-super-Mare	Several, mostly red-brown and green beads, and badly made	Iron Age fort occupied into the Roman period. These beads found in surface soil	Dymond, C. W., *Worlebury* (Bristol, 1902), pl. x, 16
Atworth	Wiltshire	Devizes	Several small examples	Roman villa site. From late Roman spread. Not closely stratified in 1974 excavations	Information from excavator

SITE AND PARISH	COUNTY	MUSEUM & NO.	DESCRIPTION AND APPROX. DIMENSIONS	ASSOCIATIONS AND REMARKS	PUBLICATION
Brixton Deverill (Cold Kitchen Hill)	Wiltshire	Salisbury and Devizes	Over 400 different colours	Mostly Romano-British finds from this site. Perhaps a Romano-Celtic temple here with beads made locally. Probably deserted by mid-4th c. A.D.	*WAM* xliii (1925–7), 83 ff.
Wick Wood, Nettleton	Wiltshire	c/o Bath and Camerton Arch. Soc.	Bottle green, translucent. 4 segments	Stratified 'before A.D. 284'	Wedlake, W. J. (1958)
Stockton Earthworks	Wiltshire	Salisbury	Several, opaque blue or green	Native and early Roman	*WAM* xliii (1925–7)
Catterick	Yorkshire	c/o D.O.E.	One segment bottle green (? blown) and 5 segments of another, wound		Information from Mr. J. Wacher

SCOTLAND

SITE AND PARISH	COUNTY	MUSEUM & NO.	DESCRIPTION AND APPROX. DIMENSIONS	ASSOCIATIONS AND REMARKS	PUBLICATION
Lochlee Crannog	Ayrshire		2 segments	Sub-Roman and post-Roman site	*PSAS* xiii (1879), 239
Skewalton	Ayrshire		Blue and green examples, wound		Smith, J., *Prehistoric Man in Ayrshire* (1895), p. 116, figs. 214 and 215
Traprain Law, Prestonkirk	E. Lothian	N.M.A.	Several examples. Semi-translucent blue. Wound. One possibly pinched	Probably from Roman period occupation	See A. H. A. Hogg in Grimes, W. F. (ed.) (1951)
Dalmeny	W. Lothian	N.M.A.	Green and blue examples. Several examples	From E.-W. orientated graves perhaps 6th c. A.D.	*PSAS* xlix (1914–15), 271
Culbin Sands	Morayshire	Miss Young's Colln., Edinburgh	One opaque yellow and one blue, 3 segments, larger than usual	Chance finds undated and almost certainly post-Roman	
Culbin Sands	Morayshire	N.M.A.	Semi-translucent blue. 2 segments. ? blown	Chance find	
Struan, Skye	Inverness-shire	N.M.A. GA1094		From Dun Beag broch occupied in Roman and post-Roman periods	*PSAS* lv (1920–1)

WALES

SITE AND PARISH	COUNTY	MUSEUM & NO.	DESCRIPTION AND APPROX. DIMENSIONS	ASSOCIATIONS AND REMARKS	PUBLICATION
Usk	Monmouthshire		Bottle green, 3 segments. Pinched	Excavated in 1970 in fort occupied from A.D. 55–60 and again in 3rd–4th c.	Information from excavator

SITE AND PARISH	COUNTY	MUSEUM & NO.	DESCRIPTION AND APPROX. DIMENSIONS	ASSOCIATIONS AND REMARKS	PUBLICATION
			(b) SEGMENTED BEADS ENCLOSING METAL FOIL		
			ENGLAND		
Fordington	Dorset	Dorchester 1846.2.15	3 segments on necklace	From mainly 3rd–4th c. A.D. Roman cemetery	See Roach Smith, C. (1852), iii, pl. ix and p. 33 and see R.C.H.M. *Dorset* ii
? Colchester	Essex	Colchester	Ten examples from unknown site	Probably Roman	Baldwin Brown, G., *Arts in Early England* (1915), p. 433, pl. 106 and p. 409, pl. 5
Burn Ground, Hampnett	Gloucester-shire				Grimes, W. F. (1939-45), 121
Cirencester	Gloucester-shire	Corinium Museum, Cirencester	2 segments of originally larger bead	From late Roman graves outside the town. ? 4th c. A.D.	Publication forthcoming
Lydney	Hereford-shire	Private museum at Lydney Park	2 examples, one 5-segmented	Presumably from the Roman temple to Nodens. Late 4th c. A.D. ?	Wheeler, R. E. M., *Excavations in Lydney Park, Gloucestershire* (1932)
Rockbourne	Hampshire	Rockbourne Villa Museum	Striated and broken off at each end. Possibly once gilded	From villa occupied through Roman period	Information from the late Mr. A. T. Morley Hewitt; see *Roman Villa Report*, 1971 (privately printed)
Winchester, Lankhills Cemetery	Hampshire		Various examples both in clear and amber coloured glass. Gold or silver foil enclosed	Necklaces 85, 215, 363, 436, and 443, all in graves variously dated within the period A.D. 310-70	Clarke, G. (forthcoming) and George Boon in *JGS* xvii (1975)
Winchester, Wolvesey Palace	Hampshire		Incomplete example	Unstratified	Information from Mr. M. Biddle
Weston-under-Penyard, Bollitree	Hereford-shire	Gloucester 1772A	One small segment	With Roman beads on necklace	*JBAA* xxvii (1871), 211 ff.
Baldock	Hertfordshire		Necklace of 41 beads	From Burial Group 89 dated from associated pottery to A.D. 160-190	*ArJ* lxxxviii (1932), 278
St. Albans	Hertfordshire	Verulamium	One gilded and one double white-metal foil segment	Thought to be 4th c. A.D. from a necklace of 55 mixed beads	*Ve*, p. 214 and fig. 47

SITE AND PARISH	COUNTY	MUSEUM & NO.	DESCRIPTION AND APPROX. DIMENSIONS	ASSOCIATIONS AND REMARKS	PUBLICATION
Bardon Mill (*Vindolanda*)	Northumberland		3 globular, perhaps originally all one bead	Stratified late 3rd–4th c. A.D.	Information from Mr. R. E. Birley
Carrawburgh	Northumberland	Chesters 614 and Box 65	About 20 beads all probably originally gilt and perhaps on a necklace	From 'Coventina's Well'. 19th c. find, approximate date A.D. 120–383	Budge, pp. E. Wallis, (1907), 65, 169, 393
Chesters	Northumberland	Chesters 614	Several beads like those from Coventina's Well (see above)	Site occupied about A.D. 122–383	
Wroxeter	Shropshire	Rowley's House Museum, Shrewsbury, D117	10 gilded beads	From the Forum with late Roman beads. Perhaps 4th c. A.D.	Unpublished
Hales Roman Villa	Staffordshire		One example	From Roman context	Information from Mr. F. H. Goodyear
Farley Heath, Albury	Surrey	Guildford	One clear bead with gold foil enclosed	Found in excavations of 1848–9. Romano-Celtic temple	*A* xxxiv (1852) and *AnJ* xviii (1938), 391
Milnthorpe	Westmorland		2 segments	On necklace not closely datable. From Dog Hole, Haverback. ? Ritual shaft burial	Information from Mr. K. P. Bland, Milnthorpe

SCOTLAND

Newstead	Roxburghshire	N.M.A.	3 or 4 broken segments	Site occupied about A.D. 80–200. Probably second half of 2nd c.	*Ne*

WALES

Coygan Camp, Laugharne	Carmarthenshire		One light grey almost opaque glass seems to be a segment	Late 3rd c. A.D.	Wainwright, G. J. (1967)
Castell Coch Fort	Glamorganshire	N.M.W.	11 beads	Roman date	Found in 1955–7. Information from G. C. Boon
Dinas Powys (Cardiff)	Glamorganshire	N.M.W.	Wire wound with 'knocked' ends	Roman or, according to Harden, Coptic. Unstratified in hill-fort with Roman and Dark Age occupation	Alcock, L. (1964), p. 186, fig. 41, no. 5
Caerleon	Monmouthshire	N.M.W.	Part of a segmented bead	From clearing of a Roman drain	Boon, G. C. (1966)
Caerleon	Monmouthshire	N.M.W.	Another, smaller	Stratified A.D. 130–230	Boon, G. C. (1966)

SITE AND PARISH	COUNTY	MUSEUM & NO.	DESCRIPTION AND APPROX. DIMENSIONS	ASSOCIATIONS AND REMARKS	PUBLICATION

CYLINDER-SHAPED AND CUT SEGMENTS BEADS

(a) BLUE CYLINDERS

ENGLAND

SITE AND PARISH	COUNTY	MUSEUM & NO.	DESCRIPTION AND APPROX. DIMENSIONS	ASSOCIATIONS AND REMARKS	PUBLICATION
Nor' nour, Scilly	Cornwall	St. Mary's, Scilly	Translucent cobalt. Diam. 4 mm. Length 2·1 cm.	Occupation through-out Roman period	*ArJ* cxxiv (1967)
Cadbury Castle, Bickleigh Bridge	Devonshire	Temporarily at Farsdon House, Cadbury	2 examples, both dark blue. Lengths 1·5 and 1·9 cm.	From a well thought to belong to 3rd c. A.D.	*PDAS* lxxxiv (1952), 109
Fordington	Dorset	Dorchester 1846.2.15	Opaque. Diam. 4 mm. Length *c.* 1 cm.	Roman cemetery. Perhaps 3rd or 4th c. A.D.	*PSAL* ii (1853), 140–1 and R.C.H.M. *Dorset* ii
Woodyates	Dorset	Salisbury	Light blue, semi-translucent with longitudinal stria-tions. Diam. 3 mm. Length 2 cm.	Romano-British settlement	Pitt-Rivers, A. H. L. F. (1892) and see *ArJ* civ (1947)
Cirencester	Gloucester-shire		Light translucent. Diam. 4 mm. Length 2·5 cm.	From Barnsley Park Roman villa, occupied 2nd–4th c. A.D.	Information from Dr. Graham Webster
Frocester	Gloucester-shire		Diam. 4 mm. Length 1·8 cm.	From Roman villa stratified 'post A.D 275'	*TBGAS* lxxxix (1970)
Rockbourne West Park Roman Villa	Hampshire	Fordingbridge	A number of trans-lucent glass and vary-ing sizes	None of these was stratified. The villa was occupied through-out the Roman period and into Saxon times	Information from the late Mr. A. T. Morley Hewitt
Winchester, Lankhills Cemetery	Hampshire		A number of trans-lucent glass and varying sizes	Necklaces 182, 215, 248, 315, 399, and 443, all from graves variously dated within the period A.D. 310–410	Clarke, G. (forthcoming)
Silchester	Hampshire	Reading	'Long blue cylinder'	On necklace not stratified	Boon, G. C. (1957) and in *A* cii (1969)
St. Albans	Hertfordshire	Verulamium	Opaque sky blue (and others). Diam. 3 mm. Length 1·7 cm.	On necklace of prob-able 4th c. date	*Ve*, figs. 214, 47 a–g

SITE AND PARISH	COUNTY	MUSEUM & NO.	DESCRIPTION AND APPROX. DIMENSIONS	ASSOCIATIONS AND REMARKS	PUBLICATION
Close ny Chollagh, Scarlett	Isle of Man		Has light greenish streaks. Diam. 0·4 cm. Length 1·4 cm.	Iron Age fort occupied into Roman period. Bead came from midden material together with a Colchester type La Tène III brooch. Late 1st c. A.D.? unless midden material was of mixed date	*PPS* xxiv (1958), 94–5
Woodeaton	Oxfordshire	A.M.	Light translucent blue. Diam. 5 mm. Length 2·2 cm.	From Romano-Celtic temple—occupation from late Iron Age to post-Roman	*O* xix (1954), 15
Brislington	Somerset	Bristol F2319	Opaque. Diam. 4 mm. Length 2 mm.	From Roman villa	*TBGAS* xxiii (1900), 289 and xxiv (1901), 283
'Mendip'	Somerset	Bristol F2086 (A. C. Pass Colln.)	Opaque. Diam. 3 mm. Length 1·7 cm.	Stray find	
Sea Mills, Bristol	Somerset	Bristol F2221	Opaque. Diam. 5 mm. Length 1·2 cm.	Roman fort at *Portus Abonae*, Claudian and later (possibly from a 1st c. A.D. storehouse)	*TBGAS* lxviii (1949), 184
Whitton	Suffolk	Ipswich	Length 1·8 cm. Semi-translucent	From Roman villa dated A.D. 130–290	*PSIA* xxi (1931–3), 240 ff.

SCOTLAND

| Traprain Law, Prestonkirk | E. Lothian | N.M.A. Excav. no. III 20223 | Broken fragment translucent | Occupation throughout Roman period | See Hogg, A. H. A. (1951) |

WALES

| Caernarvon | Caernarvonshire | Segontium Museum, Caernarvon | Royal blue. Diam. 5 mm. Length 2 cm. Another smaller and less regular | Unstratified from Roman fort | Unpublished. Information from G. C. Boon |

(b) GREEN CYLINDERS (for Segments, see below, pp. 211–12)

ENGLAND

| Calcot or Henxworth | Bedfordshire | | '6 long glass beads of green colour' | With Samian ware from Roman burials | Stukeley, W. *Itinerarium Curiosum* (1776), p. 78 |
| Santon Downham | Cambridgeshire | C.M. | Opaque green. Diam. 4 mm. Length 8 mm. | With rich 1st c. A.D. burial | Fox, C. (1923) *passim* |

SITE AND PARISH	COUNTY	MUSEUM & NO.	DESCRIPTION AND APPROX. DIMENSIONS	ASSOCIATIONS AND REMARKS	PUBLICATION
Nor' nour, Scilly	Cornwall	St. Mary's, Scilly	Probably broken at one end. Opaque yellow-green. Diam. 3 mm. Length 1 cm. And another fragment, bright bottle green	Site 1, Room. 2. Site occupied for most of Roman period. Information from Miss Dudley 1962. Second example probably with 2nd c. A.D. coins from later excavation	*ArJ* cxxiv (1967)
Little Chester, Derby	Derbyshire	Derby	Translucent bottle glass. Length *c.* 1·2 cm.	From late Roman site. Unstratified	Information from Mr. Christopher Green
Woodcuts	Dorset	Salisbury	2 specimens, one broken in half longitudinally. Diams. 3 and 5 mm. Lengths 2 and 2·2 cm. Both translucent	From Romano-British settlement	Pitt-Rivers, A. H. L. S. (1887) and *ArJ* civ (1947)
Colliton Park Villa, Dorchester	Dorset	Dorchester	Several examples. Two in translucent sea-green glass. Lengths 1 and 2 cm. Diams. 2 and 5 mm.	From Roman villa late 2nd c. A.D. with subsequent additions	R.C.H.M. *Dorset* ii
Maiden Castle, Winterbourne Monkton	Dorset	Dorchester	Blue-green	From 'Belgic' level, now redated post 50 B.C.	*MC*
Poundbury, nr. Dorchester	Dorset	Dorchester	Necklace of 78 of these with 3 small square-sectioned blue beads	From late Roman grave	Information from Mr. C. J. S. Green
South Shields	Durham	South Shields and University Museum, Newcastle-upon-Tyne	3 or 4 examples of various dimensions	From Roman fort occupied A.D. 122–369	*JRS* lvii (1967) and Richmond, I. A. (1954)
Cirencester	Gloucester-shire		One translucent sea-green. Length 2 cm. Another bottle green, length 7 mm.	From Barnsley Park Roman villa occupied 2nd–4th c. A.D.	Information from Dr. Graham Webster
Cirencester	Gloucester-shire	B906	Several segments	Unstratified in Roman town	
Portchester	Hampshire		Two rather greenish-blue. One 1 cm. long and another slightly larger	Both from late Roman levels	Information from Prof. Barry Cunliffe
Rockbourne West Park Roman Villa	Hampshire	Fordingbridge	2 light green beads. Diams. 3 m. Lengths 1·5 and 2·1 cm.	Roman villa occupied throughout Roman and into Saxon times	Information from the late Mr. A. T. Morley Hewitt

SITE AND PARISH	COUNTY	MUSEUM & NO.	DESCRIPTION AND APPROX. DIMENSIONS	ASSOCIATIONS AND REMARKS	PUBLICATION
Rockbourne West Park Roman Villa	Hampshire	Fordingbridge	Roughly wound and opaque dark green	Thought to be Constantine	Information from the late Mr. A. T. Morley Hewitt
Winchester, Lankhills Cemetery	Hampshire		A number of translucent and opaque glass, and of various sizes	Necklaces 85, 140, 215, 248, 269, 315, 363, 399, 443, and 583, all from graves variously dated within the period A.D. 310–410	Clarke, G. (forthcoming)
Kenchester	Herefordshire	Hereford 6058	Semi-translucent, one end broken. Diam. 6 mm. Length 1·5 cm.	The occupation of this Roman town is thought to have ended about A.D. 390	TWNFC (1916) and (1926)
St. Albans	Hertfordshire	Verulamium 30.209	Diam. 5 mm. Length 1 cm.	Site A. Building 2, Room 2, Level 2	See Anthony, Ilid, Verulamium (1970)
St. Albans	Hertfordshire	Verulamium 33.192	Oval in section. Max. diam. 4 mm. Length 2·3 cm.		
St. Albans	Hertfordshire	Verulamium 33.700	Another example on its original wire, opaque. Diam. 3 mm. Length 5 mm.		
Richborough, Ash	Kent	Richborough 4623	Bright bluish-green, semi-translucent. Diam. 4 mm. Length 1·2 cm.		Information from Dr. G. C. Dunning
Manton	Lincolnshire	Scunthorpe	Diam. 4 mm. Length 1·2 cm. Broken	Hut sites. Occupation throughout Roman and into Saxon period	Information from Mr. R. H. Arrand
Chesters Fort	Northumberland	Chesters 2783	2 examples. Both opaque and of usual dimensions but broken	Probably dates from between A.D. 122–383	Information from Dr. G. Simpson
Great Chesters	Northumberland	University Museum, Newcastle-upon-Tyne	Bottle green translucent. Length c. 1·2 cm.	From Roman Aesica	
Housesteads	Northumberland	University Museum, Newcastle-upon-Tyne	Translucent bottle green, one 2 cm. long and three others	From Roman site of Borcovicium	
Bradley Hill, Somerton	Somerset		Broken almost opaque green, striated. Existing length 1·7 cm. Diam. 5 mm. Perf. diam. 1 mm.	From homestead of 4th–5th c. date	Preliminary report in C.B.A. Groups XII and XIII, Arch. Rev. 7 (1972), 39–41
Lamyatt Beacon	Somerset		Light bottle green, translucent. Length 8 mm.	From Romano-Celtic temple of 2nd–4th c. A.D.	Information from Mrs. Crystal Bennett

SITE AND PARISH	COUNTY	MUSEUM & NO.	DESCRIPTION AND APPROX. DIMENSIONS	ASSOCIATIONS AND REMARKS	PUBLICATION
Hepworth	Suffolk	Ipswich 959.143	Semi-translucent. Length 2·2 cm.	Roman	Information from Ipswich Museum
Overton Down	Wiltshire		One opaque. Length 6 mm. 2 others	From site XII, late Roman	*WAM* lxii (1967), 16 ff.
Catterick	Yorkshire		One rather flattened cylinder and one segment	Roman	Information from Mr. J. Wacher

IRELAND

Lagore Crannog, Dunshaughlin	Co. Meath		Diam. 4 mm. Length 2·3 cm.	Unstratified, in post-Roman site which yielded pre-Roman beads as well. This example could be early Roman or post-Roman	*PRIA* liii C (1950–1), 136

SCOTLAND

Traprain Law, Prestonkirk	E. Lothian	N.M.A.	Small opaque green and two similar found in second level in 1915	Roman period	*PSAS* liv (1919–20), 89
Newstead	Roxburghshire	N.M.A. FRA907	Diam. 3 mm. Length 9 mm.	Occupation about A.D. 80–200	*Ne*

SEGMENTS OF CYLINDER BEADS
(Opaque or translucent green)

ENGLAND

Wood Farm, Haversham	Buckinghamshire	Aylesbury	Diam. and length 4 mm.	Roman site	
Poundbury Camp, Dorchester	Dorset	Dorchester	Necklace with 3 cube shaped beads and 78 cut green segments	In a 4th c. A.D. Christian cemetery	Information from Mr. Christopher Green, 1973
Cirencester (Watermoor Cemetery)	Gloucestershire	Gloucester 539–41	Opaque. Diam. 5 mm.	Roman and post-Roman	*AnJ* xlix (1969), 222 and earlier reports
Cirencester	Gloucestershire	Cirencester B901	On a wire with 2 melon beads	From Roman town	*AnJ* xlix (1969), 222 and earlier reports
Frocester	Gloucestershire		Semi-translucent green. Diam. 4 mm.	Unstratified but post-A.D. 275	*TBGAS* lxxxix (1970)
Silchester	Hampshire	Reading	Small segment	Necklace. Not dated	See Boon, G. C. (1957) and in *A* cii (1969)
Winchester, Lankhills Cemetery	Hampshire		Many, listed above under blue and green glass cylinder beads		Clarke, G. (forthcoming)

SITE AND PARISH	COUNTY	MUSEUM & NO.	DESCRIPTION AND APPROX. DIMENSIONS	ASSOCIATIONS AND REMARKS	PUBLICATION
St. Albans	Hertfordshire	Verulamium	Opaque. Diam. 5 mm.	From Park Street villa excavated 1944, Room V	
Ospringe	Kent	Maison Dieu Museum, Ospringe	No colour noted	Group XCIX with beaker of *c.* A.D. 140–190	*Os*
Chesters Fort	Northumberland	Chesters Museum 614	Opaque. Diam. 5 mm.	Found in 19th c. Site occupied *c.* A.D. 122–383	
Housesteads	Northumberland	University Museum, Newcastle-upon-Tyne	Opaque. Diam. 4 mm.	Roman site	
Shakenoak, Wilcote	Oxfordshire		6 examples, all opaque green	Dated A.D. 360–80	Brodribb, A. C. C., Hands, A. R. and Walker, D. R., *Shakenoak* i (1968), fig. 26, 20
Lansdown, Bath	Somerset	Bath	Opaque. Diam. 8 mm.	Upper Langridge Farm. The same site produced a cable bead of probably early Roman date	
West Coker	Somerset	Yeovil	No information	Roman villa	Site described in *PSNHAS* lxi (1916), 162
Wick Wood, Nettleton	Wiltshire	Nos. 824, 264A and 440		Romano-British. Several examples dated post A.D. 330	Information from Mr. W. J. Wedlake
Overton Down	Wiltshire		3 small segments, all opaque green	Site XII. Late Roman	*WAM* lxii (1967), 16 ff.
Huntcliff, Saltburn	Yorkshire	? Middlesbrough	2 examples, both opaque	From Roman signal station. Late Roman	
Scarborough	Yorkshire	Scarborough 1869–72–38	Opaque. Diam. 4 mm.	Signal station. Occupied A.D. 369 to opening of 5th c.	*ArJ* lxxxix (1932), 206

SCOTLAND

Traprain Law, Prestonkirk	E. Lothian	N.M.A.	Several examples	Roman period	See refs. to this site in Rivet, A. L. F. (ed.) (1966)

SQUARE SECTIONED BEADS, LONG OR CUBE-SHAPED
(mostly blue or green)

ENGLAND

Nor' nour, Scilly	Cornwall	St. Mary's, Scilly	2 small examples, one opaque blue. Diam. 2 mm. Length 6 mm. The other badly made and greener. Another colourless, flattened	Roman site lasting through to 4th c. A.D.	*ArJ* cxxiv (1967), 1 ff.

SITE AND PARISH	COUNTY	MUSEUM & NO.	DESCRIPTION AND APPROX. DIMENSIONS	ASSOCIATIONS AND REMARKS	PUBLICATION
Probus	Cornwall	Truro	Bottle glass. Length 1·8 cm. Width 4 mm.	From Carvossa Romano-British Camp. Occupied into 4th or 5th c. A.D. Perhaps made from reused Roman glass	Information from Mr. H. L. Douch
Little Chester, Derby	Derbyshire	Derby	Opaque blue. Length 7 mm. Diam. 3 mm.	From bottom of 4th c. A.D. ditch	Information from Mr. Christopher Green
Colliton Park, Dorchester	Dorset	Dorchester	One opaque blue, length 5 mm. One striated translucent sea-green, length 2·1 cm. Another small with one end only square in section	From Roman villa. Mostly late occupation, but begun in late 2nd c. A.D.	R.C.H.M. *Dorset* ii
Poundbury Camp, Dorchester	Dorset	Dorchester	3 cube-shaped beads, translucent cobalt	On necklace in 4th c. A.D. Christian cemetery with 78 segments of opaque green cylinder beads	Information from Mr. Christopher Green, 1973
South Shields	Durham	South Shields Museum	Blue iridescent. Diam. 4 mm. Length 2·6 cm.	Roman fort. Occupation *c.* A.D. 122–369	Richmond, I. A. (1954)
Frocester	Gloucestershire		3 examples of different sizes. Two have rounded section at one end	Stratified late 3rd– late 4th c. A.D. in Roman villa	*TBGAS* lxxxix (1970)
Kingscote Roman Villa	Gloucestershire		2 or more small blue examples	Surface finds from late Roman area of settlement	Information from Mr. Graham Walker
Rockbourne West Park Villa	Hampshire	Rockbourne Roman Villa Museum	Several small chips, blue opaque	From villa occupied throughout Roman period	Information from the late Mr. A. T. Morley Hewitt
Winchester, Lankhills Cemetery	Hampshire	Winchester	Various small examples of necklaces	Necklaces 363, 560, and 583, all in graves variously dated to *c.* A.D. 350–80	Clarke, G. (forthcoming), figs. 90, d, 98, c, b
Croft Ambrey, Croft	Herefordshire	Hereford	Necklace with small sky-blue beads on wire	Iron Age hill-fort with later occupation. This find is probably Roman	Stanford, S. C. (1974) and in *TWNFC* xxxix (1967), 31–9
Kenchester	Herefordshire	Hereford	2 examples. One opaque sky blue. Diam. 4 mm. Length 3 cm. Another smaller and more cobalt	Roman town occupied into late 4th c. A.D.	*TWNFC*, 1916 and 1926

SITE AND PARISH	COUNTY	MUSEUM & NO.	DESCRIPTION AND APPROX. DIMENSIONS	ASSOCIATIONS AND REMARKS	PUBLICATION
Weston-under-Penyard, Bollitree	Herefordshire	Gloucester 1772	Long green opaque. Others flatter sections	On necklace	*JBAA* xxvii (1871), 211
St. Albans	Hertfordshire	Verulamium	Light blue opaque. Diam. 3 mm. Length 5 mm.	Necklace of probably 4th c. date	*Ve*, p. 214, fig. 47g
Bardon Mill (*Vindolanda*)	Northumberland		Dark opaque turquoise. Diam. 4 mm. Length 1·4 cm.	Stratified late 3rd–4th c. A. D.	Information from Mr. R. E. Birley
Great Chesters	Northumberland	University Museum, Newcastle-upon-Tyne	Bright peacock blue opaque. Diam. 4 mm. Length 2 mm. Another longer, blue	Roman site	
Lamyatt Beacon, Lamyatt	Somerset		2 small opaque blue examples	Surface collection from site of Romano-Celtic temple frequented from *c.* A.D. 300 into 5th c.	Mr. Jones Colln. Kindly submitted by Mr. Roger Leech
Whitton	Suffolk	Ipswich	One small example	Roman villa occupied *c.* A.D. 130–290	*PSIA* xxi (1931–3), 240 ff.
Wick Wood, Nettleton	Wiltshire	c/o Bath and Camerton Arch. Soc. 288	Several very small examples. Green opaque	Romano-British necklace 'Before A.D. 284'	Information from Mr. W. J. Wedlake
Stockton Earthworks	Wiltshire	Salisbury	Pale blue translucent. Diam. 2 mm. Length 6 mm.	Belgic or Roman	*WAM* xliii (1927), 185 and pl. viii
Huntcliff, Saltburn	Yorkshire	? Middlesbrough	Broken, bright peacock blue. Diam. 4 mm. Length 1·5 cm.	Signal station occupied A.D. 369 to early 5th c.	*JRS* ii (1912), 215, and *ArJ* lxxxix (1932), 203
Templebrough Roman Fort	Yorkshire	Rotherham	Opaque azure	Excavated subsequently to main excavation. Probably 1st or 2nd c. A.D.	May, T. (1922)

IRELAND

Tara	Co. Meath	Dublin	Small opaque light blue. Diam. 3 mm. Length 5 mm.	From the Rath of the Synods which produced Roman pottery of 1st–3rd c. A.D. This bead may be Roman	Ó Ríordáin, S. P. (1964)

SCOTLAND

Covesea	Morayshire	N.M.A. HM212	Long, battered. Light blue-green. Diam. 5 mm. Length 3 cm.	Occupation in Roman period. Site included imported 2nd c. A.D. glass	*PSAS* lxv (1930–1) 177

SITE AND PARISH	COUNTY	MUSEUM & NO.	DESCRIPTION AND APPROX. DIMENSIONS	ASSOCIATIONS AND REMARKS	PUBLICATION
			WALES		
Coygan Camp, Laugharne	Carmarthenshire		Badly made dark almost opaque blue. Diam. 4 mm. Length 6 mm. Half another, and another smaller translucent light blue	Late 3rd c. A.D. stratified. All badly made and perhaps local products	Wainwright, G. J. (1967)
Caerleon	Monmouthshire		Small opaque emerald green. Diam. 2 mm. Length 5 mm.	Stratified c. A.D. 230–96 (from Broadway Drain)	Boon, G. C. (1972)
Caerwent (Pound Lane)	Monmouthshire		Bright green. Diam. 4 mm. Length 2·1 cm.	From late Roman stratum	Information from Dr. G. C. Dunning

LONG POLYGONAL BEADS

(opaque emerald green if not stated)
(See Exotic Roman Beads, p. 231)

SITE AND PARISH	COUNTY	MUSEUM & NO.	DESCRIPTION AND APPROX. DIMENSIONS	ASSOCIATIONS AND REMARKS	PUBLICATION
			ENGLAND		
Poundbury Camp, Dorchester	Dorset	Dorchester	Translucent bottle green. Length 7 mm. Hexagonal	3rd to 4th c. A.D.	Information from Mr. Christopher Green
South Shields	Durham	University Museum, Newcastle-upon-Tyne	One hexagonal turquoise. Diam. 6 mm. Length 2·6 cm. Another, smaller, green	Fort occupied c. A.D. 122 to 4th c.	See Richmond, I. A. (1954)
Colchester	Essex	B.M.	Hexagonal (2 others in B.M.)	Roman period pre-A.D. 61	*AnJ* ix (1929), 38
Mount Bures	Essex		Octagonal. Large size shown in illustration may not be correct. Length 2 cm.	Belgic burial with fire-dogs, etc., c. 10 B.C.–A.D. 50	Roach Smith, C. (1852), ii. For discussion see *A* ci (1967), 1 ff.
Wickford, Beauchamps	Essex	? Southend-on-Sea	Hexagonal. Emerald green, opaque	Roman	Information from Mr. W. Rodwell
Cirencester	Gloucestershire	Gloucester 539.41	Several examples. Green. Rather blurred angles. Hexagonal. Length 9 mm.	From Watermoor Cemetery. Roman period	*AnJ* xlix (1969) and earlier refs.
Cirencester	Gloucestershire	Cirencester B966	Rich translucent bottle green. Hexagonal	Unstratified from Roman town	*AnJ* xlix (1969)
Winchester, Lankhills Cemetery	Hampshire		Hexagonal, various sizes, blue, translucent green, opaque green	Necklaces 85, 140, 215, 363, 399, 424, and 436, all from graves variously dated within the period A.D. 310–70	Clarke, G. (forthcoming)

SITE AND PARISH	COUNTY	MUSEUM & NO.	DESCRIPTION AND APPROX. DIMENSIONS	ASSOCIATIONS AND REMARKS	PUBLICATION
St. Albans	Hertfordshire	Verulamium 38.64	Hexagonal opaque green. Rather large. Length 1·2 cm. Width 8 mm.	Roman town. Stratified A.D. 360–70	Frere, S. (1972), fig. 79, no. 75
St. Albans	Hertfordshire	Verulamium 38.64	Hexagonal opaque. Large in diameter. Length 9 mm.	Roman villa, Park Street	See refs. in Anthony, Ilid, *Verulamium* (1970)
Water Newton	Huntingdon-shire		One hexagonal		Beck's notes in C.M.
Richborough	Kent	Richborough 2361	Translucent green. Hexagonal	Unstratified from Roman and Saxon site	*Rich* iv, 244
Richborough	Kent	Richborough 1359	Small opaque green. Hexagonal. Length 4 mm.	3rd or 4th c. A.D.	*Rich* iv, 254
Richborough	Kent	Richborough 2880	Semi-translucent bright green with gold iridescence. Length 10 mm.	From inner stone fort ditch post Carausius	*Rich* iv, 243
Southfleet	Kent		A number on gold chain	3rd c. A.D.	Beck's notes in C.M.
Carrawburgh	Northumber-land	Chesters 62	One opaque green. Hexagonal. Length 16 mm. 5 other examples	Coventina's Well. Date approx. A.D. 122–383 (John Clayton excavations)	
Chesters Roman fort	Northumber-land	Chesters 1361	Pentagonal. Shiny opaque dark green. Length 1·2 cm. Slight break 'collar' at one end	From group: 'chiefly from Cilurnum' occupation about A.D. 122–383	
Corbridge	Northumber-land	Corstopitum 1140 and 754	2 examples opaque green	Occupation of the site from 1st to 5th c. A.D.	
Ilchester Mead	Somerset	Yeovil Borough Museum	Bright translucent green. Broken. ? Pentagonal or hex-agonal	From Roman villa	Interim report in *SDNQ* xxvi (1951–4), 213–15
Lamyatt Beacon	Somerset		Hexagonal. Green. Length 8 mm.	From Romano-Celtic temple begun about A.D. 300	Information from Mrs. Crystal Bennett and Mr. Roger Leech
Felixstowe	Suffolk	B.M.	One hexagonal		Beck's notes in C.M.
Icklingham	Suffolk	Bury St. Edmunds	Hexagonal	From hoard dated c. A.D. 400	
Whitton	Suffolk	? Ipswich	Hexagonal	From Castle Hill Roman villa, occu-pied c. A.D. 130–290	*PSIA* xxi (1931–3), 240 ff.

SITE AND PARISH	COUNTY	MUSEUM & NO.	DESCRIPTION AND APPROX. DIMENSIONS	ASSOCIATIONS AND REMARKS	PUBLICATION
Kirkby Thore	Westmorland		Green. Hexagonal	Several on a gold wire necklace found with dragonesque brooch, etc.	Way collection of drawings under *Fibulae* in the S.A.L. Library
Overton Down	Wiltshire		Small translucent, pentagonal, bottle green	From Site XII. Late Roman	*WAM* lxii (1967), 16 ff.
Wick Wood, Nettleton	Wiltshire	Bath and Camerton Arch. Soc. 2009	Translucent bottle green. Hexagonal. Length 1 cm.	From post-Roman layer perhaps containing Roman material	Information from Mr. W. J. Wedlake
Wick Wood, Nettleton	Wiltshire	Bath and Camerton Arch. Soc. 1915	Semi-translucent green. Hexagonal but flattened. Length 8 mm.	'after A.D. 330'	Information from Mr. W. J. Wedlake
Wick Wood, Nettleton	Wiltshire	Bath and Camerton Arch. Soc. 1510	Hexagonal. Opaque green. Length 7 mm.	'pre-Constantinian'	Information from Mr. W. J. Wedlake
Catterick	Yorkshire		Bright emerald green. Semi-translucent. Hexagonal. Large. Length 1 cm.	Roman period	Information from Mr. J. Wacher
Scarborough	Yorkshire	Scarborough 1869. 72.3	Translucent greenish blue. Hexagonal. Length 9 mm.	From Roman signal station occupied *c.* A.D. 370–400	

SCOTLAND

SITE AND PARISH	COUNTY	MUSEUM & NO.	DESCRIPTION AND APPROX. DIMENSIONS	ASSOCIATIONS AND REMARKS	PUBLICATION
Traprain Law, Prestonkirk	E. Lothian	N.M.A.	Several, hexagonal, green or blue-green	From native fort occupied during Roman period. From Level II. Not closely datable within Roman times	*PSAS* lvii (1922–3), 212
Covesea	Morayshire	N.M.A. 213	Large. Semi-translucent. Pentagonal. Dark green. Length 1 cm.	From cave occupied during Roman period. It produced, *inter alia*, a fragment of 2nd c. A.D. imported glass	*PSAS* lxv (1930–1), 177
Dun Beag Broch, Skye	Inverness-shire	N.M.A. GA1109, 1110	One bright blue cobalt to opaque. Hexagonal. Length 4 mm. Another more globular	From a broch with Dark Ages occupation	*PSAS* lv (1920), 110

SITE AND PARISH	COUNTY	MUSEUM & NO.	DESCRIPTION AND APPROX. DIMENSIONS	ASSOCIATIONS AND REMARKS	PUBLICATION
			WALES		
Whitton, nr. Barry	Glamorgan-shire		Pentagonal. Slight collar at each end perhaps where broken off. Bright opaque yellow core radiating to each angle. Covering translucent green glass reflecting yellow through	Unstratified in villa occupied from c. 1st c. B.C. to A.D. 300	Information from Dr. Michael Jarrett
Caerleon	Monmouth-shire	N.M.W. 63.228.B, G7	Large. Pentagonal. Translucent emerald green over opaque yellow core. Break 'collar' at one end. Length 1·1 cm.	Antonine. From Building X	Boon, G. C. (1972)
Caerleon	Monmouth-shire	N.M.W. 54.389A, G110	Octagonal. Small. Opaque green. Length 8 mm.	Stratified c. A.D. 130–230	Boon, G. C. (1972)
Caerwent	Monmouth-shire	Newport	Pentagonal. Green. Length 1·1 cm.	With pottery of prob- ably late 1st c. A.D. (Pound Lane)	Information from Dr. G. C. Dunning, see also A lxxx (1930), 239
Caernarvon	Caernarvon-shire	Segontium Museum, Caernarvon	Translucent with 5 or 6 sides. Badly made	Unstratified in Roman fort	Unpublished. Information from G. C. Boon

SMALL BICONICAL BEADS

(I) BLUE

ENGLAND

SITE AND PARISH	COUNTY	MUSEUM & NO.	DESCRIPTION AND APPROX. DIMENSIONS	ASSOCIATIONS AND REMARKS	PUBLICATION
Grove Hill, Tingewick	Buckingham-shire	Aylesbury	On chain	From Romano-British villa	
Porthmeor	Cornwall	West Cornwall Field Club	Translucent. Diam. under 5 mm.	From Hut 12 in site of long occupation	JRIC xxiv (1933–36)
Probus	Cornwall	Truro	Diam. 8 mm. Width 7 mm. Very small perforation	From Romano-British site of Carvossa	Information from Mr. H. L. Douch
Uplyme, Holcombe	Devon	Sidmouth	One very small trans-lucent and another, larger	Unstratified in Roman villa	PDAS xxxii (1974)
Badbury Rings, Wimborne	Dorset	Dorchester 1937.57. 2–3	Bright translucent dark cobalt. Diam. c. 4 mm.	Lent by Mr. W.C. Wallace	
Maiden Castle, Winterbourne Monkton	Dorset	Dorchester	Dark blue. Diam. 7 mm.	From 'Belgo-Roman' level c. A.D. 25–70	Wheeler, R. E. M. (1943), p. 291 and fig. 98, no. 5

SITE AND PARISH	COUNTY	MUSEUM & NO.	DESCRIPTION AND APPROX. DIMENSIONS	ASSOCIATIONS AND REMARKS	PUBLICATION
Fordington	Dorset	Dorchester 1846.2.15	Small	From Roman period cemetery. Possibly 3rd–4th c. A.D.	Roach Smith, C. (1852), iii, pl. ix and p. 33, and R.C.H.M. *Dorset* ii
Cirencester (Barnsley Park)	Gloucester-shire		6 examples, diam. about 5 mm.	From Roman villa, 'probably 3rd–4th c.'	Information from Dr. Graham Webster
Frocester	Gloucester-shire		4 small examples	3 from mid-4th c. A.D. levels of Roman villa	*TBGAS* lxxxix (1970)
Weston-under-Penyard, Bollitree	Herefordshire	Gloucester 1769 and and 1771	2 examples, one opaque. Diam. 6 mm.	Roman period	*JBAA* xxvii(1871), 207
Richborough, Ash	Kent	Richborough 2107	Light cobalt translucent. Diam. 6 mm.	From middle layer of inner stone fort ditch, probably post-Carausius	*Rich* iv, 246
Bardon Mill (*Vindolanda*)	Northumber-land		Translucent blue. Larger than usual. Diam. 1 cm.	Stratified late 3rd–4th c. A.D.	Information from Dr. R. E. Birley
Chesters Fort	Northumber-land	Chesters 614	About 5 examples. One opaque and one translucent. Diam. 6 mm. and 2 or 3 very small examples	Found in 19th c. by John Clayton in excavations. Probably date between A.D. 122 and 383	
Lamyatt Beacon	Somerset		Irregular, translucent. Diam. 9 mm. Two others similar	From Romano-Celtic temple at Lamyatt Beacon begun about A.D. 300	Information from Mrs. Crystal Bennett and Mr. Roger Leech
Cold Kitchen Hill, Brixton Deverill	Wiltshire	Devizes	2 examples	Unassociated from hill which produced large numbers of Roman beads	For site see *WAM* xliii (1926)
Stockton Earthworks	Wiltshire	Salisbury	Bright translucent cobalt. Diam. 5 mm.	Belgic-Roman site	*WAM* xliii (1926), 389
Larkhill, nr. Durrington Walls	Wiltshire		Blue glass	Probably 4th c. A.D. pit. Feature 188	*WAM* lxvi (1972), 119, fig. 29.9
Catterick	Yorkshire		Bright translucent cobalt. Diam. 5 mm.	Roman	Information from Mr. J. Wacher

SCOTLAND

SITE AND PARISH	COUNTY	MUSEUM & NO.	DESCRIPTION AND APPROX. DIMENSIONS	ASSOCIATIONS AND REMARKS	PUBLICATION
Traprain Law, Prestonkirk	E. Lothian	N.M.A. FR519	Translucent bright greenish blue. Diam. 4 mm.	Native hill-fort. Occupied late 1st – 4th c. A.D.	For references see Rivet, A.L.F. (ed.), (1966)

SITE AND PARISH	COUNTY	MUSEUM & NO.	DESCRIPTION AND APPROX. DIMENSIONS	ASSOCIATIONS AND REMARKS	PUBLICATION
Hownam	Roxburgh-shire	N.M.A. HH532	Opaque. Shows signs of coiling. Diam. 8 mm.	Unstratified in hill-fort. This seems to be made by coiling. It has a larger per-foration than most in this class and may be late or post-Roman in date	*PSAS* lxxxii (1947–8), 220

(II) OTHER COLOURS

ENGLAND

Witham	Essex	? Southend-on-Sea	Semi-translucent green. Diam. 4 mm.	From Romano-British site	Awaiting publication
Cirencester	Gloucester-shire	Cirencester	Green	From Roman town	*AnJ* xlix (1969) and earlier refs.
Wick Wood, Nettleton	Wiltshire		4 similar, apparently opaque black.	From level dated 'after A.D. 330'	Information from Mr. W. J. Wedlake
Wick Wood, Nettleton	Wiltshire		Another very small green bead	Late 4th c. A.D.	Information from Mr. W. J. Wedlake
Catterick	Yorkshire		Opaque emerald green. Rather flat. Diam. 5 mm.	Roman period	Information from Mr. J. Wacher

SCOTLAND

Dun Ardtreck, Skye	Inverness-shire	Glasgow SF28	Opaque terracotta-colour. Diam. 1 cm. Ht. 4 mm. Perf. diam. 4 mm.	From a gallery-walled fort, perhaps 1st c. B.C. to 1st c. A.D.	Preliminary report in *An* xxxix (1965), and xliii (1969), 23

(III) VERY SMALL BICONICAL BEADS (VARIOUS COLOURS)

ENGLAND

Fordington	Dorset	Dorchester 1046.2.15	Very small translu-cent yellow, green and blue and bottle-green with other beads on a long necklace (pl. *IV b*)	Clearly a late Roman necklace. Many of the beads have analogies from 4th c. A.D. sites. See also R.C.H.M. *Dorset*, ii	Some of the finds published by Roach Smith, C. (1852), iii
Wycomb	Gloucester-shire	c/o W. L. Cox, Charlton Kings	One blue and one green opaque	Found on surface of field with other beads (4th c. A.D. and Saxon)	Information from finder
Winchester, Lankhills Cemetery	Hampshire	Winchester	Large number from late Roman burials. Opaque green, blue and yellow translu-cent	Necklaces 28, 85, 182, 192, 215, 248, 353, 363, 425, 443, and 583, all from graves variously dated within the period A.D. 310–80	Clarke, G. (forth-coming)

SITE AND PARISH	COUNTY	MUSEUM & NO.	DESCRIPTION AND APPROX. DIMENSIONS	ASSOCIATIONS AND REMARKS	PUBLICATION
Icklingham	Suffolk	A.M. 1927.700	Necklace with one translucent yellow, 7 green translucent and 62 blue and a faceted bead	From Lackford Hills. Probably 4th c. A.D. Bought. 'Found by a gravel digger at Lackford Hills.' The association as a necklace seems to be probable	MS. notes of J. Warren of Ixworth (1859, 9 Feb.) in A.M.
Cold Kitchen Hill, Brixton Deverill	Wiltshire	Devizes	One blue translucent	Nearly all late Roman beads from this ? sacred site	*WAM* xliii and xliv and *UCH Wilts.* i

LONG BICONICAL BEADS
(Various colours, opaque and translucent)

ENGLAND

Holcombe	Devon	Sidmouth	Opaque cobalt blue. Length 1·1 cm.	Unstratified	*PDAS* xxxii (1974)
Dorchester	Dorset	Dorchester	Several examples, blue-green or colourless	On necklace from Poundbury Camp. Late Roman	Information from excavator 1971
Bagendon	Gloucester-shire	Cheltenham	Opaque terracotta-coloured like Wick Wood beads below. Length 9 mm.	Belgic site, probably 1st c. A.D.	Clifford, E. M. (1961)
Cirencester	Gloucester-shire	Cirencester	Several blue examples	Unstratified in Roman town	*AnJ* xlix (1969) and earlier refs.
Frocester	Gloucester-shire		Length 1 cm. Almost opaque turquoise blue	Probably 3rd–4th c. A.D.	*TBGAS* lxxxix (1970)
Portchester	Hampshire		2 dull almost opaque blue examples. Length 1 cm.	From late Roman levels	Information from Prof. Barry Cunliffe
Rockbourne	Hampshire	Fordingbridge	Almost opaque cobalt. Length over 10 mm.	Unstratified in Roman villa occupied throughout Roman period	Information from the late Mr. A. T. Morley Hewitt
Silchester	Hampshire	Reading	Length 1·2 cm.	Necklace with hexagonal beads and other types from Roman and pre-Roman town	
Kenchester	Herefordshire	Hereford	Opaque blue. Length 1·6 cm.	Roman site occupied up to about A.D. 390	*TWNFC*, 1916 and 1926
Weston-under-Penyard, Bollitree	Herefordshire	Gloucester 1772	Opaque, atypical and angular. Length 1·5 cm.	Necklace with other Roman beads of various types	*JBAA* xxvii (1871), 211 ff.

SITE AND PARISH	COUNTY	MUSEUM & NO.	DESCRIPTION AND APPROX. DIMENSIONS	ASSOCIATIONS AND REMARKS	PUBLICATION
St. Albans	Hertfordshire	Verulamium T34:545	Opaque blue. Length 1 cm.	From the Roman theatre, mid-2nd – early 4th c. A.D.	*A* lxxxiv (1934)
St. Albans	Hertfordshire	Verulamium 30, 125	Blue. Length 1 cm.	Roman	
Ospringe	Kent	Maison Dieu, Ospringe	Length 1·3 cm.	Group 99, nos. 339–40. Necklace dated A.D. 140–90 from bulbous beaker	*Os*, pp. 34–5
Strood	Kent	Humphry Wickham Colln. (perhaps lost)	Opaque Samian red	Roman burial ground ranging from 1st–4th c. A.D.	Roach Smith, C. (1848), p. 17, pl. ii
Bardon Mill (*Vindolanda*)	Northumberland		4 or 5 almost opaque blue beads about 1·5 cm. and 1·8 cm. long but various sizes	Stratified late 3rd–4th c. A.D.	Information from Mr. R. E. Birley
Chesters Fort	Northumberland	Chesters 1362	Pale blue translucent and flat. Atypical. Length 1·6 cm.	Roman. (This could be classified with heart-shaped and flat beads)	
Stonham Aspal	Suffolk	Ipswich 965–45	Blue. Broken at end. Length 1·4 cm.	From ditch round early 3rd c. A.D. bath building	*PSIA* xxx (1966), 240, fig. 38e
Lower Beeding (Money Mound)	Sussex		Blue. Length 1·1 cm. Wide and flattish. Badly made	Among Romano-British objects deposited in earlier barrow	*SAC* cv (1967), 18, fig. 3
Nr. Rugby (*Tripontium*)	Warwickshire		6 translucent bottle-green beads, originally translucent. Length about 8 mm.	On necklace with red and white chevron beads (see below), bronze bangles and iron buttons on female burial	*TPBAS* lxxxv (1972), 131
Wick Wood, Nettleton	Wiltshire	c/o Bath and Camerton Arch. Soc.	3 opaque terracotta-coloured beads with striated surfaces. All about 6–9 mm. long	Stratified in Romano-British site, 'before A.D. 284'	Information from Mr. W. J. Wedlake

LONG BLUE BICONICAL OR SQUARE-SECTIONED BEADS WITH RED AND WHITE BAND OR CHEVRON

ENGLAND

Nor' nour, Scilly	Cornwall	St. Mary's, Scilly	Small with single wave in red, bordered in white	From Roman site unstratified	Main report published in *ArJ* cxxiv (1967), 1 ff.
Fordington, Dorchester	Dorset	Dorchester	2 possible examples on long necklace. The red has quite disappeared	Necklace probably 3rd–4th c. A.D. Probably intrusive (pl. *IVb*)	R.C.H.M. *Dorset*

SITE AND PARISH	COUNTY	MUSEUM & NO.	DESCRIPTION AND APPROX. DIMENSIONS	ASSOCIATIONS AND REMARKS	PUBLICATION
Tarrant Hinton	Dorset	Wimborne	Rounded biconical bead. Length *c.* 1 cm.	Found on Roman site 1975–76	Excavations in progress
Rockbourne	Hampshire	Roman Villa Museum, Rockbourne	Long, rather biconical, with single red wave outlined in white. Length 1·2 cm.	Unstratified in villa occupied throughout Roman period	Information from the late Mr. A. T. Morley Hewitt
St. Albans	Hertfordshire	Verulamium 232		From woman's grave near N.W. gate. Late Roman, probably 4th c. A.D.	*Ve*, p. 214, fig. 47, no. 67n.
Ospringe	Kent	Maison Dieu, Ospringe	Several small beads with single red wave outlined in white	From an unrecorded grave with 3rd–4th c. A.D. finger ring, bracelets, etc.	
Bardon Mill (*Vindolanda*)	Northumberland		2 small examples	Stratified late 3rd–4th c. A.D.	Information from Mr. R. E. Birley
Great Chesters	Northumberland	University Museum, Newcastle-upon-Tyne	Length 1·1 cm. with one red band edged in white	Unstratified from Roman site	
Stouting	Sussex	C.M., Beck Colln. 1704b	Larger than normal red band bordered in red. Max. diam. 6 mm. Length 1·5 cm.	This came from a colln. with many Anglo-Saxon beads	
Nr Rugby (*Tripontium*)	Warwickshire		9 examples, all long biconical with single chevron. Average length 8 mm.	With 6 long biconical green beads of same size. With female burial with bronze bangles and iron buttons	*TPBAS* lxxxv (1972), 131
Cold Kitchen Hill, Brixton Deverill	Wiltshire	Devizes	Rather biconical. Length 1 cm. Single chevron	Unassociated, from hill producing large quantities of Roman period beads	For site see *WAM* xliii (1926)
Wick Wood, Nettleton	Wiltshire	Bath and Camerton Arch. Soc.	2 small and typical examples on a necklace	Dated 'before 284' A.D.	Information from Mr. W. J. Wedlake

SCOTLAND

Traprain Law, Prestonkirk	E. Lothian	N.M.A. 1923.270, small example	One example with single red wave with white border. One, longer, with two similar waves	Not stratified on site occupied throughout Roman period	Larger example, *PSAS* lvii (1922–3), 225 and fig. 22, p. 212

SITE AND PARISH	COUNTY	MUSEUM & NO.	DESCRIPTION AND APPROX. DIMENSIONS	ASSOCIATIONS AND REMARKS	PUBLICATION

OBLONG (ROUND SECTIONED)

(A) SKY BLUE OPAQUE

ENGLAND

Wilderspool, Warrington	Cheshire–Lancashire border	Warrington 27113	Opaque light sky blue. Diam. 8 mm. Length 1·1 cm. Very small perforation	From Roman industrial site	For site see May, T. (1904) and Thompson, F. H. (1965)
Weston-under-Penyard, Bollitree	Herefordshire	Gloucester 1772	Opaque light sky blue. Diam. 5 mm. Length 1·8 cm. Small perforation	Necklace from Roman site	*JBAA* xxvii (1871), 211 ff.

SCOTLAND

Selkirk area	Selkirkshire	Mr. Mason's Colln., Selkirk	Opaque light sky blue. Evidently wound. Diam. 5 mm. Length 1·8 cm. Small perforation	Most of the finds in this colln. come from Roman sites	

(B) OTHER COLOURS

One 'black' example comes from Dun Beag, Skye (N.M.A., no. GA1107) from broch with Dark Ages occupation (*PSAS* lv (1920–1), 110), and another, also 'black' but smaller, from Gloucester (stray find, Gloucester Museum 1290) from Roman and post-Roman site. Both of these are perhaps more probably post-Roman in date.

UNDECORATED HEART–OR PEAR-SHAPED BEADS AND RELATED ROUND BEADS WITH FLAT SECTIONS

ENGLAND

Sennen, Maen	Cornwall	c/o West Cornwall Field Club	Translucent light green. Broken and atypical	From hill-fort. Seems broken but possibly this type	*WCFC*, N.S., i, no. 3 (1954–5)
Fordington, Dorchester	Dorset	Dorchester 1846.2.15	Light cobalt translucent about 1 cm. diam.	From Roman period cemetery	Roach Smith, C. (1852), iii, p. 33 and pl. ix
South Shields	Durham	University Museum, Newcastle-upon-Tyne	Translucent natural glass. Heart-shaped Max. diam. 1 cm. Length 1·2 cm.	Roman fort occupied A.D. 122–369	Richmond, I. A. (1954) and *JRS* lvii (1967)
Cirencester	Gloucester-shire	Cirencester C951	Pear-shaped. Bright dark cobalt. Flattish section and small perforation	Unstratified in Roman town	*AnJ* xlix (1969) and earlier refs.

SITE AND PARISH	COUNTY	MUSEUM & NO.	DESCRIPTION AND APPROX. DIMENSIONS	ASSOCIATIONS AND REMARKS	PUBLICATION
Frocester	Gloucester-shire		Pear-shaped, colourless. Length 1·2 cm.	Not clearly stratified in villa occupied from c. A.D. 275	*TBGAS* lxxxix (1970)
Frocester	Gloucester-shire		Two small round beads with flat sections	Stratified late 3rd c. A.D. from Frocester Court Roman Villa	*Ibid.*
Wolham	Gloucester-shire	Gloucester 36/1942	Triangular green, translucent. Diam. 2·3 cm.	From Roman and post-Roman site	
Owslebury	Hampshire		Round, bright, almost opaque cobalt with flat section. Diam. 7 mm.	Probably 4th c. A.D.	First report in *AnJ* xlviii (1968), 18 ff.
Portchester	Hampshire		Small almost opaque cobalt heart-shaped with diamond-shaped perforation	Late Roman deposit in Saxon shore-fort built late 3rd c. A.D.	See *AnJ* xlix (1969), 62
Rockbourne	Hampshire	Roman Villa Museum, Rock-bourne	Translucent natural glass. Pear-shaped. Length 1·1 cm. Flat section	Villa occupied throughout Roman period	Information from the late Mr. A. T. Morley Hewitt
Winchester, Lankhills Cemetery	Hampshire		Translucent, light blue glass. Length 0·8 cm.	Necklace 363, from Grave 336, dated c. A.D. 350–70	Clarke, G. (forth-coming)
Kenchester	Herefordshire	Hereford	Translucent natural glass. Wide heart-shaped. Length 1·3 cm. and flattish section	From Roman town occupied till about A.D. 390	*TWNFC* 1916 and 1926
St. Albans	Hertfordshire	Verulamium	Translucent pale green. Oval. Diam. 1·4 cm.	Evidently on a necklace with other Roman beads. Probably 4th c. A.D.	*Ve*, not shown in fig. 47 where representative selection only illustrated
Godman-chester	Huntingdon-shire		Light blue, pear-shaped with round section. Length 9 mm.	Late 1st or early 2nd c. A.D. Roman	*PCAS* liv (1960), 57 and 22
Manchester (Castlefields)	Lancashire		Heart-shaped. Natural glass. Approx. diam. 1·1 cm. Length 1·4 cm.	From Roman fort	*A* xxxiv (1852), pl. v
Wilderspool, Warrington	Lancashire–Cheshire border	Warrington 386.'06	Wide pear-shaped. Very fractured. Translucent bright clear glass. Max. diam. 13 mm. Ht. 15 mm.	Roman industrial site	May, T. (1904) and Thompson, F. H. (1965)

SITE AND PARISH	COUNTY	MUSEUM & NO.	DESCRIPTION AND APPROX. DIMENSIONS	ASSOCIATIONS AND REMARKS	PUBLICATION
Chesters Fort	Northumberland	Chesters Museum 614	Translucent cobalt blue. Heart-shaped. Max. diam. 1 cm. Length 1·2 cm.	Probable date A.D. 122–383	
Chesters Fort	Northumberland	Chesters Museum 614	Another smaller heart-shaped	Probable date A.D. 122–383	
Great Chesters	Northumberland	Chesters Museum 2508	Light blue translucent. Heart-shaped. Max. diam. 1·3 cm. Length 1·5 cm. Small perforation	Probable date A.D. 122–383	
Bath	Somerset	Bath	Bright translucent blue. Irregular and perhaps accidentally heart-shaped. Length 7 mm.	From Roman baths begun at end of 1st c. A.D. and frequented through Roman period	See Cunliffe, B., *Roman Bath Discovered* (1971) and refs.
Camerton	Somerset	Bristol F753	Circular translucent natural glass. Flat section and very small perforation. Diam. 1 cm. Length 1·3 cm.	Roman and post-Roman site	Wedlake, W. J (1958)
Ham Hill, Montacute	Somerset	Taunton	Bottle glass. Oval. Length 1·3 cm. Another	Iron Age hill-fort with later Roman occupation. Unstratified. Several with late Roman beads	For site, see *VCH Somerset* i, p. 295
Lamyatt Beacon	Somerset	c/o Mrs. Crystal Bennett, Bruton, and Mr. Roger Leech	Small, round, translucent green with flat section. Diam. 7 mm. Another similar but oval	From Romano-Celtic temple probably begun c. A.D. 300 and frequented into 5th c.	See Lewis, M. J. T., *Temples in Roman Britain* (1970)
Castle Hill, Whitton	Suffolk	Ipswich 1948.116	Translucent bottle glass. Oval with flat section. Length 1·4 cm. Width 9 mm.	Roman villa thought to be dated c. A.D. 130–290. On necklace with all globular beads	*PSIA* xxi (1931–3), 249 ff.
Lakenheath	Suffolk	C.M., Beck Colln. 1735	Translucent green oval. Length 1 cm.		
Lower Beeding (Money Mound)	Sussex		Clear colourless glass. Heart-shaped. Length 7 mm.	Early barrow with deposit of Romano-British objects in it	*SAC* cv (1967), 18, fig. 3
Stockton Earthworks	Wiltshire	Salisbury	Black circular flat bead. Diam. 8 mm.	Probably Roman period. Belgic-Roman site	*WAM* xliii (1925–6), 389
Stockton Earthworks	Wiltshire	Salisbury	Translucent bottle glass. Length 1 cm. Width 7 mm.	As above	*Ibid.*

SITE AND PARISH	COUNTY	MUSEUM & NO.	DESCRIPTION AND APPROX. DIMENSIONS	ASSOCIATIONS AND REMARKS	PUBLICATION
			SCOTLAND		
Nr. Coulter	Lanarkshire	N.M.A., Sim Colln. FJ32	Bright green translucent rather heart-shaped. Length 1·2 cm.	Possibly post-Roman	
			WALES		
Whitton, nr. Barry	Glamorgan	N.M.W.	Irregular, badly made. Bottle glass. Round section. Length 1·3 cm.	Site occupied c. 1st c. B.C. to A.D. 300	Information from Dr. Michael Jarrett

FACETED BEADS
(Square section with diamond-shaped facets)

SITE AND PARISH	COUNTY	MUSEUM & NO.	DESCRIPTION AND APPROX. DIMENSIONS	ASSOCIATIONS AND REMARKS	PUBLICATION
			ENGLAND		
Cirencester	Gloucestershire	Corinium Museum, Cirencester	Bright translucent blue. Length 8 mm.	4th or early 5th c. A.D. from burial, excavated 1973	Awaiting publication
Cirencester	Gloucestershire	Corinium Museum, Cirencester	Large bead. Blue. Length 1 cm. Ht. 9 mm.	On a wire with 2 melon beads and one cut green cylinder	
Wycombe	Gloucestershire	c/o W. L. Cox, Charlton Kings, Cheltenham	Length 7 mm. Ht. 5 mm. Blue	Surface find with other beads (4th c. and Saxon) in field	Information from finder
Winchester, Lankhills Cemetery	Hampshire	Winchester	Several cube-shaped blue and green examples about 6 mm. long	Necklace 140, 363, 424, and 436, all in graves dated to A.D. 350–70	Clarke, G. (forthcoming)
Bradley Hill, Somerton	Somerset		Translucent blue. Square. 5 mm. long	With a burial. From homestead site with accompanying East-West graves. Beginning not later than A.D. 370 and running into the 5th c.	C.B.A. groups XII and XIII, *Arch. Rev.* vii (1972), 39–41
Lufton	Somerset	Yeovil Borough Museum	Bright translucent blue	From same horizon as a coin of Constantine II as Caesar (A.D. 330–335)	*PSANHS* cxvi (1971–2), 66, fig. 5
Mendip	Somerset	A. C. Pass Colln., Bristol F2089	Long. Translucent green. Length 1·2 cm. Ht. 5 mm. Perf. diam. 1 mm.	From a collection containing many Roman beads	

SITE AND PARISH	COUNTY	MUSEUM & NO.	DESCRIPTION AND APPROX. DIMENSIONS	ASSOCIATIONS AND REMARKS	PUBLICATION
Icklingham, Lackford Hills	Suffolk	A.M. 1927.700. (Some other beads from the site are at Bury St. Edmunds)	One translucent blue. Length 8 mm. Ht. 7 mm.	From a necklace with very small biconical beads and tiny cylinder beads. The find was made in 1859 and is obviously 4th–5th c. A.D.	Joseph Warren's MS. daybook in the library of the A.M.

GLASS MELON BEADS

ENGLAND

SITE AND PARISH	COUNTY	MUSEUM & NO.	DESCRIPTION AND APPROX. DIMENSIONS	ASSOCIATIONS AND REMARKS	PUBLICATION
Dunstable	Bedfordshire		Blue glass	From well-filling of *c.* 2nd c. A.D. Site abandoned about 100 years later	*BAJ* (1922), fig. 5, no. 3 and p. 30
Nanstallon	Cornwall		2 cobalt melon beads. Diam. 2.2 cm.	From 1st c. A.D. deposit	*Brit* iii (1972), 94
Woodcuts	Dorset		Dense green	Unstratified but probably 1st c. A.D.	Pitt-Rivers, A. H. L. F. (1887), p. xliv, no. 15
Sutton Walls	Herefordshire		Dark blue. Diam. *c.* 2·5 cm.	Unstratified in Iron Age and Roman fort	*ArJ* cx (1953), 61–2
St. Albans	Hertfordshire	Verulamium	Deep blue glass	Stratified A.D. 130–150	Frere, S. (1972), p. 213 and fig. 79, no. 70
Manchester	Lancashire	Manchester	One example. Small. Blue	Flavian fort subsequently reduced in size	Bruton, F. A., *The Roman Fort at Manchester* (1909), p. 126
Ribchester	Lancashire	Ribchester	Deep blue. Gadroons begin well below perforation. Large	Flavian and Antonine fort with later occupation	*JRS* xxxv (1945), 15. See also Frere, S. (1967), *passim*
Leicester (Jewry Wall)	Leicestershire	Leicester	Light blue	Level VII. Early 3rd c. A.D.	Kenyon, K. M. (1948), fig. 93.9
Lincoln	Lincolnshire	Lincoln	One blue and one green	Blue from mainly 1st c. A.D. fill, and another, green, from mixed Roman soil	*ArJ* cxvii (1960), 68
Lincoln	Lincolnshire	Lincoln	Blue	1st c. A.D.	civ (1973), 173
London	London	Formerly Guildhall Museum, 3956, 2616, 2652, 19041	All blue except 3956 (light green). 19041 is fragment of large bead *c.* 3·5 cm. diam. and wide perforation	All unstratified except 19041 from Bucklersbury House site, 1955. Lower filling of Walbrook, 1st–2nd c. A.D.	Information from Mr. Hugh Chapman
Corbridge	Northumberland	Newcastle-upon-Tyne	Dark blue glass	From the Corbridge hoard of 1964	*AA*, 4th s., xlvi (1968), 119

SITE AND PARISH	COUNTY	MUSEUM & NO.	DESCRIPTION AND APPROX. DIMENSIONS	ASSOCIATIONS AND REMARKS	PUBLICATION
Ebchester	Northumberland		Half a deep blue glass melon bead	Early Roman	*AA*, 5th s., vii (1975), 78
Great Chesters	Northumberland	Newcastle-upon-Tyne 1956.63A	Half bead in dark blue opaque glass		
Housesteads	Northumberland	Newcastle-upon-Tyne 1956.151.24.A	Fragment of dark blue bead		
Milking Gap, High Shield	Northumberland	University Museum, Newcastle-upon-Tyne	Two fragmentary translucent blue beads, *c.* 3 cm. diam.	This site was occupied from about A.D. 122–80 at latest	*AA*, 4th s., xv (1938), 346
Wick Wood, Nettleton	Wilts.	c/o Bath and Camerton Arch. Soc.	Fragment of large blue melon bead	Romano-British	Information from Mr. W. J. Wedlake
Chichester	Sussex	Chichester	Blue	From Grave 228 associated with late Antonine pottery	Down, A. and Rule, M., *Chichester Excavations*, i (1971)
Wick Wood, Nettleton	Wiltshire	c/o Bath and Camerton Arch. Soc.	Fragment. Large. Blue	Cutting A, layer 2	Information from Mr. W. J. Wedlake
Castleford	Yorkshire		At least 6 blue glass melon beads and lumps of the same glass as waste	A Roman site, perhaps making beads among its products	Information from excavator
Edlington Wood, nr. Doncaster	Yorkshire		Fragment, dark blue glass melon bead, gadroons start well below the perforation	Probably Hadrianic–Antonine	Grimes, W. F. (ed.) (1951)
Rotherham (Templebrough)	Yorkshire	Rotherham	Several examples	From excavations of 1921. Two forts both before Hadrian	May, T. (1922)

SCOTLAND

SITE AND PARISH	COUNTY	MUSEUM & NO.	DESCRIPTION AND APPROX. DIMENSIONS	ASSOCIATIONS AND REMARKS	PUBLICATION
	'Aberdeenshire'	N.M.A. (Rae Colln.) FJ75	Opaque. Roughly made. Turquoise glass	No details	
Castle Hill, Dalry	Ayrshire	N.M.A. HH365	Dark blue glass. Diam. 2·5 cm.	Fort occupied during late 1st–early 2nd c. A.D. and again in about 8th–9th c.	*PSAS* liii (1918), 123
Lochlee Crannog, Tarbolton	Ayrshire		No colour specified. Diam. *c.* 1·5 cm.	Roman period not closely dated	*PSAS* xiii (1874), 239
Barburgh Mill, Nithsdale	Dumfriesshire		Roughly made, small, pale blue. Diam. *c.* 1·1 cm.	From Roman fortlet of Antonine date	Forthcoming in *PSAS*. Information from Roger Miket
Birrens	Dumfriesshire		One dark and one greenish	Roman fort	*PSAS* xxx (1896), 79

SITE AND PARISH	COUNTY	MUSEUM & NO.	DESCRIPTION AND APPROX. DIMENSIONS	ASSOCIATIONS AND REMARKS	PUBLICATION
Traprain Law, Prestonkirk	E. Lothian	N.M.A.	Blue melon. Possibly others not recorded, and 2 badly made green fragments	From Iron Age fort occupied throughout Roman period	*PSAS* lvii (1923), 212 and fig. 19, no. 76 and *ibid.* lv (1920–1), 198
Camphouse	Roxburgh-shire		Blue glass	With finds suggesting 1st–2nd c. A.D.	
Newstead	Roxburgh-shire	N.M.A.	Several examples in blue and green	Mainly of Flavian date	*Ne*, p. xci
Blackwood Hill, Keir Hill, Gargunnock	Stirlingshire	N.M.A.	Dark blue translucent. Diam. *c*. 3 cm.	From homestead of uncertain date, probably before A.D. 80. Beads exactly like Newstead ones	*PSAS* xci (1957–8), 82

WALES

SITE AND PARISH	COUNTY	MUSEUM & NO.	DESCRIPTION AND APPROX. DIMENSIONS	ASSOCIATIONS AND REMARKS	PUBLICATION
Brecon Gaer	Brecknockshire			Fort built *c*. A.D. 75	*Y Cymmrodor*, xxxvii (1926), 120–1
Caerhun	Caernarvon-shire		Various examples	The fort was dismantled in the Antonine period	Baillie-Reynolds, P. K. (1938), fig. 49
Pen Llystyn	Caernarvon-shire		'Hand crimped glass.' Diam. *c*. 2·2 cm.	From Roman fort occupied A.D. 78–90	*ArJ* cxxv (1968), 180, Gb2 and pl. xvi c
Caernarvon	Caernarvon-shire	Segontium (Caernarvon)	Several examples of blue paste or glass	Fort built around A.D. 75 and later modified	Wheeler, R. E. M., *Segontium* (1926)
Whitton, nr. Barry	Glamorgan-shire	N.M.W.	Dark olive green. Diam. *c*. 2 cm.	From Roman villa occupied until about A.D. 300. Unstratified	Information from Dr. M. Jarrett
Tomen-y-mur	Merioneth-shire		Half-bead. Medium blue, translucent. Diam. *c*. 3 cm.	Fort occupied *c*. A.D. 75–140	Information from Dr. M. Jarrett
Abergavenny	Monmouth-shire				*MAn* ii (1965–8), fig. 10, no. 9
Caerleon	Monmouth-shire		Several examples	Timber period of fort A.D. 75–105	*AC* lxxxvii (1932), 92, fig. 40, 1–3
Caerleon	Monmouth-shire	N.M.W.	Several more examples	Dated A.D. 75–100 (2) and one probably Hadrian or Trajan	Boon, G. C. (1972)
Caerleon	Monmouth-shire	N.M.W.	Black opaque with irregular concentric bands round circumference	From main lateral drain to S.W. of legionary fortress, *c*. A.D. 140	Boon, G. C. (1972)

THE SCHEDULES: ROMAN PERIOD
EXOTIC BEADS OF THE ROMAN PERIOD

SITE AND PARISH	COUNTY	MUSEUM & NO.	DESCRIPTION AND APPROX. DIMENSIONS	ASSOCIATIONS AND REMARKS	PUBLICATION
			ENGLAND		
Bracknell	Berkshire	C.M., Beck Colln., 2247	'Black' irregular oval bead with flat section and band of blue above the circumference. Diam. 1·3 cm. Ht. 1·2 cm. Small perforation	Comparable to beads from Kenchester (Herefordshire) from Roman context. Both beads may be imports from Germanic contexts. See also Housesteads (Northumberland)	Not published
Pangbourne	Berkshire	C.M., Beck Colln., 1696	Long dark blue bead 3·3 cm. by 1·3 cm. Central zig-zag and end bands. Colour missing	This bead may compare with Lankhills and Cirencester beads of 4th c. A.D. date	Unpublished
Bradwell, nr. Milton Keynes	Buckingham-shire		Square-sectioned part of translucent green bead with irregular opaque red bands and yellow spots. Cf. another somewhat similar found recently at Chelmsford (unpublished)	From Roman villa, probably 4th c. A.D.	Green, M., *The Bradwell Roman Villa* (first interim report). Milton Keynes Development Corporation
Willingham	Cambridge-shire	C.M. 1918–160.9–15	Very like a late La Tène bead from Adria, Italy (Grave 1904/83). Illustrated by Haevernick, T. E. (1960), Tav. 16. Large annular opaque blue black with several inlaid wavy white lines round sides. Diam. 3·8 cm. Ht. 1·4 cm. Perf. diam. 1·1 cm.	With sceptre-head, etc., either of Commodus (A.D. 161–92) or Antoninus Pius (A.D. 138–61). Almost surely a Celtic bead used in a later context	*AnJ* vi (1926), 178; *JRS* xxiii (1923), 91 and xxxix (1949), 19
Chester	Cheshire	Chester	Azure glass with white opaque wave and above it a painted gold band. Diam. 1 cm. Ht. 1 cm. Cf. Bromham, below	Found with coin of Vespasian in Water Tower Street, 1914	

SITE AND PARISH	COUNTY	MUSEUM & NO.	DESCRIPTION AND APPROX. DIMENSIONS	ASSOCIATIONS AND REMARKS	PUBLICATION
Colliton Park, Dorchester	Dorset	Dorchester	Small globular black bead with crossing white swags. Yellow rings round black eyes enclosed	From Roman villa. Possibly 4th–5th c. A.D. from German or N. European source	R.C.H.M. *Dorset* ii
Poundbury Camp, Dorchester	Dorset	Dorchester	Flat hexagonal bead like Samatian beads from Richborough and Chesters, but blue in colour and opaque. Length and height *c.* 9·0 mm.	From late Roman graves	Information from excavator
South Shields	Durham	South Shields	Translucent light greenish bottle-glass with opaque white around perforation and circumferential bands of finely twisted white, red and blue. Diam. 2·5 cm. Ht. 1·1 cm. Perf. diam. 1 cm.	From Roman fort with Spanish, Palmyrene, and Tigris area elements. Occupied *c.* 122–369	The site is published in *AA*, 4th s., xi (1934), 83–102
Colchester	Essex	Colchester, Group 94	Biconical bead inlaid all over with tiny black, white and yellow mosaic tesserae. Max. diam. 1·2 cm. Ht. 1·1 cm. Perf. diam. 4 mm.	Imported from Egypt? Thought to have been found with coin of Nero (A.D. 54–68) but these Groups are not reliable and on the Continent this type of mosaic bead is usually late Roman	May, T. (1930), p. 279
Colchester	Essex	Colchester 518	Bright semi-translucent cobalt with decoration of opaque white vertical S-shaped lines between pairs of diagonal lines. Diam. 2·6 cm. Ht. 1·1 cm. Perf. diam. 1·2 cm.	With remains of box, rings, mirror, etc., dated *c.* A.D. 50–60. Joslin Group 107. (Not totally reliable)	May, T. (1930)
Colchester	Essex	Colchester	Dark brown annular with badly applied yellow decoration, nearly worn away. Diam. 2·9 cm. Ht. 1·1 cm. Perf. diam. 1·4 cm.	Said to be from Group 94, dated A.D. 54–68. (These groups are not reliable)	May, T. (1930)

SITE AND PARISH	COUNTY	MUSEUM & NO.	DESCRIPTION AND APPROX. DIMENSIONS	ASSOCIATIONS AND REMARKS	PUBLICATION
Barnsley	Gloucester-shire	Corinium Museum, Cirencester, A320	Globular black bead with white and sky blue swags and opaque yellow eyes with brown centres	From Barnsley Roman villa. Prob-ably 4th–5th c. A.D. See remarks on Ciren-cester beads, and on the bead from Lankhills, Winchester	*TBGAS* lxxxvi (1967)
Cirencester	Gloucester-shire	Corinium Museum, Cirencester	Long barrel-shaped black bead with irregular yellow zig-zag and stripes. Another similar, white decoration	Both these beads must compare with Lank-hills, below. Intrusive elements from Teu-tonic sources. Late Roman graves	Publication in preparation, 1975
Cirencester	Gloucester-shire		Appears to be part of a small jug-shaped bead with broken neck and handle. Bluish purple with white wave. Ht. *c.* 1·2 cm.	Cf. Keller, E. (1971), Abb. 27, no. 24 (late Roman from S. Bavaria)	Buckman and Newmarch, *Illustrations of the Remains of Roman Art in Cirencester* (1850), p. 97, fig. a
Wolham	Gloucester-shire	Gloucester 36/1942	Flat triangular bead, translucent greenish-blue. Each side measures *c.* 2·6 cm.	Not associated and may not be Roman	Information from Dr. O. H. Wild
Woolaston, Chesters Roman Villa	Gloucester-shire	Lost	Apparently two beads, both poly-chrome with dark core and 'wedge-shaped' pieces of red glass (translucent) enclosed in oval yellow glass. Larger bead *c.* 2·5 cm. long and 1·8 wide	From a Roman villa occupied into late, possibly post-Roman period. Cf. no. 5 in Leeds, E. T. and Harden, D. B., *The Anglo-Saxon Cemetery at Abingdon, Berks.* (1936), pl. 6	*AC* xciii (1938), 121–2. Fully described but not illustrated
Winchester, Lankhills Cemetery	Hampshire	Winchester	(i) Large pear-shaped bead in trans-lucent dark brown glass with white opaque swags enclos-ing yellow round brown eyes overlaid by red opaque trail	From necklace 436, Grave 323, a foreign grave dated *c.* A.D. 350–70. Widespread Continental parallels beyond the Imperial Frontiers, for which see Lankhills report	Clarke, G. (forth-coming), fig. 8, f
			(ii) 2 green tapered beads	From necklaces 28 and 353, in Graves 40 and 336, two foreign graves dated within the period A.D. 350-90. Cf. Bath	*Ibid.* figs. 69, d, 90, f

SITE AND PARISH	COUNTY	MUSEUM & NO.	DESCRIPTION AND APPROX. DIMENSIONS	ASSOCIATIONS AND REMARKS	PUBLICATION
Kenchester	Herefordshire	Hereford 6058	Glossy, black, round with flat sections. Blue band around circumference. Diam. 1·1 cm. Ht. 1·3 cm. Small perforation	Occupation of this town to at least late 4th c. A.D. Similar to bead from Bracknell, Berks. (unpublished)	For site see *TWNFC*, 1916 and 1926
St. Albans	Hertfordshire		Green emerald coloured glass with a bluish streak. Prism-shaped, 2·7 mm. long and 1·8 cm. wide	Probably Sarmatian. From 4th c. A.D. necklace	*Ve*, fig. 47, a and p. 214
Richborough, Ash	Kent	Richborough	Flat hexagonal or prism-shaped green stone or glass bead of similar type to one from Chesters, below. Small perforation. Incomplete	Perhaps a Sarmatian import. See Chesters, below	*Rich* iv, p. 239
Leicester (Jewry Wall)	Leicestershire	Leicester	Dark blue globular with light thin band wound once from perforation around circumference. Diam. 1·3 cm. Ht. 1 cm. Perf. diam. 2 mm.	From disturbed level	Kenyon, K. M. (1948), p. 269 and fig. 93.5
Chesters Fort	Northumberland	Chesters Museum	Flat hexagonal or prism-shaped bead with 2 long sides similar to Richborough and Verulamium beads, above. Ht. 1·3 cm. Length 2 cm. Small perforation	Opaque and abraded stone or glass. Perhaps Sarmatian (information from Dr. Grace Simpson)	See for type. Párduez in *AH* xxv (1941), 56 ff. and Taf. 24, 25
Housesteads	Northumberland	University Museum, Newcastle-upon-Tyne	Glossy, 'black', round with flat section. White band around circumference	Unstratified from Roman site. Early excavations. Cf. examples from Kenchester and Bracknell, Berks.	
Shakenoak Farm, Wilcote	Oxfordshire		Harden described as follows: 'Fragment of bead of mosaic glass, oblate with large hole. Made from pieces of blue and white marbled mosaic and red, green and white streaky glass by a native workman using waste Roman mosaic glass fragments'	Probably late 3rd c. A.D.	Brodribb, A. C. C. Hands, A. R. and Walker, A. D. *Excavations at Shakenoak Farm near Wilcote, Oxfordshire*, ii (1971), 106

SITE AND PARISH	COUNTY	MUSEUM & NO.	DESCRIPTION AND APPROX. DIMENSIONS	ASSOCIATIONS AND REMARKS	PUBLICATION
Bath	Somerset	Roman Baths Museum	Large pear-shaped bead of brown glass. Applied opaque blue swags enclosing yellow rings round brown eyes	From temple site under Pump Room. Bead very like the Lankhills (Winchester) bead of foreign origin	Information from Prof. Barry Cunliffe (unpublished)
Wookey Hole	Somerset	Bristol	Small blackish oval bead with blue band around girth at right angles to perforation. Diam. 1.2 cm.	'Later 3rd century'	Information from G. C. Boon and Professor Tratman, 1975
Icklingham (Lackford Hills)	Suffolk	A.M. 1927.700	'Black glass ring about 1⅞″ in diameter' (nearly 5 cm.)	With 4th c. A.D. beads on necklace. Found in 1859	Joseph Warren's MS. notebook in the A.M.
Bromham	Wiltshire	Devizes 27C	Globular, light opaque with decorative bands in opaque pink around speckled gold painted band. Some mixed glass. Diam. 1.5 cm. Ht. 1.4 cm. Max. perf. 3mm.	From site of Roman villa, 1911. (Cf. Chester, above)	
Aldborough	Yorkshire		Rather large globular bead. Ground in dark green covered with white glass, with irregular red lines. Yellow line round perforation at top and bottom. Diam. 1.5 cm. Ht. 1.7 cm. Perf. diam. 3 mm.	Found with Roman coins in 1843	*A* xxxiv (1852), pl. v, no. 7. Another exactly similar and perhaps the same bead shown in the Nightingale Colln. Drawings in the S.A.L.
York	Yorkshire	York	Decorated with swags and eyes	Probably an intrusive bead. Dated 4th c. A.D.	Poorly described in R.C.H.M. *York* i (1962), fig. 58, p. 74 and p. 140 b

SCOTLAND

Dunadd	Argyllshire	Glasgow ? HPO275	Long drum-shaped bead with yellow collar at each end. 'Black' ground with white chevrons. Length 1.4 cm. Width 1 cm.	This site is reputed to have been occupied from the 5th c. A.D. as a (Scottic) Dalriadic stronghold. An identical bead is said to have come from Aubigny-en-Artois (Pas-de-Calais) with a Roman coin of *c.* A.D. 300 and another in a N. French tomb with a coin of Gratian (*c.* A.D. 380) but with red ground instead of black	*PSAS* lxiv (1930), 116, fig. 3 and 119. See Boulanger, Cl. (1902–05)

SITE AND PARISH	COUNTY	MUSEUM & NO.	DESCRIPTION AND APPROX. DIMENSIONS	ASSOCIATIONS AND REMARKS	PUBLICATION
Newstead, Melrose	Roxburgh-shire	N.M.A. FRA904	Opaque bright red with yellow girth band decorated with green herring-bone. Diam. 1·3 cm. Ht. 1·1 cm. Perf. diam. 8 mm.	'Outside the North Gate of Roman town.' Occupation c. A.D. 80–200	Ne
Newstead	Roxburgh-shire	Mr. Mason's Colln., Selkirk (1954)	Part of long tubular bead 10 mm. diam. and broken off at 1·5 cm. length. Perf. diam. 4 mm. Semi-translucent yellow glass with opaque yellow zigzags around it at right angles to the perforation	This rather damaged bead cannot be closely paralleled but is not unlike some of the variants from Meare	
Newstead	Roxburgh-shire	Mr. Mason's Colln., Selkirk	Bright red globular with four yellow girth bands on sides. Each band has central black line. Diam. 1·5 cm. Ht. 1·3 cm. Perf. diam. 3 mm.	Surface find in Roman site	Unpublished

WALES

SITE AND PARISH	COUNTY	MUSEUM & NO.	DESCRIPTION AND APPROX. DIMENSIONS	ASSOCIATIONS AND REMARKS	PUBLICATION
Caerhun	Caernarvon-shire	Segontium Museum, Caernarvon	Annular green glass with dark blue wave edged with red	This fort was dismantled in the Antonine period	Baillie-Reynolds, P. K. (1938)
Caernarvon	Caernarvon-shire	Segontium Museum, Caernarvon	Half a natural greenish translucent annular bead. Opaque white irregular trail interspersed with opaque blue dots. Diam. 2·2 cm. Ht. 1 cm. Perf. diam. 5 mm.	Unstratified from Roman fort	Unpublished. Information from G. C. Boon
Caernarvon	Caernarvon-shire	Segontium Museum, Caernarvon	Very dark green bead, seemingly black, with opaque white and red irregular swags and opaque yellow spots, one containing opaque green eye. Irregular globular about 1 cm. diam.	Unstratified from Roman fort (? post-Roman)	Unpublished. Information from G. C. Boon

SITE AND PARISH	COUNTY	MUSEUM & NO.	DESCRIPTION AND APPROX. DIMENSIONS	ASSOCIATIONS AND REMARKS	PUBLICATION
Caernarvon	Caernarvonshire	Segontium Museum, Caernarvon	Slightly biconical dark green almost black bead with unmarvered wave decoration in opaque red. Diam. 1·4 cm. Ht. 8 mm. Perf. diam. 5 mm.	Unstratified from Roman fort (? post-Roman)	Unpublished. Information from G. C. Boon
Carmarthen	Carmarthenshire	N.M.W.	Half Prussian blue annular bead with marvered opaque white circumferential bands. Diam. 2·7 cm. Ht. 1·3 cm. Perf. diam. 1·3 cm.	The earliest material from this Roman site is not very early Flavian, and this bead may pre-date it	Information from Mr. G. C. Boon
Whitton, nr. Barry	Glamorganshire	Cardiff	Part of light translucent cobalt annular bead with glossy 'black' blob. Original diam. 1·5 cm. Ht. 4 mm. Perf. diam. 6 mm.	From Roman villa. On surface of rubble roadway	Report forthcoming
Caerleon	Monmouthshire	Caerleon 54, 389A (G113)	Opaque 'black' gadrooned bead with opaque white roughly horizontal lines round it. Diam. 2·1 cm. Ht. 1·4 cm. Perf. diam. 6 mm.	'Near the legionary fortress' in main lateral drain of c. A.D. 130–230. A somewhat comparable bead came from a mid-5th c. context at Krefeld-Gellep (no. 1462). See Pirling, R. (1966)	Information from G. C. Boon
Caerleon	Monmouthshire	Caerleon 62, 2656, G18	Part only of small translucent blue bead with remains of stratified eyes (colour missing)	Late 3rd c. A.D.	Boon, G. C. (1966), pp. 104 ff.
Usk (near)	Monmouthshire		'Blue-green glass coated entirely with yellow and dull red lines running diagonally, the irregular series of which is broken by cracks in the coating like faults in geology'	? From the Roman site	Lee, J. E., Catalogue of the Caerleon Museum (1862), p. 55

GENERAL INDEX

INDEX OF SCHEDULES

(for museums *see* Museums in General Index)